www.wadsworth.com

wadsworth.com is the World Wide Web site for Wadsworth and is your direct source to dozens of online resources.

At *wadsworth.com* you can find out about supplements, demonstration software, and student resources. You can also send email to many of our authors and preview new publications and exciting new technologies.

wadsworth.com
Changing the way the world learns®

From the Wadsworth Series in Mass Communication and Journalism

General Mass Communication

Anokwa, Kwadwo, Lin, Carolyn, Salwen, Michael, *International Communication: Issues and Controversies*
Biagi, Shirley, *Media/Impact: An Introduction to Mass Media*, 6th Ed.
Bucy, Erik, *Living in the Information Age: A New Media Reader*
Craft, John, Frederic Leigh, and Donald Godfrey, *Electronic Media*
Day, Louis, *Ethics in Media Communications: Cases and Controversies*, 4th Ed.
Dennis, Everette E., and John C. Merrill, *Media Debates: Great Issues for the Digital Age*, 4th Ed.
Fortner, Robert S., *International Communications: History, Conflict, and Control of the Global Metropolis*
Gillmor, Donald, Jerome Barron, and Todd Simon, *Mass Communication Law: Cases and Comment*, 6th Ed.
Gillmor, Donald, Jerome Barron, Todd Simon, and Herbert Terry, *Fundamentals of Mass Communication Law*
Hilmes, Michele, *Only Connect: A Cultural History of Broadcasting in the United States*
Hilmes, Michele, *Connections: A Broadcast History Reader*
Jamieson, Kathleen Hall, and Karlyn Kohrs Campbell, *The Interplay of Influence*, 5th Ed.
Kamalipour, Yahya K., *Global Communication*
Lester, Paul, *Visual Communication*, 3rd Ed.
Overbeck, Wayne, *Major Principles of Media Law*, 2003 Edition
Sparks, Glenn G., *Media Effects Research: A Basic Overview*
Straubhaar, Joseph, and Robert LaRose, *Media Now: Communications Media in the Information Age*, 3rd Ed.
Whetmore, Edward Jay, *Mediamerica, Mediaworld: Form, Content, and Consequence of Mass Communication*, Updated 5th Ed.
Zelezny, John D., *Communications Law: Liberties, Restraints, and the Modern Media*, 3rd Ed.
Zelezny, John D., *Cases in Communications Law*, 3rd Ed.

Journalism

Adams, Paul, *Writing Right for Today's Mass Media: A Textbook and Workbook with Language Exercises*
Anderson, Douglas, *Contemporary Sports Reporting*, 2nd Ed.
Bowles, Dorothy, and Diane L. Borden, *Creative Editing*, 3rd Ed.
Chance, Jean, and William McKeen, *Literary Journalism: A Reader*
Dorn, Raymond, *How to Design and Improve Magazine Layouts*, 2nd Ed.
Fischer, Heintz-Dietrich, *Sports Journalism at Its Best: Pulitzer Prize-Winning Articles, Cartoons, and Photographs*
Fisher, Lionel, *The Craft of Corporate Journalism*
Gaines, William, *Investigative Reporting for Print and Broadcast*, 2nd Ed.
Hilliard, Robert L., *Writing for Television, Radio, and New Media*, 7th Ed.
Kessler, Lauren, and Duncan McDonald, *When Words Collide*, 5th Ed.
Klement, Alice M., and Carolyn Burrows Matalene, *Telling Stories/Taking Risks: Journalism Writing at the Century's Edge*
Laakaniemi, Ray, *Newswriting in Transition*
Miller, Lisa, *Power Journalism: Computer-Assisted Reporting*
Rich, Carole, *Writing and Reporting News: A Coaching Method*, 4th Ed.
Wilber, Rick, and Randy Miller, *Modern Media Writing*

Photojournalism and Photography

Parrish, Fred S., *Photojournalism: An Introduction*

Public Relations and Advertising

Hendrix, Jerry A., *Public Relations Cases*, 5th Ed.
Hunt, Todd, Grunig, James, *Public Relations Techniques*
Jewler, Jerome A., and Bonnie L. Drewniany, *Creative Strategy in Advertising*, 7th Ed.
Newsom, Doug, and Bob Carrell, *Public Relations Writing: Form and Style*, 6th Ed.
Newsom, Doug, Judy VanSlyke Turk, and Dean Kruckeberg, *This Is PR: The Realities of Public Relations*, 7th Ed.
Sivulka, Juliann, *Soap, Sex, and Cigarettes: A Cultural History of American Advertising*
Woods, Gail Baker, *Advertising and Marketing to the New Majority: A Case Study Approach*

Research and Theory

Babbie, Earl, *The Practice of Social Research*, 8th Ed.
Baran, Stanley, and Dennis Davis, *Mass Communication Theory: Foundations, Ferment, and Future*, 3rd Ed.
Rubenstein, Sondra, *Surveying Public Opinion*
Rubin, Rebecca B., Alan M. Rubin, and Linda J. Piele, *Communication Research: Strategies and Sources*, 5th Ed.
Wimmer, Roger D., and Joseph R. Dominick, *Mass Media Research: An Introduction*, 7th Ed.

Modern Media Writing

Rick Wilber
University of South Florida

Randy Miller
University of South Florida

THOMSON
—————✦—————™
WADSWORTH

Australia • Canada • Mexico • Singapore • Spain
United Kingdom • United States

THOMSON

WADSWORTH ™

Publisher: Holly J. Allen
Assistant Editor: Nicole George
Editorial Assistant: Amber Fawson
Technology Project Manager: Jeanette Wiseman
Marketing Manager: Kimberly Russell
Marketing Assistant: Neena Chandra
Advertising Project Manager: Shemika Britt
Project Manager, Editorial Production: Paula Berman

Print/Media Buyer: Barbara Britton
Permissions Editor: Bob Kauser
Production Service and Compositor:
    Delgado Design, Inc.
Text Designer: Delgado Design, Inc.
Cover Designer: Ross Carron
Cover Image: PhotoDisc
Text and Cover Printer: Webcom

Printed in Canada
  5 6 7 07

For more information about our products,
contact us at:
Thomson Learning Academic Resource Center
1-800-423-0563
For permission to use material from this text,
contact us by:
Phone: 1-800-730-2214
Fax: 1-800-730-2215
Web: http://www.thomsonrights.com

Library of Congress Control Number: 2002110782

ISBN-13: 978-0-534-52047-2
ISBN-10: 0-534-52047-2

Wadsworth/Thomson Learning
10 Davis Drive
Belmont, CA 94002-3098
USA

Asia
Thomson Learning
5 Shenton Way #01-01
UIC Building
Singapore 068808

Australia
Nelson Thomson Learning
102 Dodds Street
South Melbourne, Victoria 3205
Australia

Canada
Nelson Thomson Learning
1120 Birchmount Road
Toronto, Ontario M1K 5G4
Canada

Europe/Middle East/Africa
Thomson Learning
High Holborn House
50/51 Bedford Row
London WC1R 4LR
United Kingdom

Latin America
Thomson Learning
Seneca, 53
Colonia Polanco
11560 Mexico D.F.
Mexico

Spain
Paraninfo Thomson Learning
Calle/Magallanes, 25
28015 Madrid, Spain

Brief Contents

Contents

Chapter 5   Research for Media Writing   90

| Chapter 8 | **Research and Writing Skills for Opinion Writing** 161 |

Chapter 12   **Research and Writing for Advertising Copywriting** 245

Preface

We have written *Modern Media Writing* to give students a useful, interesting and approachable introduction to various kinds of non-fiction writing for the media. With newswriting at its core, the text begins with a brief history of the news and then progresses through the essentials of leads, basic structures, research and interviewing to a series of chapters that offer guidance in particular kinds of media writing, including feature writing, broadcast writing, opinion writing, writing for public relations, writing for the Internet and advertising copywriting.

There are a number of special elements to this text that we think will make it especially appealing to students and instructors. Among these are:

▶ The CD-ROM that is packaged with each textbook. This CD-ROM gives students a number of useful exercises in reporting and writing for the media. Of special note are numerous sound files, which give students the unusual opportunity to hear interviews take place and then to take notes for their stories by actually listening to subjects speak.

▶ An appendix that serves as a guide to the basics of style for media writers, as well as a chapter devoted to grammar and writing trouble spots.

▶ Numerous "Day in the Life of . . ." features from practicing media writers and editors.

▶ Information on writing for online publications. Of special interest is Chapter 10, Writing for the Web, which includes coverage of media convergence in the newsrooms of media outlets in Houston, Tampa, Orlando, Sarasota and elsewhere.

▶ A historical overview in Chapter 1, which gives students a context from which to view modern media writing and its concept of what makes something newsworthy.

▶ Internet links, especially the live links found in the CD-ROM.

▶ The Glossary of Common Terms, which should prove especially useful for students encountering media writing for the first time.

Modern Media Writing covers an ambitiously large amount of material, and so we realize the book offers more material than students may be able to cover in one semester or quarter. Some instructors, we suspect, may well choose to select certain chapters to cover in more depth and leave other chapters for another semester. The wide range of material reflects our hope that this book will be useful for several different kinds of introductory reporting and writing courses, including what is called, on many campuses, "Media Writing" or (where we teach) "Writing for the Mass Media," as well as more traditional beginning reporting or beginning journalism courses.

The book begins in Chapter 1 with a compact history of media writing and how the media's concept of news has changed over the years. This material is intended to help students establish a context for understanding the needs of various media. The discussion at the chapter's end, comparing how news is defined by the various media, from traditional print and broadcast media to today's online publications, should help students see how the varying needs of each medium help define the news value of any potential story.

Chapter 2 helps students understand how media stories are organized. The chapter discusses basic structures for the news story for print, broadcast and public relations, starting with the inverted pyramid and then moving forward into more complex structures for various kinds of media writing. The chapter also discusses nutgraphs, anecdotes, quote blocks, sound bites and other structural elements of media writing. There are examples of the work of professional media writers and a special "Tips and Tactics" section from *Houston Chronicle* Assistant Sports Editor David Barron.

Chapter 3 discusses common language trouble spots for media-writing students, including noun-pronoun and noun-verb agreement, misplaced modifiers, tense shifts, misused words and phrases, clichés, jargon and more. Instructors who feel their students need more guidance in the essentials of grammar and style for media writers may want to utilize Appendix B, which offers a refresher course in vexing issues from spelling and capitalization to punctuation style.

Chapter 4 takes a close look at the importance of the lead paragraph in a media story, using a variety of examples from newspapers and other media to help students identify various kinds of leads, and then, importantly, gives them guidance on how to write effective leads.

Chapter 5 offers information on the basics of research as a function of reporting. The chapter offers not only a how-to guide to research, but includes, as well, a number of sources for research information, including useful online links. In addition, there is a special "Tips and Tactics" segment on the use and abuse of statistics, and an enlightening "Day in the Life of . . ." feature from media-relations writer Charles Stovall, who provides important research support for many journalists.

Chapter 6 then takes the next step in reporting by focusing on interviewing, and includes information not only on how to conduct interviews but also on how to use quoted material. We are aware that there may be some disagreements on how journalists translate the spoken word into the written word, and we urge instructors to discuss that issue, in particular, with their would-be media writers. The chapter has examples of the work of professional practitioners and also an interesting "Day in the Life of . . ." feature from *St. Petersburg Times* reporter Roger Mills.

Students should find Chapter 7 interesting with its focus on feature writing, since it not only discusses traditional kinds of feature writing for newspapers, but also guides the students through the basics of feature writing for magazines and offers an interesting look at feature writing for online publications. The chapter also discusses the special kinds of reporting needed to write effective features for any medium and pays attention to freelance writing, a career aim for many students. Once again, there are examples of the work of professional feature writers and an interesting "Day in the Life of . . ." feature, this one from *Los Angeles Times* feature writer Shari Roan.

Chapter 8 offers students a look at various kinds of opinion writing. The basics of editorial and column writing are covered, with material from several top editorialists and columnists. In addition, the chapter discusses other forms of opinion writing in the media, including criticism and reviews for newspapers, broadcast and on-line publications. There are numerous examples from practicing editorialists and columnists, and a "Day in the Life of . . ." segment from newspaper columnist Cragg Hines of the *Houston Chronicle*.

Chapter 9 discusses broadcast writing, paying attention to radio's needs but focusing more on newswriting for television, including such essential material as reporting skills for broadcasters, basic formats for broadcast newswriting and broadcast writing's essential differences from print newswriting. Special sections deal with numbers and with blocking and counter blocking. Again, there are several examples of the work of professional practitioners, as well as a "Day in the Life of . . ." feature, this one from investigative reporter Robin Guess.

Chapter 10 discusses writing for Internet publication, noting that while the basics of good journalism remain the same, there are specific needs for reporting and writing for Web sites. While there is material on this newest form of media writing throughout the text, this particular chapter offers a specific, narrow focus on an area of media writing that many students find interesting, and where they may well build their careers. As in many other chapters, there are examples and quotes from professional practitioners and a "Day in the Life of . . ." segment, this one from CNN.com feature writer Jamie Allen.

In many colleges and universities, public relations majors now make up a significant percentage of overall mass media majors, and so the book offers, in Chapter 11, a complete chapter devoted to writing for public relations. Here, students will find information on writing and editing press releases, annual reports, company brochures, corporate magazines, video news releases and other forms of internal and external writing for public relations. As with other chapters, there are several examples of the work of professional practitioners and also some interesting "Day in the Life of . . ." material, in this case one from publication-information officer Marilyn Bartell and another from freelance writer Nancy Reynolds.

Chapter 12's focus on advertising copywriting gives a broad overview of the kinds of writing that take place in the advertising world. The acronym *HUBBA, HUBBA* should help students remember some of the basic needs of the advertising professional, and a "Day in the Life of . . ." feature by advertising copywriter Ray Straub gives students a glimpse of what life is like for one such professional.

One of the more common failings for beginning writers is their lack of appreciation for the necessary hard work of editing and revision, and so Chapter 13 focuses on those skills, giving the students advice on some useful basic techniques for revising their own work for print, broadcast and online work. There is a discussion, as well, on how writers work with editors to produce the best possible stories. Included are samples of stories from first draft to publication, a special "Tips and Tactics" segment with two top newspaper editors, and an informative "Day in the Life of . . ." segment from freelance magazine editor Nan Woitas.

Chapter 14 discusses legal and ethical concerns for the beginning media writer, including the basics of libel and copyright law and a discussion of media ethics.

Three appendices at the end of the book give additional instruction.

Appendix A contains the ethical codes of the Society of Professional Journalists, the Public Relations Society of America, the American Association of Advertising Agencies and the National Association of Broadcasters.

Appendix B is a guided tour through some of the more troublesome areas of journalism style, using numerous examples of problems and solutions to them. The appendix includes lengthy lists of commonly misspelled words, common capitalization problems, common punctuation problems and more.

Appendix C holds a discussion of media careers, not only offering advice on career building, but also giving students an idea of salary ranges, career paths and the like. Several recent graduates who are enjoying success in the media add their thoughts to this appendix, including newspaper reporter John Wing and magazine writer Lisa Costantini.

Finally, there is a Glossary of common terms.

Acknowledgments

We wish to offer our deepest thanks and gratitude to the writers and editors who were so willing to share their work by taking part in *Modern Media Writing*. These include (in no particular order) editorial writer Stephen Henderson of *The Baltimore Sun,* Jamie Allen of CNN.com, public relations practitioner Marilyn Bartell, magazine writer and editor Lisa Costantini, columnist Cragg Hines of the *Houston Chronicle,* editor Phil Mintz of *Newsday,* public relations practitioner Nancy Reynolds, reporter Shari Roan of the *Los Angeles Times,* copy editor Tom Seals of *The Kansas City Star,* advertising copywriter Ray Straub, reporter John Wing of *The Tampa Tribune,* and magazine freelancer Nan Woitas, *Tampa Tribune* reporter Jennifer Barrs, public relations practitioner Bob Wilber, assistant sports editor David Barron of the *Houston Chronicle,* public relations practitioner Frank R. Stansberry, television news reporter Glen Selig, *Minneapolis Star Tribune* reporter Warren Wolfe, editor Morgan McGinley of *The Day* of New London, Conn., Bobbi Olson at the *Los Angeles Times,* movie critic Steve Persall of the *St. Petersburg Times,* online editor Mark Kelly and editor Charles N. Brown of *Locus* magazine, freelance writer Nick DiChario, public relations writer and editor Renee Buchanan, advertising copywriter Debra Jason, *Baltimore Sun* reporter Del Quentin Wilber, *Detroit Free Press* columnist and Poynter Fellow Mike Wendland, writer and editor Joan Hammond, and reporter Art Campos of *The Sacramento Bee.*

Each one of them found the time to discuss his or her work, and in many cases they also took part in lengthy online or telephone interviews and then read and revised chapters in which their work was mentioned or their quotes were used. Many of them offered advice on how to improve the book as the manuscript progressed, and we deeply appreciate their comments.

We are also especially grateful to those writers and editors who took the time to write a "Day in the Life of . . ." segment. Each of these segments adds to the text an invaluable sense of what "real world" media writing is really like and we are confident that students will gain much from encountering the stories these media writers and editors have shared.

Hundreds of our students over the past few years have seen various of the chapters of this text, and it is in large part through their reaction to the material that we shaped and refined *Modern Media Writing* into this published version. To all those students we offer our thanks. We are most appreciative of all they have taught us.

We could not have had more supportive leadership than that from Dr. Edward Jay Friedlander, director of the School of Mass Communications at the University of South Florida. His guidance was priceless, and his support of the time and effort involved during the many semesters of work that went into this text was crucial to the successful completion of the textbook. We also thank the very talented Dr. Ken Killebrew, who wrote Chapter 9 for us despite a busy schedule of teaching, the directing of our department's graduate program, and the demands of his own writing.

Dr. Humphrey Regis, who handles the challenging task of designing and administering our department's introductory writing class, was especially helpful to us in innumerable conversations about the writing skills of the modern student. In addition, many of our faculty colleagues were most supportive, especially Dr. Larry Leslie, Dr. Dan Bagley, Dr. Ken Killebrew, Kim Golombisky and Dr. Scott Liu.

In addition, the front office staff of Cathy D'Azzo, Lisa Croy and Marcia Stein provided constant timely support and a cheerful reaction to our sometimes harried requests and we thank them enormously for their calm, patient efforts in our behalf. Also, Charles McKenzie, graduate student extraordinaire, was most helpful during the crucial final crunch approaching publication, and we are most appreciative.

The CD-ROM that accompanies this textbook was made possible through the expert technical help of Jason Funderburk from the University of South Florida's Educational Outreach Department, and his work with the technical team at Wadsworth and we greatly appreciate their efforts.

Our team at Wadsworth was the perfect blend of patience and motivation. Editors Karen Austin and Holly Allen offered expert advice which was absolutely invaluable to the entire process. We would also like to thank Nicole George, senior assistant editor, and Jeanette Wiseman, senior technology manager for their help with the instructor and student resources, including the CD-ROM with exercises. In addition, the production team at Delgado Design was extremely helpful, patient and supportive in walking us through the myriad details of the book's production, from the copyediting through proofs. We are grateful for the calm guidance, sharp eyes and wonderfully talented design skills of Ed Smith, Linda Stern, and Marilyn Granald, in particular.

Finally, we thank the following reviewers for their insight and valuable comments: Betsy B. Alderman, University of Tennessee at Chattanooga; Randy Bobbitt, Marshall University; Barbara Bullington, East Carolina University; Donald Challenger, Syracuse University/Utica College; Dan Close, Wichita State University; Frank D. Durham, University of Iowa; Sandra Fowler, Salem State College; Gail Henson, Bellarmine University; W. Wat Hopkins, Virginia Polytechnic Institute and State University; Jerry Howard, University of Oklahoma; Dianne Lamb, Georgia Southern University; Marsha Little Matthews, East Central University; Charles Okigbo, North Dakota State University; Jon M. Smith, Southern Utah University; Herb Strentz, Drake University; Wayne Wanta, University of Florida; Henry Wefing, Westfield State College.

1

Changing Definitions of the News

You've just finished interviewing your college president after she threw out the first pitch of the softball season for your college team's inaugural game in the new stadium. As you walk into the office of the campus newspaper, you're convinced that you can write a terrific story about the president and her new plan to improve the quality of education on campus while keeping costs down.

The third part of her seven-part plan, though, is to form a committee to consider alternatives to the tenure process for professors. As you look over your notes and start to write your lead paragraph, you begin to wonder what the faculty will think about the tenure issue, so you make a few phone calls before writing the story. Two hours later, at 5 p.m., you've turned in a story that you think is really solid.

Later that night on the local television news, there's a 30-second story about the president, but it focuses on the new stadium for the softball team and shows only that first pitch. A brief mention is made of her seven-point plan.

1

The next morning your story appears, and before you have a chance to rub the sleep from your eyes the phone is ringing. The president and her staff are furious with you. Of all the various things she discussed with you, why did you think the tenure issue was the most important one? The president had made it clear that the proposed salary raise for faculty and staff was at the top her list, and yet you nearly ignored that, the president's assistant argues.

The assistant makes it clear that you will meet with the president at 10 a.m. and you had better have some answers. A few minutes later the phone rings again. It's your editor at the *Daily*, who seemed to like the story fine late last night but now wants to talk about it. She wants to meet with you at 9:30 a.m. sharp.

The phone rings again. It's the faculty adviser to the *Daily*, and he wants to meet with you at 9 a.m. He'll back you all the way on this, but he wants to know why you thought a tenure committee was the most important thing in this story when the budget crisis is clearly the top issue.

Whew, you think, your head spinning with all this hubbub. What a day *this* is going to be.

Welcome to the news business.

Defining the News

As our mythical beginning journalist has just discovered, defining just what we mean by the word *news* can be a difficult task, one that gets even harder when you try to rank the value of elements within a news story. The public and the media often disagree on what makes something or someone newsworthy, and journalists sometimes disagree among themselves as well.

Different media each have their own idea of what's news and what isn't. Television's idea of news frequently differs from newspapers' idea of news, and both of those frequently differ from what radio finds newsworthy. Public relations practitioners frequently operate under an entirely different set of circumstances and have still another idea of what is the news.

Compounding all this, even within each medium there are disagreements about what makes something or someone newsworthy. One newspaper may find coverage of the trial of a famous athlete for murder to be consistently worth the front page. Another paper may quickly move the trial from the front page to an inside page. Yet another paper may move the trial coverage to a "briefs" section or drop it entirely until the trial's conclusion. The same sorts of differences occur daily in local and national television news. One network's lead story sometimes doesn't make it onto another network's news program at all, or merits just a brief mention.

Nevertheless, if you compare several daily newspapers, or your various local television news shows, or the networks on a daily basis, you will see a lot more agreement than disagreement, both inside each medium and among the various media.

Most newspapers agree on their basic concepts of what's worth the front page and what merits being on an inside page, and most television stations jockey to find fresh angles on news items that they generally agree are worth covering.

So, while those of us in the media argue and disagree on many aspects of what defines *news* and what contributes to the news value of something or someone, there are some important areas of general agreement.

To understand what those areas of general agreement are, it will be helpful for you to gain a little perspective on how we arrived at the concept of news as we think of it in the United States.

The English and Colonial Press

In Colonial days, the first printing presses were used for books, not newspapers. Newspapers had been around since the early 1600s in England, first with the *corantos,* which were published irregularly in London and were mainly concerned with war news and the political intrigues of Europe.

Later that same century, the *diurnals* were published daily. These diurnals began as official reports on Parliament's deliberations, but grew into more independent publications by the time of John Thomas' *Diurnall Occurrences,* which first appeared in November of 1641.

By the mid-1600s, Oliver Cromwell came to power and tightly restricted this emerging press, limiting it to officially sanctioned publications. The Restoration, in 1660, brought Charles II to power and with him the generally recognized first true newspaper, *The Oxford Gazette*, in 1665. The paper was printed twice a week, by royal authority, and so contained as news whatever the court thought newsworthy, usually the perceived successes of the Crown. When the royal court, which had been in Oxford to avoid a plague in London, moved back to the capital, the paper became *The London Gazette*.

Several decades later, in 1702, *The Daily Courant* appeared in London; it not only qualified as the first daily newspaper, but is famous for having an editor, Samuel Buckley, who insisted on his paper's reporting only factual news. This was a major departure, since earlier publications had readily printed opinion (usually government-approved opinion, at that) as fact.

Another important figure in early newspapers was Daniel Defoe, more famous now for his novels *Robinson Crusoe* and *Moll Flanders,* but well-known in his own day as a journalist and editorial writer.

Some other famous names you may have encountered in English classes as poets, satirists, or essayists, but who certainly qualify as journalists, are Jonathan Swift, Richard Steele and Joseph Addison, and Samuel Johnson.

In the American Colonies, it wasn't until the early 1700s that the first newspaper appeared. *The Boston News-Letter*, edited by John Campbell and printed by Bartholomew Green, began on April 24, 1704. An earlier attempt at a newspaper, the four-page *Publick Occurrences, Both Foreign and Domestick*, had been published by Benjamin Harris in 1690; but Harris had failed to obtain permission from the Colonial governor, and his newspaper was banned after the first issue. *The Boston News-Letter*, then, was the first successful American newspaper, and it is interesting to see what Campbell thought of as news in his paper.

As you can see from the illustration, much of the content of *The Boston News-Letter* was reprinted from London newspapers and so was already at least several weeks old. These dispatches typically covered war news from the Continent or political news from Parliament and the Crown. This first issue contained stories about rebellious Scotland and troubles with France.

The local news, you will notice, is considerably more timely and includes the same sort of material you can find today in your local newspaper. There are notices of births and deaths, advertisements for property sales, reports of local crimes, and coverage of Colonial politics.

The political coverage is cautious, since Campbell had his paper approved by the governor. Later in the 1700s, as the Colonies approached the American Revolution, other editors became considerably less cautious and their ideas of what constituted the news began to change.

James Franklin, Benjamin's older brother, began publishing *The New England Courant* in 1721, and right from the start *The Courant* had some very different ideas about what was newsworthy. For one thing, Franklin was determined to print his paper without the permission of authorities. By 1722 he was in jail for contempt, but on his release he went right back to printing facts and opinions that were unpopular with the political leadership of the colony.

Also, Franklin was a crusader, and he was unafraid to take the lead in shaping community thought on pressing issues. James and his teenage brother Benjamin (usually writing under a pseudonym) regularly crusaded for one thing or another in the pages of *The Courant*.

By 1729, Benjamin Franklin had moved to Philadelphia and had begun his own career as a journalist as editor of *The Pennsylvania Gazette*. Franklin succeeded as a newspaper editor and a printer of *Poor Richard's Almanack* and other books, winning new respectability for the role of journalists and thereby influencing the field enormously.

Courtesy of the Massachusetts Historical Society

The Boston News-Letter, *the first successful American newspaper, began publication on April 24, 1704.*

In this era, then, the concept of news began as a simple one that reflected political censorship and the availability of shipping news from abroad and politically acceptable local news. Most of these first newspapers had a circulation of no more than several hundred readers.

But, by the time the Colonial era ended with the start of the American Revolution, the concept of news had changed to something considerably more energetic and independent, and circulation was on the rise, too.

Beginning with James Franklin's willingness to take on causes, newspapers became increasingly strong in their support of the independence movement or their support for the Crown. Important journalists like rebel editors Samuel Adams and Isaiah Thomas, Tory editor James Rivington, and Colonial Whig writer John Dickinson each used newspapers to try to sway popular opinion in the years leading up to 1776.

Adams is the most famous of the group, and his success at persuasion through such newspapers as the *Boston Gazette and Country Journal* and the *Independent Advertiser* was a significant factor in the Colonies' actually going to war rather than continuing to negotiate with the Crown.

For Adams and the other Sons of Liberty, like Paul Revere and Isaiah Thomas, the news was whatever helped their cause. In that sense they were certainly propagandists, manipulating the news for their own purpose. Adams, in particular, was willing to use personal attacks against the aristocracy as an important tool in his writing. In that sense, the modern era of journalism, which frequently gets uncomfortably personal with its attacks on political figures, is a reflection of the very beginnings of American journalism.

After the war, the political struggle between Alexander Hamilton's Federalists (who wanted something resembling England's aristocracy to run the new nation with a firm hand) and Thomas Jefferson's Anti-Federalists (who wanted the rural landowners to run a decentralized new nation with strong states' rights) dominated newspapers' interests, so most nonlocal news came in the form of highly charged political commentary.

John Fenno edited the *Gazette of the United States*, the primary newspaper for the Federalist position, and Philip Freneau, editor of the *National Gazette*, spoke for the Anti-Federalist position. In both cases, the editor's idea of what was news was strongly influenced by politics. Personal attacks—some of them quite vicious—were common.

By 1798, with Federalist president John Adams in control and preparing for a possible war with France that sparked heated opposition from the Anti-Federalists, Congress passed the Alien and Sedition Acts, the first official efforts by the federal government to censor the press and control its critics (though it also firmly established the truth as a defense for statements made against the government or its officials).

There was a tremendous uproar over the Sedition Act in particular, since it clearly was aimed at stifling dissent. Several editors went to jail, and public reaction against the act was strong. Within a short time, the

Sedition Act expired and it was not renewed, and all those jailed were pardoned by the new president, Thomas Jefferson.

The 19th-Century Press

The new century brought with it enormous growth in the media, starting with the frontier journalism of the early part of the century and progressing through the penny press era, the invention of the telegraph, the Civil War, and then the incredible changes brought by the telephone and, by century's end, the beginnings of radio.

All of these innovations changed the concept of news. To the frontier journalist putting out a small weekly newspaper in a burgeoning Western town, the news was usually very local and as rough-hewn as the ambitious and rugged people who read the paper. But in America's more urban East, it was the Industrial Revolution that brought the greatest changes in the concept of news.

In Boston, New York and other large cities in the East, a combination of circumstances brought the news to the masses for the first time. First, these major cities grew rapidly as Americans moved in from the farms to work in the new factories. The emergence of schooling for these urban children meant rapidly increasing rates of literacy. Also, the same steam power that drove the huge machines in the factory could also be harnessed for printing presses.

By 1833, Benjamin Day began publishing *The New York Sun* and selling it for a penny on street corners every day. The era of the penny press was born as a number of competitors quickly emerged.

To appeal to this mass readership, Day and others became increasingly sensationalistic, printing lurid accounts of crime and mayhem in the streets and embellishing national and international news, as well. Circulation, which had been in the hundreds for most newspapers before this era, shot up into the thousands and then the tens of thousands as the newspapers engaged in circulation wars, each trying to outdo the other in this sensationalist approach to the news.

The Granger Collection, New York

The New York Sun *brought a new medium to the masses.*

By 1844, the invention of the telegraph by Samuel F. B. Morse brought another shift in thinking about what constituted news. With the telegraph, information from distant parts of the country that once took weeks to arrive could now be transmitted in seconds. The public had a large appetite for this new type of immediate news, especially for coverage of the Mexican War in 1846, where the first American war correspondents covered the fighting on a daily basis.

In 1849 the precursor to the Associated Press was formed, and another change in the definition of news took place. As members of a news cooperative, Associated Press newspapers shared stories, thereby enlarging the sources of news far beyond what local reporters and occasional correspondents could cover. As a result, newspapers could include more timely stories about national, and even international, occurrences.

In this same general time period, the abolitionist press arose, giving voice to the anti-slavery movement. Led by writer and editor Frederick Douglass and his newspaper, *The Northern Star* (shortened later to *The North Star*), these newspapers pushed for freedom for slaves in the years leading up to the Civil War. Douglass himself was an escaped slave.

During the Civil War, newspapers in both the North and the South hired many correspondents (called "specials" at the time) to cover the war news. Both sides had news cooperatives, so newspapers shared stories filed by their correspondents. The North's cooperative was the Associated Press, or AP. The news cooperative for the Confederacy was the Press Association, or PA.

The Granger Collection, New York

Frederick Douglass' The North Star began a rich tradition of newspapers that sought the African-American reader.

Reporters from both sides of the conflict faced enormous dangers in their reporting and difficulties in transmitting their stories as well. The high toll rates to use the telegraph lines to file stories, and the possibility that the lines might be cut by the enemy at any time, helped push reporters toward a style of newswriting called "the inverted pyramid," influencing not only what stories were thought of as newsworthy but also how those stories were constructed. You can read more about the inverted pyramid style of newswriting in Chapter 2.

After the war came a huge expansion of the newspaper industry, marked by brisk competition among a great number of newspapers in every large city. This competition eventually led to the yellow press era in newspapers, a time marked by large circulation and financial success, but one also marked by sensationalism and a wildly self-promotional concept of the news.

Hulton Archive/Getty Images

Harper's Weekly *began in the 19th century and continues in publication today as* Harper's Magazine.

The two most successful and competitive publishers of the era were Joseph Pulitzer and William Randolph Hearst. Pulitzer, with the St. Louis *Post-Dispatch* and then later the *New York World*, grabbed and held reader interest with everything from heated pro-war stories (many of them exaggerations or outright inventions) about the coming Spanish-American War, to the sponsorship of Nellie Bly as she attempted to beat Jules Verne's fictional characters' feat of traveling around the world in 80 days.

Hearst was Pulitzer's arch rival, and determined to outdo Pulitzer in every way. Starting with *The San Francisco Examiner* and then later the *New York Journal*, Hearst published newspapers that screamed for the readers' attention with sensational stories of crime, war and violence.

Hearst occasionally hired reporters away from Pulitzer's paper, and even stole Pulitzer's innovative comic strip, "Hogan's Alley," which included a character named the Yellow Kid. When Pulitzer continued to publish the comic with a new artist, the battle over the Yellow Kid soon

The Granger Collection, New York

The Yellow Kid symbolized the journalism of post-Civil War America.

became attached to the excesses of both publishers, and the tag "yellow journalism" was born. After the Spanish-American War, Pulitzer renounced this kind of news coverage and began to champion a higher calling for newspapers. In 1915, as he was dying, he endowed the Pulitzer Prize for excellence in journalism.

Public Relations

Around this same time period the practice of public relations was beginning to emerge as a legitimate tool for media influence. People like circus-act promoter P. T. Barnum and Wild West Show promoter William F. (Buffalo Bill) Cody laid some early groundwork for public relations, but it was Ivy Ledbetter Lee who is considered one of the founders of modern public relations.

In a famous case, Lee (a former reporter), convinced the Pennsylvania Railroad that the best way to react to a deadly train crash was to admit the mistake, try to correct the problems that had led to it, and let the newspapers in on the whole story, rather than trying to hide the crash from public scrutiny. The honesty of the approach worked, and Lee became the first famous public relations practitioner, even managing to change the public image of John D. Rockefeller from that of a financial tyrant to that of a notable philanthropist.

Another important early founder of modern public relations was Edward L. Bernays, who in the 1920s helped legitimize the field not only through his professional work, but also by writing the field's first textbook, *Crystallizing Public Opinion*, which quickly became a standard text. Bernays also taught the first public relations class, at New York University, in 1923.

20th-Century News

Another journalistic style that marked the news in the early part of the new century was muckraking. The Muckrakers primarily published in the flourishing magazine industry of the time and focused their attention on the nation's economic and social ills. Writers and editors like Ida M. Tarbell, Upton Sinclair and Robert J. Collier crusaded for things like governmental controls over monopolistic companies and against things like patent medicines and unsanitary practices in the meat-packing industry. This view of the news as a source for public improvement is still found in both broadcast and print media.

The use of public relations as a source for news—and sometimes a manipulator of the news—emerged at this time, too, with the Creel Committee during World War I.

Shortly after President Woodrow Wilson asked Congress to declare war in April of 1917, he appointed newspaper editor George Creel to head the Committee on Public Information. Creel's committee set up strict policies to communicate the government's news to the media of the time, while it also instructed newspapers and magazines on what kind of war news should be withheld. In addition, the committee issued its own publication, the *Official Bulletin*, which covered the war effort daily.

Generally, the Creel Committee received high marks for its work, both in its effort to swing American public opinion solidly behind the war effort and for its work with the media to provide news about the war while not jeopardizing military operations.

After the war, a prosperous United States entered the Roaring '20s, and the age of jazz journalism—not too far different from the sensationalist days of Hearst and Pulitzer—was a result.

Radio was enjoying its first burst of success in the 1920s, competing with newspapers for both audience and advertisers. In competing with the immediacy and intimacy of radio's spoken words, some newspapers—led by the nation's first tabloid, the New York *Daily News*—became highly sensational. Others followed, and the label "tabloid" has followed (often unfairly) those smaller-sized newspapers since.

During the late 1920s and then through the 1930s, several inventors on both sides of the Atlantic succeeded in developing a workable method of transmitting moving pictures in much the same way that radio transmitted sound. This new medium of television was to have a profound effect on the news in the years ahead, but was too expensive for most Americans during the Great Depression and so temporarily languished.

Radio, however, blossomed into a powerful news medium during the 1930s, and an especially important one as European tensions rose and a large-scale war seemed inevitable. While newspapers could bring a reader in-depth information and analysis on a daily basis, only radio could bring virtually instantaneous information from Europe and President Franklin Roosevelt's White House.

Starting with the Spanish Civil War and then through the latter part of the decade, reporters like H. V. Kaltenborn and Edward R. Murrow became famous for their live reports from the battlefields and negotiating tables of Europe. Radio was primarily an entertainment medium

Peter Stackpole/TimePix

*Life helped popularize magazine
photojournalism, a colorful, visual
approach to delivering the news.*

with a wide range of comedies, dramas, variety shows and the like. But it was a perfect medium for the drama of the world's building tensions, too, and so its news focus stayed on these dramatic events. The concept of "live" news coverage, so important to television's idea of what makes something newsworthy today, comes from this 1930s-to-1940s era of radio news.

Also, during the late 1920s and early 1930s, magazines became interested in the news. Prior to this time, virtually all the major magazines were feature-oriented, with heavy doses of fiction to go along with articles that primarily entertained. Then, in 1923, Henry Luce and Briton Hadden started *Time* magazine, a weekly devoted to keeping America informed of national and international events. By 1929, *Time*'s circulation reached nearly 250,000 and a spin-off, *The March of Time*, was begun on radio. Competitors followed. *Newsweek* started in 1933, and *Business Week* (which had its own ideas on what was newsworthy) began in 1929.

Life and *Look* also began in this area, contributing the art and craft of photojournalism to the news mix, and documentary filmmakers like John Grierson and Robert Flaherty even brought the news concept to film.

With the outbreak of World War II at the end of the decade, both newspapers and radio focused their attention on the war effort. Daily newspaper stories detailed as much information as the military censors would allow from the front while radio sometimes brought the actual sounds of war right into America's living rooms.

War correspondent Ernie Pyle, justifiably the most famous correspondent of the war, thought the real news of the war was the soldiers who fought it. Pyle most frequently reported on the men in the foxholes and regularly risked his life to interview them. He was killed on Ie Shima, in the Pacific Theater, in 1945. Pyle's closely personal look at where the real news was during the war had an impact that is still with us in contemporary newspaper and television coverage of war.

Post-World War II America soon found itself in the Cold War and worried about the spread of Communism. This concern had a strong influence on what the media considered newsworthy on the international scene, where the focus stayed on the Union of Soviet Socialist Republics and the People's Republic of China and their confrontations with the United States and its allies.

But it was the arrival of television in the 1950s that sparked the most dramatic change in newspapers and magazines and what they thought newsworthy. Television boomed after the war, with tens of thousands of newly prosperous Americans buying TV sets, and new stations going on the air by the dozens.

Faced with this chaotic growth, the Federal Communications Commission (FCC) froze all new station allocations in 1948 until 1952, in an effort to get the new medium reasonably organized and to make technical decisions about station allocations and the system to be used for color telecasts. When the freeze was lifted, television very quickly became successful, so successful that the other media were forced to react to this new phenomenon.

Newspapers found that television's ability to tell the news immediately was a match for that of radio, and television added a visual component, as well. This forced newspapers into some dramatic changes in what was thought of as news.

For one thing, newspapers realized they had to be more visual to compete, so photojournalism received a boost in interest. Also, newspapers slowly came to realize that just because they couldn't be *first* with the news, that didn't mean they couldn't be the best, the most complete or the most entertaining.

Finally, newspapers also slowly came to realize that breaking the newspaper into sections made it easier for readers to find what they wanted in their paper and, importantly, made it easier for advertisers to reach exactly the audience they wanted to reach.

This trend toward sectionalizing the newspaper began in the 1950s, picked up steam in the 1960s and 1970s, and has accelerated significantly in the past 25 years, along with other innovations like color photography and highly effective graphics.

For newspapers, this means the idea of what is newsworthy has expanded in the past few decades to include a great deal more feature writing, a huge increase in the newspaper's visual appeal, an increase in specialized sections, and a noticeable increase in news analysis and opinion. All this is in response to audience changes that began with television's arrival in 1952.

Modern Changes in News Content

In terms of news content, the Vietnam War, the Watergate scandal and the Gary Hart political campaign all prompted changes in what was considered news.

As the Vietnam conflict heated up in the mid-1960s, a number of national news media outlets began to focus increasing attention on Southeast Asia. The media in Vietnam had far fewer constraints on their war coverage than most media in previous wars, and the results were telling. Not only did newspapers and magazines have correspondents in the middle of the conflict, but also live or very recent television footage seemed to bring the media's perspective on the war right into America's homes.

As a result, perceived differences between the government's optimism about the war effort and the media's more pessimistic portrayal of how things were going (including considerable footage of killed or wounded American soldiers) helped fuel a great deal of anti-war activism. By the late 1960s this activism reached a peak, with major demonstrations (all covered live by the media) against the war. By the time the United States pulled out of Vietnam in 1975, the war was widely unpopular.

During that same mid-1970s period, a bungled break-in at Democratic Party headquarters in the Watergate complex in Washington, D.C., escalated into President Richard Nixon's resignation. The investigative reporting of Bob Woodward and Carl Bernstein of *The Washington Post* was clearly the major factor in Nixon's decision.

These two events—the Vietnam War and the Watergate scandal—had a dramatic, if temporary, impact on what the media considered newsworthy. War correspondents learned to expect virtually complete freedom to do their reporting even in the middle of a war zone, and investigative reporting became a dominant trend in national political news coverage. Both of these news trends have since faded, but for a decade they heavily influenced our concept of news.

Another major shift in our thinking about news happened during the 1988 presidential campaign, when Democratic candidate Gary Hart of Colorado, a married man, was accused of having an affair. Hart denied the allegations and challenged reporters to provide evidence of any inappropriate behavior. *The Miami Herald* took up Hart's challenge and *did* find the proof in the form of photographs and witnesses, and the Hart campaign collapsed as a result.

Following the Hart reporting, more and more often the media began to look closely at the private lives of political figures. Where once the concept of news in politics was devoted primarily to issues, and often protective of political figures' private lives, after the Hart campaign the media began generally to think of the private lives of political figures as perfectly newsworthy. By the 1990s, these kinds of issues were a regular and major part of the news.

For magazines, television's ability to reach millions of viewers meant that advertisers could reach a mass audience at a cost per thousand (CPM, or the cost to reach 1,000 viewers) that was significantly less expensive than the CPM for magazines.*

---

* "M" is the Roman numeral for "1,000."

The large mass-audience magazines tried various techniques to compete, including cut-rate subscriptions, but nothing quite worked. By the end of the decade most of the large, mass-audience magazines such as *Collier's, Life, Look* and *The Saturday Evening Post*, were either gone or in steep decline.

The answer, for magazines, turned out to be specialization, which meant, for advertisers, a relatively high CPM, but a very *effective* CPM, with little waste. What better place for an automaker to advertise its top-of-the-line automobile than a golf magazine, for instance, where the affluent readership was likely to consider buying that type of car?

This meant, for magazines, that what was newsworthy for a particular magazine became sharply defined in terms of a narrow readership. That trend continued through the 1990s and will probably increase during the new century, becoming even more specialized through the use of new technologies. Even news magazines—*Time, Newsweek* and *U.S. News & World Report*—can be thought of as narrow in that sense, appealing to an audience that wants a weekly wrap-up of world and national news.

For radio, television's impact was profound. Not only did television steal radio's audience, it stole its programming as well. Prior to the early 1950s, radio's programming was similar to what television's is today—a mix of comedies, dramas, variety shows (a form now virtually extinct on television) and news.

When television really arrived during the 1950s, many of the radio shows became television shows. For a few years, the shows were on both media; then low ratings killed them, one by one, on radio. News shows suffered just as badly as the rest, and by the end of the decade it was difficult to find a news show on radio, where once these shows had been an important part of radio's mix.

For more than 30 years, radio devoted the great majority of its programming to music. Then, beginning in the late 1980s (after the FCC dropped the fairness doctrine in 1987, which required broadcasters to offer reply time to all responsible parties when controversial political issues were being discussed), talk radio emerged as a major force on AM radio. Talk radio, primarily concerned with persuasion rather than information, is the major news component of commercial radio today, with a few public affairs programs, the occasional big-city all-news station, and NPR's *All Things Considered* the rare alternatives.

Current and Future Trends

A slow but persistent general decline in both the number of newspapers and their circulations pushes today's newspapers to tinker with their idea of just what the news is. Finding ways to combat that disturbing trend is an ongoing battle in the newspaper business.

One potential solution is the move toward *civic journalism*, a nickname for the kind of newspaper reporting that takes sides on public issues, not just on the editorial and op-ed pages, but even on page one. Led by papers like *The Wichita Eagle* and *The Miami Herald*, civic journalism seeks to place the newspaper into public efforts to combat crime, improve education and the like.

This can be a risky trend, since it threatens to dislodge newspapers' hard-won stance as neutral observers. But it also holds real promise as a way to regain the public's confidence in newspapers and win back disenchanted readers.

Another potential solution is the digital newspaper, one that comes to you through your home computer and offers an intriguing blend of immediacy, depth and consumer choice.

In broadcast, current trends seem to focus on violence and crime, though there are wide variations across the country in terms of local news broadcasts. Certainly another dominant theme is broadcast's version of civic journalism, which often involves local investigative teams, consumer reports, and special health or education reports. Television news always seeks to connect as strongly as it can with the needs of its audience, and local ratings keep a constant eye on each station's success or failure at making that connection.

On the national level, the broadcast networks continue to focus on major national and international political news, and to mix that in with national economic news, and reporting on crime, accidents and disasters of national scope.

A trend during the 1990s that has continued into the new century is the so-called tabloid television news shows like *Hard Copy* and *Inside Edition*, which focus on the more sensational aspects of crime and scandal.

Also, the success of Cable News Network (CNN) and its offshoot CNN Headline News have had an impact on the news, providing, as they do, 24-hour coverage. CNN doesn't expect a huge prime-time audience, as the network news shows must. Instead, CNN aims by its steady presence to become a first stop for anyone seeking up-to-date news, and so capture an adequate audience at a wide variety of time slots during the day.

More recently, Fox News has become a major source of news and commentary for many Americans by combining more typical reporting with a variety of news-talk shows led by popular, and sometimes abrasive, hosts.

News Today

So, what is news today? For a newspaper reporter, the news is usually local and frequently tied to a specific section of the newspaper (the business section, for instance, or a particular suburban area's section). The expectations for a news reporter are that the story will be tightly written, accurate, fair and complete. It can be difficult to get all four goals accomplished when you have to meet a pressing deadline and you have a limited amount of space for the story.

For a television reporter, brevity is even more of a concern, since it is unusual for a particular story to get more than 30 seconds or a

Newspapers like The Tampa Tribune *published extra editions after the terrorist attacks of Sept. 11, 2001, and followed up with extensive coverage on Sept. 12.*

minute at most of air time. Again, the expectations are focused on brevity, accuracy, fairness and completeness. And with television, the visual component is extremely important also, as is the timing of the story. If two events seem equally newsworthy and only one will get on the air, the more visual of the two will most likely be aired. Similarly, television news understandably wants to play to its strengths, so a live report is more newsworthy than a taped one, and the more personal a story is (that is, the more it involves people and strong emotions) the better. A live, highly visual report that involves people in a dramatic context is, arguably, the best story of all for television.

The differences between newspapers and television are clear. A dramatic rescue from a burning building, though routine for the firefighters involved, may be extremely newsworthy by television's standards. For a newspaper, the same rescue may merit no more than a brief in the metro section of the paper. If one of the newspaper's photographers happened to get a good shot, that will probably run prominently, perhaps on page one. But, the accompanying story will probably be a small one, since it is the rescue, not the news value of the fire, that gives the story impact. On radio, the story will probably get no more than a mention during a news wrap-up show.

The differences between the two dominant news media—newspapers and television—help explain why their definitions of news differ. There are, of course, many cases of overlap, where a major story is not only the lead item on the evening news but also the lead story on page one of your local paper. But, there are just as many events that have important news value in one medium and little or no news value at all in the other.

Think back to your interview with your college president after she threw out the first pitch of the softball season in the new stadium.

For television, that first pitch was the most visual element of the story, and the local station keyed its story to that visual element, barely mentioning the president's seven-point plan. To you, on the other hand, the first pitch was unimportant. It was the president's plan that mattered, and her plans for changing tenure that mattered the most.

That's a huge difference. Further, even within your college newspaper there were disagreements. Your editor thought one thing; you thought another; the advisor thought something else again.

And to outsiders, your decision on what was most newsworthy didn't make much sense at all to some, but great sense to others. The president and her staff thought the news lay elsewhere, for instance, but you can bet that many of your college faculty agreed with your opinion that the tenure issue was the most important item.

It's all worrisomely indefinite, as you discovered. One medium's lead item is another's least important one, or doesn't make the news at all. And within a medium, one editor's opinion may, at times, differ from that of another editor or of the reporter.

What are you to do, then? The idea of news doesn't seem dependable at all. It's changed widely over the years, and yet after nearly 300 years of discussion, there's still disagreement.

Well, the situation is not quite as chaotic as it seems. Certainly within each medium there is wide agreement on what news means, and even a general agreement on how to rank items within a particular news event when you're writing a story (for more on this ranking process, see Chapter 6). And while the print and broadcast media have some areas of disagreement when it comes to the news, they have a number of areas of broad agreement as well.

Here's a ranked list for a generally agreed-upon set of standards for rating the news value of something or someone, from a newspaper's perspective:

1. *The news is unusual.* Readers are generally not interested in normal, everyday occurrences. It is the events that depart from the norm that are interesting. A story on the dozens or hundreds of airplanes taking off and landing each day at your local airport would have little news value (though it might make a nice feature story once every two or three years). A plane crash, though, or even the threat of one (from, say, engine trouble) is *very* newsworthy—in part because it is so unusual.

2. *The news is local.* If a large warehouse burns down in your town, causing damage but injuring no one, the fire will probably have news value for your local paper. In a smaller city, it will be page one news. The newspaper in the next town, however, may find very little news value in the fire. The newspaper in a town 200 miles away will probably find no news value in the story at all.

3. *The news is timely.* That same fire has a great deal of news value in the next day's paper, but the value declines rapidly from there. Three or four days later it typically has no news value at all.

4. *The news involves prominent people.* Readers are interested in prominent people, from politicians to rock stars to athletes. Your next-door neighbor's arrest for driving while intoxicated probably has little news value for the local paper. However, if your next-door neighbor is the mayor or the shortstop of your local baseball team, the news value of the story rises rapidly.

5. *The news quickly informs and explains.* Readers expect to be quickly informed by their newspaper, and they expect that

information to explain and clarify the news. The more information you can present, and the better you can explain it, the more news value the story has.

6. *The news is about people.* Readers like to read about people. They connect best to those stories that show the human side of the news. A dry recitation of economic numbers may numb a reader. A story that shows the effect of those numbers on a typical family has more news value.

7. *The news has a broad, general appeal.* For newspapers, the news must appeal to a general audience, one that includes all the various elements of human society in your town. The broader the story's appeal, the greater its news value.

And here's a list from a magazine's perspective:

1. *The news is specific to that magazine's interest.* Magazines are almost always aimed at a specific and narrow audience, and the news value of a given story is directly related to the story's appeal to that narrow audience. Wise magazine writers pay close attention to the magazine's needs when constructing their stories, hoping to maximize the news value for that particular readership.

2. *The news involves prominent people.* Just as in newspapers, readers care about prominent people. In magazines, though, the specific interest of the magazine sharply defines who is prominent. A surfing magazine won't find much news value in a U.S. senator, unless he or she is a surfer or involved in legislation having to do with surfing.

3. *The news entertains as it informs and explains.* For magazines, entertainment is often at least as important as informing and explaining. A story that entertains the reader as it discusses a relevant issue has more impact, and so more news value, than one that dryly informs.

And here's a list from the perspective of broadcast television:

1. *The news is visual.* For television, the visual image is often the key element in weighing the news value of otherwise equal events. A warehouse fire, with its strong visual appeal, usually has more news value than a speech or lecture.

2. *The news is live.* Television's immediacy is part of its powerful appeal. Live events usually have far more news value than taped events.

3. *The news is local (or national and/or international for network news).* Television, like newspapers, deals with proximity as a news value. The closer an event is to your town, the more news value it has. The news value of many events declines sharply outside the immediate TV market area.

4. *The news is personal.* Television shows human emotion better than newspapers, magazines or radio. The more emotionally personal the news event is (showing elation or fear or sorrow or anger on a subject's face, for instance), the more news value it has.

5. *The news is unusual.* Like newspapers, television gives news value to the unusual, though this ranks lower than other news value elements for television.

6. *The news involves prominent people.* Just like for newspapers, the more prominent a subject is, the greater the news value. For television, add in the visual element (clips from a famous athlete or a Hollywood star, for instance) and the news value increases even more.

Agreements and Disagreements

You can see that there are several areas of general agreement about what gives something or someone news value:

▶ *Prominent individuals* have news value.

▶ *Unusual* occurrences or people have news value.

▶ *Timeliness* gives added news value.

▶ *Proximity* to the media outlet gives added news value.

▶ *Personal (human) interest* angles to the story give added news value.

The ranking of these elements changes from medium to medium, but a general, unranked list would include all the items just mentioned.

Importantly, these news values are rarely isolated. That is, most news events or newsworthy people include several of the listed news value. In many respects, the more of these values the event has, the greater the news value.

It's also very important to see how these rankings of news value are changing with the emergence of the Internet and new-media convergence. As you will see in Chapter 10, the immediacy of new-media publications and online versions of traditional publications has an impact on the news value of that publication.

Summary

The concept of what news is has changed over the centuries. Early newspapers were often censored by government, but by the early 1700s in the American Colonies independent editors were publishing whatever they thought was news.

During the 1800s the arrival of the Industrial Revolution brought large audiences for newspapers. By the 1920s radio had arrived with its own ideas of what was newsworthy, and by the 1950s television's rise changed the concept of news again.

Today, the different media each have their own ideas of what makes something newsworthy, with television most interested in dramatic and often live images, newspapers most interested in personalities and the unusual, and magazines most interested in specific news relevant to their specialized audiences. Radio is most interested in sports and opinion, though some stations still provide timely coverage of breaking news.

Key Points

▶ The idea of news varies from medium to medium.

▶ The idea of news has changed over time.

▶ The various media agree on certain news values.

▶ The idea of news is changing again with the arrival of the information age.

Web Links

Here are a few interesting sites on the Internet where you can find out more about media history and news value.

http://www.nscee.edu/unlv/Colleges/Greenspun/Journalism_History
http://www.mediahistory.com/
http://www.scripps.ohiou.edu/mediahistory/
http://www.newspapers.com

InfoTrac College Edition Readings

For additional readings, go to **www.infotrac-college.com**, enter your password, and search for the following articles by title or author's name.

► "Network Anchors See a Diminished World: Nightly News Loses Viewers and Substance," *Columbia Journalism Review*, March–April 2002 v40 i6 p52.

► "Improving the News," James S. Ettema, *Quill*, June 2001 v89 i5 p54.

► "Merging Media to Create an Interactive Market," Jack Fuller, *Nieman Reports*, Winter 2000 v54 i4 p33.

► "A Case Study: How to Get on (or Stay off) the Front Page," Randall S. Sumpter, *Newspaper Research Journal*, Summer 2000 v21 i3 p39.

Exercises

Go to your CD-ROM to complete the following exercises:

► Exercise 1.1

► Exercise 1.2

For more chapter review, use the following resources on your *Modern Media Writing* CD-ROM:

► *InfoTrac College Edition* Exercises (included in the exercises of some chapters)

► Key Points

► Weblinks

► A link to the **Modern Media Writing Web** Site at the Wadsworth Communication Cafe, which offers activities at **http://communication.wadsworth.com/wilber_miller**.

Basic Structures for Media Writing

No doubt you've noticed that your professors use different lecture styles. Dr. Neatfreak, for example, emphasizes the important points of the lecture by writing key words on the blackboard and meticulously following a set of charts on the overhead projector.

Dr. Nytol, though, chases rabbits, rambling from one anecdote to another before culminating in a desperate rush to fill in important points in those final five minutes while students rustle their backpacks and shuffle their feet in anticipation of escape.

Your class notes for each professor may look the same, but you've learned that your study habits need to differ for each. Dr. Neatfreak has organized her lectures clearly, and you can follow that outline if you're a conscientious notetaker. But your notes for Dr. Nytol need to emphasize the rapidly delivered, but important, material at the end rather than following the anecdotes, if you're going to have the material you'll need later for a test. If you were to study heavily the beginning of Dr. Nytol's lectures, you might well be learning material that won't appear on the exams.

Beginning reporters often make a similar mistake when they park themselves in front of a keyboard to start turning their notes into a story. They open their notepads and begin describing the response the first source made to the first interview question. Then they trace their path through the first source's quotes, and only after exhausting those do they consider what a second source said. They repeat the pattern, following the second interview in exact order before moving to the notes from the third interview.

This may seem to you, at first glance, like a perfectly logical way of organizing the information in a story. It is, after all, an entirely natural pattern. But it is almost certainly not the best approach for your story.

The Inverted Pyramid

During the Civil War, war correspondents from both the North and the South were faced with a problem. Using the telegraph, they could easily write a detailed account of the day's news from the front. But they could rarely be certain that the troops of one side wouldn't cut the wires in order to prevent their enemy from using them.

As a result, the correspondents began to emphasize the day's most important happenings at the beginning of their dispatches in case the wires went down during their transmission. This form of storytelling—building a structure from most important information to least important—became known as the *inverted pyramid*. (See Figure 2.1.)

Or so the stories tell us.

Some journalism historians, more cynical (and perhaps more accurate), point out that the inverted pyramid structure made it more economical for the burgeoning wire services of the latter half of the 19th century to save money on telegraph costs. Also, these historians

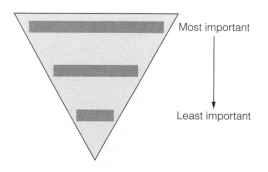

FIGURE 2.1 *The inverted pyramid structure*

point out that plenty of post–Civil War stories were written in nothing resembling an inverted pyramid. Indeed, the inverted pyramid actually seems to be a perfect design for newspaper writing after the invention of typesetting machines more than 30 years *after* the Civil War. With such technology, typesetters found it simple to stop when a page was filled to capacity.

No matter exactly how the inverted pyramid form came to be, it remains a staple in all kinds of news writing. Most newspaper editors today will expect you to be able to craft an inverted pyramid story, and if you're writing news releases, your success may well depend on how well you've mastered the inverted pyramid form. Television reporters, who face tight constraints of time, must be able to give their audience the most important point to a story at its very beginning and then mention in declining order whatever less important points there is time for.

The Magic Formula

Beginning writers sometimes believe that a magic formula for importance exists and that if they could just figure out that formula, then writing would be simple. Alas, even with something as basic as the inverted pyramid, the formula isn't magic at all. Instead, figuring out what is important requires solid reporting and a sense of news values from you.

In Chapter 1, you learned a number of factors that go into deciding what's newsworthy and what isn't, and that list should help you decide what belongs at the top of a story and what comes after that, in order.

But every story differs somewhat, depending on the medium you're working in and the publication's or station's needs. So, while you can certainly use the basic news values—prominent individuals, unusual nature, timeliness, proximity, human interest and others—to help determine what fact is most important in a particular story, you should expect variations in how an editor wants those elements put together.

Usually, the most important element of a story will be the one that affects the most people or affects only a few people but affects them drastically. To help you figure out which element that is, some writing coaches favor this little exercise: Imagine you're calling a friend or a family member about the story, but you have only 15 seconds before the phone line is shut down to tell that person one thing about the happening. What would you say before the phone line died? That element may be the most important one in your story, and thus the one that you will spotlight in your beginning. We call that beginning the "lead" (pronounced "leed"). (Some news organizations spell this as *lede* to differentiate it from *lead* (pronounced "led"), an abbreviation for *leading*, the term for the spacing of lines in printed stories.)

But the inverted pyramid doesn't stop there. You will need to rank all your information in order of importance and then build a structure that uses effective transitions (more about them later in this chapter) to guide the reader through it.

Also, you want to make sure that information supporting your lead follows soon after. Or, perhaps, after you've told why the story is important, you will want to explain some of the story's background fairly quickly. If you're covering a trial, for instance, you'll want the reader to know that the trial has to do with a particular crime that the defendant is accused of having committed.

The least important facts you've gathered end the story. You won't need to think even for a second about how to end an inverted pyramid story. The last paragraph contains the least important fact or aspect of the story, and the story usually ends flatly right there, with no concluding paragraph.

Pretend you've been assigned to cover a county commission meeting. At that meeting, these items catch your attention and you jot them down in your notepad.

- ▶ Commissioners Nagle and Gilliam insulted one another during a discussion.

- ▶ The commission voted 5–0 to triple the county licensing fees for tattoo parlors.

- ▶ The commission debated and tabled a proposal to build a sidewalk for one block of Bagley Avenue.

- ▶ The commission voted 3–2 to impose a half-cent sales tax on clothing for a new jail facility.

- ▶ The commission unanimously approved three easements—two for subdivisions and one for Sepulveda's Tex-Mex Restaurant.

Here's how your story might look:

KIRKWOOD — The county commission last night narrowly passed a half-cent sales tax on clothing that will provide needed funds for a new jail facility.

Councilman Gus Gilliam broke a 2–2 tie among the commissioners by approving the tax despite objections from representatives of several major clothing retailers within the county.

"The citizenry has clearly expressed its desire for increased jail capacity," Gilliam said. "The sales tax on clothing is the least onerous way to quickly raise the funding."

Commissioners Martha Milton and James Holmes voted to pass the tax while Esther Nagle and Gonzalo De-Leon voted against it.

The commissioners agreed unanimously to triple licensing fees for tattoo parlors in the county, despite objections from several local tattoo artists and customers.

(continued)

(continued)

"They always take it out on the young people," said college student Jennifer Bellini, who sported a spider-web design on both elbows.

Commissioner DeLeon claimed that the fee would eliminate the fly-by-night nature of some new businesses. "Besides, we haven't increased the fee since the first parlor opened years and years ago," he said.

The commission didn't take action on requests from Oak Haven residents on a sidewalk for the 5700 block of Bagley Avenue.

"Some kid's going to get killed on his way to the Circle K if you're not careful," said Janice McDowell, a resident of the nearby Oak Haven Estates subdivision.

You can see that for this story, you would almost certainly lead with the half-cent tax for the jail. Readers will want to know about their tax statements and how this jail might specifically help reduce crime. That vote would affect almost every reader in the county.

Two other items would compete for the next slot in the inverted pyramid: the tattoo parlor license fee and the sidewalk. Neither is likely to affect the entire county, but the license fee might mean an increase in the cost of tattoos or the closing of local businesses. The sidewalk sounds pretty dull, but may signal some other problem. Do residents want the sidewalk so schoolchildren won't have to step into Bagley Avenue traffic? Or will it help storefront businesses?

The other two items probably aren't very important at all. Oh, Nagle and Gilliam could be former allies on the commission and the insults could signal a split. Or you might decide the insults are just typical politician behavior. The easements (an easement is a right that one person has to use land owned by another for a specific, limited purpose) might mean that Sepulveda's wants to expand into property used as a food bank for the homeless. But easements such as these usually mean that the restaurant wants a second entrance to its parking lot or that the subdivision wants to widen the entrance past county codes. Conceivably, a good reporter could find stories in both items, but neither would be likely to bump any of the other three from the upper part of the pyramid (unless the insults were particularly vicious).

Keep in mind that you need not want to include every fact in your story.

Public Relations

Jennifer Barrs covers country music for *The Tampa Tribune*, a newspaper located in a market that sees plenty of country music performers every year. As a reporter and reviewer, Barrs receives press releases and press kits from the public relations practitioners representing these musicians. She's learned what works.

"I need the basics—what time is the concert, where, admission prices," she says. "I appreciate a beautifully written story on how this star learned to play guitar and I appreciate the quotes, but I would rather know the basic information; I shouldn't have to call the publicist back and ask when the concert will be held."

Why don't more press releases contain the basic information?

"Three out of four don't have basic information and they don't start the release with it," she says. "Too many releases read like advertising copy."

Advertising tries to sell a product to a customer. But, as corporate consultant Frank R. Stansberry explains, public relations has a different purpose.

"Public relations is interested in creating an environment in which the company's goals can be achieved," says Stansberry, who worked for Coca-Cola USA as the manager of guest affairs at Epcot Center in Orlando.

Stansberry often talks to beginning public relations students about the importance of adopting journalistic writing techniques.

"Since you're playing on the media's court, you might as well play by their rules," he says.

Plus, he adds, writing in the inverted pyramid form forces the public relations writer to decide what's really important, while also making that information more acceptable to a journalist.

A writer like Barrs receives dozens of releases daily. A release that gets its point across immediately has a better chance of catching her attention than purple prose without basic facts.

You'll see a lot more about writing for public relations in Chapter 11.

Pyramid Problems

The inverted pyramid's strength is that it lets the reader know immediately what is important. It wastes no time in catching the reader's interest with catchy description or lyrical narration or uninformative shock. There are other kinds of leads that you've read about that try for these effects, but the inverted pyramid lead doesn't. Instead, it says, This is the news, reader, and *this* is the most important part of it.

The inverted pyramid structure also provides another service for readers after they move past the lead: It allows the reader to scan key points of each story without having to search for the news.

Readers, in fact, can follow along as far as they wish and get maximum news for their effort. If they read half of a story, they have the most important information contained in one-half of the story.

The inverted pyramid also serves as a standard, and that makes it very important for you to learn how to write the news in this structure. Musicians may love to reach the limits of their instruments, but they must also practice the basics. Professional musicians practice for hours each day—and they usually begin a practice with scales. Basic, everyday scales. In different keys. In different octaves.

The inverted pyramid is like a musical scale in that it is the basic structure for newspaper stories and press releases. Television news, as you've seen, also relies on the basic premise of presenting the important facts first in a story. Certainly, you as a beginning writer, need to master this form. But you should also realize its limitations.

Foremost, the inverted pyramid doesn't lend much drama or tension to your writing. Consider this inverted-pyramid lead to the events in the film *Casablanca*.

> MOROCCO — Restaurateur Rick Blaine shot the villain, allowed his lost love to flee Casablanca with her husband, and then departed into the fog to join the anti-Nazi underground.

That gives the news, certainly, but it saps every last bit of the dramatic tension from that great film. The inverted pyramid works well in summarizing the main point of a news event, but it doesn't do a very good job of storytelling.

Of course, not every event is dramatic. Our fictional county commission meeting probably didn't have much tension. But imagine you go to a basketball game where the home team blows a big lead before winning on a shot at the buzzer, the noise almost deafening you as the students swarm the court and trade high-fives before carrying off the player who sank the winning shot.

Here's the inverted pyramid approach to that story:

> The Owls defeated the Coyotes 71–70 in the final seconds here last night at Smith Gym.
>
> Michael Kilgore scored 15 points, but none as important as his successful jumper as the buzzer sounded to end the game.

That inverted pyramid summary lead just doesn't convey the emotion of the event, but it does give the final score. In Chapter 4, you can read several other ways to start this story that offer considerably greater excitement.

The inverted pyramid approach also allows editors to cut from the bottom of the story without losing important information. This mattered when stories were typed on dependable manual typewriters and the typed pages were carried by copy boys to the back of the shop, where Linotype operators would set the stories in rows of recently molten lead ("line of type," hence the trademarked name Linotype). An editing change in the middle of the story meant considerable effort on the part of those operators, slowing down the newspaper's production.

However, in a time when computer technology has supplanted hot lead, editors can much more easily trim a story in the middle or rearrange paragraphs or perform other structural changes that required considerable effort in the hot-metal days. So, the inverted pyramid structure has lost its technological advantage.

And the inverted pyramid has another, more telling problem, says writing coach Don Fry. In his teaching sessions at newspapers around the country, he points out to writers that the inverted pyramid structure means that information eventually gets duller and duller as the reader goes through the story. And why subject the reader to dull information?

Chronological Order

The most traditional way to organize a story is through chronology: first, second, next. According to one version, the Book of Genesis starts "In the beginning, there was God" and traces days one through seven.

Telling a story from the beginning allows readers to follow along in a familiar pattern that they can easily understand. It also allows you to build to a climax at the end. In a chronology, what comes last is often the lead in an inverted pyramid story.

The chronological structure has its limits, though. The story must have some element of chronology in it, for instance, or the form won't work.

Many television news stories are too brief to build any tension, though some reporters use chronology in detailing crime stories. Television and print reporters almost never use chronology in detailing a speech or a sports event or stories like our earlier story of the county commission meeting.

One of the more common traps that beginning writers fall into is trying to build a chronology around a speech, depending on the speaker to have structured the chronology from most important to least important.

Unfortunately for reporters, many speakers use their openings to build to later, more important points. They prefer to warm up the audience or help themselves relieve their own fears of public speaking. Suppose the most important part of a speech comes two-thirds of the way through. Your readers are unlikely to fight through to the good stuff on Page 3 if you have a straight chronological approach to writing the story about that speech.

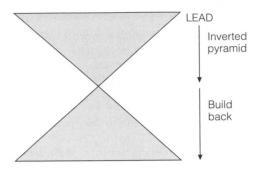

FIGURE 2.2 *The hourglass structure*

You also won't see many city council stories start with the Pledge of Allegiance, or many sports stories begin with the first points scored in a high-scoring game.

A Pair of Glass Structures

Two hybrid structures may help you write news stories that take advantage of modern technology while still retaining some of the impact of the inverted pyramid form.

The hourglass structure shown in figure 2.2, mixes an inverted pyramid beginning with a pyramid structure at the end.

Thanks to the portable computer, this form has become useful because reporters can file ongoing information, perhaps chronologically, from the site of the story (the pyramid structure at the base) before topping the story with the most important information in inverted pyramid fashion.

If you are asked to cover a night event (a game or a political rally) on deadline, you might write about some of the earlier events as they occur and file them with your office. Then you might top the story with an inverted pyramid lead or a descriptive lead and follow-up paragraphs.

Here's an example:

She can't pull objects from the sky with a gold lasso or deflect bullets with shiny wrist bands, but Donna Stilwell is a superhero no less. At least in the eyes of her husband, who has only tire-mark abrasions, bruises and a broken arm to show for a mishap that could have been far more serious.

Last Sunday, Richard Stilwell was working underneath a van in his driveway when the linkage slipped and the vehicle rolled on top of him. In a feat of remarkable strength, Donna Stilwell lifted the weight of the frame off her husband's body, allowing him to slip out from under it.

"If it wasn't for her, who knows what would have happened," said

Richard Stilwell, recovering at their home in Bow yesterday after two days in the hospital. "I can't believe she did that."

Neither can Wonder Woman herself. "I don't know how I did it. I just lifted. It didn't feel that heavy," said Donna Stilwell, who, for curiosity's sake, attempted a repeat performance yesterday. The 5-foot-2-inch, 110-pound woman couldn't heft the vehicle even half an inch.

"I really think it was adrenaline," she said.

Certainly it was more than a hearty helping of spinach. "It seemed like somewhat of a Herculean effort," said Scott Devanney, the doctor who set Stilwell's broken arm Sunday night. "He told me his wife picked the van off of him, and I said, 'This lady right here?'"

In his years of medical practice, Devanney has never heard of such a feat firsthand. "You hear about it happening, but I've never actually had a patient who experienced it," he said. "It's pretty amazing. She may have saved his life."

It's hard to say what would have happened if Stilwell had been pinned under the van for any length of time, Devanney said.

The chronology begins here. ▶ Stilwell had the van, a full-size Dodge Ram, up on ramps and was making adjustments to the transmission he'd just replaced when the vehicle slipped out of gear and started rolling down the steep driveway. He tried to get out of the way but wasn't fast enough. The van's under parts rolled him on his stomach, and its front tire came to rest on his upper thigh.

Hearing her husband's cries, Donna Stilwell ran outside.

Richard Stilwell can't believe his wife didn't panic. "If the cat gets hurt, she goes into hysterics," he said.

"He told me to go get the neighbor, but I was like, 'No, we have to move the van,'" Donna Stilwell said.

Unfortunately, the keys weren't in the ignition. Donna Stilwell ran inside, called the neighbor and grabbed the keys. A former truck driver, she had no trouble easing the van forward off her husband's leg. But their troubles weren't over. Richard Stilwell was now pinned, belly down, beneath the vehicle's frame—and in a great deal of pain.

"I said, 'Well, you're going to have to pick it up,'" Richard Stilwell said.

So she did.

Grabbing hold of the van beneath the front wheelwell, Donna Stilwell lifted the van enough for her husband to roll all the way underneath it—Richard Stilwell estimates 4 or 5 inches, though no one was there with a tape measure. She then hopped back in the driver's seat and carefully backed down the driveway. Paramedics soon arrived and took Stilwell to Concord Hospital, where he was treated for a broken arm, bruises and abrasions. He's on painkillers to ease the throbbing in his arms, head, chest and leg.

Donna Stilwell is no worse for the wear.

It's hard to say just how much weight the quiet, petite woman lifted. Richard Stilwell figures the van, which is full of tools, weighs 4,000 to 5,000 pounds.

Raising that type of vehicle high enough for a person to slip out from under the frame would not require lifting the entire vehicle off the ground, said Dan Weed, a Concord mechanic. Rather, you would have to lift the weight of the body off the suspension.

"It's possible," Weed said. "But it takes a lot to do it with a van that big."

Donna Stilwell says she had plenty of motivation. "It's pretty scary seeing your husband pinned under the car," she said.

Just imagine what she could do with a couple of those spiffy wrist bands.

Sarah Earle, *Concord Monitor*

The Stilwell story actually uses a slightly different structure—the champagne glass—which also includes an inverted pyramid begin-

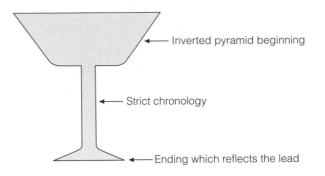

FIGURE 2.3 *The champagne-glass structure*

ning, but follows with a defined chronology before ending with important information, usually related to your lead. The form is shown in Figure 2.3.

Again, this structure allows a reporter to compose the chronology as it happens before concentrating on the lead and, in this case, the ending. In the Stilwell story, the first paragraph to mention Dan Weed begins the defined ending.

Because the beginning and end of the story both include important information, you will usually want to tie your ending to your beginning. This technique is sometimes called a "circle kicker" (*kicker* is an old newspaper term for "ending"). The writer tries to bring the reader back to the beginning with the ending.

In the following example from *The Philadelphia Inquirer*, reporter Jennifer Weiner writes about reaction to the death of Grateful Dead leader Jerry Garcia. Notice how the concepts of family and loss show up in the lead and in the ending:

They knew it was coming. Given their hero's much-publicized history of drug use and ill health, how could they not?

Still, yesterday afternoon, fans of the Grateful Dead were struggling to come to grips with the passing of Jerry Garcia—the band's lead guitarist, its sometime singer and its heart.

"Everyone knew Jerry was sick. We just wanted to see him get fatter and older and retire to his ranch in Marin," said John Rockwell of Springfield, Delaware County, veteran of more than 400 shows. "But, in a way, I guess that's what he did."

* * *

For some, the music was only a part of what it meant to be a Deadhead and of what Jerry Garcia's death has taken away from them.

Randi Horn of Northeast Philadelphia left work early yesterday—she'd been crying since her coworkers took her aside and told her the news, and her stomach hurt from the sobs.

"I blasted his tapes on the way home thinking, 'This is what I'll miss,'" she said. "I'd been having a rough year, and I'd think, 'Well, I'll catch a few shows in September and be OK.' Now I won't have that either."

◀ *After backgrounding the circumstances of the death and continuing reactions of famous and not-so-famous Deadheads, Weiner closes her story with these paragraphs.*

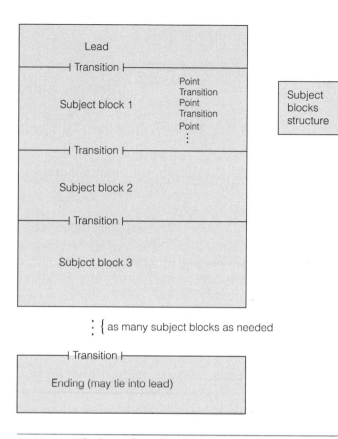

FIGURE 2.4 *The key-subject-blocks structure*

Remember, that a basic inverted pyramid story doesn't require an ending. But writers who use the glass forms are usually trying to keep the reader involved throughout the story.

A broadcast reporter will often want to finish a story with an ending that ties into the opening, but usually doesn't have time to develop a long chronology or to impart the relatively minor information needed in the glass forms.

Public relations practitioners often find the glass forms more effective for in-house communication than the inverted pyramid, which works best for media releases. Readers of the organization's own magazine, sometimes called a "house organ," aren't as hurried as morning newspaper readers and can be expected to read to the end of the story. Such readers don't need the inverted pyramid's heavy information load right up front and are looking for each story to be entertaining as well as informative.

Key-Subject Blocks

You probably have already used this form while writing for other classes, but it is a useful way to organize information in certain news stories as well. The form basically begins with an attention-grabbing summary and then illustrates key points or subject areas one at a time before providing an ending that ties back to the beginning. You might think of the key-subject-blocks form as looking like the illustration in Figure 2.4.

One way to approach this method is to think of subheads. You might organize a feature on campus-area restaurants under these subject headings: Chinese, Mexican, Pizza, Hamburgers. Or a feature on a political candidate's platforms might be organized with these headings: Economy, Education, Abortion, Crime.

A writer won't usually insert the actual subheads into his or her copy, but having them in mind clearly organizes the story's flow.

The key-subject-blocks method works especially well for longer stories because it helps keep the story flowing. Using subject blocks removes the responsibility of ranking information by importance. Each subject block is relatively as important as the others. Thus, the writer only needs to organize material into suitable blocks and string them together with solid transitions.

You won't actually spend a lot of effort in thinking about various story structures as you gain experience. With a little practice, the structures will start to become second nature to you, freeing you up to give more thought to your reporting and other elements of the craft of your writing.

You should remember that the structure's main purpose is to help you organize material for a particular audience. Don't fret about constructing the perfect inverted pyramid or champagne-glass story. Instead, concentrate on telling a great story.

Transitions

Beginning writers often turn in stories that seem disconnected. The stories resemble nothing so much as stacks of facts and quotes piled atop each other. This pile of stuff desperately needs transitions to help guide the reader from one thought to the next. After placing information in some sort of logical order, you have to tie it together for the reader.

The metaphor of tying together is appropriate for transition writing. Think of transitions as the duct tape that keeps your facts and quotes from falling apart.

You may use any or all of the transition devices that follow.

▶ *Repeated words, thoughts or concepts.* In the paragraph after the heading "Transitions" above, the word *piled* is mentioned in the second sentence and then *pile* appears in the third sentence. One easy way to tie a story together is to use repetition throughout. As you browse some of the stories in this textbook, notice the ways that words, thoughts and concepts are carried from one paragraph to the next.

▶ *Transition words.* As mentioned in "Grammar Terms" **Chapter 3**, certain words serve as transitional devices by themselves. The most common of these are the *coordinating conjunctions* and the *conjunctive adverbs*. These words serve to keep track of the scene for the readers.

▶ *Time and place words.* Writers can also keep the reader informed by using words and phrases that track time and place. *In Manhattan, Across town, After midnight, At 3:15 p.m.,* and *Somewhere over Kansas* are examples of these kinds of phrases.

▶ *Numbers.* The use of ordinal numbers—*first, second, third*—can provide order to your story.

In some instances, writers will simply use one or more of these phrases to convey transition, but often they will use transition sentences. These usually involve the repetition of some word, phrase or concept in order to move on to the next point.

Occasionally, though, beginning writers lapse into what we call "television transitions." This device works well for broadcast stories, but leads to trouble for print stories. You are almost certainly familiar with these transitions:

Howard Troxler is the humorous political columnist for the *St. Petersburg Times.*

Owl Goingback is an author of several Native American–based fantasy novels.

One Writer's Approach to Structures

David Barron hears voices in his head, or at least he does when he starts to assemble a news story.

"The thing I always try to picture is Walter Cronkite [the long-time CBS news commentator] reading my story," he said. "If I can see Cronkite reading it in his and-that's-the-way-it-is voice, then I know that I'm on the right track.

"I think you ought to rely on keeping it conversational with someone's voice running through your head without sounding stupid."

Barron, assistant sports editor of the *Houston Chronicle,* has worked as a news reporter, assistant city editor, wire-service reporter, and magazine writer during his 20 years in journalism. That's long enough to learn to do more than follow the basic advice of mentally composing the lead while driving back to the office. Barron often mentally sketches out the first five or six paragraphs and tries to have an idea where the rest of the story is going.

"If you can master the structure of the story, then you've got everything else licked," he said. "A lot of the trick is using linear thinking to get from one point to the next."

The biggest problem that Barron notices as an editor who also writes is that some reporters flit around the story in ineffective bursts.

"We call them choppy stories," Barron said. "Ideas are not fully developed, but you'll get 30 percent of the idea, then go on to something completely unrelated and then come back with another 20 percent of the idea and so on.

"Choppy's not real good."

Barron knows that the lead is important: It not only it engages the reader; it also sets the structure for the rest of the story. Consider his following lead on one of his first sports stories written for the *Chronicle* at a time when the staff may have wondered whether he could write.

Andre Ware and Anthony Thompson finished No. 1 and No. 2 respectively in this year's Heisman Trophy voting.

Nigel Clay and Bernard Hall are No. 184913 and No. 184915 respectively in the Oklahoma Department of Corrections.

Paula Clemens is the company's training and quality coordinator.

These work only in broadcast stories where the verbal description can be matched with a picture of either Troxler wearing his trademark bow tie, Goingback dressed in traditional tribal wear, or Clemens dressed in a business suit. In print, they don't work because the visual (or verbal, in radio) element is not present.

Finally (to use a popular transition word), transitions are important at a deeper level for writers who embark on feature stories. Not

From this lead, it's clear that Barron's structure will contrast the success of Ware and Thompson with the failures of Clay and Hall, who could have been star players.

Even while Barron gathers information for his stories, he's trying to figure out which quotes will help the story and how he can build his story around them.

"If you know what structure you're going to use, then you don't even have to begin with the lead," Barron said. "If I get blocked on the lead, and [that] still happens occasionally, I will write the second half of the story or a segment somewhere in the middle in order to use this quote, which will lead to this transition.

"Soon, most of the story is written, and then the lead seems to follow."

During his days as assistant city editor for the *Waco Tribune-Herald,* Barron got a crash course in using transitions. The editors decided to run a long feature piece titled "A Minute in Waco," and the entire staff, including copy editors, section editors and anyone else breathing in the newsroom, was assigned a specific location to cover at exactly 2 p.m.

Except for Barron.

He stayed in the newsroom and waited while the reporters returned to the office and hammered out two-and three-paragraph vignettes about a minute in a convenience store or about how swim-suit-clad students were placidly studying at the university marina.

And Barron had to assemble the pieces into a narrative, using dozens and dozens of transitions to take readers from football practice to a funeral home to a kindergarten.

"You get pretty good at it when you have to use a transitional device every two or three paragraphs for a 100-inch-plus story," Barron said.

However, he thinks longer stories with a lengthier theme base ought to be structured in block fashion.

"When you're getting into 40- to 50-inch stories, it helps to think in blocks with three dashes, if not subheads," Barron said.

Barron likes the inverted pyramid approach to basic news stories.

"I'm basically wire-service-oriented [after working for United Press International—UPI] when it comes to breaking news," Barron said. "What I do is write a lead, two or at most three paragraphs of background and hit them with a quote and then build around the quotes."

But he realizes that the approach doesn't always work on feature stories.

only must feature writers tie together the paragraphs with transitions, but they must also make sure that the theme flows through the story. In Jamie Allen's story on Michael Clarke Duncan ("*Green Mile*'s Giant Has Taken Massive Strides," in Chapter 7), for example, notice how often Allen contrasts Duncan's imposing physical presence with his softer, emotional side. Good features carry themes like this one throughout the story. That doesn't happen accidentally. Therefore, the feature writer decides what the story is about and then toils to carry through that theme from the beginning until the end of the piece.

"You think in staccato in a news story—more like Dan Rather than Charles Kuralt—but you think long-term on features," Barron said. "Features are more often structured from idea to idea while news is structured fact to fact."

Barron shows the difference between the two with an example about a second-day news story (breaking news is often called "first-day" in newspaper journalism) about a killer tornado in Texas. Since Barron has covered Texas high school football for the *Chronicle* (and edits *Texas Football* magazine, a publication that includes a summary of hundreds of high school teams), he wondered whether any football players had died in the calamity. As a sports editor, he thought the piece might make an interesting story.

He compared the casualty list with his *Texas Football* list, learning that 12 teen-agers had died in the tornado and that six had been football players. He made some telephone calls and began his story like this:

> Jarrell's Cougars will open the 1997 football season against Bruceville-Eddy.
> No one has suggested canceling the game; high school football, after all, is what transfixes young Texans even when part of their town doesn't exist anymore.
> Fifty boys, about one-half of the kids in the school and probably 70 to 80 percent of the boys, planned on donning helmets this fall for coach Terry Burke.

Now the number will be 44.

"The next fact I wanted to establish was about two brothers who were killed in the storm," Barron said. "They saw the tornado, wanted to go home, but since they knew about trailers in storms, they went to a friend's house instead. The tornado destroyed the house and, it turned out, didn't even touch the trailer.

"A straight news lead just doesn't work here," he said, giving a sample news lead. "Six Jarrell football players died in yesterday's storm, including two brothers who sought shelter in a friend's house instead of a trailer that went untouched."

The feature lead begins a series of blocks designed to emphasize the end of the block, rather than the important-facts-first structure of an inverted pyramid structure.

The problem with endings that Barron sees as an editor is that his sportswriters tend to put them on game stories, the basic news of the sports page.

"One of our writers has even made a verb of it," Barron said. "He'll complain that 'you end-cut my story again.' But in a game story or any basic news story structure, you can't worry about the ending. If you are really concerned about your ending as a writer, and I have been, then the best advice is to talk to the desk and make sure that they cut something in the middle." ∎

Reprinted by permission.

Summary

Any communicator consciously chooses the order in which information is presented. The professional communicator chooses that order in the best way to reach that audience. For most news stories, writers will choose to structure information by its importance. In others, writers will construct the story chronologically. And in other cases, the writer will choose to use subject blocks as an organizing device.

As you improve as a communicator, you will want to master each of these storytelling forms. Then you can use them in different situations to most effectively reach your audience.

Key Points

The inverted pyramid is the most common form for news stories. It requires the reporter to begin with the most important information and then to present facts in order of their importance.

> ► The call-a-friend technique can help beginners determine the relative importance of different elements of the story.

> ► Most press releases should be written in inverted pyramid structure.

> ► Chronologies work when a strong narrative element is present. If a story builds to a climax, it may be a candidate to be presented chronologically.

> ► Hourglass and champagne-glass structures combine the inverted pyramid structure with chronology.

> ► Key-subject-blocks structure allows a writer to group information by subject. It is most effective in longer print stories and in broadcast writing.

Web Links

Here are a few interesting sites on the Internet where you can find out more about structures for media writing.

www.newsthinking.com
www.copydesk.org
www.newswriting.com
www.case.org/current/index/periodicals/writing.cfm

InfoTrac College Edition Readings

For additional readings, go to **www.infotrac-college.com**, enter your password, and search for the following articles by title or author's name.

> ► "How to Avoid Transition Trauma," Bharti Kirchner, *Writer,* Nov 1997 v110 n11 p13.

> ► "What Do Garages and Good Writing Have in Common?" (Tips for avoiding backed-in sentences), Paula LaRocque, *Quill,* July-August 1993 v81 n6 p26.

▶ "Structuring Stories for Meaning: Your Character Gets to the Point Where Something Changes" (Nieman Narrative Journalism Conference), Jon Franklin, *Nieman Reports,* Spring 2002 v56 i1 p47.

▶ "Endings: The Inverted Pyramid Makes Endings Impossible" (Nieman Narrative Journalism Conference), Bruce DeSilva, *Nieman Reports*, Spring 2002 v56 i1 p47.

Exercises

Go to your CD-ROM to complete the following exercises:

▶ Exercise 2.1

▶ Exercise 2.2

▶ Exercise 2.3

Grammar and Style Trouble Spots

The process of media writing begins with your knowledge of the basics of spelling, capitalization and punctuation for journalists. Think of these basics as the bricks with which you will build your story: If the bricks aren't solid, the story won't stand.

But that's only the start. Once you have your words in order (that is, they are spelled correctly and capitalized where appropriate) and your punctuation in good shape, then you begin the process of putting together sentences, paragraphs and the groups of paragraphs that become your story.

This construction process for your story has rules that are meant to help you and your reader communicate successfully. The rules are important. Think of playing a game of poker if there were no rules, or if the rules were too vague. If any card could have a variety of numbers attached to it (if all cards were, in essence, wild cards), then

43

you simply wouldn't be able to play. You would have chaos instead of friendly competition.

Similarly, imagine a tennis match where each player set his or her own rules on how to play before each match, or even each point. Play would be impossible.

In much the same way, if you and your reader don't share a basic understanding of the rules of writing, you can't communicate. Since you are the one constructing the message, the responsibility is yours. You must understand the rules so that you can say exactly what you mean to say.

Happily, you have encountered these rules in elementary school, high school and other college courses, and you probably know how to apply them. Moreover, if you read often and well, you have seen them applied correctly so many times that you use them quite effortlessly.

But not all of us read as much as we should, not even among media-writing students. Also, sometimes the rules for media writing are different from the rules you learned for English class. So here's a refresher course, focusing on common grammar and style trouble spots for beginning media writers. If you can get a good grip on these trouble spots, and you do a good job with your spelling, capitalization and punctuation, you're probably ready to write good, clean copy that communicates well with your audience—and that's what media writing is all about.

Remember, these problems are rarely tricky, and they most often crop up through sloppy writing and the writer's inability or unwillingness to edit and revise his or her own work. For some advice on how to edit and revise your own writing, see Chapter 13. For explanations and examples of the grammar terms used in this discussion, turn to the "Grammar Terms" section at the end of this chapter.

Agreement Troubles

A major problem area for beginning media writers is the connection between nouns and pronouns, and between nouns and verbs.

It's simple, really. A noun and its pronoun must agree in gender (male or female or neither), number (singular or plural) and person (first, second or third).

Similarly, the subject of a sentence and the verb of a sentence must agree. The problem here is usually one of number; that is, a singular noun must have a singular verb. In many cases, as you'll see, collective nouns (*team, committee, panel,* and the like) fool the writer (and the occasional editor) into thinking they take a plural verb form. Be wary.

Noun–Pronoun Problems

The important point to remember with noun–pronoun problems is that the pronoun must agree with its antecedent (the *antecedent* is the original noun that the pronoun refers back to). Take a look at this sentence:

> If a *student* is late for this examination, *they* will be penalized a full grade point.

You can see that the *they* following the comma is incorrect, since the first part of the sentence made it clear that only one student ("If *a student* is late") is being discussed. Thus, the correct version of the sentence would look like this:

> If *a student* is late for this examination, *he or she* will be penalized a full grade point. (More about the *he or she* construction a bit later.)

Or, you can make the whole thing plural, like this:

> If *students* are late for this examination, *they* will be penalized a full grade point.

See how *students* and *they* agree in being plural?

Collective Nouns

One form that is a bit trickier is the collective noun, such words as *team, committee, panel, staff*. The general rule is that the collective noun takes a singular pronoun, as long as the noun is being used in a collective (that is, singular) sense.

> UCLA's football *team* won *its* final game of the regular season.

You can see that the "team" under discussion is a single entity, a unified "team," and so the pronoun (*its*) is also singular.

Occasionally, a collective noun is used in a discussion about individual members of that group. In that case, you can use a plural pronoun.

> The *team* put on *their* socks before the game.

> The *family* ate *their* sandwiches during the long car drive.

> The *audience* applauded *their* favorite performers.

Even here, some editors will prefer that you avoid the agreement issue by rewriting the sentences.

Each player put on *her* socks before the game.

The *family* ate sandwiches during the long car drive.

The *audience* applauded the performers.

Some sports nicknames are difficult collectives to figure, as in the Crimson Tide, the Green Wave, the Lightning, the Magic, the Galaxy and the like. The general rule is that these names should take the singular pronoun ("The Galaxy won *its* game"), but some sportswriters and editors choose to use the plural ("The Galaxy won *their* game").

In practice, the decision on singular or plural usage is decided by the editor of each publication. In the Tampa Bay area of Florida, for instance, the National Hockey League team, the Lightning, takes the collective singular in the *St. Petersburg Times* ("The Lightning won *its* game last night") and the plural ("The Lightning won *their* game last night") in *The Tampa Tribune*. You will simply have to learn how your newspaper, magazine or agency handles each case and abide by that decision.

Remember, the plural nickname of a team will always take the plural pronoun:

The Badgers won *their* Big Ten opener.

The Yankees finished second in *their* division.

The Packers are heavily favored in *their* next game.

Subject–Verb Problems

Subject–verb agreement problems are similar in many respects to noun–pronoun agreement problems; in both cases the two elements have to be in agreement. Subject–verb problems are typically problems of *number;* that is, you have a sentence that has a singular subject and you mistakenly use a plural verb. Most often, the singular subject seems to be plural through the sentence's construction, frequently because of a prepositional phrase.

Saturday's *game,* of the past 11 games, *is* the key to the whole season for the Ramblers.

The insertion of the phrase "of the past 11 games" can confuse you, but *game* is the subject of this sentence. It is singular, so the verb, *is,* must be singular, too.

Only *one* of the team's three pitchers *is* ready for today's game.

Again, the phrase *of the team's three pitchers* confuses an otherwise obvious construction. *One* is the subject, and so the verb remains singular (*is*).

Remember that when you connect two or more nouns in a subject, you make the subject plural:

> *Apples and oranges* are on the plate.

The subject, *Apples and oranges,* is plural. It therefore takes a plural verb, *are.*

Misplaced Modifiers

Misplaced modifiers are especially serious for writers because they may change the actual meaning of the sentence. It's one thing to make an error that sounds wrong and makes your writing look clumsy. It's another thing entirely to make an error that changes the meaning of your sentence.

Dangling participles are at the top of the list of misplaced modifiers. It's all too easy to connect a participle to the wrong noun:

> *Driving hard down the lane,* the basket was Thompson's fifth of the game.

The writer meant to say that Thompson drove down the lane and scored a basket, and that the basket was Thompson's fifth of the game. But what the writer actually said here was that the basket did the driving down the lane. *Driving hard down the lane* is a participle phrase (see the discussion of participles and gerunds in the section "Grammar Terms" at the end of this chapter) that modifies the nearest noun or pronoun, in this case *the basket.* So, what the sentence means is that the basket did the driving. That's the sort of confusion you absolutely want to avoid in your writing.

To avoid dangling participles, simply make sure the participle phrase is followed directly by the word it is modifying:

> Driving hard down the lane, Thompson scored his fifth basket of the game.

Other misplaced modifiers are equally confusing, and frequently inadvertently funny. Take a look at this:

> The puppy walked right up to Jane as Greg noticed that she was dirty and so thin that her ribs showed.

The writer probably did not mean to say that Jane was dirty and thin, but that's what the sentence means.

Shifts in Person or Tense

A troublesome area for beginning writers is keeping track of person (first, second or third), tense (present, past or future), and point of view.

While the most common form for media writing is third person, past tense, you can occasionally use other forms. The important concern is consistency. Once you have the reader started in your story, you should stick with the person, tense and point of view that you've chosen; otherwise, the reader can be easily confused.

Person

To avoid confusing your audience, you need to stick with whatever person you choose to write in. In media writing, the most common mode for stories is third person. Occasionally there are stories that call for the second person. Rarely, there are stories where the first person is appropriate.

First, from *The Salt Lake Tribune* (May 27, 1997) here is an example of a typical third-person news story:

> Consultants believe there are enough Wasatch Front commuters willing to park their cars and ride a train to make commuter rail a reality within the next year.
>
> A new study shows some 3,500 work-related commuter trips would be made daily on such a line between Brigham City and Payson, and that represents enough riders to cover—through fares alone—more than a quarter of the system's annual operating expenses.
>
> Another 525 daily trips would be made by tourists, students, shoppers and people visiting physicians, lawyers and dentists, says the study conducted by transportation consulting firm DeLeuw, Cather & Co.
>
> Reprinted by permission.

You can see that the reporter remains invisible in this story, and that the pronouns *I* (first person) and *you* (second person) never appear. When people are referred to in this fashion ("Consultants believe") and *I* and *you* are not in the story, it's a third-person story. This is, by far, the most common way to write newspaper and magazine stories, including virtually all news stories and most feature stories.

Now, take a look at this story from the *Los Angeles Times* (April 28, 1997):

> Imagine that you've been fatally injured in a car wreck and your doctor offers to implant your brain in another perfectly healthy body. When you wake up from the operation, who will you be? Yourself, with a new body? Or the person whose body you inhabit—with memories of being someone else?
>
> Or this about this: You are told that tonight your brain will be transplanted into someone else's body, and that person's brain will be implanted in yours. Tomorrow, one of the two will be tortured. If you had a choice, which would you want tortured: the other body with the transplanted brain, or your present body with the other person's brain?
>
> Your answer will depend on whether you think the self is embodied in the body, or is mainly in the brain.

In this story, written in the second person, you can see that the reporter seems to be carrying on a conversation with the reader and refers to that reader as "you" throughout the story.

This form is more personal (and thus is quite common in broadcast media writing, as you'll see in Chapter 9) and so is somewhat unusual in newspaper writing. Newspapers usually present their material in a much less personal, more institutional voice (see Chapter 7 for an explanation of *voice*). The form does appear occasionally in newspapers, however, as the preceding example proves, and is reasonably common in magazine writing. Some experts think second-person stories may become more common in newspaper writing in the future as newspapers try new techniques for reaching out to readers.

Note: As you can read in the discussion of voice and tone in Chapter 7, second person does have its drawbacks. Make sure to take a look at them in that chapter.

Now, take a look at this story from *The Tampa Tribune* (March 25, 1997):

> On a perfect spring day in St. Petersburg, I get mail from my parents. I open up the large, padded envelope and my father's personal history tumbles out—photographs and baseball cards from the game's golden era: the 1930s, '40s and '50s.
>
> Del Wilber, my father, spent his whole life in The Game, from his start in the minors in Fostoria, Ohio, in 1938 through a career in the major leagues and then on into coaching, managing and scouting until he retired in 1988.

As you can readily see, the writer is very strongly present in this story, using the first-person "I" in the very first sentence. First-person stories, always very personal in tone, use *I* or *we* or *us* and try to get the reader to share with the writer the story's impact.

First-person is rare in newspapers (other than in opinion pieces, where it crops up more often), but is found relatively often in magazines. Like second-person, it lends itself to the broadcast media and is found there frequently.

Note that first-person stories are very demanding in several respects, not the least of which is your ability to tell the story without sounding annoyingly egocentric.

It's worth adding that first-person stories, like second-person stories, are beginning to appear more often in newspaper feature sections as newspapers search for ways to more effectively connect with their readers.

Each of these—first person, second person and third person—has its place in certain kinds of media writing, with third person certainly the dominant form. Not only does third person lend itself best to that institutional voice we've talked about, but first person is troublesome to some editors who feel that first person calls attention to the writer at the expense of the story's content and that second person too easily lapses into a kind of lecturing tone, in which the writer is telling "you" what you should think about something or someone.

The major problem beginners run into is not just that they attempt first- or second-person stories, but that they try to mix first-person or second-person material into a third-person story. Take a look at this excerpt:

> On a perfect spring day in St. Petersburg, Rick Wilber received mail from his parents. I open up the large, padded envelope and my father's personal history tumbles out—photographs and baseball cards from the game's golden era: the 1930s, '40s and '50s.
>
> Del Wilber, his father, spent his whole life in The Game, from his start in the minors in Fostoria, Ohio, in 1938 through a career in the major leagues and then on into coaching, managing and scouting until he retired in 1938.

You can see how confusing the story gets when you mix first-person or second-person material into a third-person story. Is the third-person "Rick Wilber" in the first sentence the same person as the "I" and "my" found in the second sentence? And, in the second paragraph, note that the first sentence has "his" three times. To whom does that pronoun refer? It's hard to say, especially for the first two uses of "his."

While journalists occasionally mix first-person and second-person material in one story, it's very unusual to combine first or second person with third person in media writing. Generally, your safest route will be to stick with third-person writing throughout a story.

Tense

Verb tenses indicate the time of an action. You will most commonly use past tense for newspaper and public relations writing. For magazine writing and for broadcast writing, you will most often use past tense but will also occasionally use present tense. In addition, you will sometimes use past perfect, present perfect, future and future perfect tenses.

Present: John *walks* to the store.

Present perfect: John *has walked* to the store.

Past: John *walked* to the store.

Past perfect: John *had walked* to the store.

Future: John *will walk* to the store.

Future perfect: John *will have walked* to the store.

Each of these tenses has its uses for you in media writing, but it's important that you not confuse the reader by mixing the tenses unclearly in one story. Generally, every story has a dominant tense, that is, a time sense in which the story takes place. Usually, that will be simple past tense. But within a given story, it's entirely possible—even likely—that you will need to go beyond that simple past tense.

Warner *admitted* that he *felt* worried about the brakes, but *had been* too busy to take the car into the shop. He *said,* "I *will take* the car into the shop tomorrow."

You can see past (*admitted, felt, said*), past perfect (*had been*), and future (*will take*) in this one short passage. As long as the reader can logically follow the time sequence, this is perfectly fine.

Sometimes, however, media writers confuse the reader with tense shifts that are unnecessary or improperly handled.

Warner says that he *feels* worried about the brakes, but *had been* too busy to have driven to the shop. He *said,* "I *will have taken* the car into the shop by tomorrow."

Whew. Compare the two passages and you can see how the writer has unnecessarily, and inappropriately, mixed tenses and turned a simple passage into a complex one that the reader must struggle to follow. Try to avoid that in your writing.

Note: Beginners sometimes mix the simple past tense *said* and the present tense *says* in the same story, and that is usually wrong. Once you've picked one form, stick with it. While the traditional form (see Chapter 5) has been *said,* in recent years it has become increasingly common for writers to use *say,* and most editors don't seem to mind. Just don't mix them unnecessarily.

Misused Words and Phrases

There are a number of words and phrases that can cause you trouble in media writing. In many cases these words or phrases have slipped into a usage that is common, but incorrect. When you use the word or phrase incorrectly, the reader may easily be confused. Did you really mean to say that the regatta, below, was full of hope? Probably not.

There's the possibility, of course, that the reader will get the meaning you intend, because he or she also misunderstands the usage in exactly the same way that you do. But counting on that sort of shared misuse is a poor way to write. It is far better to learn the correct version and use that, or even just avoid the word or phrase altogether and so sidestep the issue.

Here's a list of commonly misused words and phrases.

Hopefully   Many beginning writers put *hopefully* at the start of a sentence, thinking it means "I hope." It doesn't. When you place *hopefully* at the start of a sentence, you are saying that the action in that sentence takes place with hope.

> **Faulty**
>> *Hopefully,* the regatta will take place despite the cold weather.

This faulty image implies that the regatta itself will somehow be full of hope. If you mean to say that the organizers hope the regatta will take place, say so.

> **Revision**
>> The organizing committee *hopes* that the regatta will take place despite the cold weather.

Your best bet with *hopefully* may be to simply avoid using the word altogether, since its common misuse has made its meaning untrustworthy for many readers.

Unique   Writers sometimes think that *unique* means "unusual," which isn't at all the actual meaning of the word. For something to be unique, it must be the only one of its kind. The word cannot be qualified: You cannot be "rather unique" or "sort of unique" or "really unique" or (worst of all) "pretty unique." This last phrase combines a misuse of *pretty* (which primarily defines some level of beauty, and only secondarily refers to a level of quality) with a misuse of *unique* (which can't be qualified).

Faulty

> It was a *really unique* half-time show, complete with sky-divers parachuting in to land on the fifty-yard line.

Unless you honestly know for a fact that this particular athletic contest was the only time, ever, anywhere, that parachutists landed at midfield during half-time, you have misspoken. If you mean to say something is unusual, say so.

Revision

> It was an *unusual* half-time show, complete with sky-divers parachuting in to land on the fifty-yard line.

As with *hopefully,* your best bet with *unique* may be to avoid using the word, since its rarely called for.

Livid Many writers seem to think that to be "livid" is to be flushed and red in the face, as in "O'Neill was livid with rage."

To be livid, however, actually means to be pale, ashen-faced, as if the blood has drained away from the face. It also means to be black-and-blue, as in a bruise. Be careful how you use the term.

Literally/figuratively These two terms are all too often confused, with writers using *literally* when they mean *figuratively*, as in, "He was *literally* blown away by the way Johnson read the final poem." (Imagine poetry that powerful!)

Remember that *literally* means that something actually happened and that the expression is not a metaphor. When you mean to use it as metaphor, use *figuratively*. So, the sentence should read as follows: "He was *figuratively* blown away by the way Johnson read the final poem."

That/which These two words are not nearly so confusing as writers sometimes make them out to be. The rule is to use *that* for essential clauses and *which* for nonessential clauses. Simply put, if you must use commas to set off the clause, then the clause is nonessential and you should use *which*. If you don't use commas to set off the clause, you should use *that*.

> The bicycle *that* has the broken chain is in the repair shop.

> The bicycle, *which* has a broken chain, is in the repair shop.

The two sentences mean entirely different things. The first sentence clearly implies that there are more bicycles and that the one with the broken chain is the one in the shop. In the second sentence, the implication is that there is just the one bicycle being discussed and it is in the repair shop.

You need to make sure you know the difference between the two uses and use the correct one.

Fewer/less If you can separate out the things under discussion (that is, you can count the individual numbers), use the word *fewer*. If you cannot separate out individual items, use the word *less*.

> There are *fewer* books in the library this year than last year.

> There is *less* water in the aquifer this year than last year.

You can separate out individual books, so you use *fewer*, and you cannot separate out individual water, so you use *less*.

Note that advertising copywriters frequently abuse this rule, as in radio stations that claim "KXXX plays less commercials." This should be "KXXX plays fewer commercials."

Awesome Current usage has changed the meaning of *awesome* from something that inspires awe or expresses awe to a weaker expression of support or delight. Avoid the new, and certainly temporary, usage.

Appropriate
Notre Dame Cathedral in Paris is an *awesome* sight.

Faulty
Kelly's new dress was, like, *awesome*.

You can readily see which sentence seems more professional and which seems flippant. Strive to be, like, professional.

Awful The primary definition of *awful* refers to something that inspires awe. It is the secondary definition that refers to something that inspires fear or is dreadful. You should not use the word as a mildly positive modifier, as in "He was an *awfully* nice guy."

Couldn't care less/could care less The two terms are not synonymous. If you *couldn't care less*, you mean that you care as little as possible. If you *could care less*, you mean it is entirely possible that you still care at some significant level. If you use the second phrase to mean the first, you are probably saying something very close to the opposite of what you intend to say. Here's an example:

> Samantha said that she *could care less* about what Austin has to say.

This sentence means that Samantha could, indeed, care less, which implies that she still does actually care. Change the sentence to this:

> Samantha said that she *couldn't care less* about what Austin has to say.

Now you are saying that Samantha's amount of caring is at the bottom, which is probably the intended meaning.

First annual For something to be "annual" it must be taking place for the second time; so it is impossible for something to be the "first annual" anything. If you mean to say that the event is intended to be annual, you have to say that: "The firefighters plan to make the picnic *an annual event*."

Gauntlet/gantlet A gauntlet is something you wear. The word originally referred to an armored glove worn by medieval knights and now means a glove with a long wrist extension. You cannot "run a gauntlet."

A gantlet is a form of punishment in which you run between two rows of people who strike you with clubs or sticks; thus, metaphorically, you can "run the gantlet" between two difficult groups or issues.

Clichés

Clichés are those words and phrases, many of them metaphors, that have been used so often that they've become nearly meaningless. You want to try to avoid them. If your writing has very many clichés it becomes boring for the reader, who wonders why he or she is reading something that has nothing new, nothing fresh to offer. In fact, writing that contains clichés often becomes unintentionally funny, since it not only sounds boring and repetitious but also frequently contains mixed metaphors (which you can read about in a bit more detail later in this chapter).

The English language is filled with clichés, so what follows is only a small start on your hunt for clichés. You can probably come up with half a dozen more for each letter of the alphabet as you read through these, and that kind of search is not a bad idea, since it will help you see how boring and void of real meaning most clichés are.

a great deal of	bombshell
acid test	calm before the storm
all too soon	clean as a whistle
armed to the teeth	clean slate
a rock and a hard place	concerted effort
back in the saddle	date with destiny
beginning of the end	dog tired

epic struggle
exercise in futility
facts and figures
fall into the habit of
fell on deaf ears
final word
get psyched
get the green light
go to great lengths
hale and hearty
handwriting on the wall
hanging in there
hard as a rock
ignorance is bliss
in the spotlight
keeled over
labor of love
last-ditch effort
leaps and bounds
mad as a hatter
mad as a hornet
mixed blessing
motley crew
name of the game
neat as a pin
night of terror
odd and sundry
on any given day
on a roll

one fell swoop
open secret
paying the price
pleased as punch
powder keg
push the envelope
reign of terror
reign supreme
right stuff
run the gantlet
score
second to none
select few
senseless murder
strike out
such is life
tight as a drum
to the tune of
untimely end
up in arms
vanish into thin air
various and sundry
walks of life
white as snow
whole nine yards
wipe the slate clean
world-class
wrestle with it
yahoo, a

Sportswriting, by the way, is notorious for its use of clichés. Some sportswriters seem to feel that the use of clichés ("Brown launched a three and drained it to ice the game") works to make their stories more vivid and entertaining. The opposite is more often true, since the use of clichés keeps the sportswriter from using better, more descriptive, language to describe a game-winning basket.

You could also argue that too many sportswriters use cliché-ridden language because it sounds more knowledgeable, more what an "insider" would say.

The problem with that philosophy is that it keeps new readers from entering the sports pages of your newspaper or magazine, hinting to them strongly that if they don't know the jargon, they shouldn't be reading the story. Most publications, and their editors, want more readers, not fewer.

Jargon

So, has your university or college prioritized its outsourcing opportunities yet? Has your local major corporation right-sized its human resources to optimize its competitive paradigm and maximize its global outreach?

In other words, have there been layoffs in your college or in your town?

Words, jargon and phrases like *outsourcing* and *right-sized* and *optimizing* and *human resources* and *prioritized*, is closely related to cliché, in the sense that these words quickly become overused and lose whatever meaning they may have had.

But jargon's main purpose is to exclude those who don't speak the jargon. In other words, those who speak the jargon (and know what it means for a company to "right-size its human resources applications") can exclude those who don't.

Your job as a media writer is to break through the jargon and turn it into plain English that your readers can understand. In newspaper and broadcast writing, in particular, you are trying to reach a mass audience with your words, and to reach that audience you need to translate the jargon into something your readers can readily understand. Take a look at this passage.

Jargon

The XYZ Corporation announced today that it will *reallocate personnel* as part of its ongoing efforts to *optimize* its global competitiveness through *outsourcing* and *right-sizing* its *human resource* base.

Whew. Try this version.

Revision

The XYZ Corporation announced today that it will immediately lay off 250 employees in an effort to stay competitive internationally.

And this could be tighter still.

Revision

The XYZ Corporation laid off 250 employees today.

For public relations and for some specialized magazines, the jargon situation becomes tricky, since your readers may be part of the group that speaks with that jargon and you will be expected to learn and use the terminology of the group. In that case, write as you must. Remember, though, that media writers communicate, so even when you must use jargon, make sure it actually says something meaningful to your audience.

Parallel Constructions

Parallel construction refers to the way you write your phrases and clauses, and how those phrases and clauses must be alike, especially in a series. When you list items in a series, all the elements in that series should be of the same grammatical construction, whether they are gerunds, infinitives, nouns, clauses or phrases. Similarly, verbs in a series should be parallel with each other in terms of tense, voice (active or passive) and mood.

Faulty Parallelism
DeWarde drove to the mall *to see* a movie, *go* shopping and then *to rent* a video.

The infinitive phrases in the series are not parallel because "*to*" is missing from the second verb, *go*.

DeWarde drove to the mall *to see* a movie, *go* shopping, and then *rented* a video.

Correct Parallelism
DeWarde drove to the mall *to see* a movie, *shop* and *rent* a video.

Here the three forms are parallel, and the sentence is easier to read and comprehend.

Mixed Metaphors

Metaphors are useful for writers; they help illuminate the unknown for the audience by comparing it to the known, as in Homer's classic "wine dark sea." Homer's readers knew the color of dark wine, and so could visualize the color of the Aegean as Homer described it through his metaphor.

But metaphors have their peril, too. Remember first that for a metaphor to be useful, it must take something known and compare it with something unknown. A metaphor or simile that uses two unknowns ("The bracken cracked like a broken hurley") may confuse readers more than help them.

Be wary, too, of those metaphors that have become clichéd, and be especially wary of mixing metaphors. When you metaphorically compare apples and oranges, you confuse the reader and you may be inadvertently funny. Take a look at this mixed metaphor, for instance:

> Knowing it was the most important speech of his life, the speaker *stepped up to the plate* and *threw a touchdown pass* to convince the House of Representatives.

You can imagine how difficult it would be for a baseball player (who "stepped up to the plate") to be the one who "threw a touchdown pass." You can hope the speaker didn't mix metaphors that painfully in the speech.

Similes, by the way, are metaphors that use the words *like* or *as* in the comparison: "The sea was *as* dark *as* wine." They, too, can be badly mixed.

Some Final Thoughts

Remember that clarity is crucial to success in your media writing, and the material you've just studied in this chapter and the previous chapter is important to your achieving that clarity in your writing. Confusion in your writing is something you very much want to avoid. If you have to fall back on claiming "You know what I mean" in your stories, then you're in trouble. Not all readers are going to successfully figure out what you "meant" to say, as opposed to what you actually said.

And finally, just for fun, here's some advice we received (unattributed) on e-mail. We hope the humor will help you remember the basics of good writing.

Rules for Writing

1. Verbs has to agree with their subjects.

2. Prepositions are not words to end sentences with.

3. And don't start a sentence with a conjunction.

4. It is wrong to ever split an infinitive.

5. Avoid clichés like the plague. They're old hat.

6. Also, avoid annoying alliteration.

7. Be more or less specific.

8. Parenthetical remarks (however relevant) are (usually) unnecessary.

9. Also too, never, ever use repetitive redundancies.

10. No sentence fragments.

11. Foreign words and phrases are not apropos.

12. Do not be redundant; do not use more words than necessary; it's highly superfluous.

13. One should never generalize.

14. Comparisons are as bad as clichés.

15. Don't use no double negatives.

16. Eschew ampersands & abbreviations, etc.

17. One-word sentences? Eliminate.

18. Analogies are like feathers on a snake.

19. The passive voice is to be ignored.

20. Eliminate commas, that are, not necessary.

21. Never use a big word when a diminutive one would suffice.

22. Kill all exclamation points!

23. Use words correctly, irregardless of how others use them.

24. We could care less about how many grains of sand there are on this beach.

25. Use the apostrophe in it's proper place and omit it when its not needed.

26. If you've heard it once, you've heard it a thousand times: Resist hyperbole; not one writer in a million can use it correctly.

27. Puns are for children, not groan readers.

28. Even if a mixed metaphor sings, it should be derailed.

29. Who needs rhetorical questions?

30. Exaggeration is a billion times worse than understatement.

Grammar Terms

The following definitions and examples will help you get the most from the information presented in this chapter.

The Parts of Speech

A *noun* is a word used to name a person, place or thing.

> *John* bought a new *car* in *Abilene*. (*John, car* and *Abilene* are nouns.)

A *pronoun* is a word used in place of a noun.

> *He* bought *his* new car at the dealership. (*He* and *his* are pronouns.)

An *antecedent* is the noun for which a pronoun stands.

> *John* bought a new car in Abilene. He bought his new car at the dealership. (*John* is the antecedent for *he* and *his*.)

An *adjective* is a word used to describe or limit the meaning of a noun or pronoun. Here are several types of adjectives.

> *Possessive: My* suit, *their* yard
>
> *Demonstrative: This* carriage, *those* people
>
> *Interrogative: Whose* cat? *Which* boy?
>
> *Articles: A* picture, *an* egg, *the* book.
>
> *Numerical: One* day, *second* inning.

A *verb* is a word or words that describe an action or a state of being.

> John *bought* a new car in Abilene. (*Bought* is the verb.)
>
> John *loves* his new car. (*Loves* is the verb.)

There are different types of verbs, including:

> *Transitive:* He *blew* the whistle. (A transitive verb takes an object—in this case, *whistle*.)
>
> *Intransitive:* The wind *whistled*. (An intransitive verb does *not* take an object.)
>
> *Linking:* He *seems* a timid student; the cake *tastes* sweet. (A linking verb shows the relation between the subject of a sentence and a predicate noun or predicate adjective.)

An *adverb* is a word used to describe or limit the meaning of a verb, an adjective or another adverb. Here are several types of adverbs.

Place: Put the cat *outside.*

Time: He was *never* healthy.

Manner: She was *secretly* envious.

Degree: I was *quite* angry.

Frequency: I *seldom* do that.

Affirmation: Certainly, I will be happy to take part.

Negation: I will *not* agree to the proposal.

Qualification or condition: However, I may agree later.

Logical relationship: I think, *therefore* I am.

A *preposition* is a word used to relate a noun or pronoun to some other word in a sentence.

John swam *in* the pool.

Jane walked *down* the road.

Prepositions usually indicate direction or position, and several word groups function as propositions. Here's a list of prepositions:

about	beyond	near
according to	down	on
among	from	over
around	in	through
because of	instead of	to
behind	into	under
beside	in view of	

A *participle* is a verb form that can be used as an adjective. The ***present participle*** is the *–ing* form of the verb. The ***past participle*** can take different forms, but most past participles end in *–ed.*

Soaring through the air, Michael Jordan dunked the ball. (*Soaring* is a present participle.)

Delighted, we watched the last few seconds. (*Delighted* is a past participle.)

A *gerund* is the present participle of a verb used as a noun:

Fishing is a bore, but I like *hiking,* (*Fishing* and *hiking* are gerunds.)

An *infinitive* is a verb preceded by *to* and used as a noun, adjective or adverb:

> *To swim* is fun. (*To swim* is a noun.)

> I have nothing *to say.*
> (*To say* is an adjective, modifying *nothing.*)

> We were ready *to begin.*
> (*To begin* is an adverb, modifying the adjective *ready.*)

An *interjection* is a word grammatically unrelated to the rest of the sentence but expressing attitude or feeling:

> *Oh!* I am hurt.

> *Now,* let me see.

> *Well,* there is one answer I can give you.

An *expletive* is the word *it* or *there* used to introduce a sentence in which the subject follows the verb:

> *It* is doubtful that he will arrive today.

> *There* are two ways of solving the problem.

The Main Elements of a Sentence

The *subject* of a sentence (or of an independent or dependent clause) is the word or words that are doing the acting (or being):

> *The Gateway Arch* in St. Louis is the nation's tallest national monument. (*The Gateway Arch* is the subject.)

The *predicate verb* is the verb that tells what the subject is doing or being:

> The Gateway Arch in St. Louis *is* the nation's tallest national monument. (*Is* is the predicate verb, telling the reader what the arch is being—that is, tall.)

A *direct object* is a word, phrase or clause that receives the action of a transitive verb:

> I followed *him.* He gave *the ball* to me.
> You may keep *whatever you find.*
> (*Him, the ball* and *whatever you find* are the direct objects.)

An *indirect object* receives indirectly the action of a transitive verb:

> Give *me* the money. (*Me* is the indirect object.)

The *object of a preposition* is the noun or pronoun that follows the preposition:

> We sat on the *porch*.
> (*Porch* is the noun following the preposition *on*.)

A *conjunction* is a word used to connect words, phrases and clauses. There are several types of conjunctions. *Coordinating conjunctions* are the words *and, but, or, nor, for* and *yet*. They are used to connect two elements of equal grammatical rank:

> Timmy *and* Ann are allowed to ride their tricycles on the sidewalk *but* not on the street. (*And* and *but* are the coordinating conjunctions.)

Correlative conjunctions include *either/or, neither/nor, both/and*, and *not only/but also*:

> You may *either* go now *or* go later.

> I *not only* like him *but also* like his brother.

Subordinating conjunctions connect a subordinate clause with a main clause or join two subordinate clauses:

> He will send for you *when* he needs you.
> (*When* connects a main clause and a subordinate clause.)

> *Although* he faltered, he reached his goal.
> (*Although* connects the subordinate clause *Although he faltered* to the main clause *he reached his goal*.)

A *conjunctive adverb* is a word that shows a logical relationship between sentences. (Because of this, you might want to consider using them for transitions in your stories. See Chapter 2.) Some conjunctive adverbs are:

accordingly	in addition	on the contrary
besides	indeed	on the other hand
consequently	meanwhile	still
for example	moreover	then
furthermore	namely	therefore
however	nevertheless	thus

A *predicate noun* is a word or phrase that renames the subject of a verb:

> Harry is a *baker.* (*Baker* renames the subject.)

A *predicate adjective* describes the subject of a verb:

> The building was *tall* (*Tall* is the predicate adjective.)

Clauses

A *clause* is a group of words that contains a subject and a predicate. There are two types of clauses—independent and dependent.

An *independent clause* (also called a *main clause*) can stand alone as a complete sentence:

> I know him well, and I recommend him highly.
> (Two independent clauses are joined by *and.*)

A *dependent clause* (also called a *subordinate clause*) has a subject and a predicate, but cannot stand alone as a complete sentence. There are adjective, adverb and noun dependent clauses:

> This is the jet *that broke the speed record.*
> (The adjective dependent clause is in italics.)

> The child smiled *when the dentist appeared.*
> (The adverb dependent clause is in italics.)

> *What Joan wants* is a better job.
> (The noun dependent clause is in italics.)

Phrases

A *phrase* is a group of closely related words not including a subject or a predicate. A phrase acts as a part of speech in a sentence. Here are some examples:

> They are building a *large new house.*
> (*Large new house* is a noun phrase.)

> We tried to find *some ripe blueberries.*
> (*Some ripe blueberries* is a noun phrase.)

> He *is working.* (*Is working* is a verb phrase.)

> They *have been hurrying.*
> (*Have been hurrying* is a verb phrase.)

The men have gone *to war.* (*To war* is a prepositional phrase.)

Mice hide *in holes and corners.*
(*In holes and corners* is a prepositional phrase.)

Solving problems is fun. (*Solving problems* is a gerund phrase.)

His favorite sport is *fishing for trout.*
(*Fishing for trout* is a gerund phrase and includes
the prepositional phrase *for trout.*)

Having caught the ball, he threw it quickly.
(*Having caught the ball* is a participial phrase.)

He saw the books *neatly arranged on the shelves.*
(*Neatly arranged on the shelves* is a participial phrase
and includes the prepositional phrase *on the shelves.*)

To read easily in a foreign language is his objective.
(*To read easily in a foreign language* is an infinitive phrase
and includes the prepositional phrase *in a foreign language.*)

The flowers *in the garden* are beautiful.
(*In the garden* is an adjectival prepositional phrase.)

Startled by the noises, the girl looked up
(*Startled by the noises* is an adjectival participial phrase.)

Now is the time *to decide.*
(*To decide* is an adjectival infinitive phrase.)

We lived there *half a year.*
(*Half a year* is an adverbial noun phrase.)

We lived *in that house.*
(*In that house* is an adverbial prepositional phrase.)

He is able *to learn quickly.*
(*To learn quickly* is an adverbial infinitive phrase.)

Summary

The basics of grammar and style are important to you. They are, after all, the building blocks you use to write your stories in a way that readers can clearly understand. Also, basics like spelling, capitalization, punctuation, noun–pronoun agreement and noun–verb agreement must be under your control before you can move on to more complex writing skills.

Many beginning media writers seem to have particular problems with certain matters of usage and a number of common errors. These kinds of mistakes are red flags for editors, and you'll want to avoid them.

Key Points

- ▶ Good spelling is essential, and *you're* spellchecker isn't always *write* so you can't trust it. Also, every student learns *they* must make their nouns and pronouns agree.

- ▶ *It's* can be used only as the contraction for *it is*.

- ▶ Sloppy writing tells editors that you can't be trusted.

- ▶ A number of style issues are different for media writers than for academic writers.

- ▶ Within media writing, too, there are occasional style differences between broadcast, newspaper, magazine, public relations and advertising. You must learn which is appropriate for your field or for your publication.

Web Links

Here are a few interesting sites on the Internet where you can find out more about matters of grammar and style. Several offer fun and challenging exercises that will help improve your grammar and style usage.

http://www.chompchomp.com/menu.htm
http://ccc.commnet.edu/grammar/
http://papyr.com/hypertextbooks/englu/s_126/book126.htm
http://www.brownlee.org/durk/grammar/

InfoTrac College Edition Readings

For additional readings, go to **www.infotrac-college.com**, enter your password, and search for the following articles by title or author's name.

- ▶ "He Said, She Says: To Set the Scene—and Grab Readers' Attentions—Present Tense Works Like a Charm. Here's How to Make Your Present Perfect," David A. Fryxell, *Writer's Digest*, Feb 1997 v77 n2 p57.

► "The Problem With Prepositions" (English grammar for newspaper copy)(Writer's Workshop Column), Jack Hart, *Editor & Publisher*, Jan 13, 1996 v129 n2 p5.

► "If You Spell *de rigueur* de rigeur, You've Got Yourself an Oy Canada" (Grammatical errors in print), Alden Wood, *Communication World*, April 2001 v18 i3 p33.

Exercises

Go to your CD-ROM to complete the following exercises:

► Exercise 3.1

► Exercise 3.2

► Exercise 3.3

► Exercise 3.4

► Exercise 3.5

► Exercise 3.6

► Exercise 3.7

► Exercise 3.8

► Exercise 3.9

Leads for Media Writing

The Importance of Importance

Kinds of Leads

Breaking Out of the Boxes

The Six Questions

Recognizing Bad Leads

The initial verbiage that confronts the various members of the author's waiting audience (hereafter "*audience*") may well, should the author of the verbiage elect to optimize the potential of retention of said audience for the remainder of the author's deathless prose, contain the sole opportunity to maintain the attention capacity of the various members of the audience.

No way.

Hmmmm. Let's try . . .

Read this sentence or we'll shoot your dog.

A little better, but not to the point. Maybe if we speak more directly . . .

Your first sentence is your best chance to get your reader's attention.

That's better; it will work, for now . . .

Professional writers often work hardest at crafting the opening sentence or sentences of a story. Some may spend 75 percent of their time (maybe even more) at the keyboard composing the opening.

Professionals know their audience. Reporters read news stories. Public relations practitioners read media releases. Advertising writers read and watch ads. Television reporters watch other reporters. People who specialize in visual tasks in any of those fields not only read, but also see how others compose, visual messages.

Professionals understand their audience. They know that no member of the audience is required to pay attention to their work, even if the professional spent days toiling over it.

69

The audience isn't your high school English teacher, whose job it was to read your essays. The audience isn't your Aunt Elizabeth, who likes you and thinks everything you've written is perfectly swell.

The audience is fickle, capricious, logical, cruel and unfeeling. It doesn't care that you spent three days tracking down that tough interview with the mayor. It doesn't care that your client made you rewrite a one-page press release five times. It doesn't care that you waited in gale-force winds to do a live shot for the late-night newscast. It doesn't even care that you put together an absolute gem that will impress the toughest judges in your field come awards time.

The audience retains the right to stop reading at any point—even in the middle of . . .

You see. That's how it is.

Look in the office-complex food court at breakfast. The young man at the corner table with the bleary eyes doesn't want to read another story about child abuse—even if you spent three weeks getting a truly interesting, heartbreaking story. The woman with the designer glasses started the piece but decided to turn directly to the editorial page. The bald guy with the colorful tie just burned his tongue on the coffee and closed his eyes as they were about to scan over your story's headline.

This condition doesn't haunt just reporters. The city editor stops halfway through the first sentence of your news release, crumples it into a ball and throws it wordlessly into the trash. Your advertisement appears on the television screen, and 57,000 clickers change to Monday night wrestling. The magazine editor reads your cover letter, is unimpressed with your craft, and stuffs a rejection slip into your envelope.

It's hard enough to keep people's attention. But if you don't get their attention in the beginning, you have zero chance of getting it again.

The Importance of Importance

You want to start with something important. In fact, it's usually going to be the most important part of your story.

In a print advertisement, the most important point is often conveyed to the reader in large, easy-to-spot type. *"Democracy Exists Everywhere In This Country But The Highway"* reads an ad for the luxury car Lexus. The copywriter thinks that the superior performance of the Lexus is the most important point for potential customers.

In a news story, writers David Ballingrud and David Dahl of the *St. Petersburg Times* thought the most important point of a story about medical problems within the Department of Veterans Affairs medical system was to show an example of the problem:

> In Miami, a dialysis patient at the Veterans Affairs Medical Center was left bleeding to death while his nurse discussed her plans for breakfast on a telephone a few steps away.
>
> *St. Petersburg Times*

If you're writing for a magazine, however, you probably won't face the time crunch that newspaper and broadcast reporters can deal with. You're less likely to depend on a basic summary lead because you have time to find a different angle.

Some of the news values you learned about in Chapter 1 play a role in determining the most important point in an assignment. You know that prominence and impact are two important news values, but you may see another, perhaps proximity, as being important.

Not every writer will see the same important point in every news story. For example, a dozen reporters covering a speech by, say, consumer advocate and former presidential candidate Ralph Nader may well come up with a dozen angles on what each thought was the most important thing Nader said.

Your job as a writer is to determine what your audience will find important. If the event is a baseball game between the San Francisco Giants and the Chicago Cubs, we know that the sports journalists from San Francisco are writing for an audience that will contain many more Giants fans than the Cubs-oriented Chicago audience. If you're the wire-service reporter for the Associated Press or a reporter for a "national" newspaper like *USA Today*, your audience is baseball fans throughout the country and your story will not center around either the Giants or Cubs.

One technique you might try is to think of describing an event to somebody in a 20-second long-distance telephone call to a close friend. You want to convey the most important information before the line goes dead. But your friend's a pretty sharp person.

You: Ralph Nader spoke on campus today.

Friend: Doesn't he do a lot of that?

Time's up. Maybe you need to convey some more information.

You: Ralph Nader spoke about consumer safety on campus today.

Friend: Was he for it or against it?

Maybe some more information is what you want.

You: Ralph Nader said that college students don't often exercise their consumer rights and that they should.

Friend: That's interesting. I want to know more.

Kinds of Leads

In Chapter 2, we discussed the introduction to a news story or press release—the lead. One of the nicer compliments a writer can receive from colleagues is "You got the lead right." Professionals consider a well-crafted lead that entices the audience into the story to be no small achievement.

Some of the approaches used by writers can be classified into types of leads. These classifications, like so much in writing, are artificial. You should consider them as guidelines rather than laws etched in stone. Sometimes beginning writers become frustrated with the lack of hard-and-fast rules about what can and can't be done in professional media writing. (We do have some hard-and-fast rules, but most of those fall into the grammar and spelling categories.) Writing is not painting by the numbers, but it's not quite throwing a bucket of paint against a slab of canvas either.

Summary Lead

The idea of a *summary lead* is to briefly summarize the most important point or points in your story. Take a look at some examples:

> Perhaps one in every 100 whites is genetically resistant to infection by the AIDS virus, two sets of researchers have found.
>
> Thomas H. Maugh II, *Los Angeles Times*

> SANTA FE — A district judge Friday sentenced an Espanola man to three years in prison for a third-degree rape conviction in a case that paved the way for the admissibility of certain DNA evidence.
>
> Minerva Canto, *Albuquerque Journal*

> The Oregon State System of Higher Education and the Oregon Public Employees Union came to a tentative agreement on a two-year contract last Friday morning after seven months of bargaining.
>
> Laura Kepshire, *Oregon Daily Emerald,*
> University of Oregon

> Terrorists hijacked four passenger jets and turned them into guided missiles yesterday, striking at U.S. government and financial capitals, in choreographed attacks that left thousands feared dead and that shredded the nation's sense of security.
>
> Mitchell Zuckoff and Matthew Brelis,
> *The Boston Globe*

> MILWAUKEE — At least 54 firetrucks were destroyed in the collapse of the World Trade Center on Sept. 11. Now the New York Fire Department is calling on a Clintonville, Wis., company for help.
>
> WRAL-TV, Raleigh, N.C.

> NEW YORK (CNN) — In an apparently coordinated terrorist attack against the United States, four commercial passenger jets crashed on Tuesday, three of them into significant landmarks.
>
> CNN.com

Examine those leads and you'll see several ideas you'll want to consider in your writing.

The leads are relatively short. A long-standing rule of thumb in journalism has limited a newspaper lead to about 35 words and a broadcast lead to about 20 words.

There are exceptions, of course. Magazine writers are usually not limited to one- or two-sentence leads, but the idea remains for the writer to gain the attention of the audience member and that task becomes harder in a flurry of words.

The relatively short length also forces you to focus on the most important point of the story. All too often, beginning writers in every mass media field overload their first sentence, trying to answer every question a reader might have.

The time of breaking news can be placed correctly either by the verb or at the end of the sentence, depending on whether it affects the meaning of the sentence. Notice in the *Albuquerque Journal* lead above what happens if the time element ("Friday") is moved to the end of the sentence: The DNA evidence becomes valid only on that Friday. If the lead begins with an introductory clause, writers may use time elements in that clause. This may be the reason the writer chooses to begin a lead with such a clause.

We find that introductory clauses are being used today more often than older journalism textbooks would like. In the *Los Angeles Times* example above, Maugh did not choose to begin with the introductory clause: "Researchers have found that . . . " but chose to emphasize what he thought was the most important point.

Relevance is the key to making an introductory clause work in a hard-news lead. If the clause places the action in a context or gives a perspective that makes sense and doesn't overwhelm the reader with too much detail, then it can work for the writer.

Most summary leads use the active voice rather than the passive voice. Active voice gets to the point more quickly than does passive voice.

Active Voice
The actor *earned* the part.

Passive Voice
The part *was earned* by the actor.

If you choose to begin your writing in the passive voice, you signal to the reader that the receiver of the action is more important than the actor. And sometimes it is.

Passive Voice
President Reagan was wounded by a gunman. (The subject, *President Reagan*, is the reciever of the action.)

Active Voice
A gunman wounded *President Reagan*. (*President Reagan*, the receiver of the action, is the object.)

Passive voice might be useful in any mass communication situation if the person receiving the action is more important than the person performing the action. An advertisement that intends to make the audience identify with "Harry" might say that "Harry was avoided by everybody" rather than "Everybody avoided Harry."

The active voice also makes it easier to use the basic subject-verb-object sentence construction.

Whatever affects the most people is often the most important point in the story. After a city council meeting, it might be important to the owner of a taco stand that the council has allowed the city to build a turn lane that will help bring customers to the stand, but it's probably more important that the council is expanding the recycling program that affects thousands of people.

As a writer, you want to take advantage of any opportunity to demonstrate impact in your writing.

Contrast Lead

Contrast engages the reader. Charles Dickens' most famous (and well-worn by future generations of writers) line in the classic *A Tale of Two Cities* is the sentence "It was the best of times, it was the worst of times."

But contrast leads can be dangerous, especially when the writer sets up a straw-man approach: "You might think that Mayor Smith is a bungling bureaucrat, but he has a heart for stray cats." The reader may very well think that Mayor Smith is no bungler and that your description is unfair. So there.

Contrast leads often show us that things aren't what they seem—and just think how many novels, movies and other fictional pieces depend on that idea. Here's a contrast lead that deals with a person:

> Ten-month-old Brandon Urban has the bright-eyed, full-cheeked face of a cherub.
>
> But his sweet features do not tell the whole story.
>
> E. Janene Nolan, *The* (Annapolis) *Capital*

Here's an example that shows contrast but isn't limited to an A-but-B approach:

> WASHINGTON — When bungling burglars broke into the Democratic headquarters in the Watergate complex on June 17, 1972, Hawaii Sen. Daniel Inouye was a second-term senator little known on the mainland.
>
> Two years later, when the scandal had shocked the nation and was about to topple the Nixon presidency, it had made a national figure of Inouye, who "served with low-keyed dignity" as the *Almanac of American Politics* put it, on the high-profile Senate Watergate Committee.
>
> Now, a quarter-century later, Inouye remembers Watergate as a "once-in-a-lifetime experience."
>
> Pete Pichaske, *Honolulu Star-Bulletin*

News Feature Leads—Description and Narrative

In what seems to be the long-distant past in American journalism, competition thrived between morning newspapers and afternoon newspapers. The morning paper arrived first with the latest news and usually used hard-news leads to reach its readers.

Then, hours later, the afternoon paper would arrive, facing a reader who, it was assumed, had already perused the morning paper. In order to compete, the afternoon paper's reporters needed to have a different approach for those stories. Often, they would write news features, focusing on the whys and hows rather than using the basic who-what summary-lead approach.

Newspapers today face competition from television, radio, cable television and the Internet, all of which can report breaking news quickly and, sometimes, in a compelling manner. Not many newspaper reporters could get away with a hard-news summary lead on a saturated story that draws major network and cable attention. But with a news feature lead, reporters are able to bring a perspective that may not have appeared yet.

The basic form of a *news feature lead* is an introductory section, or lead, followed by a *nut graph,* a paragraph that states briefly the focus of the story. It's vital that writers include the nut graph, since the story becomes an exercise in futility without it. Imagine an advertisement that smothers the audience in 15 adjectives about a product, but never lets us know whether the product is a fountain pen, a shampoo or a new alcohol-free beer. Reporters do the same when they write a feature lead and forget to tell us the point of the story.

Feature leads can be categorized in two basic groups: descriptive and narrative. Each can powerfully evoke emotion when written well. But when the description doesn't lead us to a key element in a story, when the narrative doesn't have anything to do with the focus or doesn't connect to the person, the news feature falls flat and the readers wonder why the writer didn't just tell them the news.

Descriptive leads paint a verbal picture for the reader, using the reporter's observation of detail to show the audience.

WILLOW — His 16 dogs arched their backs and threw themselves into harness, eyes white and teeth bared with an overwhelming desire to run. Handlers crouched alongside, struggling to hold the team in place as the huskies yammered and howled and bit at the air.

In moments, these dogs would launch the 25th Iditarod Trail Sled Dog Race to Nome, dashing across Willow Lake down a quarter-mile-long chute lined with thousands of shouting, clapping fans. A helicopter circled overhead, a television crew crowded around, loudspeakers blared commentary and patriotic songs.

Amid the clamor stood 80-year-old Joe Redington, the founder of the race and the first participating musher to wear ceremonial bib No. 1. While everyone in sight scrambled like mad, Redington stood calmly, a slight smile playing on his face.

He was as serene as a seasoned old lead dog, ignoring the antics of wrestling pups.

The crowd counted down from five and his handlers sprang back, but Redington's expression never changed. When his dogs surged into a sprint, Redington simply stepped to the runners and held on, the smile intact as he swept down the raceway that curved through the crowd onto the trail toward Susitna River and beyond.

Redington's departure set the tone. Under brilliant sunshine that masked cold, crisp temperatures, the annual 1,100-mile race across Alaska began Sunday at the Willow Community Center in a festival of happy mushers and smooth-running huskies.

Doug O'Harra, *Anchorage Daily News*

Perhaps the writer needs to emphasize details and capitalize on strong verbs and razor-sharp nouns in that kind of description. But not every descriptive lead paints the whole picture. Sometimes the focus lets the reader internalize one—and only one—specific detail:

Before he finally decided to give up pitching, Jon Peters could hear bone grating against bone when he tried to extend his right arm.

If you can't conceive of the pain, at least try to imagine the sound.

David Barron, *Houston Chronicle*

A medium like television supplies some detail through camera work—and lots of detail when the producer and camera operator can look beyond the basics. In radio, meanwhile, vivid description can work together with accurate sound effects to tell a story.

In this example, KQED-FM reporters find an apt analogy to introduce a piece on a small town in California.

They look like big bugs—maybe grasshoppers—dipping and rising endlessly. These are called pumping units by people who know the oil business. And they do here in Taft—a Kern County town sitting right on top of the largest, richest known oil deposit in the continental U.S., the Midway-Sunset Field.

The purpose of a *narrative lead* is to tell a compelling story and put the reader right beside the action as you describe it.

JARRELL — Keith Bukowsky raced death to save his family.

As he watched the deadly, twisting fury bear down on Jarrell, on his neighbors, Bukowsky used a cellular phone in his truck as he raced along Interstate 35 to call his children and sister-in-law and her kids to tell them to get to his mother's stone house southwest of Jarrell.

They would be safe in the closets, he told them.

Then he raced to his mother's house.

"When I pulled up to the house in my dump truck, I saw the tornado about a thousand feet away," he said. "It looked awesome and dangerous. I thought it was going to hit us."

Get out of the house, he screamed. They did, then sped away from the house in a car.

"They say you're not supposed to run from a tornado," Bukowsky said, "but I think we did the right thing."

In the neighborhood they left just west of I-35, as many as 31 people, maybe more, died or would die in the deadliest tornado in Texas in 10 years.

Claire Osborn, Greg Easterly, Pamela Ward, *Austin American-Statesman*

Narratives can be constructed with what fiction writers call "interior monologue," though writers should base such a narrative on interview questions, rather than presumptions. Here's how a different narrative approach puts the reader in the story:

ST. PETERSBURG — Alone in his living room, wheezing and trembling, a frail man watches the triumphant politicians on his television set.

Their giddy words float through the dimness. The tobacco industry has surrendered, they are saying. The old man raises the volume. He has waited for this moment.

He listens closely to the terms of surrender. Big Tobacco will pay hundreds of billions. The industry will be regulated, punished, reformed.

He expects to feel satisfaction.

But as the politicians speak, it dawns on the man with bitter clarity: He has been sacrificed by those smiling faces. They have won, and maybe even the country as a whole has won, but not him.

No denying it.

He has been used as a bargaining chip by powerful people who know nothing of his suffering.

David Barstow, *St. Petersburg Times*

In order for a narrative lead to work, the story ought to be compelling or ought to serve as an example of the point or central issue of a story. You want to have a beginning and ending to the story that will seize the audience's attention.

Shocker and Teaser Leads

These two devices are seen in advertising and public relations writing as well as news writing. The *shocker lead* begins with a bold or odd opener in order to hit the audience like a triple mocha cappuccino.

Getting away with murder is not the exception in Los Angeles County. It is the rule.

Los Angeles Times

In the following lead, the shocker hits in the second paragraph:

YANTIS, Texas — Bryan McCreight grew some of the largest sweet potatoes in northeast Texas this year. Big bulging tubers, some the size of a man's arm bicep and all.

"It just makes you sick," said Mr. McCreight.

You see, big is bad in the sweet potato business. And the fertile, sandy loam fields surrounding Lake Fork Reservoir 75 miles east of Dallas have been transformed into a sea of orange, near-worthless potatoes that won't find a market.

Steven H. Lee, *The Dallas Morning News*

Teaser leads, on the other hand, are meant to grab the reader's attention by promising a revelation later in the story. As with many feature leads, you may find yourself addicted to these, since they give a certain satisfaction to the readers and to the writer.

But watch out. The teaser can easily become what New Hampshire professor and editor Jane Harrigan calls "the mystery lead." Mystery lead writers try to withhold the identity of something for several paragraphs. The biggest problem with mystery leads, Harrigan says, is that they too often are given away in the headline. We would add that they also sometimes try to carry the mystery so far into the story that the solution becomes obvious to everybody. Teasers, therefore, should get to the nut graph relatively soon and shouldn't be spoiled by a copy editor's headline.

When D. C. (Pepper) Clements and Harold (Pee Wee) Adanandus were students at Sam Huston (cq) College in Austin in the fall of 1944, they had no idea that they were going to cross paths with one of the most important figures of the 20th century.

Clements and Adanandus, graduates of Waco's Moore High School, had just finished the football season at Sam Huston and were wondering who was going to coach the basketball team.

When they returned from the Christmas holidays, they got their answer: a young man named Jackie Robinson.

John Werner, *Waco Tribune-Herald*

A Roseville police officer got more than he expected with his soft-shell taco during a recent dinner break.

Officer Joe Spark was preparing to eat a taco from Taco John's, 3338 Rice St., in Little Canada, Feb. 16, when he noticed a dark green substance "which looked and smelled like marijuana," according to a criminal complaint filed in Ramsey County.

St. Paul Pioneer Press

Teaser leads are particularly effective when they get your audience to ask a key question. In the Jackie Robinson lead, the reader should ask "Who?" and in the taco story, the reader should ask "What?" In the following lead, you can see that the teaser can induce readers into playing detective with a "How?" question.

Detectives say a simple traffic stop helped them crack a months-old mystery of disappearing cars at a local dealership.

Paulo Lima, *The Tampa Tribune*

Wordplay Leads

When Kenn Finkel served as sports editor for the now-defunct *Dallas Times Herald*, he issued edicts about what couldn't appear in the section. His staff called them "Finkelisms," and one of the more painful was a ban on puns in stories.

The Texas Rangers could no longer "Cruz" to win in headlines even if a player named Cruz had four home runs. Finkel also banned the use of holiday-based puns because he had seen one too many Christmas-comes-early leads.

We're no Scrooges, but we would caution you to use puns and other clever word tricks carefully. When they work, you're the envy of the office, but when they don't, you wind up with egg on your face, . . . er, on the short end of the stick, . . . uhhh, wishing you'd tried something else.

One device you should begin to develop is the craft of turning a cliché into your own. Instead of writing that something was as "flat as a pancake," you could describe it as "flat as a plate of old Pepsi." You'll also want to consider words that convey two meanings—see Michelle Kaufman's use of the word *baggage* in her lead shown later in this chapter, in the section "Breaking Out of the Boxes," as an example.

If you have to strain for the pun or if you reach for an unwieldy comparison, describing a losing football team as "a sputtering jalopy" (not the worst analogy, but your editor will ask why a jalopy), then it's best to start over. Learning that fine line is particularly hard in advertising and sportswriting, it seems, because those areas seem to encourage wordplay.

But when wordplay works, it appeals to the word lover inside almost every mass communicator. If the city council unanimously votes to come into federal compliance by banning smoking in city hall, you could write "No smoke got in the council's *ayes* today" and delight in the chuckles and the moans throughout the office.

Puns aren't the only way that writers call upon to use wordplay effectively. Consider these leads:

> TAMPA — Look heavenward tonight and you'll see a sight that comes around, well, once in a blue moon. At 11:58 p.m., the moon will wax full for the second time this month.
> But it won't wax poetic.
>
> Jackie Ripley, *St. Petersburg Times*

> Not long ago, Phillies home games meant salad days for the pizza and steak shops around Veterans Stadium. Even if the team wasn't on a roll, these places were packed like a good hoagie before and after games.
> "Used to be that when there was Phillies games, they'd be lined up outside," said a waitress at Celebre's Pizza in a Packer Avenue shopping center, one block west of Broad Street.
> Now on game nights these tiny restaurants frequently are as empty as the Vet's upper-deck seats, their employees as blue.
>
> Frank Fitzgerald, *The Philadelphia Inquirer*

Question Leads

We'll steal our best advice on *question leads* from David Letterman, the TV show host, who has been known to say, "Remember, we're professionals; kids, don't try this at home."

Brian Crites, *The Kansas City Star*

Kansas City Star *assistant business editor Gina Henderson writes a story in the newsroom.*

It's not that question leads are the source of all evil in the newsroom; it's simply that it's much easier to write a bad one than a good one. And they have the potato-chip effect on beginning writers—one is never enough.

Writers all too often fail to answer the question posed in the lead—an excellent indication that the question could be removed with no problem. Some editors have been known to rail—at least they did in the old days when editors railed—about reporters who are supposed to answer questions in their stories rather than ask them. Even worse, lots of amateur writers love question leads and you could wind up guilty by association.

Still, sometimes a question lead lends the proper tone to a story, as does this one by writer Patty Ryan:

> Is the Pope Catholic?
> Not always.
>
> Patty Ryan, *The Tampa Tribune*

Or this one, which is also used to set a tone for the story:

> So, who's this Nicandro Castaneda guy?
>
> And where's "Susan," the mysterious Austin flight attendant of his dreams? And what did he say to Susan at the Gigglin' Marlin bar in Cabo San Lucas, Baja California Sur, that brought an end to their intense starry-eyed conversation?
>
> Don't know what we're talking about? Turn to Castaneda's full-page advertisement—titled "Desperately Seeking Susan"—in the June 13 *Austin Chronicle* or the quarter-page ad on Page F11 of the Classified section of Sunday's *American-Statesman*. Austinites, it seems, are both intrigued and baffled by a man who is spending more than $5,000 to find a woman he met in a bar.
>
> Conversations in restaurants and offices split two ways: Some (Meg Ryan movie fans) want to believe it's romance. Others (daytime talk-show watchers) aren't so sure.
>
> Hank Stuever, *Austin American-Statesman*

Quote Leads

Quote leads are also seldom used in print reporting, and your instructor may cringe at their very existence, but they are sometimes effective when a writer opts to use one. To make a quote lead work, you need a great quote that somehow contains enough context to make the issue clear to the reader without sounding like an economics lecture. Come to think of it, a quote that leads a story needs to be slightly better than great.

Writers are usually better at summarizing and describing a scene than the people they quote are. But every now and then, one of those quote leads jumps from the back of the closet and the writer goes with it, as in this story from Associated Press writer Martha Mendoza:

ROSWELL, N.M. — "I'll tell you one thing. They didn't have big eyes or big, stringy fingers," 80-year-old Frank Kaufmann says of the aliens. "No, ma'am. These were trim, good-looking people."

In 1947, Kaufmann and a handful of other men stationed at the Roswell Army Air Field stumbled onto what they say was wreckage of a spaceship northwest of town.

www.nando.net

Anecdotal Leads

Anecdotes are tales from someone's life that can illuminate a story. They are best when they illustrate the writer's point about a subject.

After the September 11 tragedies, several news organizations devoted space to telling the stories of the victims. *Newsday,* the newspaper on Long Island, New York, maintains an archive of these stories on its Web site, newsday.com. Here's an example from that series of an anecdotal lead:

On the day Eileen Varacchi met the man who would become her husband, he was fooling around in biology class at Syosset High School. She was drawn to his sense of humor. He was mischievous, the class clown. A week after they met, he got kicked out of class after one of his antics.

On the day Frederick Varacchi died, he was engaged in more serious business, as chief operating officer of Can-

tor Fitzgerald, the global trading company located on the 105th floor of Tower One, just above where the first plane hit. Roughly 700 Cantor Fitzgerald employees are unaccounted for.

"I hoped for days, but nobody from his floor, none of the wives, heard anything," said Eileen Varacchi, of Greenwich, Conn. "I was just hoping for one person that he sat near. There was nobody."

Breaking Out of the Boxes

Some leads above, you may have noticed, actually combine two or more of those categories. Luckily, there's no lead police watching over the terminals. Here are a couple of other combination leads:

The sports uniforms were left in the locker room. Instead, they wore gowns and suits and ties. The usual sneakers gave way to high heels and dress shoes. And this time, they didn't have to sweat and scream to win.

Hillsborough public and private high

school coaches were treated to live music, a steak dinner, dancing and prize drawings that ranged from cars and weekend trips to cash Saturday at the eighth annual Coaches Banquet and Dance.

Juliana Lopes, *St. Petersburg Times*

Lopes' lead combines description with contrast in order to show the stark difference between coaches at work and at a formal dinner. In Michelle Kaufman's lead here, she not only mixes description and contrast, but also has narrative elements and uses the word *baggage* in wordplay, meaning not only "luggage," but also problems that the men carry with them.

MIAMI — They showed up at the Miami Airport Marriott five summers ago with lots of baggage. They had been eight of the NBA's most promising players—former first-round draft choices, 7-footers with million-dollar salaries, talented men who had grown accustomed to the world of limos, groupies, television cameras and mansions.

One by one, they stepped up to the registration desk, their names well-known to any basketball fan— Roy Tarpley, Richard Dumas, Chris Washburn.

They spent the next three months playing at Florida International University's Golden Panther Arena and Palm Beach Community College for $350 a week, in front of crowds that sometimes didn't reach three digits. There were no cheerleaders, no national media, no catered meals, no Ferraris.

Those men dazzled the faithful crowds with behind-the-back passes and dunks. They won consecutive U.S. Basketball League championships in 1992 and 1993.

But their toughest opponent is one they're still trying to beat—substance abuse.

Michelle Kaufman, *The Miami Herald*

The Six Questions

You've probably heard that the journalist tends to ask six questions: *who, what, when, where, why* and *how*. Professionals almost never try to overstuff the first sentence with all six elements. Instead, they choose the more important elements for a particular lead and hold the others for later in the story, if they apply.

Who

Writers almost always use *who* in the lead. Good writing always includes people. When writers are faced with complex stories about governmental misuse of bonds or the effects of the futures market on the economy, they are often well-served to focus on people rather than statistics or the broadest picture possible.

As a writer, you'll have to decide how to identify the person or persons in the lead. Part of your decision will be based on the kind of lead you choose to write, and part of the decision will be based on whether your audience could reasonably expect to know the person.

If the subject is a national or local celebrity, then the decision becomes easy. We expect readers to know George W. Bush, Michael Jordan, Tiger Woods, Julia Roberts, Tom Hanks and the town's mayor. But should the audience know Stephen Chew, a psychology professor at Samford University, who has won a major national grant for teaching?

We would expect only audiences of Samford students and faculty or psychology professors would know Professor Chew by name. For other audiences, we would probably use a *blind identifier* and call him "a Samford University professor" or a "psychology professor" or a "42-year-old Birmingham man" depending on which fits the story best and which media outlet we work for.

On the otherhand, you could choose to take a feature style approach to the subject by using "Stephen Chew" in your lead. Here are three approaches you could take on the story:

This lead is probably appropriate for Alabama news outlets. ▶	BIRMINGHAM — A Samford University professor is one of six educators honored with a national award this week. Psychology professor Stephen Chew, 42, has won a $10,000 grant from the Pew Center for outstanding teaching.
This lead is probably appropriate for Samford's public relations news release or the campus newspaper. ▶	Psychology professor Stephen Chew has been named as one of only six educators nationwide honored with a Pew Center teaching award.
This feature lead is appropriate for a Birmingham news outlet. ▶	Stephen Chew's office wall features a formal stiff beige card, four-by-six, that states "I would not have graduated without your teaching. Before, statistics were a foreign language. Now I'm fluent." For the Samford University professor, good teaching has led to a national honor.

In a news feature approach, the writer will almost always use the names on first reference with the idea that this will humanize people to readers.

What

Telling your reader what happened is essential to any good summary lead. In other kinds of more feature style leads, you may wait a few sentences to get to the *what*, but you'll never wait long, since *what* is an essential element in your storytelling. You can find the answer to *what* in all the other leads given in this chapter, but here are two more examples:

> The University of Colorado violated its own policy on beer sales during Saturday's game at Mile High Stadium against Colorado State, CU Regent Bob Sievers said Tuesday.
>
> *The Denver Post*

> Community activist Larry Bush, along with more than 50 individuals and area businesses, says he is filing a formal complaint with the Federal Communications Commission detailing the controversy surrounding KDGS-FM 93.9 disc jockey Kidd Chris.
>
> *The Wichita Eagle*

When

Writers occasionally use *when* as the focus of their leads, but more often worry about where to place the time element into a lead. Rarely is it important enough to be placed at the beginning of the first sentence:

> On Monday, high school English teacher Gerry Dalby will collect a teacher-of-the-year award.

Conceivably, it may be important that Mrs. Dalby gets the money on Monday, but it's more likely that the what element is more important than the exact day.

Where do you place the time element? Usually writers put it near the verb or at the end of the lead sentence. The choice isn't a flip one. The lead "The Board of Regents approved plans to double student tuition *on Monday*" can be read as if only tuition paid on Monday will be doubled. There you would choose to place the time near the verb; "The Regents *on Monday* approved . . . ."

Where

Like when, the *where* element only occasionally surfaces as the most important point in a summary lead, but it's often present somewhere in the lead.

Some of the blind identifier guidelines pertain to where as well. How exactly do you identify a place in a lead and indeed in a story? If Ralph Nader is speaking on the University of Dayton campus, which is the best option for where?

At the University of Dayton campus . . .

In the Nutter Center on the University of Dayton . . .

In the University Lecture Hall, room 115 . . .

In Dayton . . .

Depending on your audience, it could be any of the four (though your professors will probably hope that you spare the reader a room number). A wire story might say "In Dayton" or, with a dateline, might skip the element entirely. The local daily or the local television news might use either the "campus" or the "Nutter Center" identifier. Perhaps the campus daily would use "In the University Lecture Hall" and the room number in an effort to be specific.

In a news feature, a descriptive lead in particular might well focus on the where question.

Why and How

Why and *how* are not often the focus of a hard-news lead on the first day of a big story, but if the story continues for several days, a reporter will often focus on, for example, how wind shear causes airplanes to crash or how the jury system works in a particular murder trial.

Your audience usually wants to know who and what before why and how. In advertising, it might be fine to tell how this razor shaves more smoothly, but you'd better get the who and what questions answered first.

Beginning writers sometimes try to squeeze these elements into a lead that focuses on who and what. They're usually mistaken to do so. Despite popular belief, a lead is not composed of all five *W*'s and the *H*. Really.

Recognizing Bad Leads

You will almost certainly want to revise your first draft of a lead. Heck, you might want to revise a bunch of them, looking for that ideal hook to reel in your audience. Here are some common problems that writers stumble across in their leads.

The Buried Lead

Beginning writers often fail to put the most important fact or angle in the lead. Consider a story about the sentence handed to a convicted murderer. If the story describes the murder in great detail and the ensuing arrest and the trial before mentioning the sentence, the writer has taken a shovel, dug a big hole and dropped the lead right into it before covering it up. That story needs to have the murderer's sentence somewhere in the lead.

Feature writers can bury a lead by failing to connect their introduction to the point. *Los Angeles Times* copy editor Bobbi Olson says that her newspaper gives writers plenty of room, but that occasionally a writer will spend 20 inches of a 40-inch story on the lead.

The No-Follow-Through lead

Sometimes writers will touch on a point in the lead, but fail to explain that point in detail or, even worse, never mention it again. This lead, for example, doesn't work if the writer fails to talk about the backup band again.

The rest of the story fails to mention the Remainders. ▶

> The Smashing Pumpkins had to work hard to better the performance of their warm-up band, the Rock City Remainders, at Saturday's concert at Market Square Arena.

This mistake is not uncommon in the stories that touch on multiple elements in the lead. The writer has to double-check that every item mentioned in the lead appears in the story. If not, it doesn't belong in the lead.

The Recycled Lead

We're not talking plagiarism here—though we have worked with at least one writer whose lead had appeared under another writer's byline a year before. Let's show you three separate leads with the same motif:

Ah, chocolate.

Ah, spring.

Ah, romantic picnics in the park.

Aw nuts, says Bobbi Olson. She's no fan of these overused "Ah" leads. Usually you can find a pretty good lead hiding in the second and third paragraphs of these. If you've seen a clichéd lead like this, you've probably tired of it after the second time. Keep an eye on your work to make sure that you don't fall into a rut with some word trick.

But the worst mistake you can make in a lead comes back to your reporting. Inaccuracy spoils the best lead ever written. Your most important point and your compelling narrative first need to be accurate.

Summary

No matter what kind of story you are writing, if the lead doesn't get the reader started into the story, the rest of your work is in vain. By work-

ing hard on beginning with something important, or capturing attention in some other way, you can ensure that the reader will continue in
the story. Just be sure the lead is appropriate and accurate.

Key Points

▶ Writers must capture the reader's attention immediately.

▶ The basic summary lead summarizes the story by putting
the most important point in the story at the beginning.

▶ Leads are not wordy, usually.

▶ Narrative leads can be effective when there is a compelling
narrative to follow.

▶ Descriptive leads work best when the writer uses excellent
detail to show the reader a verbal picture.

▶ Don't overstuff a lead with all five *W*'s and one *H*. Usually
some of those elements can wait.

▶ You should be aware of some of the classic lead problems
and learn to avoid them, but remember the biggest problem
of all is inaccuracy.

Web Links

Here are a few interesting sites on the Internet where you can find out
more information or see more examples of various kinds of leads.

http://www.newspapers.com/
http://www.msnbc.com/news/NW-front_Front.asp

InfoTrac College Edition Readings

For additional readings, go to **www.infotrac-college.com**, enter your
password, and search for the following articles by title or author's name.

▶ "Writing Compelling Article Leads," Steve Weinberg,
Writer, Nov. 1995 v108 n11 p18.

▶ "Hooking the Reader Depends on Variety of Well-Written
Leads; Writer's Success Hinges Not on One Style But Several,"
Paula LaRocque, *Quill,* July-August 1995 v83 n6 p41.

▶ "First Things First" (Writing news leads), Jack Hart, *Editor & Publisher,* Feb. 12, 1994, v127 n7 p 29.

Exercises

Go to your CD-ROM to complete the following exercises:

▶ Exercise 4.1

▶ Exercise 4.2

▶ Exercise 4.3

▶ Exercise 4.4

5

Research for Media Writing

You can write, you tell yourself while hunched uncomfortably in the ill-constructed plastic chair. And, you're willing to put in the hours. So why are you here in the unemployment office again?

It was a simple mistake. Well, actually several simple mistakes.

Like the first day when you got that really big scoop on the drunk-driving charge against the Rev. Martin Counts, one of the country's best-known ministers. Your boss was really displeased when it turned out the charge was actually filed against Marvin Counts, a fellow with a string of 39 drunk-driving arrests to his name.

Sure, you could have done a little more research by double-checking the police blotter and calling the minister's church to confirm, but you were busy, darn it.

Then there was the affair with the press release that had somebody's age wrong. Somebody important, your boss said. Somebody important enough (though you'd never heard of her) that there had been 20 stories on the person over the years that never once missed the age. Until now.

Stupid press release, you mutter in your best Homer Simpson voice.

The person in the next chair leans over and says, "Don't mutter out loud. I'm a copywriter thinking of my next ad campaign. Can I help it if my agency didn't appreciate my envelope-pushing campaign for that new line of menswear? Oh sure, they said my creative masterpieces were aimed at 16-year-olds and that the research showed that only men 50 and older were interested in the clothes. They just don't appreciate genius."

The person on your other side speaks up. "Oh, I agree. My public relations agency just dumped me simply because I wasn't reading the research reports. I never could understand statistics, which don't really tell you anything anyway. They said I shot from the hip too much."

And so the three of you shift in your uncomfortable chairs and wait.

Reporting skills are necessary for any media writer, and in the process of going from an idea to a published story, reporting is at the front, where it all begins. There are two major aspects to reporting: research and interviewing. Those are the skills you will learn about, and practice, in this chapter and the next.

Research Skills

Research skills consist of all information-gathering skills other than interviewing. As you start your media writing career, you will quickly find that solid research *before* you ever sit down to write, or even conduct an interview, is crucial to good media writing. If you haven't done enough research, you are unlikely to write an acceptable story.

Research provides factual information that you may directly use in your story. Take a look at the story by Delbert Quentin Wilber on page 274. The material in that fine 1A story didn't just appear for the writer; it came about as the result of solid research that included a reading of court documents, extensive interviews with a number of different people involved in the case, and heavy use of the newspaper's library.

"Once you get into a story like this, or any story really, you find that it's the research that makes the story trustworthy for the reader," says Wilber. "I always find, too, that finding out one thing always leads you to discover more—so good research leads to even more research, and that's great for the quality of the story."

Research, as Wilber notes, provides important background information that allows you to do a better job of further reporting, including interviewing. Research, then, helps you do some of the following:

▶ Find background material, which includes small details and interesting facts and anecdotes. These freshen your story and add to your credibility.

▶ Get ideas for new interview questions, which is helpful in making your story different from the last dozen written about a subject.

▶ Locate current information on a subject, which allows you to avoid sounding like a stuffy history text.

▶ Explore areas where previous information conflicts with other information, which keeps you from repeating previously printed mistakes.

▶ Unearth mistakes in stories or press releases, which keeps you from blindly putting false information before the public.

▶ Avoid your own errors—the most important task. In any mass communication field, any lack of accuracy leads to a lack of credibility. Your audience wants information it can trust. And it will respond to any inaccuracy it can find.

A reporter who makes a factual error can expect some sharp-eyed reader to find the error and call the editor about it. A broadcaster who gets a name or fact wrong may hear from hundreds of listeners or viewers. A public relations practitioner who gets information wrong will no doubt hear from the client, since the client's reputation is at stake.

In advertising, too, research is crucial, since it not only gives the ad copywriter the information he or she needs to come up with a useful idea that will help sell the product, it also provides important information that may actually appear in the ad.

If, for instance, an assignment requires the title of Toni Morrison's first novel or the price of gasoline in 1976 or what critics have said about the television show *Buffy, the Vampire Slayer,* then it's your responsibility to find that information.

Sources for Research Information

A good reporter quickly learns the sources for the research information that will suit his or her needs. Here are just a few of the basics.

Dictionaries and Telephone Books

One overlooked source for information should be somewhere on your work desk. Not only do dictionaries provide correct spellings and definitions, but some also contain helpful tables and lists. For example, in the back of *Merriam-Webster's Collegiate Dictionary, Tenth Edition,* you will find these lists:

▶ Foreign words and phrases (when someone mentions *sic transit gloria mundi,* you can look it up there),

▶ Biographical names (where you could, for instance, look up the historical figures of William Wallace and Francis Marion, so you'd be better prepared for that interview with Mel Gibson),

▶ Geographical names (exactly where is Lake Baikal?)

The telephone book is also helpful. It gives you the correct spelling of names, addresses and phone numbers of businesses. Some mass media supervisors insist that writers look up in the phone book every name that comes up in a story, and frequently these editors also require reporters to call and verify every phone number that is mentioned in any story.

Criss-Cross Directory

A *criss-cross directory*, also called a "city directory," is valuable for reporters because it lists entries by address and telephone exchange rather than alphabetically. If you need to know who lives at 5501 Loblolly Court, across the street from your story subject, a criss-cross directory will give you that information. If you need to know who has the phone number 555-2368 rather than 555-2367, the criss-cross directory lists those in numerical order.

Criss-cross services are now available on some Internet search engines. For example, the Excite engine's People Finder can give you a person's name with an address linked to all of the other names and addresses on that street.

The Library or "Morgue"

Until the last decade or so, most news organizations hired a few staffers to serve as librarians, responsible for clipping and filing stories as well as maintaining reference material like phone books from other cities. In the newspaper business, the room where this material was stored was called the "morgue."

The name itself was spooky and romantic. It was the place where old stories went to be clipped from the newspaper and placed into file cabinets to await the day when some reporter would rummage through the yellowed newsprint to find background information for a new story.

Sigh. It *was* romantic, and veteran reporters remember the hands-on appeal of the newspaper morgue with a certain nostalgia.

But it was also time-consuming, prone to filing errors, and cumbersome to use. In some smaller news organizations, the morgue may have meant a stack of unclipped papers piled on a cabinet.

These days, news organizations have pretty much put the morgue into the file cabinet and adopted the electronic library. Now reporters can access some old stories from their desks by using a computer. In fact, some reporters can access their organization's news library from laptops without ever visiting the office.

In television, wise station managers arrange for someone to maintain video libraries, which include not only old broadcasts but also video clips of celebrities and important stories. Public relations practitioners need access to old news and to former campaigns. Advertising workers also need access to old campaigns.

All may also need general reference materials, from atlases and specialized dictionaries to trade association phone lists and more complex works like *Contemporary Authors,* which includes writers from Stephen King to T. Coraghessan Boyle.

Librarians now do their clipping with word processing software, rather than with scissors; but the idea of keeping old information easily accessible is still important. Still, most newspapers haven't put a lot of older stories into the electronic library. If you need to find out news coverage from before the early 1980s, in most places, you may still need to summon your courage and enter the morgue.

Lexis-Nexis

Lexis-Nexis may be accessed through Mead Data Central's Meadnet, available if your organization pays Mead Data Central. It doesn't come cheaply, which means that libraries, universities, large legal firms and large news organizations are much more likely to become subscribers.

Lexis is a vast reference network of legal information. Attorneys and law clerks are more likely to use this source regularly, but reporters can check the results of court cases and law review articles here. It's a valuable source for reporters and others who need to check legal references.

Nexis, however, probably gets much more attention from print and broadcast reporters, public relations practitioners, and advertising copywriters. Nexis is a vast database of news that has appeared in thousands of newspapers, magazines, and newsletters, including transcripts of some broadcast news programs.

After signing on, you will decide which categories, known as "libraries" and "files" in Nexis, to examine. Your choices include news, business, company, industry, people, political, international, legal, medical and patent. Within these libraries are specific databases.

Because each search costs money and because Nexis cuts off searches at 1,000 hits, you may want a librarian to help you use good search strategies to narrow your focus. A search for political consultant James Carville, for instance, would easily exhaust your 1,000 hits, but if you need to focus on his views on Louisiana politics, a search that uses both terms—*Carville* and *Louisiana*—should yield better results.

The utility of Nexis seems apparent for reporters, but those working in advertising and public relations can make good use of the service as well. Advertising copywriters base their work around facts, and Nexis is an excellent source of factual information. Public relations practitioners can scan news stories and also get an in-depth picture of opinion by searching for editorial and opinion pieces on a subject.

The Internet

The question is not, Is there information on the Internet? but rather, How can you get to the information you need? And as most of you know, that's a difficult question.

Like other computer users, reporters sometimes get frustrated while dealing with the Internet, but they are, by each month, more willing to take a plunge into vast, confusing cyberspace. They can find "expert" sources on subjects and arcane details that can boggle the mind of newcomers to the Net.

Reporters love search engines such as Webcrawler, Excite, Google, and Alta Vista, which allow people to type in one or more terms. (The current favorite is Google because of its more relevant returns.) The engine then searches for matching terms throughout the World Wide Web and/or the Internet and posts the results. If you wish to visit a located site, you merely point at the appropriate link and press the appropriate button or key.

But almost all of you already know that.

What you want is a better understanding of Boolean logic, which can help pinpoint searches more easily. Boolean logic narrows a search with the terms *AND, OR, BUT,* and *NOT.* For example, if you want to search for the musician Seal, you would be advised to use a search term like "Seal AND music AND concert." If you use only "Seal," you're going to have to scan past dozens of stories about Greenpeace, marine biology and the San Francisco Giants' mascot.

Once you've found information on the Internet, you have reached the toughest point. Now you have to swallow all your excitement and take a deep breath. Because the Internet is unregulated for the most part and because anyone with a computer and modem can post on it, you need to be extremely cautious about the information you find. The information, no matter how official the site looks, could very well be wrong. You should always double-check the "facts" you've found from the Internet.

Mass communicators can improve their chances of finding accurate information through listservs and newsgroups, which are two specific areas where experts and aficionados gather. Though they don't guarantee the accuracy of all information, listservs and newsgroups can guide you to some experts. A little time spent browsing will probably tell you about the relative trustworthiness of certain posts.

Listservs focus on a certain topic and require you to subscribe by sending an e-mail message to a listserve. SUBSCRIBE JOURNET, for example, gives you access to a discussion group about journalism and journalism education. Individual members post messages to the entire group, which appear in the other members' e-mail queues. Some of these groups are very busy and can fill an e-mail system overnight. Fortunately, you merely need to send a message to the same listserv asking to UNSUB the group. (Remember this instruction because list members may be too busy to answer every person who wishes to leave the list but doesn't remember how to do that.)

Newsgroups are accessible through Usenet, a subdivision of the Internet, or through a commercial service such as America Online or CompuServe. These groups are often unmoderated and open to virtually anyone who can wield a mouse. There are thousands of newsgroups available; you may wish to visit sites like alt.activism, alt.books, alt.culture.Australia, alt.x-files, alt.pop-up-trailers, rec.sport.college basketball, alt.tv.pinky-and-the-brain or alt.backrubs.

Though some who post messages in newsgroups are extremely knowledgeable, others are, well, fountains of misinformation. Let the reporter beware. We highly recommend that before using a post, you request from the author permission to quote the post in an assignment and that you make that request via e-mail rather than in a post. Sometimes you will find that the "author" has posted a controversial message from someone else's account.

We also recommend making interview requests via e-mail rather than in posts; after all, reporters rarely shout interview requests across crowded rooms.

News Releases

Reporters need releases and appreciate a newsy release that contains important information and covers enough background information that the reporter doesn't have to spend the day looking up information in the electronic library.

If you're a newspaper or magazine reporter, you will have developed a healthy skepticism concerning the facts presented in a press release. But if the story seems important, if it has news value and the source has proven itself trustworthy, then you may very well follow up on the release with a story of your own that validates the press release's information.

From the perspective of the public relations practitioner who wrote the release, seeing the newspapers or local broadcast stations do their own version of the story is a sign of success. You've convinced the media that your client has news value, and you've gotten the news out there that the client wanted seen.

If you're a reporter working at a small publication, you are probably going to be even more dependent on well-written releases. Most small publications need material—they often have no wire service to provide news—and public relations practitioners often see their work reprinted word-for-word in some of these smaller newspapers.

When one of this book's authors worked for a biweekly newspaper, he was always happy to see releases from the Texas Parks and Wildlife Department. They were well-written, timely and trustworthy, and they covered hunting and fishing issues well enough that he didn't have to spend much time chasing down that information himself.

The broadcast version of a press release is called a *video news release* (VNR) and usually contains a videotaped story suitable for broadcast. You may have seen some of these on local newscasts, especially daytime and weekend news programs that need to fill space. These, again, should have some newsworthy element and should look as professionally produced as a newsroom story. VNRs are also sometimes used for their video segments while reporters or producers write local news stories about the subject.

Tips and Tactics

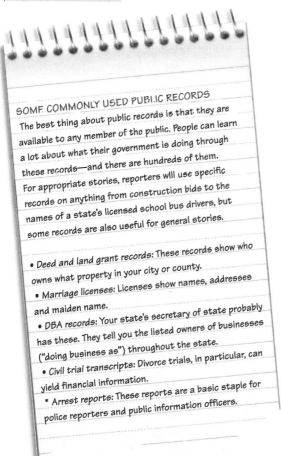

SOME COMMONLY USED PUBLIC RECORDS

The best thing about public records is that they are available to any member of the public. People can learn a lot about what their government is doing through these records—and there are hundreds of them. For appropriate stories, reporters will use specific records on anything from construction bids to the names of a state's licensed school bus drivers, but some records are also useful for general stories.

• Deed and land grant records: These records show who owns what property in your city or county.
• Marriage licenses: Licenses show names, addresses and maiden name.
• DBA records: Your state's secretary of state probably has these. They tell you the listed owners of businesses ("doing business as") throughout the state.
• Civil trial transcripts: Divorce trials, in particular, can yield financial information.
* Arrest reports: These reports are a basic staple for police reporters and public information officers.

Public Records

You can learn a lot about somebody by visiting the county courthouse. Does she own property in the county? Does he have a mortgage on a house? Who owned the house before him? Has she been in court? Does he have a marriage license from the county? What political party does she belong to? Does he hold a county occupational permit? What is the name of her cat, and does her pet license include a phone number that is unlisted everywhere else?

Depending on the access provided by each individual state's *sunshine* (or *open records*) *laws*, any member of the public can find information like this at the county courthouse. These records are open to the public and available for the asking.

If you're willing to invest some time and to request information from the state government, you can learn even more about someone. In some states, you can request information from the department of motor vehicles and receive photocopies of driver's licenses. (California, for one, has closed access to driver's license records, and you should check your state's access.) You can find the names of a corporation's officers or ownership information about a local nightclub.

Re: Freedom of Information Act request

Dear (FOI officer):

I request that a copy of the following documents
(or documents containing the following information)
be provided to me: (identify as specifically as
possible).

In order to help to determine my status to assess
fees, you should know that I am (insert description
of requester and purpose of request such as 'a
representative of the name of newspaper, broadcast
station, etc.) and this request is made as part of
newsgathering and not for commercial use.

(You may also offer to pay fees up to a certain
amount or you may request a fee waiver.)

Thank you for your consideration of this request.

Sincerely,

Your name

FIGURE 5.1 *Sample letter of request*

The federal government will also provide some information to the public through the Freedom of Information Act (FOIA). You may request information about a subject through the government, and the government may be able to find that information. The more precise your request, the easier it will be to fill the request. Figure 5.1 shows an example of an FOIA request letter.

Not every record kept by county, state and federal government agencies is open to your scrutiny. Law enforcement investigations that remain open, for example, are exempt from public record statutes as are records from juvenile courts.

Good reporters, though, learn how to navigate public records to get information that, at first glance, seems closed. For example, the Internal Revenue Service will not release any individual income tax information (and well it shouldn't), but if a person has been through a divorce trial, income tax information may be included in the court record. And court records are generally open to the public.

The availability of public records may sound somewhat scary. Indeed, sunshine laws often clash with our concept of individual privacy. But sunshine laws also prevent government agencies from operating in shadowy secrecy (hence, the term *sunshine law*). Sunshine laws allow the public to investigate for themselves. You can find out the history and cost of property yourself rather than trusting a seller to be completely honest. You can check to see how many lawsuits have been filed against that local company that wants you to buy its product.

Numbers and Polls

You will certainly run across numbers in your research. In fact, you may well be asked to conduct some research that yields numbers. Since some of you entered mass communication to avoid ever finding another *x* or *y*, this may seem frightening.

But there's a reason for you to enter the bramble patch of conducting valid research. Once you know the basic terminology, you will be able to use research products much more effectively.

In newswriting for print or broadcast, you will better understand the numbers you find (or receive in a press release) if you have at least a minimal background in statistics.

If you don't have that basic understanding, then your ability to recognize, analyze and write about the news is weakened.

If you're entering advertising or public relations, this kind of research is an important part of the process of doing your job. In advertising, for example, you will become familiar with STARCH numbers. In public relations, you will need to be able to gauge public opinion and to evaluate how effectively your last campaign worked.

One of the most common research devices that you'll need to understand is the survey. Advertisers use various forms to check public opinion of products and campaigns. News media use ratings services and readership surveys to fine-tune their products. And public relations practitioners find that nothing is quite able to describe public opinion better than a systematic means of measuring what a public thinks.

Tips and Tactics

The Numbers Game

For many of us in mass communication, at some point we found ourselves helpless in a math class. Maybe it was algebra or geometry or calculus, but at some point we found the numeric world to be a sheer glass cliff, slick and unstable. Yeah, a slick glass cliff with pterodactyls swooping down to pluck us off one by one to a horrid, terrible . . .

We're *word* people, not numbers people.

At some point, however, we must conquer our fear of numbers, even if we never conquer calculus. Reporters are faced with interpreting budgets and understanding municipal bonds; copywriters are asked to interpret numerical goals; corporate communicators have to understand and then explain annual reports.

Here are six (I had to count twice) basics in understanding numbers.

The Average

Average does not always mean the arithmetic average that we may be most familiar with. That average, called the *mean*, is the sum of all the observations divided by the number of observations. If, however, we look at the midpoint of a group of numbers, that's the *median*. Occasionally, both are used in certain situations. And they aren't always the same.

Look at the numbers 3, 6, 13, 25 and 33. The mean is 16 (3 + 6 + 13 + 25 + 33 = 80; 80 ÷ 5 = 16). But the median (the number that is in the middle of these five numbers) is 13. Don't expect your source to always explain which is used. Also, the *mode* is the most common finding in a group of numbers and might sometimes be considered an average.

Percentages, Percentiles, Percent Change

You probably have a good grasp of *percentages*. If you got 48 of 50 test questions correct, you scored 96 percent. However, if half of the class scored a 96, you would be located at the 50th percentile. *Percentiles,*

(continued)

(continued)

then, tell us where a score ranks in comparison with other scores. The real nightmare comes with *percentage change*—a task that challenges reporters daily. If a city cuts its recycling budget from $50,000 to $40,000, what percentage change occurred?

The formula is the new number divided by the old number minus 1.

$$\frac{\$40,000}{\$50,000} = .8$$

$$.8 - 1 = -.2$$

To convert the answer to a percentage, multiply by 100:

$$-.2\,(100) = -20$$

Therefore, the recycling budget has been cut by 20 percent. This computation may look easy, but news reporters have had to make thousands of corrections after doing the arithmetic incorrectly.

Standard Deviations

Occasionally you will run across a report that makes use of *standard deviations,* which are a way to measure variance. This measurement is based on the classic theoretical bell curve.

IQ tests are the easiest way to show how standard deviations work. By definition, the mean for certain IQ tests is 100. The standard deviation is 15, which means a certain number of people—68 percent—will have an IQ from 85 to 115. At two standard deviations, 95 percent of people will have IQ scores from 70 to 130. The remaining 5 percent are way out there on the ends of the bell curve. Thus, if someone reports a standard deviation of more than 2, you know you have a rare case.

Margin of Error

Why don't pollsters interview 50,000 people for national elections? They don't have to. Probability theory tells them that they can predict within certain boundaries how an election will come out on the basis of a sample of 1,000 to 1,200 people. The idea is that by polling a certain number of people, you can predict (well, at least 19 of 20 times) how a given population will vote with a certain degree of accuracy. The probability does not increase incrementally, so a sample of 1,600 is more accurate than a sample of 800 people, but it is not twice as accurate.

How to Use Information

Please pay close attention to the following warning.

Be careful. Now that you know where to find information, you must face the dangerous part of background research—using the information correctly.

After you've spent time rummaging through cyberspace or the morgue or the criss-cross directory, there is a real temptation to show off your excellent research skills in your story. These stories become cluttered with excessive and much-too-long quotes from other publications, with lots of biographical information that readers may not want to hack their way past, and with details that detract from instead of enhancing your writing.

You've written term papers, and you probably have assignments to write research papers this semester. You probably understand the concept of footnotes and probably know that those are very important in research papers. In mass communication writing, it's important to

That degree of accuracy is usually called the *margin of error*. Reporters usually state this in the number of percentage points, plus or minus. Let's say that Candidate Miller gets 55 percent in an election poll and Candidate Smith gets 45 percent. If the polling organization has interviewed enough people to claim a 4 percent margin of error, then Candidate Miller can start buying the champagne because Smith can't get more than 49 percent and Miller would get no worse than 51 percent (unless things change, as they usually do).

In the 2000 presidential election, before the voters made their choice, most national polls found neither Al Gore nor George Bush was able to claim a large enough lead to escape the margin of error, and thus the race was too close to call ahead of Election Day.

The Gambler's Fallacy

You just watched your friend flip a coin with heads coming up 9 times in a row. You know the odds are astronomical against anyone flipping 10 straight heads, so you bet your new DVD player against her. That night, as you beg her for mercy, you realize that though the odds of flipping 10 heads in a row is astronomical, each individual flip in that run has a 50–50 chance of coming up heads. In other words, the odds of flipping 10 heads in a row are exactly equal to the odds of flipping 9 heads in a row and then a tail.

The coin has no memory. It doesn't know what it's done. You have fallen prey to the gambler's fallacy. Maybe she'll let you watch if you bring the snacks.

Specialized Numbers

Certain mass communication areas require knowledge of special numbers. A broadcast journalist would do well to take a crash course in how ratings numbers are calculated. An advertising copywriter should know what some of those STARCH numbers explain. A sports reporter must be able to interpret ERA—earned run average—and other statistics. Business reporters have plenty of numbers to figure out—price-earnings ratios, profit margins, annual budgets. In fact, the business reporter, more than anyone in the newsroom, must be able to walk up to the sheer glass cliff and find a way to climb it.

Almost all of them do. With no pterodactyl bites, either. ■

attribute information, but it's also important to reduce needless clutter from your copy.

► Avoid long quotes from other publications: if your boss wanted to publish those, she would just run the other writer's story instead.

► When you do use quotes from other sources, try not to use many of them.

► Watch out for big blocks of biographical information in your story. (In fact, some public relations practitioners compose a separate biography page to avoid clutter.)

Remember, the purpose of research is not to show off how much you learned, but rather to add specific information to a story where it's needed (and only where it's needed) and to prepare for and add to your interviews, which probably will comprise the most important part of your story.

Your Brain: Database and Critical-Thinking Central

Mass communicators who know details and trivia and have some understanding of what's going on in the world are valuable to their companies. Potential newsroom employees often must take current events tests and general knowledge tests.

Editors and others bemoan the lack of cultural literacy, a term from E. D. Hirsch's book of the same name. They think it's important to understand some general concepts and to identify certain historical figures.

Editors and other supervisors would also like employees to enter the newsroom with literacy in popular culture. They think it's important to be able to identify, say, Michael Stipe as the lead singer for REM, to know the nickname of Chicago's professional basketball team (the Bulls), and to discern between *Gilligan's Island* and *Gulliver's Travels*. They like generalists, people who know a little bit about a lot.

However, what they usually find are potential employees who are reasonably intelligent, but don't seem to know much outside of areas they're interested in. Some of these folks can tell you the name of every *Brady Bunch* character who ever appeared on the show, but can't tell the difference between World War I and World War II.

That's a pity. Because the more information you understand, the better you can perform an important task: evaluating information and using critical thinking to improve your assignments.

For example, one of this book's authors once copy-edited a story about a historic resort that had been refurbished and was up for sale. In its heyday during the 1920s and 1930s, it had been a popular hangout for celebrities and gangsters, who would come South to relax. The story described one of those gangsters, Alvin (Creepy) Karpis, who vowed revenge after his fellow gang members were killed in an FBI raid.

The story said that Karpis had vowed to kill President Franklin Roosevelt and that Roosevelt flew to New Orleans to personally arrest Karpis, with the help of federal agents.

Hmmmmmm. Think for a moment or two. You might have a couple of questions about that anecdote: (1) Presidents don't usually arrest people. Why was this a special case? (2) We know now (though the public, for the most part in the '30s, didn't know) that Roosevelt had suffered polio and spent much of his time in a wheelchair. Would someone who had limited mobility actually try to arrest a top gangster?

The author dug through the morgue and found the Alvin Karpis file. It contained an old wire story clipped many years before by an anonymous librarian that explained that Karpis had not threatened Roosevelt, but rather FBI director J. Edgar Hoover and that Hoover had flown to New Orleans to personally arrest the gangster.

And that's how using critical thinking can save a story.

Avoiding Dumb Questions Through Research

Your mother told you, your high school English teacher told you and your scoutmaster told you that there was no such thing as a dumb question if you didn't know the answer. They were wrong. Unfortunately, for a mass media writer, dumb questions can absolutely stall an interview before it begins.

So what might a dumb question sound like? Here are four of them.

So, Pat Conroy, you're a well-known author.
What books have you written?

So, Meg Ryan, you're a famous actor.
What movies have you appeared in?

So, Mr. Kareem Abdul-Jabbar, what sport did you play?

Senator Jesse Helms, what state do you represent?
And what is your party affiliation?

Maybe you don't know that Pat Conroy is the author of several highly regarded books, including *The Prince of Tides* and *The Great Santini*. Maybe you wouldn't know some of Meg Ryan's big screen roles in *When Harry Met Sally* and *Sleepless in Seattle*. You might not even know Kareem Abdul-Jabbar, the 7-foot basketball star who played for Milwaukee and Los Angeles from jockey Pat Day. Maybe you missed government class the day the teacher talked about North Carolina Republican Jesse Helms.

Too bad. They're still dumb questions—not because you didn't know, but because you didn't look them up.

Two Not-Dumb-at-All Questions

Finally, as we prepare to enter the interviewing chapter, we want to assure you that every "dumb" question may not be so dumb.

Consider, for example, when a reporter interviewed a secretary for a feature story about her victory in a secretarial competition. He waited in the office, saw her name painted on her office's glass door, and when she invited him to enter, he saw the name on her desk nameplate.

He conducted the interview and wrote the story. After it was published, he called her to check her reaction to the story.

It was fine, she said, except that you misspelled my name.

After the queasy feeling hit his stomach, he managed to reply, "But I saw your name on the door and on your nameplate . . ."

The secretary began laughing. It seems the painter had misspelled her name, and her officemates had thought that funny enough to buy her a gag gift, a nameplate with the same misspelling.

The reporter could have kicked himself for not asking a "dumb" question. How do you spell your name? is basic research. And think what a great idea that gag gift is for a fresh angle to the story, too.

Embarrassing questions don't qualify as dumb, either. At a Washington press conference some time ago, reporter Linda Ellerbee recalled in her book *And So It Goes* that former first lady Betty Ford was wrapping up a standard news conference. The Washington

David Brody

A Day in the Life of...

Media-Relations Writer
Charles Stovall

Working in media relations at a major theme park in the Orlando area, I see my job as being a resource for media writers from all over the world. I help provide them with information, usually through our extensive Web site. It's a job that changes every day, of course, but a typical day might go something like this.

By 8:30 a.m. I'm in the office and answering e-mail and voice mail. I receive about 100 pieces of e-mail per day. Most journalists now use e-mail as one of their primary means of communication, and it has made answering simple questions about the theme parks infinitely easier. Some journalists still prefer to use the phone. I answer 10–15 voice mails per day. Most are simple questions dealing with a fact or two about the resort, but some require in-depth research and outside information from experts throughout the company.

By 9 a.m. I'm busy checking on outstanding releases and photos. Press releases and photos are principal means of getting information to reporters. Most of the publicists in our department have publicity duties for a specific theme

park or resort in the complex. As "manager" of the publicity for a specific part, I assist journalists who are doing stories on my individual park or where my park is included in a bigger story. I write most of the press releases and supervise most of the photography that is used for publicizing that park, its attractions and events. A good press release–photo combination should give reporters a base of knowledge about a given event or product, painting a complete picture for the reporter.

At 10:30 a.m. I usually confer with the New Media team. Two major research tools we create specifically for journalists are our media-only Web site and an annual CD-ROM focusing on new attractions and events. The Web site is a password-protected site designed specifically for journalists. It contains press releases, high-resolution photos and multimedia clips. It is a huge time saver for us, as journalists can get answers to their questions and find information anytime. The CD-ROM is also a very effective resource tool for journalists. In addition to being a resource for journalists working on a current story, it also presents story ideas for journalists who might not be familiar with the theme park, might have not been to our theme parks in a few years or might be looking for a new story angle.

At noon it's time for lunch, but that doesn't mean any time off. My lunch hour usually means taking part in a media tour. Relationship building is the hallmark of our success, both with tra-

media regulars had asked the usual questions and were ready to go when Ford took one last question from a newcomer in the back of the room.

"Have you or any of your children used marijuana?"

Ellerbee recalls the media regulars stifling giggles and dismay. If there had been a comic-strip balloon over the reporters' heads, it would have said, "What a dumb question."

Except that Ford said, "Yes."

Some dumb questions can be pretty darn smart.

---

ditional media outlets and new media outlets. And it can be a lot of fun. One of the biggest "perks" to my job is being able to take time with media people and show them rides, attractions, shows, resorts or restaurants that our guests enjoy. With an entertainment offering such as a theme park, experiencing the product is a vital part of the story-gathering process of reporters. It is my job to make sure not only that reporters have a good experience, but that their experience is relevant to their story and has made the best use of their (usually) limited time.

By 2:30 p.m. I'm involved in Web monitoring. One of the ways we measure whether a publicity campaign or event has been successful is through recapping and measurement. We collect media coverage and evaluate it for its "media value." Traditional print and broadcast media have established media values based on circulation and TV viewership; we're basically calculating what our advertising department would have to pay for the newspaper space or air time we are given. The public relations community has never formally addressed online media value. Our new media team has established a set of values based on variable values of online advertising and CPM (cost per thousand) impressions, a standard used *in* online ad buying.

An hour and a half later, around 4 p.m., I'm in the International Meeting. One of the growth opportunities that our theme park is addressing is international markets. A core team of interna-

tional publicists has joined our domestic media relations department. The team helps us learn how international guests and journalists think; and we support their efforts abroad, helping to launch campaigns in Europe, Asia, Latin America and South America.

At 6 p.m. it's time for dinner, but a great many of our media relationship building opportunities fall outside of the 9-to-5, Monday-through-Friday workweek. Working nights and weekends is a must for any publicist. At a theme park, most of the events are fun (dinners at theme park restaurants, dessert parties at resorts, watching fireworks); so it's not as much of a burden as it might seem.

It's a full day, and it's important to remember that in my job much of what I do actually falls outside the daily routine as I've just described it. At a theme park, every day is an adventure; so you can't pin everything down into a set schedule. My daily routine can consist of everything from huge press events for hundreds of media people that take up entire weeks (sometimes months) of my schedule to individual media visits and intimate media weekends where we design a tour around a journalist's particular interests. We produce media events and stunts. We even host celebrities on our property, with handprint ceremonies, motorcades and other special events surrounding their visits. My job may be a lot of things, but dull is never one of them. ■

Summary

Researching helps writers find information that they can include within a story, use to craft interview questions, or use to develop story ideas. However, the most important reason to research subjects is to avoid errors. Some common research tools include dictionaries, phone books and maps; the Internet and electronic databases are also sources.

How much research is enough? Writers should do as much research as possible, given the restraints of time and availability. But you will find the restraints loosen when you gain confidence in approaching stories through research.

Key Points

Research may begin with easy-to-use tools like dictionaries and phone books, but will probably also include trips to the morgue or the modern electronic library.

▶ Learning Internet research skills is vital, but remember to carefully evaluate information gleaned from cyberspace.

▶ Public records are extremely important sources for many public affairs stories.

▶ Press releases must be accurate since many reporters will take information from them for distribution to their audience.

▶ In an interview setting, a dumb question is one that you should have been able to answer through basic research.

Web Links

Here are a few interesting sites on the Internet where you can find out more about research.

http://www.gao.gov/
http://www.muckraker.org/
http://www.webgator.org/
http://www.nicar.org/
http://www.ire.org/
http://ww.iabc.org/links

InfoTrac College Edition Readings

For additional readings, go to **www.infotrac-college.com**, enter your password, and search for the following articles by title or author's name.

▶ "Negotiating for Electronic Records: Doing Your Homework Will Help Get the Data You Need," Jennifer LaFleur, *Quill,* June 2002 v90 i5 p65.

▶ "Loaded Questions; Bad Numbers" (Evaluation of surveys done by St. Louis *Post*), Terry Jones, *St. Louis Journalism Review,* March 2001 v31 i234 p13.

▶ "Databases Offer More Than Statistics: Raw Data Can Sometimes Add to Stories in Unexpected Ways" (Mastering the art), Jennifer Lafleur, *Quill,* Jan. 2002 v90 i1 p42.

▶ "A Librarian's Plea to Journalists: Give Us a Clue!" Donald Altschiller, *Columbia Journalism Review,* March–April 2002 v40 i6 p70.

Exercises

Go to your CD-ROM to complete the following exercises:

▶ Exercise 5.1

▶ Exercise 5.2

▶ Exercise 5.3

▶ Exercise 5.4

▶ Exercise 5.5

6

Interviewing Skills for Media Writers

t's your first day on the job at the *Daily Sun*. You're a little nervous, but you're also confident that you're ready for this.

You worked for your school paper for two years; you did a solid summer internship at a good paper; you were a sports stringer for one semester and sold the same paper two freelance feature articles after that.

There were dozens of applicants for this general-assignment reporting job, you remind yourself as you sit down at your desk, and you were the one who got hired.

Sure, you're in a bureau out in the boondocks, but it won't be long, you figure, before you'll earn your way downtown to where the *real* action is.

You spend the morning filling out forms for the human resources department, and then your editor calls you over for a chat. This is it, your first assignment.

Your editor looks harried. It's been a wild day, she tells you, and now it's just gotten wilder. The city manager for your small suburban town has been under fire lately, accused of harassing his female employees. Two of them quit several weeks ago, and today they filed charges. The city manager just called. He wants to do an interview. He wants to set the record straight.

And you're the only reporter available.

The city manager will see you at 2 p.m., and right now it's noon. His office is only 10 minutes away, so that gives you almost two hours to get ready. You should be back at the office by 3 or 3:30, your editor says, and your deadline is 6 p.m., so you'll have 2 ½ hours or so to write the story.

Fifteen inches, your editor says. That's how much copy she wants, exactly 15 inches. Not 10 inches. Not 20 inches. Now get busy.

How do you prepare for this interview? How do you handle being face to face with the city manager, an old pro who's been in the office for years? How can you make sure you get useful quotes? Finally, how do you use the quotes in an accurate and fair manner?

You need to answer these questions and others before you turn in your story. How well you answer them will determine just how good your story is.

For a newspaper reporter, a magazine writer, a public relations practitioner or even a broadcast reporter (there are more details on interviewing skills for broadcast reporters in Chapter 9) these basic questions about interviewing remain the same. Interviewing, you see, is a skill that requires that you prepare carefully, handle the interview with care, and obtain useful quotes that you can use in a fair and accurate manner in your story.

PHUFA

You can use this little mnemonic device to help remember what you need to know for a successful interview—think *PHUFA* (foo-fa). That is, *P*repare carefully, so that you *H*andle the interview well and get *U*seful quotes that you use in a *F*air and *A*ccurate manner.

Tips and Tactics

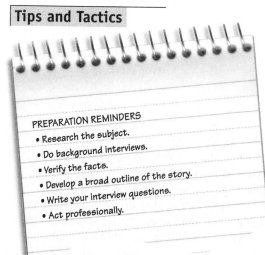

PREPARATION REMINDERS
- Research the subject.
- Do background interviews.
- Verify the facts.
- Develop a broad outline of the story.
- Write your interview questions.
- Act professionally.

Prepare Carefully

Preparation is crucial to effective interviewing. No matter which medium you work in, you need to have planned ahead for the interview or you will probably do a poor job the rest of the way. The reporter who hasn't done his or her preparation is likely to be the one who asks the famous novelist questions like "So, what's your latest book about?"

Those kinds of "dumb" questions (see Chapter 5 about researching) not only provide you with information that you should have found out beforehand, but they may well spoil the interview before it really gets underway because they send a clear message to the person being interviewed that you haven't done your homework and you aren't ready for the interview. As a result, you may very well get either a flat response that gives you precious little information or a simplistic answer that might be good for background information but won't be very useful for you as you write your story.

Research the subject. Do your research first, finding out everything you can about the person you will be interviewing. You need to know all the basics, including the correct spelling of the name, the exact job title, and any other relevant facts that you can find out. Married? Children? How long in the current job? How long in the area?

Then you need to find out other, more particular information that relates to your story. In the case of our mythical city manager, for instance, you need to know the names and details of the people who have accused him of harassment and exactly what they say occurred.

To get this information, you will typically start with your own newspaper's library and then expand your research from there. You certainly might wish to examine the public records at the courthouse for trial transcripts and other information. You might consult biographical reference books. You might choose to interview a public information officer or one of the city manager's office staff for some information. (There is more information on these research techniques in Chapter 5.)

Do background interviews. For a major interview you may very well do a number of interviews with people familiar with the subject. Perhaps one or two of them will tell you something that makes it into your story. But even if their information doesn't wind up fitting into your story, what they say about the subject will give you useful background information that will help you during the major interview.

Start with those people you have easiest access to, such as reporters or columnists with your own paper who have written previous pieces about the subject. In the case of the city manager, perhaps one of your newspaper's reporters or columnists has done a previous story. What they have to say will probably be very useful (and you can probably reach your own fellow staffers easily through your computer system's e-mail).

Next, consider talking to others who might have something worthwhile to say about the city manager, including other city managers in the area, other officials with his city, and even the city manager's own office help. Secretaries, when they are willing and able to speak to you, are usually filled with useful information. For a newspaper story in our example, you won't have much time for all of this, but even background information from a few sources will help you.

For a magazine interview this kind of background interviewing becomes much more important, and you will have the time to get several of these pre-interview interviews done.

Verify the facts. When it comes to your preparation, remember that getting close on any of these details isn't good enough. If the person's name is Johnston, and you spell it *Johnson,* you have made a very serious error, one that will have your editor screaming at you. Do this very often and your editor will know you can't be trusted, and that's a sure way to convince the boss that you ought to be in another line of work.

One of the authors of this book remembers with considerable embarrassment the time, early in his writing career, when he wrote a freelance feature story for a major daily newspaper on a man named Fleischman, spelling the name *Fleishman,* without the *c*. The editor in charge of that section of the newspaper never bought another piece from the writer, so that single missing letter turned out to be an expensive one.

Develop a broad outline of the story. Once you have gathered your information, and you trust its accuracy, you can start in on the next step, getting your questions ready for the interview.

You should think through your story, at least well enough so that you have a broad idea of the kinds of information you need to get from the subject you will be talking to. In most cases, the *news hook* (see your glossary for a definition of the term) will make this obvious for you. With our mythical city manager, for instance, you will need to ask questions about the alleged harassment and his explanation of the incidents.

In a few cases—with a feature story, for instance—this may not be quite so obvious, and you will need to actually outline broadly how you think the story is going to look when it's done. As soon as you begin that outlining process, you will readily see where the quotes will fit in, and you can make sure to ask the questions that will give you the quotes for those spots.

Write your interview questions. For most beginning media writers, your best bet will be to write out beforehand the actual questions you plan to ask. Many times during an interview the subject will say something interesting to you that takes the discussion off in a new direction. That's fine, but you will still need to make sure you get the answers you need, and having your most important questions right there in your notebook will help remind you of that as the interview takes place.

Art Campos, a reporter for *The Sacramento Bee*, remembers that "When I started reporting, I always wrote out my questions," he says. "Now that I've had 25 years in this business, I know the questions that need to be asked, but when you're starting out, you need to write them down so you won't forget. As I learned early on, if you don't write them out, you *will* forget."

You don't have to always write down a lot of questions; in many cases just five or six will do. For the city manager story, for instance, you might have jotted down the following questions.

▶ Plans for legal action?

▶ Response to specific allegations?

▶ Plans for changes in your department?

▶ Response to statements from mayor and city council?

▶ Response to recent editorial in the paper (or previous stories)?

▶ OK to call back for details/double-check?

An important reminder: Make sure the last question you ask is this one: "Is it all right if I call you back if I have any other questions or I need to double-check these quotes?"

As Campos advises, "Afterward, always promise to call them back. If it was a face-to-face interview, ask for their phone number. Say something polite and nonthreatening, like 'I promise not to bug you, but I may need to call you back.'"

Most of the time, Campos says, the subject is happy to hear your request, since it indicates how serious you are about accuracy. You can read one of Campos' stories for *The Sacramento Bee*, "Growth Builds Roseville's Budget," in the "Writers at Work: Media Samples" section of this chapter.

It's also a good idea to ask subjects "Is there anything you'd like to add?" at the end of an interview. Sometimes they will volunteer information you hadn't thought to ask or give you another person who can help your story.

As you'll see, there are special considerations for interviewing people who have often been interviewed, but the essential need to be prepared remains. Jamie Allen, a senior writer for CNN.com, frequently interviews famous personalities. For those kinds of interviews, Allen says, "First, I study the product the interviewee is selling. If he's starring in or directing a movie, I see that movie and read the press notes, writing down questions as I go along. How did you shoot that scene? What were you trying to convey with this character? Was it difficult for you to do that scene where you knocked that guy's brains all over the boat, or did you enjoy it? Did you get seasick when you were out on that boat?

"If she has written a book, I read as much as I can of the book and the reviews of it. If the writer is well-known, I'll read past articles on her to gather tidbits of info that might lead to questions that stray from the questions they've been asked far too many times."

In either case, Allen says, "The thing I really try to do is give the reader a snapshot of who this person is, rather than what it is the person's selling. I see the movie or book as a window for us to take a moment and find out a little bit about this person. If we're going to spend our dollars to see these people or read their thoughts, shouldn't we know something about them that makes them like us, or not like us at all? So after I ask the traditional questions about their product, I start to dig into their past—perhaps there's something in their upbringing that relates to their product. Perhaps they have a funny story to tell. Perhaps they refuse to talk about their childhood because it was so rotten. Whatever: it's a quick way to learn about someone."

You can read one of the stories that resulted from Allen's interview techniques in the "Writers at Work: Media Samples" section of Chapter 7.

Act Professionally. Remember, too, that you should also practice professional behavior in requesting the interview. Almost always, you should call ahead, identify yourself and ask for an interview. Give the subject an idea what the story will concern. Then, don't be late for the appointment. It is a good idea to arrive early in many cases because you might be allowed extra interview time.

You should also dress appropriately. Television requires certain standards from its reporters for on-air purposes, but print reporters should also look professional, depending on the subject. If you are going to cover someone involved in business, wear business clothes. On the other hand, if you are interviewing rock musicians, your best power suit might be out of place.

Handle the Interview Well

You are in charge of the interview.

That's an important thing for you to remember. You are the one who needs information for your story, and so you need to control the interview well enough to get that information.

As you can see on page 181, this need to control the interview can change a bit when you are writing for public relations, but for most interviews you need to be the person in charge of the conversation.

This doesn't mean you're not polite, even quite nice, during the interview. And it doesn't mean that you don't let the conversation wander into other areas when you have the time. After all, you may get something useful from the new discussion, and sometimes letting your subjects ramble on helps loosen them up so that you get better responses from your later, more important, questions.

But it *does* mean you have to make sure certain things are accomplished over the course of the few minutes you may have to ask questions and jot down quotes. If you let the subject control the interview, you are likely to get either *canned* quotes (that is, quotes that the subject has prepared in advance) or information that isn't useful to you once you start writing the story.

In the case of the city manager, for instance, he will be trying to express his innocence and perhaps attack those who have accused him. If you let him control the interview, you may not get the answers you need to some of the tougher questions you need to ask.

Similarly, if you are interviewing a movie star or a pop music performer, you can bet that he or she will try to promote the latest movie or compact disk, and if it's an athlete, he or she will often have been interviewed so often that the quotes you get, if you're not careful, will come in the form of tried-and-true sports clichés—"We knew we had to come out and play them tough in the second half." Those are the kinds of clichéd quotes you'll want to avoid.

Also, it can be difficult interviewing a famous personality. As CNN.com's Jamie Allen notes, even veteran journalists occasionally find themselves in awe of the person they are interviewing.

"Yes, there are times when I get nervous," admits Allen, "like when I met John Travolta. You have to understand," Allen says, "I was a kid in the '70s, and Travolta was the king of cool, starring in *Grease, Welcome Back, Kotter,* and *Saturday Night Fever.* But you can't be in awe of your subject if you want to be taken seriously as a journalist, obviously. You have to remove yourself from the idea of who they are, or who you think they are. They're only human. And you have a job to do—collect information on this person and give it to the audience, calmly, sanely, evenly.

"And with Travolta, there was an issue at hand. He was promoting *Battlefield Earth,* based on the L. Ron Hubbard novel. Hubbard founded Scientology, and Travolta is a well-known subscriber to those beliefs. So the question had to be asked: Was Travolta trying to promote Hubbard's views through a movie? He denied he was trying to do that. The point, though, is that you have to see through the star power to focus on the real story.

"So what I do is remind myself of something fundamental, the oft-repeated line in *The Godfather*—'This is not personal; it's business'—and just like any businessperson does when she starts a meeting, I make some funny reference to something, to cut the tension. Even if it's not funny at all, as long as I'm not trying too hard, the celebrity appreciates it and the conversation is on, and secretly, you've just taken control of the meeting, because you don't seem nervous."

Allen adds, "Another way to get someone to open up, believe it or not, is to offer them something about yourself. For instance, when I talk to writers, I always tell them something about my writing habits, and then they reciprocate.

"The thing is," he notes, "most celebrities or authors that I have interviewed desperately want to be treated like a normal person. If you treat them like a normal person, they respect you and they give you good answers. Usually."

A word of warning: Athletes, performers, business people—anyone you interview will have his or her own agenda that may or may not be the same as yours. This leads to occasional conflicts between you and your subject.

What *you* want to achieve in an interview is a productive conversation between you and the subject, one where you lead the conversation and wind up with information that you can use in your story.

What the *subject* wants, on the other hand, is sometimes something very different, ranging from "good press" to making an effort to sway public opinion on a given topic.

The result of this conflict may be a story that seems inaccurate or unfair to the person you have interviewed. You did a half-hour interview, the subject may say, and yet you used only two quotes, and neither one of them seemed to have anything at all to do with the point the subject wanted to make. To the subject, that doesn't seem fair.

From your perspective as the writer, of course, that half-hour interview produced exactly the two quotes you needed for your story, and two good quotes from an interview of that length isn't all that unusual.

To solve this in-built conflict, you will be wise to let the subject know before or during the interview exactly what you have in mind. If you tell him or her that you plan to use just a few quotes and that you're mainly interested in hearing about one narrow aspect of the story, then there shouldn't be any unpleasant surprises when the story appears.

Useful Quotes

Related to the idea of your being in charge of the interview, is the knowledge that you need to finish the interview with useful quotes, material that you will be able to use in your story.

How can you know what kinds of quotes will work best when it comes down to writing? Generally, in news stories your quotes will serve to expand upon facts you present in the story, so, as you saw in the section on preparation, you need to have thought through what the important facts are and make sure you ask questions that expand on that material. Try to get several quotes in response to each of your questions, because that will give you more options later, as you write the story.

For instance, in your mythical story on the troubled city manager, in response to your first question—"Plans for legal action?"—you might have gotten the following quotes:

> "I haven't sued yet, but my lawyer tells me I have a case, so I'm considering it."

> "These people have dragged my good name through the mud, and I'm considering taking legal action."

> "There's nothing to stop me from filing my own lawsuit, you know. These people have slandered me and I may sue them for that. I've had a long and productive career with the city, and I'm not going to allow them to ruin it."

When you're back in the office and writing your story, you will probably write a paragraph that goes something like this:

> Jones denies the charges and says he's considering filing a suit of his own against his accusers.

At that point, you will use one of the three quotes to expand on that lead-in. Of the three quotes, which one do you use?

Because you have three, you are able to pick the best one and slot it into the story. It is *very* important to remember that the more quotes you have for a particular spot in the story, the better your story is likely to be.

As Art Campos of *The Sacramento Bee* notes, "Remember that the general rule of thumb is always to get more information than you can possibly use. For quotes, that means you ought to have plenty to choose from, even if you can only use a few."

If in each spot where you need to use a quote you have several to choose from, and so can choose the very best one, then the odds are that you'll have a much better story than the writer who has just one quote for that spot and must use it, whether it's just right or not.

To get those quotes, you should not hesitate (when time permits) to rephrase your question and get another response from the subject. And if your subject goes on at length about something, let the subject continue as long as you can, knowing that each quote improves your later chances to write a good story.

Unfortunately, in many cases you won't have the luxury of time. Frequently, in fact, you will have to get these quotes by doing several short interviews, often over the telephone.

"When you're on deadline," Campos says, "You have to hustle in and hustle out. You can't conduct a long interview."

To do that, Campos advises, have those prepared questions ready and "look for three or four good quotes to use in a typical 15-inch story."

Tips and Tactics

To Tape or Not?

Should you use a tape recorder for your interviews? For most beginning reporters, taking complete and accurate notes becomes a difficult task. Sources are not professors who will repeat key points and write them on the board. At the same time, tape recorders bring their own problems to the question.

You should begin to work on your note-taking skills. For most reporters and other media workers, this means that you will have to practice, practice, and practice. You will want to develop your own shorthand form to eliminate the need to get every word down. The CD-ROM workbook that accompanies the textbook provides an excellent opportunity for you to work on this skill.

Many newspaper reporters use tape recorders. So do virtually all magazine writers. But you can find a marked difference in how they use them.

Because of longer deadlines, magazine writers can take the time to type each word of the interview into note form. But newspaper reporters don't have that luxury. Instead, they need to be able to find key quotes in a hurry.

One strategy is to jot the counter number into your notebook when you hear a good quote; you must not take the time to run through the tape to find the best quote in the interview.

You should also back up your tape recorder by taking notes anyway. Because tape recorders are mechanical devices that run on batteries (and because it's just your luck, darn it), your absolutely wonderful interview with Bono of U-2 fizzled because the tape recorder didn't work. Be prepared by taking notes. ■

For longer stories, whether they are news stories or features, you need to have a lot more interviewing. Feature writer Warren Wolfe of the Minneapolis *Star Tribune* tries to get his subjects involved in comfortable conversations, and then takes notes rapidly as the conversation goes along.

In his story "New Type of Eldercare Hostel Focuses on Volunteer Projects,"in the "Writers at Work: Media Samples" section of Chapter 7, for instance, Wolfe recalls seeing one subject working near a window. "I just sat down with Dorothy Lindeman and talked with her while she was working. We just chatted. For instance, I asked her what it was that led her to apply and about what it felt like to be there."

The conversation went on for more than 20 minutes. From that lengthy conversation, Wolfe wound up with just two quotes that he used directly in the story, but they were just the right quotes in just the right spot in the story. That kind of reporting is what separates a merely mediocre story from a really good one.

In nontelephone interviews, and especially in longer interviews, it is just as important to jot down the details surrounding the interview as it is to get the quotes themselves from the subject. Make sure you get all the sights and sounds you can while doing the interview. Just as with the quotes, the amount of detail that you get should greatly exceed your available space.

"I jot down the details, a lot more details than I can fit in," says

Wolfe. "Then, when I start to write, I hope to have whatever details I need right there in my notes."

Fairness and *Accuracy*

Remember always that while the quotes you choose have to be useful for your story, they also must be accurate and fair to the subject. Accuracy in quotation isn't quite as simple as it may sound to you. Spoken English and written English are not quite the same. Listen to any conversation between two of your friends, and then imagine how those words would look written down in quote form.

> "So, like, did you, um, you know, see what Donny did last night? I mean, you know, it was, like, really awesome. He is just, like, the nicest guy, you know?"

You can see that too much of this kind of quotation use quickly becomes a labor to read.

Even in more formal interview situations, many people have a number of tricky verbal usages in their conversation that you will have to deal with in converting their words into written form.

What do you do with the local politician, for instance, who peppers his speech with a word like *well,* for example? Do you write them all into the quote, so it looks like this:

> "Well, there are, well, more issues here than, well, most of my constituents, well, realize."

Or do you clean up his copy as you convert it, making the quote more readable:

> "Well, there are more issues here than most of my constituents realize."

Most editors will choose the second, cleaned-up, version.

Remember also that there are ethnic and cultural aspects of the language that you will have to contend with as you take quotes from an interview source. How much cleanup do you do with quotes from a recent immigrant, for instance, or from an inner-city resident speaking in a local slang? Or from a hockey player whose first language is French and whose English is far from perfect?

Broadcast reporters have it easy in this regard, since they can simply take the subject's responses, edit them down into a few seconds of airtime, and let them run.

But newspaper and magazine writers as well as public relations writers have to contend with the sometimes difficult conversion process. There are no hard-and-fast rules for this conversion, and you will have to handle each one individually.

The general rule is that your quotes in a story should reflect ethnic or cultural considerations only when they are relevant and significant to the story. The use of special spellings for dialect or slang is even more infrequent, acceptable only in rare circumstances when they are of considerable importance to the story.

As a result, most reporters would choose to compromise. With the recent immigrant, for instance, they would keep the word choice and word order in the quotes, since those reflect the subject's personality. But they would avoid any special spelling or other odd constructions that might seem demeaning. The same holds true for the inner-city resident, the hockey player or anyone else you are quoting.

Fairness and accuracy also require you to keep your quotes in context. This is a major source of friction between reporters and their interview subjects. The context of a quote is all the material surrounding that quote, not only the rest of the interview itself, but also elements like the setting where the interview took place and the tone of voice of the subject.

If you are not careful about context, the meaning that your reader gets from the quote and the meaning that the subject intended may not mesh. In fact, if you're not careful, the quote may seem to say quite the opposite of what the subject meant it to say.

Sarcasm, in particular, is usually understandable in a broadcast interview, but can be completely misunderstood in print. For example, after a heated political campaign, the winning candidate says, with a wide grin on his face, to a television reporter, "Sure, I feel just terrible that my opponent's multimillion-dollar campaign didn't bring him victory."

The viewer knows that the winner doesn't feel terrible at all about his opponent's loss. But in print the next day, if you're not careful about context, the quote simply says, "Sure, I feel just terrible that my opponent's multimillion-dollar campaign didn't bring him victory."

To make that quote understandable, you need to tell the reader about the sarcasm. Explaining it in the attribution: "Jones said sarcastically that he feels 'just terrible' that his opponent's 'multimillion-dollar campaign didn't bring him victory.'" Or you could mention the wide grin, hoping that that alone would suffice to make clear the intended sarcasm.

Fairness and accuracy also require you to treat your interview subjects fairly in those cases where they were unable to be interviewed. When your story says that the person was "unavailable for comment" or that the person "refused to comment," you are clearly implying that the interview was dodged by the person you sought to interview.

If that person could simply not be reached in time to meet your deadline, a specific explanation why is probably better: "Jones was on a business trip in Spain and could not be reached for comment."

When the Time Crunch Hits

It's happened to almost everyone who has worked in the mass media. You sit innocently at your desk, when your supervisor calls with just the barest bones of an assignment that needs to be done immediately. You don't have time to cruise the Internet or even make a quick run at the electronic library; truth be told, you barely have time to get to the parking lot and to the interview.

You arrive at the interview, hoping to at least skim through a press release, but there's no time. Now what to do? If you're at a press conference, other reporters may ask questions and you should be able to build on those. If, however, you're at a one-on-one interview, you probably should admit your situation and ask for help. Some sources will be helpful; others will not.

You're not doomed to sound stupid, though it would be helpful if you had some idea of just who it was you were interviewing. (If you don't know, it's probably best to confess that up front.) If you know, for example, that you are interviewing a political figure who has written a book, you can gear your questions appropriately. "Tell me about the book" would be a good starting point.

From there, you will need to listen to the answers and build questions around the responses. "You said that Social Security is in serious trouble. Why and what can be done about it?" are examples of this kind of question.

Other questions can come from your own knowledge of a topic. Interviewers who follow the news closely—as many media people do—can probably come up with news events that fit the interview. "What about Secretary of State Colin Powell's recent comments on the subject?" you might ask.

Realize that some reporters under a time crunch will wait until after the interview to fill in gaps with research. For example, one writer interviewed the author Elmore Leonard, who has written some wickedly funny and offbeat crime novels and some powerful Western novels as well. He prepared for the interview by catching up on recent reviews of Leonard's work, reading recent stories about Leonard and reviewing his general knowledge of publishing.

When he returned to the office, after the interview, he realized he didn't have Leonard's age. He knew that he shouldn't disturb a literary celebrity like Leonard at home, so he checked the press release and some stories in the newspaper library.

Unfortunately, he found three different ages listed for Leonard. Now, he was forced to call Leonard, who was somewhat miffed by the question until the writer explained the problem. Since fiction writers have to be accurate, too, Leonard understood and told the writer which age to use.

How to Use Quotes in Your Copy

After you choose which quote to use as you write your story, you'll need to use it correctly. Beginning reporters sometimes stumble over the punctuation in quotes and sometimes find trouble, as well, with the required parallel construction between the quotes and the story they're writing.

The most common quote used in newspaper style will have you introducing the first sentence of a quote, followed by an attribution (that is, the name of the person you're quoting). If the quote continues, then you will usually continue the quote in the second sentence, as in the following:

One Sentence Quote
"We are certainly going to support this initiative," Mayor Smith said.

Multi-Sentence Quote
"We think this initiative will reduce petty crime in the neighborhood," Mayor Smith said. "The police also think that crimes against persons will drop considerably."

The format emphasizes what is said, but doesn't leave the reader guessing who said it until the end of the paragraph.

There are a number of variations on this basic format, however. In magazine writing, the attribution often comes before the quote. In newspapers, you will occasionally use the attribution at the beginning of the quote, especially when the person speaking is new to the reader. Writers also do this when they use quotes from two different people without a transition sentence. Remember that each new speaker starts a new paragraph.

Attribution Before Quote
Baseball coach Eddie Cardieri, who does have two sons playing in high school, said, "Because of my recruiting responsibilities, I don't get to watch Nick and Joel as often as I would like."

"We really should be able to leave campus for lunch," said student council member Will Albritton. "It is really not fair for the administration to punish us."

Principal Beltz said, "It isn't a question of fairness. It's a question of the nearest restaurants being almost a mile away."

Also, occasionally you will use partial quotes, though some editors don't approve of them. You should avoid them when they repeat mundane phrases like this one:

Cardieri said he spends "a lot of time" recruiting.

But an unusual or specific phrase might be spared the editor's delete button:

Cardieri said he spent "exactly 888 hours" recruiting last season.

In writing dialogue for fiction, you frequently allow the style of the quote to make clear the person speaking and so you don't use the attribution.

But you're not writing fiction, you're writing for newspapers, magazines or public relations, and so, in the interest of clarity, you almost always need to use the proper attribution. Here are some of the basic rules on quote use.

Complete-Sentence Quote

Any quote that stands alone as a complete sentence (see "Grammar Terms" in Chapter 3 for an explanation of what constitutes a complete sentence) inside another sentence requires a capital letter to start the new sentence:

John Jacobs, assistant director, said, "The program will survive these cuts. Of that you can be certain."

Janet Jacobi said, "We're confident that the new guidelines will solve the problem."

Partial Quote

Any quote that is *not* a complete sentence begins with a lowercase letter:

John Jacobs, assistant director, said that his program will "survive these cuts," at least for the next year.

Janet Jacobi said she was convinced that the new guidelines would "solve the problem."

In some cases, partial quotes are useful in that they allow you around some otherwise tricky grammatical problems.

Multi-Paragraph Quote

When a long quote is more than one paragraph long, you *do not* close the quote at the end of the first paragraph, but you *do* open the quote again at the start of next paragraph:

> "Well, I certainly think we'll survive these cuts, at least for the coming year," said John Jacobs, assistant director. "But beyond that? I just don't know.
>
> "The income from our new online service is minimal right now, but we're hoping that within a year or two the revenue from that service will compensate for the current cuts."

Many editors don't like quotes that run past one paragraph in length and will ask you to break up the long quote into two or more shorter ones, complete with new attributions, as in this example:

> "Well, I certainly think we'll survive these cuts, at least for the coming year," said assistant director John Jacobs. "But beyond that? I just don't know."
>
> Jacobs added, "The income from our new online service is minimal right now, but we're hoping that within a year or two the revenue from that service will compensate for the current cuts."

Quote as Part of a Sentence

Any quotes you use inside a sentence must fit the grammatical logic of that sentence. Sometimes the grammatical structure of the quote doesn't mesh with the grammatical structure of the story you are working on. In that case, to make the quote successfully mesh with the story, you have to either drop the quote marks and make the subject's words into a paraphrase or you must insert a parenthetical word or expression to make the meaning clear.

Quote Inside a Quote

When there is a quote inside a quote, use single quote marks to open and close the interior quote. At the end of the quote, you may have to use both single and double quote marks to complete the quote. This can happen in feature writing, especially, when someone is telling a story, as in this example:

> Smith recalled the time he met Jimmy Carter. "I was walking down the main street in Plains, and there was

Mr. Carter, just a month or two after he'd left office. 'Hi, Sir,' I said to him, and 'Hello, Smitty, how's that farm coming along?' he asked me right back. I told him, 'Sir, that little farm of mine is doing just fine, thanks. I hope you and the family are doing fine, too.' "

Writers at Work: Media Samples

Growth Builds Roseville's Budget

By Art Campos
Bee Staff Writer

The continuing growth in Roseville is translating into big bucks for the city's coffers.

Fueled by a 21 percent increase in new businesses over the past year, the city's 1997–98 fiscal year budget is being pegged at $175 million. That's $22 million more than the previous budget.

City Manager Al Johnson said the new development pays for its impact, leading to new parks, roads and other infrastructure.

In addition, sales tax revenue from existing businesses and the fact that Roseville owns and operates its own electric, water, refuse and regional wastewater facilities are contributing to the financial boom, Johnson said.

"We're experiencing a period of strong economic development," he said. "All sectors of our economy—sales, office, industrial and residential development—are expanding."

Roseville, which has 63,000 residents, is even gaining ground on the county of Placer when comparing dollar figures. Placer County, which has 209,000 residents, is proposing a 1997–98 budget of $216 million. Last year, Placer County's budget was $238 million, but a major reason for the higher figure was capital improvement project allocations. Those funds have now been spent or set aside.

Johnson said the 14 percent increase in Roseville's budget will result in three new parks next year and will allow the city to finish building its new police station in February.

"There is a high expectation that we keep services at a high level in this city," Johnson said. "These improvements are a continuation of those expectations."

Overall, Roseville will see an increase of $13 million next year in its capital improvement budget—from $29 million to $42 million.

In addition to building the three parks and the police station, Roseville is planning to spend $9 million for construction of two electrical power substations and $5 million to begin designing a new wastewater treatment plant.

An additional $9.3 million will be spent for the widening projects on Atlantic Street and the intersection of Sunrise Avenue and Douglas Boulevard and for design and environmental work for the Roseville Parkway overcrossing at Interstate 80. Flood control improvements in Roseville creeks will account for another $1 million.

Johnson said Roseville will maintain its normal 10 percent reserve in the next budget and that the city's full-time equivalent employee staff will increase by less than 1 percent—from 833 employees to 839. Roseville's general fund will carry $46 million next year. That portion of the budget supports police, fire, library, parks, recreation and general government services.

The proposed budget is being unveiled at three workshops in the next two weeks. The first will be Thursday, July 1. The others will be on Monday, June 23, and Tuesday, June 24.

Each workshop will begin at 4:30 p.m. and will be in the City Council chambers, 311 Vernon St.

From *The Sacramento Bee*, June 15, 1997
Reprinted by permission.

A Day in the Life of...

Sportswriter Roger Mills
St. Petersburg Times

For the average sports journalist, particularly someone covering professional sports, the day-to-day process of acquiring information through interviews is dictated by knowledge of routine and the acquisition of insight.

Knowing how to play the game and who to play it with are determined not by the interviewers, but by the very people they are interviewing. Over the years, I thankfully have learned that knowing the rituals isn't just important; it's absolutely crucial.

Never is this more important than during deadline situations on late game nights. Under supreme constraints of time and sensitive emotions, sports journalists must not only understand the rituals but use them in their favor.

I remember once watching a football player put cream on his skin after his shower, long after midnight, while the reporters waited frantically to speak to him. Failure at that point to know not to interrupt the lotioning process, even if it was eroding valuable deadline seconds, would have resulted in a negative outcome.

Truth is, as interviewers, we have little control and on late night, deadline situations, where chaos reigns, we have even less.

Perhaps because of the thriving egos of creative people in general, coming to terms with this dynamic, which I call Interview Rule No.1, isn't easy.

Before pursuing a story, before chasing a subject, sports reporters must be prepared to surrender some, if not all, control of the direction of the interview. Yes, there are ways to stay on track. Yes, there are ways to move into more sensitive subjects. But the sooner you accept what little juice you have in your battery, the better the chance of getting what you want in the time frame you prefer.

Let's face it. It's a game that goes something like this: You need them. They know you need them. They don't directly need you. So, whatever it is you want, you have to play their game to get it.

Now, the reality is that most professional athletes are accommodating to the media. I have found that despite a less than savory public image enhanced by frequent video clips of outbursts, pro athletes and coaches don't all have adversarial relationships with the media. Most of them, in fact, not only accept that you have a job to do, but they understand that treating the media with respect can help shape their individual public image. They are taught that a forthright and candid interviewee, regardless of the sensitivity of the subject matter, routinely will find him or herself appearing more favorably in the final product.

Consider this second dynamic, Interview Rule No. 2. Writers must accept that they are human and therefore make subjective decisions, no matter how hard they strive for objectivity. How you ask a question, what verbs you use in your paraphrase, what adverbs and adjectives creep into your copy, are directly influenced by the chemistry between interviewee and interviewer.

The bottom line is that we are inclined to be more understanding to a subject who is a pleasant interview than to one who isn't. It will not change the theme of our work, but it can influence the means by which we tell the story.

With this in mind, back to the daily ritual of covering an NFL team, remembering how much more intense situations are on game nights.

My professional day begins whenever I get a chance to read my paper and compare it to that of my competitor. This is obviously a biased perspective, but considering the feverish nature with which sports fans consume the news, being first to have a story drives how you go about getting the material, deciphering it and producing it. It's a race and there are no silver medals.

Since so much time during the season is spent with the team, the regular writers have a workroom or office on team property and we are usually there from 10 a.m. to about 8 p.m., sometimes later. Being on site has its benefits. It sheds some of the "us-against-them" preconceived notions players may have and allows, through sheer proximity, the opportunity for chance encounters, where some of the most valuable interviews are conducted.

In the NFL, as it likely is in political circles and court cases, the media have a set time during which there is availability. Commonly during lunch time hours, 12 noon to 12:45 p.m., we begin the process of trying to find players and coaches and trying to extract from them, in as elaborate detail as possible, whatever we're pursuing that day.

There are two interview formats, each with some merit: group interviews, which tend to lean toward quantity; and one-on-one interviews, which lean toward quality.

Keeping in mind that time is short and they are not obligated to meet us halfway (remember Rule No.1), the group interviews begin at noon sharp. As a group, reporters bounce from player to player, coach to coach, asking questions, listening to responses asked by other reporters and generally absorbing whatever morsels of information they can.

The microcassette recorder has made this very simple, and using the device is virtually a necessity in modern writing circles. It helps ensure credibility, prevents mistakes and minimizes lawsuits.

The key in the group session is to keep the session going by keeping it informal, relaxed, entertaining. Out of casual conversations, even those on the record, come some of the best perspectives. Not a lot can be revealed when the subject of the interview thinks he is on the witness stand.

In the midst of the midday mayhem, frequently comes an opportunity for a more accommodating and personal one-on-one. More so than in any other situation, the success of this interview is directly proportional to the mood of the interviewee.

Regardless of the goal, my tradition has been always to start with something nonthreatening, the softballs so to speak. The weather, the poli-

tics, the award shows on television the night before, the country's fascination with *Star Wars*. Whatever it takes. Success as an interviewer, particularly in the limited time frame I face daily, hangs in large part on the subject's ability to view you not as a reporter, but more as an acquaintance.

As long as I remember Rule No.2, then I want that mutual feeling of acquaintance. I want a football player to think he has something in common with me. I want a football player to talk about the ways to stop a child from wetting his bed. With germane life experiences, he will be more likely, then, to discuss ways to prevent the other team from scoring.

News flash: While the game clearly is stacked in favor of the athlete, it still is a game and we reporters know how to play.

And then there is this final interview strategy I call upon every day: do some homework. Knowing the whims and fancies of someone you're interviewing is an ounce of prevention. Things can go awry. Sensitive subjects can trigger responses that terminate an interview. Previous knowledge, of some degree, helps build credibility and open doors for casual conversation.

Competent approaches to one-on-one interviews are particularly helpful in developing sources. No better sources than people in the heart of the war. You must earn their trust and often that means using judgment over what is said versus what is printed, mostly, honoring material told off the record.

I don't know everything and if I did I would have no need for the interview. But appearing to be completely in the dark limits your ability to see the light. In other words, subjects are less willing to share perspectives that are dear to them, if you have no chance of understanding and/or appreciating them.

Once all the material is acquired, my work is really just beginning. After lunch, the process of transcribing tape or revisiting notes to place them in a more usable format, gives the writer a chance to begin her own form of editing and affords her the opportunity to distance herself from the acquaintance mode. I have always been amazed at how different people sound on play-back or how impersonal responses seem upon a second look.

I won't finish until late in the afternoon when the final story is put to bed, but daily I'm reminded that any interview, two fleeting minutes in an elevator or one hour at a buffet table, has its value if information and anecdotes are exchanged.   ■

Roger Mills is a sportswriter for the St. Petersburg Times, *covering the Tampa Bay Buccaneers and other sports teams.*

Summary

Successful interviewing is important to your ability to find facts and support them with quotes. Some interviews are done for purposes of background information, while other interviews are meant to obtain quotes you can use in your story. Remember the acronym *PHUFA* (*P*re-pare carefully so that you *H*andle the interview well and get *U*seful quotes that you use *F*airly and *A*ccurately).

Proper use of quotes includes understanding the basic use of quote marks, including quotes inside quotes, quotes with multiple para-graphs, partial quotes, and complete sentences inside quotes.

Key Points

▶ Preparation is important.

▶ Remember who is in charge.

▶ Remember your needs

▶ Be fair in your quote selection.

▶ Be accurate in your reporting.

Web Links

Here are some interesting sites on the Internet where you can find out more about interviewing skills.

http://www.inlandpress.org/archive/newsed/cop.htm
http://www.utexas.edu/coc/journalism/SOURCE/journal_links/tips.html
http://www.ccom.ua.edu/News/Alumni/waldron041800.html

InfoTrac College Edition Readings

For additional readings, go to **www.infotrac-college.com**, enter your password, and search for the following articles by title or author's name.

- ▶ "Keyboard One-on-One" (Conducting interviews through e-mail), Lenore Wright, *Writer,* Nov. 2001 v114 i11 p16.

- ▶ "Studs Terkel: On the Art of Interviewing," Ronald Kovach, *Writer,* May 2002 v115 i5 p26.

- ▶ "Interviewing the Interviewer" (Interview with Terry Gross), Thomas Kunkel, *American Journalism Review,* July 2001 v23 i6 p57.

Exercises

Go to your CD-ROM to complete the following exercises:

- ▶ Exercise 6.1
- ▶ Exercise 6.2
- ▶ Exercise 6.3
- ▶ Exercise 6.4
- ▶ Exercise 6.5
- ▶ Exercise 6.6

7

Reporting and Writing the Feature Story

You listened to what your professors had to say about the importance of clips to go along with your résumé, and so you marched over to the office of the campus newspaper and asked for a chance to write a story. Now, it's noon on a Wednesday, and you've just received your first assignment.

"We could use a feature on the opening of the new campus bookstore," the editor says. Then she adds, "It'll be a sidebar, so keep it at 15 inches, and we need it done by 5 p.m. Oh, and keep it light."

"Got it," you say, and head out to the door, knowing you're going to have to go back to that textbook you haven't read closely enough and find out a few things. What the heck is a sidebar, for one thing? And how many words are there in 15 inches, for another? And most importantly, what exactly is a feature, and what did she mean by keeping it light?

What Is a Feature Story?

First, let's define our terms. What is a feature story? Well, the term *feature story* as it is used today can be defined as much by what it is *not* as by what it *is*.

Closely Tied to the News of the Day

Feature stories *are* typically timely, but the timeliness is usually much broader, with the editor thinking in terms of weeks, months or even (in the case of some magazines) years. In daily newspapers, most feature sections operate on a schedule that is planned several weeks (and often several months) in advance. Monthly magazines typically look six to nine months in advance or more. Even in new media, the schedule is days or weeks ahead of the day when the story goes up on the Web site.

This kind of scheduling means that the breaking news of the day rarely is reflected in the feature section of a newspaper or the contents of most magazines, though there are exceptions in publications like the weekly newsmagazines and with online magazines.

Interested in Informing the Reader of News Details

Because they are not closely tied to the breaking news of the day, most feature stories assume that readers have already read the hard details and now are looking for other kinds of information. For instance, if the National Aeronautics and Space Administration (NASA) launches a probe to the planet Mars, the basic news stories will follow the success or failure of the launch and provide details on the mission, including the time of the launch, the time required for the probe to travel to Mars, the planned exploration of Mars that the probe will undertake, and the like.

Feature stories on that same mission might include a profile on any one of the scientists who designed the probe or on key NASA personnel involved in the launch. Other feature stories that might come from such a mission include pieces on what it takes to launch a rocket from the Kennedy Space Center (KSC), what it is like to live in the area, a detailed sidebar on the development of the probe itself, or of the rocket that launches it, or on any of dozens of other perfectly fine ideas.

The point is that the feature stories that come from such a launch are going to be detailed, certainly. But they are not going to be detailed looks about the news event itself, but rather about the people, places, things and events that surround the event.

Is Not Written in the Inverted Pyramid Structure

The inverted pyramid structure, as you read in Chapter 2, is especially useful in presenting readers with a large amount of necessary information in a compact, very quickly read fashion. Media writers know when they write an inverted pyramid story that the great majority of readers will not read the story to the end. Many readers, in fact, will not get far past the headline and the lead paragraph.

Feature writers, on the other hand, can count on many of their readers sticking with the story right to the end. Since the reader is not just reading the story for a few quick details, but reading it in a more complete, even leisurely fashion, the story's structure can reflect that. As you'll see later, the feature story's middle and end are just as important as its beginning for the feature writer.

Likely to Be Focused on Personalities and Human Interest

A news story may be about a wildfire in the West, a train derailment in the East, a winter storm in the Midwest or any of thousands of other events. And while these happenings frequently affect people, they don't have to have human impact to be considered newsworthy.

Certainly, the human element adds news value to a story. An earthquake in crowded Southern California that topples bridges but takes no lives will probably not be as newsworthy as a quake in the same area that claims a thousand fatalities. But a quake in an isolated valley, where it does no damage at all, will not have as much news value as one in the Los Angeles area that causes extensive road and building damage, even without human casualties.

For a feature writer, there is always a human connection. For a feature writer, the earthquake in the isolated valley wouldn't be much of a story unless it affected someone. If there is no human connection, then the writer might personify the earthquake, that is, turn it into a person for purposes of telling the story.

> The series of small quakes rumbled through the valley just before dawn, shaking the town four times, as if a giant walked down the middle of Main Street, step by thunderous step.

Likely to Have Descriptive Writing

Description is often useful in a variety of media stories, but especially so in feature stories, where the longer length of many features and the added interest in making sure the writing is entertaining, prompts writers to include description.

> The first two Elderhostels have begun documenting the collections of dolls, furniture, jewelry, quilts and silver. Workers fill out inventory sheets, photograph each item with a digital camera, then download the image into a computer and type in the description.
>
> "But there's so much more to do," said Pat Moberg of Minneapolis. "The 16 sets of china, thousands of books,

(continued)

(continued)
the photos, the personal papers, cloth-ing, hats and those *Wizard of Oz* things."

Somewhere along the line, Laura Jane Musser struck up a friendship with actress Margaret Hamilton, who played the Wicked Witch of the West in the movie.

A shelf in the Musser mansion is lined with Hamilton's autographed photos and a dozen knickknacks illus-trating scenes from the film.

Warren Wolfe,
Star Tribune (Minneapolis)
Reprinted by permission.

You can see that the descriptive details add a lot to the story, giving the reader a good visual image of the material being catalogued. Remember that description can be more than just visual. What you hear, what you touch, what you smell, can be just as interesting to the reader as what you see. Don't be afraid to include relevant details from the other senses in your description.

Likely to Use Narrative (Storytelling) Techniques

News stories usually follow the inverted pyramid or some variation of it that strives to get the hard information to the reader as quickly as possible.

Feature stories, on the other hand, because of their interest in enter-taining the reader, frequently use narrative techniques. By that we mean that features tell a *story*, in some respects in much the same way a work of fiction does.

As you can see in the feature stories reprinted in the "Writers at Work: Media Samples" section at the end of this chapter, the story-telling of a good feature has a beginning, a middle and an end, and they are all of roughly equal value to the reader. That's very different from a news story, where the most important part is clearly the beginning and the value declines from there to the least important, at the end.

A Working Definition

There is a lot of variety within the general term *feature story*, of course. Some features are related to a news story. Other features are essentially timeless. Some may be narrowly focused on a magazine's or newspaper's special needs, while others may be far more general in their appeal. But they all try to connect with the reader in a way that is different from a news story, a way that has more description, a greater sense of human interest, and more of an emotional connection.

This interest in the emotional side of the story changes both the way you go about your reporting for a feature story and the way you go about your writing.

A workable definition of a feature story, then, might be something like this:

> *A feature story is a work of nonfiction meant to entertain and inform the reader while paying special attention to the human-interest aspects of storytelling.*

News Features and Independent Features

There are two categories of feature stories—**news features** and **independent features**. *News features* are feature stories that are tied to the news of the day. Frequently, newspapers use these features as the human-interest angle on the main news story and run them off to the side of the main news story in the design of the page. In newspaper writing, these stories are called *sidebars*.

A *sidebar* typically is shorter than the main news story and is usually tightly focused on one human-interest angle on the story. If the news story is about a major downtown fire, for instance, a sidebar might be about the daring firefighter who made a life-saving rescue, or the sad death of a loved one in the fire, or the history of the building that burned (focusing on the interesting people who lived or worked there, most likely).

An *independent feature* is one that stands alone and is not tied to a news story. This kind of story is usually found in the feature section or some other special section (such as the gardening section, the sports section, or the business section) and frequently is longer than a sidebar might be.

To get and hold reader interest, newspaper editors and designers like to package the news; that is, they like to find themes that help stories interrelate on a page or in a section. So sidebars are common, and even independent features are often packaged with other, similar stories.

Special Reporting Needs for Features

The research and interviewing skills that you learned about in Chapter 5 and 6 are perfectly fine for writing feature stories—for starters. But the wise feature writer is one who knows that the needs of the feature story put a new level of importance on reporting. Now not only must you do a good job getting quotes from your interviews and getting facts from your research, but you must also get the sights and sounds that you may use in your descriptive passages. Feature writers also look constantly for the human aspects of the story and for those elements of the story that lend themselves to entertaining, narrative writing.

Anecdotes

Sometimes these elements come in the form of anecdotes. *Anecdotes* are those small stories within the story that help make your work more interesting for readers. As you can see in the story by CNN.com's Jamie Allen on actor Michael Clarke Duncan, "*Green Mile*'s Giant Has Taken Massive Strides," in the "Writers at Work: Media Samples" section at the end of this chapter, for instance, an anecdote can begin a story:

ATLANTA (CNN) — Past the middle-aged Southern belles exiting a formal luncheon and speaking in drawls as they wait for their valet-parked cars, through the Ritz-Carlton's lobby distinguished by oil paintings on mahogany paneling and populated with tired white businessmen dressed in dark suits, up the elevator to the 19th floor, in a small suite of this hotel in Atlanta's ritzy Buckhead neighborhood, a 6-foot-5-inch, 315-pound black man is sitting in a chair, crying. Michael Clarke Duncan's tree-trunk fingers are pushing into his closed eyes, but it's like trying to hold back rain. The tears are flowing around the actor's fingers, down his molasses cheeks, in crystalline rivulets.

Reporters witnessing the scene are getting a little misty, too.

It's all very familiar. The day before, a similar scene played out at a press screening of the new Frank Darabont movie *The Green Mile:* Flickering on the white screen, there Duncan was, playing a 7-foot-tall death-row inmate named John Coffey who has angelic healing powers. He and Tom Hanks' character were trading tears over the evil mysteries that taint this world. And the media were all sitting there, watching Duncan, as they're watching him now, and wiping their eyes.

But in this case, at the Ritz-Carlton, Duncan's tears are not an act, and they're the best kind. He has just learned, in a brilliant display of end-of-the-interview timing by his manager, that he has been nominated for a NAACP Image Award for his *Green Mile* performance. It's the first time the 36-year-old actor has been acknowledged for his work, and it could be an omen. Duncan has drawn alongside two-time Academy Award-winner Hanks in the category of Oscar buzz. But more than that—as everyone in the hotel suite knows—this moment is a universe away from the days when Duncan was digging ditches for a living in Chicago, when Hollywood was merely a storyline of the daydreams that got him through each shift of hard labor.

Duncan lifts his massive form and walks to the suite's bathroom to gather himself. When he comes back, he's slightly embarrassed by his emotional display. "I'm sorry," he says. "I apologize for that. Oh, man."

Reprinted by permission.

This powerful anecdote *shows* the reader about Duncan's emotional honesty rather than just *tells* the reader. As you've seen in Chapter 6, a lead that uses an anecdote in this fashion is called a "narrative lead."

Specific Details

Before you can use descriptive details in a feature story, you have to notice them when you are doing your reporting for the story and jot them down in your notes. Veteran media writers make sure to spend the time and effort it takes to get these descriptive details into their notes before they begin their writing of a story.

For his feature story "New Type of Elderhostel Focuses on Volunteer Projects," in the "Writers at Work: Media Samples" section at the end of the chapter, *Star Tribune* (Minneapolis) reporter Warren Wolfe remembers his actions before and after doing his interviews for the story: "I just wandered around and jotted down the details, more details than I could possibly fit into the story."

As a result of having those details in his notes, he was able to note in his story, for instance:

> From the mansion's sun room, Mac McKusick had little time for the sun-dappled view of the Mississippi River. He was intent on cataloging the silver dishes found that day in the butler's pantry.

You can see Wolfe knew it was the sun room that the man was in, that the room had a view of the "sun-dappled . . . Mississippi River," that McKusick was "cataloging the silver dishes," and that the dishes had been found "in the butler's pantry."

None of those factual details came automatically. In each case, Wolfe had to notice the detail, and then jot it down in his notes. Paying particular attention to details is a crucial aspect of reporting for feature stories.

Emotional Values

It is very easy to overdo the emotional content of a story. If you try too hard for an emotional connection, the story becomes sentimental or maudlin. Usually, if the reader realizes that you are trying for emotional impact, you have tried too hard.

Good media writers know that the emotional connection needs to come through naturally, as an integral part of the story. As a reporter, you must have noticed not only those things that carry obvious emotional value, like the words that are spoken, but also those things that carry more subtle emotional values, such as facial expressions, tone of voice, body language, the direction in which someone's eyes look, the way people move their hands or feet. Noting down a nervous gesture (such as a person's habit of frequently winding a lock of hair around a finger) and then using it later in the story may help the reader understand the emotions going on within that person.

Take another look at the head paragraph in writer Jamie Allen's story on actor Michael Clarke Duncan (quoted under "Anecdotes" above) and notice how these kinds of details are used in the sentence "Michael Clarke Duncan's tree-trunk fingers are pushing into his closed eyes, but it's like trying to hold back rain" and elsewhere throughout the story.

Sensory Images

The sensory images that surround your story can add a lot to the reader's understanding and appreciation of the people, places and things you talk about in a feature. You probably already use a number of these visual details in your writing, but don't forget that the other senses are useful as well. Sound, smell, touch and even taste often add useful detail to a story. To say that the person you are doing a profile on was drinking a cup of coffee in her office during the interview is one thing; to say that the person "sipped on a cup of dark, bitter coffee" is another (and think of the emotional subtleties of "dark, bitter" coffee).

Did the subject have a radio on during the interview? What kind of music was playing, or was it on a talk show? Did her office smell of old coffee? Did she smell of cigarettes?

You need to note the answers to those questions in your notepad, as well as jotting down everything—what kinds of pictures she has on her walls, what kind of desk she uses, what kind of computer sits on that desk, and much, much more.

This will keep you busy taking notes during your interview, which is one reason that many feature writers use a tape recorder for such interviews, allowing the recorder to do the work of capturing the words that are spoken while the reporter captures the rest on his or her notepad.

Writing Feature Stories for Newspapers

As you read in Chapter 1, the concept of news in newspaper writing has changed over the years. During the 19th century, news was often whatever the highly opinionated editor or publisher of the newspaper said it was. In those days, editors and writers all too often weren't afraid to invent the news if that meant they could sell more newspapers than the competition. James Gordon Bennett, Jr., founder of the *New York Evening Telegram,* for instance, sent the journalist Henry M. Stanley to Africa in search of David Livingstone, the explorer; and Joseph Pulitzer sent Nellie Bly around the world in 80 days (and she actually made it in 72).

Throughout the 20th century, our modern ideas of what constitutes the news slowly took hold, so that by the 1930s, 1940s and 1950s a lot less invention and a lot more legitimate news dominated the space in newspapers. There were lighter stories, those stories printed more as entertainment than for their hard-news value. These typically ran in what were known as the "women's page" of the paper—a section devoted to society news and occasional profiles on people involved in charitable causes or on artists and writers visiting the city.

By the late 1960s a number of papers, led at first by *The Washing-*

ton Post and its "Style" section, began to greatly expand these pages, widening their scope dramatically. The rebirth of the newspaper feature story came about as those sections quickly established themselves in virtually every newspaper. The name varied from paper to paper ("Style" and "Lifestyle" were popular names, as were more local names like "Baylife" or "Metrolife"), but the kinds of stories were usually the same. They were ambitiously written stories meant to entertain as much as to inform, and they were usually in one of the following forms.

Profiles

A *profile feature* is one that tells the reader about someone interesting. Most newspaper profiles are about 30 column inches long, or about like five double-spaced manuscript pages. That's not a lot of space to say something, so newspaper feature writers have learned to focus tightly on those elements that make the person interesting for readers.

Usually, the person being profiled:

▶ Is already newsworthy, perhaps is a local or visiting author, actor, politician, or beauty queen.

▶ Has undiscovered news value that the feature story brings to light, for example, a heroic World War II military veteran or an award winner who has received little local attention.

▶ Serves as a good example of something that has its own established interest, such as a physically handicapped student succeeding in school or a single mom receiving her bachelor's degree after years of part-time study.

First-Person and Participatory First-Person Stories

The *first-person story* is still rare in newspapers, though it is now found more often than in times past. The *participatory first-person story* is one of the most likely forms to make it into print in a daily paper. When a feature writer sky-dives for the first time, or takes scuba lessons, or plays a game of tennis against a top touring pro, or plays chess against a grand master, or simply tries to program his own new VCR, the story can be entertaining, and informative, for the reader.

Writers usually enjoy these kinds of stories, and often a newspaper will have a particularly ambitious or daring writer who begins to specialize in the form.

The participatory feature often works best when the writer is *not* particularly adept at whatever the action is, since the point is usually for the writer to be Everyman, serving as a kind of surrogate for the common reader who would never think of jumping out of an airplane but enjoys reading about some other novice who is willing to do so.

How-to Stories

The *how-to story* is often found in home and garden sections of newspapers, and usually focuses on advice for the reader, often with illustrative graphics that lay out just how to build that perfect rock garden or do a smooth job of recaulking the bathtub.

The form is more difficult than many beginning (and some veteran) writers realize, since it requires a certain skill to explain in a few words tasks that are frequently rather complex. In many cases, newspapers rely on nationally syndicated writers for these kinds of features, since the writers not only have perfected this difficult form, but also have built up a loyal following among readers.

Hobby or Occupation Features

Hobby or *occupation features* are usually closely related to profiles, in the sense that the story focuses on some person with an interesting hobby or occupation. A profile on a local man who has an expansive model railroad collection in his basement, for example, will provide plenty of information on the trains (what types, how many, how many feet of track, and the like) but will also give the reader a good look at the sort of person who enjoys model railroading as a hobby.

Similarly, a feature story that focuses on a woman who is a professional umpire will detail her career, but will also discuss the sort of personality that enjoys that particular kind of occupation.

Travel Stories

The Sunday travel section is one of the best-read parts of many Sunday newspapers, and *travel features* remain a part of the paper where freelancers have a good chance to sell a story to the paper (there's more on freelancing later in this chapter).

Most newspaper travel stories are called *destination stories;* that is, they are stories that assume that the newspaper's readers might actually want to go to that place, and so they include important key facts about the destination as part of the story. Destination stories must be entertaining, of course, and give the reader a sense of the place. For the media writer, the challenge comes from being able to both entertain and inform about a particular destination, and yet make the story fit into a newspaper's typically tight space, usually no more than 30–35 inches for a typical Sunday feature.

Newspapers do occasionally run other types of travel stories, including the literary/escapist story, but usually less often than the destination pieces.

Special Section Stories

Specific sections of a daily newspaper regularly carry feature stories that come from the special interest of that section.

The Business section. In many papers, the business section is now a tabloid *insert paper* at the start of the business week, regularly publishes profiles of local, regional or national businesspeople. In addition, the business section may run interesting features about new businesses in the area or about changes in an older, established business. Another common business feature is *advice stories*, usually on personal finance issues, such as 401(k) plans, stock market tips, and the like.

Science features. Increasingly popular in newspapers, science features usually appear in a once-a-week science page. Profiles on interesting personalities in science are common, but the most frequent (and useful) features are those that explain a complex scientific program or issue to the common reader.

These *explanatory science features* require a writer who understands the science and can translate it into common language for the regular newspaper reader. That isn't an easy task.

Health and medicine features. Similar to science features in that they are frequently explanatory, health and medicine features treat a complex issue in a manner accessible to the common reader.

A major difference, though, is that health and medicine features usually connect much more directly to the reader than many science stories. Readers are likely to face health and medicine issues regularly, and so their interest level is high. Features that help explain hospital and health insurance costs are likely to be well read. Similarly, features that discuss health issues such as breast cancer or prostate cancer find an interested readership.

"Health features provide an opportunity to go beyond the breaking news story on a new development in medicine," says *Los Angeles Times* Health Writer Shari Roan. "Since feature writers have a little more time to plan a piece—and usually more space—we can put health and medical news into context for the reader, explaining in greater detail what the news means and how it affects the lives of ordinary people. A health feature typically contains information that readers will find useful."

The importance of health issues, says Roan, means that "the best health features have a strong news peg. They often break new ground by reporting on important trends or controversies in health and medicine. For this reason, health features can become candidates for front-page placement in many newspapers."

You can read one of Roan's health features, "Cyber Analysis," in the "Writers at Work: Media Samples" section at the end of this chapter.

Accuracy, of course, is paramount in these stories, and the entertainment value must always take a back seat to the accuracy. As in science stories, these features require a writer who fully understands what he or she is writing about, and so many newspapers settle on one expert writer to cover these issues, writing both news stories and informative features.

Sports features. Until recent years sports features consisted mostly of profiles on athletes and coaches. These stories usually tried to show the human side of the athlete, the side the typical sports fan rarely sees. To write a feature of this nature, the writer would typically spend enough off-the-field time with the athlete to get to know him or her better as a person, not as just a sports performer.

These kinds of sports profiles are still being written, and they remain popular with newspaper readers.

However, media writers writing about sports have also become increasingly interested in the economic and social aspects of professional and amateur sports. In this kind of story, the business feature, the profile and the sports feature frequently blend into one, as in a story, perhaps, about a new free agent baseball player signed for $8 million with the local team. How does the athlete feel about this? How does this level of pay affect his teammates? How does the expenditure affect the owner's ability to run the team at a profit? What do the fans think? These and many similar questions can be answered in such a feature story.

Entertainment features. Most frequently, entertainment features are profiles about a star performer, whether in movies and television or in the music business or book publishing. These features usually come about because the star has a new product out (a new book, a new film, a new compact disk) and wants to promote that product by doing a series of newspaper interviews around the country.

For a media writer in a hurry to meet a daily deadline, these features are a breeze. Usually done over the telephone with a 15- or 20-minute interview, they are highly formulaic and tightly focused on the new product. The performer is pleased, since the story serves as a free promotional device. The media writer is happy because it was an easy interview (the performer, after all, has been doing several of these a day for a week or so) with good quotes (the performer will certainly have some quotes ready).

The problem comes when you're an ambitious media writer trying for something more from the interview than the typical story. In that case, you may run into a conflict with the performer. You would like information about those recent drug charges, and he just wants to talk about the new movie.

Your best bet in these circumstances will be to cover the ground the performer wants to cover first, and then try for some new material.

For more information on these kinds of features, see Chapter 6 on interviewing, where CNN.com Senior Writer Jamie Allen talks about the interviewing process.

Serialized features. A new trend that goes all the way back to the 19th century in newspaper writing is the serialized feature. These long feature stories are often spread out over five, six or even more installments in the paper and require the same sort of reporting and writing effort as a book for the reporter (or, frequently, the reporting team) lucky enough to be given the time to write them.

In the early days of newspapers and magazines, serialized features were common, and often included fiction. Charles Dickens, for instance, first published many of his novels magazine-style, as serialized installments. Only later were these installments brought together into finished novels. Similarly, Upton Sinclair's muckraking classic *The Jungle* was first printed in newspaper installments.

Remember, all of these categories are arbitrary, and they frequently overlap. A profile on a scientist, for instance, will fit into both of those categories. And if you go skydiving and do a first-person story on that activity, the story will be first-person, participatory, hobby or occupation, and maybe even a how-to, all at once.

Writing Feature Stories for Magazines

Feature writing for magazines differs from newspaper feature writing not so much in the kinds of features you write, but in how you write them. There are four main areas of difference—time, space, voice and competition.

Time

When you write newspaper feature stories, you are frequently under daily deadline pressure and almost always under at least weekly deadline pressure. Many feature writers for newspapers are expected to write at least several stories a week, and often more than that. This means you have relatively little time to do your reporting and writing. These constraints mean that the full day you'd like to have spent with the conductor of the local symphony orchestra, for instance, becomes instead a hurried 45 minutes (or worse, a 15-minute phone call).

Then, as you write the piece, you can feel your deadline approaching. You'd like to revise the story a few times, bringing it to perfection. But you don't have the time. Even if you did have the time to revise extensively, you tell yourself, you didn't have the time to do all the reporting and interviewing you needed anyway, so you might as well just finish it and let it go. There's always another story tomorrow.

For magazine feature writers, that all changes. If you are a staff writer you usually have a lead time of several weeks, and for major stories you are expected to devote most of your time to working on that one story. This means that your editor expects you to spend whatever time it takes to do the story right. Spend that full day with the symphony conductor. In fact, spend several full days and really get to know her.

When it comes to writing, you will have the time as a staffer to write several complete drafts of the story, so the revision process becomes very important to you (you can read more about revising in Chapter 13).

If you are a freelancer, your time is your own, and while you may have to budget carefully (since many freelancers are working on several stories at once), you still will be expected to spend all the time it takes to get the story done right, just as if you were a staff writer. As you will see in Chapter 13, the revision process for freelancers is crucial, and you will have to make sure you find the time (and acquire the skill) to revise well.

Space

Newspaper feature writers know that space is tightly limited in a typical daily newspaper, so, for instance, the 40-inch story you'd like to write on that new conductor just won't fit. Instead, you have a mere 18 inches (or about three double-spaced manuscript pages) of space, and much that you'd like to say just can't be said.

Instead, to make things fit, you delete a number of the conductor's quotes, get rid of some of your best description, drop that great anecdote about her days back in St. Louis, and manage to squeeze the story into the 18 inches you have.

As a magazine feature writer, you will usually have a lot more space in which to work. Two-thousand-word stories (about eight double-spaced manuscript pages worth) remain common in magazine feature writing, so plan on using the best of those conductor's quotes, a good bit of the relevant description, and a few of those terrific anecdotes about her youth, her first job, and the time she conducted that orchestra under the Eiffel Tower in Paris.

Magazine writers and editors complain that, even in their business, space restrictions are becoming more common, so perhaps you'll find a 1,500-word limit, instead of 2,000. But even that is more space than most newspaper feature writers get; so enjoy the room, and remember, always, that if you haven't done a good job of reporting, you won't have enough good material to use in all that space.

A special note: Beginning writers frequently find that making their stories long enough is the problem. As your career progresses, you should find that things switch and that keeping the story short enough becomes the problem. Eight pages may sound like a lot of space to you, perhaps even too much. But before long, that will sound like barely enough space to get the job done, especially when it comes to writing feature stories.

Voice

Voice, as a writing term (not a grammar term), can refer to the way the story sounds to the reader. That is, who is it that readers hear speaking to them when they read a story? Most of the stories you write most of the time for a newspaper should have an *institutional voice:* The stories sound like part of that day's newspaper to readers. As a newspaper writer, you are expected to stay out of the story and, instead, let the subject act and speak. This *institutional voice* is important to newspapers, where personal opinion should stay out of the stories so the reader can trust the neutrality of the reporting found in the newspaper.

Magazines, on the other hand, often encourage writers to find their own voice. That is, the magazine editor wants readers to hear you, as the writer. The editor wants the reader to "hear" a distinct person, not an institution, as the story is being read.

For this reason, magazine stories are much more likely to be in first person than newspaper stories. The first person *I* and *we* is extremely rare in newspaper writing, and considerably more common in magazine writing. Read the magazine piece "One More Step" in the "Writers at Work: Media Samples" section at the end of this chapter, to see an example of voice in magazine writing.

Competition

When you write for magazines, you are likely to be writing as a freelancer, trying to sell your story to a magazine editor. As you make that effort, you will be competing against dozens, even hundreds, of other writers all trying to do the same thing. This is every different from the way newspaper feature writers work. They know the story they are writing will appear in print. For a magazine feature writer, publication is often not nearly so certain.

A magazine feature writer must first either sell the idea using a *query letter* to the editor, or sell the complete story. In either case, the competition drives the magazine writer to search for salable points in the story. For the magazine feature writer, the idea needs to be fresh, or at least a fresh angle to an old idea. Then the writing, and self-editing, must be very, very good. You can read more about this editing and revision process for magazine writers in Chapter 13.

Writing Feature Stories for Online Publications

Feature writing for online publications can be a challenging blend of newspaper and magazine work, with a large dose of broadcast-style audio and video sometimes thrown in, too.

You'll find that online publications are often very much like magazines in that you have more space to work with and you are usually expected to write with a strong personal voice. Frequently, too, you will be freelancing to an online publication and so will face the same competition that other nonstaff magazine writers face.

However, online writers quickly discover that the 24-hour nature of the medium means that they face deadlines as severe as those for newspaper feature writers. In fact, since some online publications put new material on their site whenever it's ready, the deadlines can, at times, be even tighter than those for newspapers. Happily (from the writer's perspective), most online publications that use feature stories settle into a regular publishing schedule that brings a little order from the chaos.

As you will see in the discussion on convergence, additional demands are often placed on online feature writers. To meet the needs of the online medium, you may be expected to record sound bites for the story and, perhaps, even record video clips. Also, you'll need to be aware of links to other sites that pertain to your story, and you will usually be asked to provide those links with your story.

Writers at Work: Media Samples

New Type of Elderhostel Focuses on Volunteer Projects

by Warren Wolfe

LITTLE FALLS, MINN. – From the mansion's sun room, Mac McKusick had little time for the sun-dappled view of the Mississippi River. He was intent on cataloging the silver dishes found that day in the butler's pantry.

"Look at this," he said, waving a hand at the tarnished but still impressive collection.

"Some of this is museum-quality sterling—not those silver-plated pieces, but these wine-glass holders and those serving bowls. Laura Jane must have eaten well."

Laura Jane Musser, the house's last resident, died in 1989, and the two grand mansions that make up this estate have been vacant ever since.

Now McKusick, a retired archaeologist from Iowa, was here for a week with 19 other older people, cataloging, preserving and documenting a century's worth of heirlooms as part of a new kind of Elderhostel program.

Traditional Elderhostel programs

typically offer educational programs for older people on college campuses. But the new Elderhostel Service Program focuses on local work projects instead of time in a classroom.

This year, more than 2,500 volunteers are paying about $400 each so they can build nature trails, stabilize beaches, teach children and tackle other projects.

The service program began four years ago with a handful of projects and now has more than 160 projects in 23 states and nine other countries. The number of participants doubled last year, though it's still tiny compared with the 250,000 who participated in traditional Elderhostels.

Long waiting list

"This place just vibrates with history," said Dorothy Lindeman, 70, a retired elementary teacher from Glencoe, Minn. She was using a tiny vacuum cleaner to dust some of Musser's collection of 300 dolls.

"I keep expecting the Mussers to walk in and demand to know what we're doing here."

The city was given the nine-acre estate in 1995 by the Musser Trust and will rent out the site for weddings, parties and small conferences, beginning this summer.

The Elderhostel is a project of St. John's University in Collegeville, the College of St. Benedict in St. Joseph and the city of Little Falls. The group offered four 20-member Elderhostel service programs this summer. All of them filled the first day of registration, leaving nearly 600 people on the waiting list.

"Older people have so much to offer—so much skill and experience—and they want to make a difference," said Laina Warsavage, who coordinates Elderhostel service programs at the national office in Boston.

"The people we're attracting want to stay involved and active," she said. "There are thousands of them out there eager to roll up their sleeves and go to work."

"So much more to do"

The Little Falls Elderhostelers eat, work and sleep in the two mansions, using the original linen sheets and monogrammed towels.

The workday is from 8:30 a.m. to 9 p.m.—except for those who insist on working even more.

"These people feel such an ownership of the project," said Deb Lehman, St. John's director of cultural programming. "Some were at work by 5:30 or worked until after 1 a.m. People even sneaked away during the farewell celebration to get just one more thing done."

The first two Elderhostels have begun documenting the collections of dolls, furniture, jewelry, quilts and silver. Workers fill out inventory sheets, photograph each item with a digital camera, then download the image into a computer and type in the description.

"But there's so much more to do," said Pat Moberg of Minneapolis. "The 16 sets of china, thousands of books, the photos, the personal papers, clothing, hats and those *Wizard of Oz* things."

Somewhere along the line, Laura Jane Musser struck up a friendship with actress Margaret Hamilton, who played the Wicked Witch of the West in the movie.

A shelf in the Musser mansion is lined with Hamilton's autographed photos and a dozen knickknacks illustrating scenes from the film.

Lumber made them rich

Charles Weyerhaeuser, 25, and R. Drew Musser, 26, moved to Little Falls in 1891 to operate the Pine Tree Lumber Co., which was started the year before by their fathers and other lumbermen.

The vast tracts of white pine were logged out by 1920, and the Pine Tree mill was closed, but the process made wealthy families even richer. The Mussers and Weyerhaeusers were important financial, social and cultural forces in the community. They brought classical music performers to town,

(continued)

(continued)

gave the city a grand piano and a music hall to house it and donated 3,000 acres for what became Itasca State Park.

The Weyerhaeusers left town when the mill closed, leaving their house to the Mussers. It was rented to Musser business associates until 1953, when Laura Jane Musser moved next door from her father's house.

A graduate of Juilliard School of Music in New York, she returned home to give music lessons and join the family tradition of supporting the community and the arts. She never married.

In a family of philanthropists, Musser apparently made her father nervous with her largesse. When he died in 1958, he left his two adopted children cash bequests but placed the rest in a trust for Laura Jane.

"She had the income from the trust, but she was often going to the lawyers for more money to do special things," said local historian Marilyn Brown, who spoke to Elderhostelers the night they arrived.

Brown once served with Musser on a committee to save the city's train depot. Musser gave scholarships to promising music students and brought artists such as soprano Marian Anderson and pianist Van Cliburn to town.

"She was a real character," Brown said. "She didn't dress to impress people. She'd walk around in an old housecoat. And she didn't keep her opinions to herself." People knew she strongly opposed the war in Vietnam and supported politicians who favored abortion rights.

"Laura Jane is smiling"

City and college officials expect they will decide in the fall to continue the experimental Elderhostel program.

Bobbie Marshall, a seamstress from Oklahoma, has no doubt.

"I'm coming back next year, so they have to keep going," she said. "Besides, somewhere up there Laura Jane is smiling at us. She would have been a great Elderhosteler."

From the *Star Tribune* (Minneapolis), June 16, 1997. Copyright 1997 Star Tribune. All rights reserved. Reprinted by permission.

One More Step

By Rick Wilber

On top of the small bookcase to the right of my writing desk sits a framed picture of my father, Del Wilber, in his Red Sox uniform. He's crouching near first base, pretending to be the umpire and waving his arms wide, palms down as I, age five, step toward the bag. I'm almost there, and in my mind I can hear him urging me on, as he's done so many times through my life: "One more step, son, one more step."

We're in Fenway Park, my dad, myself and my older brother, and we're all wearing our Red Sox uniforms. My number on the back is 2/3. My brother's says 1/3. My father's uniform number, the one he wore during his three years as a back-up catcher for the Sox, is 33.

The year is 1953, and my father, thirty-four years old, is near the end of his playing career. He appeared in 58 games that year, catching in 28 and hitting .241. By the next year, he was down to 24 appearances, caught in just 18 games and hit a meager .131, and his playing career was over. He moved after that into coaching, managing, scouting—the typical list of baseball jobs that follow a smart catcher's retirement from active play.

This picture, this moment, is one of many we have of him. In another, an old wire-service photo from that same year, he's making a tag on Yogi Berra. The picture freezes him in mid-air, diving back toward the plate after coming off the line to catch the throw from right. The combination of grace and power, the blend of strength and agility that any big-league catcher must have, jumps off that old photograph at me.

Dad made the play, the caption tells me, and Yogi was out.

* * *

The spinal canal narrows in many people as they age. This is called spinal stenosis, and its symptoms range from a stiff lower back with some soreness, to, in some cases, debilitating pain. This narrowing is often degenerative.

Those who suffer from spinal stenosis feel a steady ache that centers on the small of the back, with more pain after any amount of exercise, even a short walk. Rest usually produces relief of that pain, so those who suffer from it tend to exercise less and rest more, beginning a cycle toward being bedridden, a kind of ambulatory entropy taking place.

* * *

My father was the star of Lincoln Park High in Detroit in three different sports in the mid-1930s. He won 11 varsity letters. He was also, I found out only in recent years, a gifted writer: editor of the school paper and sports editor of the local town paper, the Lincoln Park News, even while he was busy playing for the baseball, football and basketball teams.

After he graduated in 1937, with no thought of college in those Depression years, he went to work in the stockroom at Ford Motor Company's River Rouge plant, unpacking crates of car-jacks and hubcaps and wheels. His father worked in the same plant, as a millwright. After just a few months in the stockroom, Dad saw an ad in a Detroit newspaper—a small filler on the sports page, as he recalls—that said the minor-league San Antonio Missions were having a tryout camp in Springfield, Illinois.

Dad and a friend (importantly, a friend with an automobile) held the dream that so many young men did in those days—to play baseball in the big leagues. So, they left work and drove to Springfield for the three-day camp, so short of cash that they slept in the car.

There were hundreds of young ballplayers at the camp the first day, a couple of hundred fewer the second day, and just a few dozen the third day. Most of them went home disappointed, their dreams gone. Dad received a contract.

By the next spring Dad was playing for Findlay, Ohio, and the summer after that for Springfield, Missouri, in the Cardinal organization. By 1941 he was ready for the big leagues, just in time for Pearl Harbor.

In 1945 he came home from the war and, like so many players of his era, picked up a career that was missing some good years. But he got back into the game, catching for the Cardinals, then with the Phillies, and then finishing his eight years as a player in the majors with the Red Sox.

Those were the Red Sox years of Williams, Dom DiMaggio, Jimmy Piersall, Sid Hudson, George Kell, Milt Bolling, Don Lenhardt, Harry Agganis. Mel Parnell was the pitching ace. Sammy White was the starting catcher. Dad, as he was for most of his career, was the back-up catcher. Far from being a star, Dad was very much a blue-collar ballplayer: hard-working, well-liked, knowledgeable. He had to earn his way onto the team each spring. It never came easy for him.

* * *

In 1959, Dad managed the Louisville Colonels of the American Association. Thirty-nine years old by then, he put himself on the active roster near season's end when injuries left him short of players.

He went three-for-ten as a pinch-hitter, including one towering home-run off Roger Craig, then pitching for St. Paul. I was there for the homer. I remember the way he rounded the bags, touching them so lightly it seemed he was floating around them before landing on homeplate with that little two-footed bounce so many players did in his era.

(continued)

(continued)

* * *

The treatment for spinal stenosis is a mixture of pain killers (ibuprofen starts the list) and physical therapy. When those don't suffice, surgery can correct the problem and is generally successful. But Dad doesn't like that idea, and his doctor agrees. The doctor tells me he doesn't think Dad could tolerate the 10-hour operation.

For now, Dad sits, mostly, or lies on his back in bed, watching televised sports and working on crosswords. A grandson of his is on the college basketball team at Eckerd College in St. Petersburg, Fla., near where I live, so he calls often to check on the boy's progress.

A freshman, the boy sits on the bench. But he's six-foot-eight and blessed with his grandfather's grace and agility. Dad and I both think he'll be a fine player in a year or two.

* * *

Dad always urged me on, even when I failed—especially when I failed. He taught me that setbacks are part of moving forward. "One more step," I recall hearing in countless Little League and high school games as I chased a flyball and tried, usually in vain, to stretch a single into a two-base hit.

Once, in Little League, I struck out in the ninth to end a rally and lose an important game. He was there, in the stands, watching, and I felt I'd let him down horribly. I stood there, at the plate, and cried, adding that dose of embarrassment to the already miserable moment.

Dad walked over to me, put his arms around my shoulders, smiled, and said, "You know, there's always tomorrow." Then he took me to get an ice cream.

Later, in college, I had a horrendous encounter with Big 10 football, the game's emotional and physical violence eating away at me until I suffered a kind of breakdown, lying in my dorm-room bed all day until time for practice, skipping all my classes, having the energy only to drag myself to the field where I obligingly collided into others until the time when I could return to my bed.

I was a quitter, then. I wanted out, and again I felt I'd let him down. But he came through for me. He seemed to understand, and supported my dropping my football scholarship. He asked only that I learn from it and try again, maybe at some other school, maybe in some other sport.

I wound up graduating on time a few years later, having paid my way through on a baseball and basketball scholarship.

* * *

Two years ago, he was still playing golf, but a broken wrist suffered in a fall in the front yard and now this spinal stenosis have slowed him down. He's gone from a cane to a walker, and now he's resisting talk about a wheelchair.

Mentally, he's as sharp as ever. He sees, I'm sure, what lies ahead, but there's no quit in him. He's a catcher, after all.

* * *

I called home one day a couple of months ago, and my mother answered the phone. Dad was out, busy. Mom had signed him up for a water exercise class at the local YMCA, one of those classes where, immersed in the supportive pool, people like my dad don't have to fight gravity to get their exercise. He grumbled, as he will, about going. But he went. His doctor thought it was a great idea, a way to gain some muscle tone without putting weight on that back.

Yesterday I called to see how he was doing. How was the pain? "Not that bad," he said.

And the water exercise? "Oh, you know. Can't find the time," he said, and let the topic go.

Mom came on the phone. "He's quit going," she said. "He says 'Not today, I don't feel like it today.'"

I thought about that after we hung up, and I found myself looking at the picture on my bookcase. I went to the files to find more. There's a whole sequence, nearly a dozen of them from that day in Fenway: posed shots of Dad, my brother and myself. In most of them he's coaching us.

He always had time for us, for me. He always backed me up, urged me on. I called him back. "Listen," I said, when he answered, "you have to go to those exercise classes."

He grumbled back at me. He gets his back worked on three times a week at a rehab clinic. That's enough, he says.

And maybe it is. But, maybe, too, he ought to be in that pool, moving around in the warm water, getting loose, feeling good, feeling the echo of those years when he could hit home runs and make diving plays at the plate. I'm going to call him now and ask him about that, try to give him some encouragement. God knows, I owe him that. C'mon, Dad, I'll tell him, one more step. Just one more step.

From *The Boston Globe Sunday Magazine,* Reprinted by permission.

Cyber Analysis

Patients wary of face-to-face therapy or simply eager for the convenience inherent in the Internet are seeking online counseling.

By Shari Roan
Times *Health Writer*

Kenny Evans knew he needed professional help for depression, but one thing always stopped him. The Russellville, Ark., man is partially paralyzed, and the idea of having to display both his physical disability and his emotional pain was enough to dissuade him from reaching out.

Then Evans, 49, discovered an Internet site operated by a Newport Beach psychologist who counsels patients computer to computer instead of face to face. For Evans, it offered a way to give therapy a try while overcoming his qualms about anonymity and privacy.

Now Evans e-mails Julie Keck whenever he feels the need, and she responds, usually within 24 hours. Evans credits Keck with helping him gain a new perspective on life.

"She is an empathetic and caring person," he says. "And I get an unconditional acceptance through her counseling."

Evans and Keck are among a growing number of patients and therapists using the Internet as an alternative to traditional in-office counseling, helping to push the mental-health field into new territory. Together with other Web sites that offer online chats with doctors, interactive health assessments, and personalized diet and fitness programs, online therapy is further establishing the Internet as a powerful provider of health information and services.

Online therapy, which typically involves an exchange of e-mails over hours or days rather than an almost simultaneous conversation, or "real time" chat, seems to capture the essence of Internet communication—anonymity, convenience and uninhibitedness. And patients and therapists say the medium helps lessen some of the stigma about mental-health counseling that can discourage some people from seeking treatment.

Americans are generally reluctant to seek out mental-health counseling and to stick with it once they start. About 30 percent of people who make a first appointment for counseling don't show up, and many people never return after a first session, says John Grohol, a psychologist in Austin, Texas, who has studied the subject.

One recent study suggests that people are less reticent about seeking mental-health information in the anonymity of the Internet. A report in *Behavioral Healthcare Tomorrow,* a professional

(continued)

(continued)

journal, found that an estimated 40 percent of all health-related Internet searches are on mental-health topics.

But online therapy is not without its critics, who cite concerns over the quality of online therapy and issues of privacy and legal protections.

Dr. Walter E. Jacobson, a Los Angeles psychiatrist, says that while online therapy may reach people who might otherwise not seek counseling, it lacks a crucial element in the relationship between patient and therapist: "A bond has to form—being able to make eye contact, how comfortable they are. You are not going to get that in e-mail. I think sometimes the treatment may be suboptimal."

Even so, Jacobson echoes other experts who say that online counseling is probably here to stay. He believes the mental-health profession needs to develop guidelines to regulate such counseling.

"Most people recognize this is one of those snowballs that you can't stop from rolling down the hill," Grohol says. "It's a question of how can you do it the most ethical and effective way possible."

Keck, a clinical psychologist who is Kenny Evans' counselor, was introduced to online therapy in 1997 after receiving an e-mail from a distraught college student named Joseph. He had picked her name from a list of psychologists and wanted to know if she would do e-mail counseling.

"I decided to try it with just that one person," Keck says. Based on that and later experiences, Keck created a Web site called CounselingCafe.com and now does 40 percent of her counseling online while also maintaining a traditional office practice. She acknowledges that there are limits to the type of counseling that can be done over the Internet.

"I call it 'e-mail counseling,'" she says. "This isn't therapy. Therapy is a lot more leading the patient to their own solutions . . . learning who they really are. E-mail counseling is more like direct advice. Anyone who says it's more than that is fooling themselves."

Joseph, who asked to be identified only by his first name, says that at the time he contacted Keck, he was spending most of his freshman year in his room due to a then-undiagnosed anxiety disorder that made him highly fearful of social interaction.

"I wanted to find help, but I was afraid of going to a public health clinic," says Joseph, now 23. "My biggest problem was the bad reputation people can get when they seek mental-health care. And, when you suffer from the disorder I have, you are nervous about the social impact of seeking therapy. So a computer was an easy way to talk to someone."

For almost a year, Keck and Joseph exchanged e-mails every few weeks. She sent him information about social anxiety and recommended books and articles. Finally, Joseph decided to seek face-to-face therapy at his school's health clinic, where his disorder was formally diagnosed. He began receiving behavioral therapy and medication.

Now recovered, Joseph says he would recommend online therapy to others as a way to get started, while adding that he believes "it's important to see someone face-to-face in the long run."

Teresa Austin, a 45-year-old school librarian on the East Coast, stumbled across an online therapy Web site one day during a troubled period when she and her husband were separated.

She exchanged e-mails with a therapist who offered advice and recommended books for the couple to read. The therapist also urged the couple to see a local marriage counselor who, Austin says, helped move them "toward a resolution."

"Many people appreciate and can benefit from limited e-mail exchanges with therapists," says Rick Harrison, a marriage-and-family therapist in Newport Beach. Harrison launched his e-therapy Web site—PsyNet.com (with the catchy home-page headline: "The Shrink Is In") in 1996.

"People aren't looking for therapy on the Internet," Harrison argues. "They are looking for fast answers to questions under the cloak of anonymity. They ask questions that they wouldn't ask face to face."

Many mental-health professionals appear to endorse limited use of the Internet. Writing last year in the journal *Cyber Psychology and Behavior,* Vicky Laszlo, a counselor based in Marlboro, N.J., says online counseling has its roots in educational Web pages and online questionnaires that screen for conditions like depression or anxiety.

Most online therapists are marriage-and-family therapists and psychologists, with almost half possessing Ph.D.s, according to Laszlo. Fewer psychiatrists appear to be seeking clients on the Internet. She said her informal survey of fees shows that therapists are charging about $18 an e-mail, on average.

Professional organizations, including the American Psychiatric Assn. and the American Psychological Assn., are monitoring the growth of online therapy.

"We get a lot of calls into the ethics office in which people say they are thinking of doing this," says Dolph Printz, director of ethics for the American Psychological Assn. "We get incredibly thoughtful and complicated questions that we simply don't have answers to."

In January, the International Society for Mental Health Online, a professional and consumer group founded in 1997, released guidelines for online therapy that deal with such issues as privacy, disclosure of the therapist's credentials and the promptness of e-mail responses. (A full list of the guidelines is available at the group's Web site: http://www.ismho.org.)

Many mental-health professionals, however, are concerned about the lack of research demonstrating the effectiveness of online therapy.

June Caldwell, a marriage-and-family counselor in Redondo Beach, started a counseling Web site with some colleagues two years ago that provides free referrals to online therapists.

"We were curious whether the Internet would be a quality way for us to do counseling," Caldwell says. "We realized there is a need. But we also realized there are a lot of people who are not serious about counseling. It became a problem as to how to sort out who is appropriate for counseling."

Caldwell says she remains uneasy with the many unresolved aspects of e-therapy, such as how to handle clients who suffer a crisis, how to ensure privacy and confidentiality and how to abide by state laws governing mental-health service practices.

Jacobson, the Los Angeles psychiatrist, says he most fears a situation in which a client becomes suicidal.

"When you're online, you can't see someone getting tense, getting upset, getting guarded," he says. "In a room, you can de-escalate. You can say, 'Let's back away,' calm them down and get to a safe place. While online, you may not know that they're freaking out. They may even be on the verge of suicide, and you can't do a thing."

Keck says she once had to ask police in a client's hometown to check on him. She insists on obtaining a client's real name, address and phone number.

But listing personal, identifying information in an e-mail that may include intimate issues of one's life is another problem in the world of e-therapy. Not only can hackers break into computer files, any printed record of the e-mail exchange (which both therapists and clients often claim they like to keep in order to review what has been discussed) might end up in the wrong hands.

"There is no confidentiality to e-mail," says Dr. Zebulon Taintor, chairman of the American Psychiatric Assn.'s Committee on Telemedicine, which favors the use of video-conferencing technology, rather than computer e-mail, for counseling sessions that take place between patients and therapists in different locations.

Since therapists must be licensed in every state in which they practice, it isn't clear whether online therapists

(continued)

(continued)

who counsel clients out of state are breaking the law.

In addition, participants may not be covered by such laws as therapist–client privilege, which protects a therapist from divulging in a court of law confidential exchanges that took place during therapy.

But the risks of using an out-of-state therapist may pale compared with the risk of using an unlicensed therapist. Online therapy is a magnet for charlatans, experts say. And it takes some effort to check out the credentials of online therapists.

At least one person is trying to help consumers locate qualified online therapists. Martha Ainsworth, an Internet consultant in Princeton, N.J., has established a Web site (http://www.metanoia.org) that lists online therapists and even ranks them based on verification of credentials and a review of their Web sites.

Like scrolling through a list of books on Amazon.com, consumers can select an appealing therapist and click into their virtual office.

The alternative? Consult with friends or a phone book for a therapist. Muster the courage to call the office. Commit to an appointment. Drive to the office. Sit in the waiting room. Take a chair across from a stranger. Not Kenny Evans.

"It is a comfort to me to be able to sit down and e-mail Dr. Keck any time of the day or night without an appointment and know that she'll respond within 24 hours or sooner," Evans says. "I think this is an idea that will only add to the mental-health field and will help shape it for the better for folks like me."

From the *Los Angeles Times,* March 6, 2000, Home Edition, Health, Part S, Page 1. Copyright © 2000 Los Angeles Times. Reprinted by permission.

What You Should Know When You Log On

By Shari Roan
Times *Health Writer*

The International Society for Mental Health Online (http://www.ismho.org) recently released principles to help protect therapists and consumers communicating online. The principles include:

• The client should be informed about the process, potential risks and benefits of the service, safeguards against risks, and alternatives to the service.

• Clients should be told that misunderstandings are possible. They should be told how quickly therapists will respond.

• The client should know the name of the counselor, the counselor's qualifications (including degree, license and certification), and any special training or degrees. The client should be told how to confirm this information with relevant institutions (such as the state licensing board).

• The counselor should remain within his or her boundaries of competence, and not attempt to address a problem online if he or she would not attempt to address the same problem in person.

• The counselor should meet any necessary requirements (such as state licensing) to provide services where he or she is located and, if necessary, where the client is located.

• The counselor and client should agree on the frequency and mode of communication, method for determining the fee, the estimated cost to the client, and the method of payment.

• The counselor should adequately evaluate the client before providing services.

- The confidentiality of the client should be protected.

- The counselor should maintain records of the online services. If those records include copies of communications with the client, the client should be informed.

- Procedures to follow in an emergency should be discussed. The counselor should obtain the name of a local health care provider who can be contacted in an emergency.

Green Mile's Giant Has Taken Massive Strides

...Working with a mouse
or
...All this Oscar talk

December 10, 1999
Web posted at: 12:07 p.m. EST
(1707 GMT)
By Jamie Allen
CNN Interactive Senior Writer

ATLANTA (CNN) — Past the middle-aged Southern belles exiting a formal luncheon and speaking in drawls as they wait for their valet-parked cars, through the Ritz-Carlton's lobby distinguished by oil paintings on mahogany paneling and populated with tired white businessmen dressed in dark suits, up the elevator to the 19th floor, in a small suite of this hotel in Atlanta's ritzy Buckhead neighborhood, a 6-foot-5-inch, 315-pound black man is sitting in a chair, crying.

Michael Clarke Duncan's tree-trunk fingers are pushing into his closed eyes, but it's like trying to hold back rain. The tears are flowing around the actor's fingers, down his molasses cheeks, in crystalline rivulets.

Reporters witnessing the scene are getting a little misty, too.

It's all very familiar. The day before, a similar scene played out at a press screening of the new Frank Darabont movie *The Green Mile:* Flickering on the white screen, there Duncan was, playing a 7-foot-tall death-row inmate named John Coffey who has angelic

healing powers. He and Tom Hanks' character were trading tears over the evil mysteries that taint this world. And the media were all sitting there, watching Duncan, as they're watching him now, and wiping their eyes.

But in this case, at the Ritz-Carlton, Duncan's tears are not an act, and they're the best kind. He has just learned, in a brilliant display of end-of-the-interview timing by his manager, that he has been nominated for a NAACP Image Award for his *Green Mile* performance. It's the first time the 36-year-old actor has been acknowledged for his work, and it could be an omen. Duncan has drawn alongside two-time Academy Award-winner Hanks in the category of Oscar buzz. But more than that—as everyone in the hotel suite knows—this moment is a universe away from the days when Duncan was digging ditches for a living in Chicago, when Hollywood was merely a storyline of the daydreams that got him through each shift of hard labor.

Duncan lifts his massive form and walks to the suite's bathroom to gather himself. When he comes back, he's slightly embarrassed by his emotional display.

"I'm sorry," he says. "I apologize for that. Oh, man."

Two mothers

Cynics who hear about Duncan's tears might presume that they are contrived. Actors must live with this suspicion their entire lives: They cry, we wonder if they're trying to promote their Oscar chances.

(continued)

(continued)

But there's something about Duncan that makes you think otherwise. Maybe it's the fact that he's a friendly guy who finally took his destiny by the shirt collar and demanded more. Or maybe it's the greeting, the way his grizzly-like hand wraps around yours and he looks you in the eye, making you forget that he could crush your hand to powder.

Of course, you can often judge a man by the way he talks about his mother, or mothers. Duncan says he has two of them. His second mother, Dolores Robinson, the one who told him about the Image nomination, and then gave him a warm hug. Duncan's first mother, Jean, now lives in Indianapolis. She raised Duncan and his older sister in Chicago without help from their father, who left the family "at an early age," Duncan says. "She takes care of me," Duncan says later.

"It was just me, my mother and my sister and we found a way to put things together," he says. "I guess that's where my tenacity came from, and that's how I made it in Hollywood—keep trying your best, and that's what my mother instilled in me."

She also gave him her soft heart.

"My mother's the emotional one," Jean's baby says. "I think she's been crying ever since I made it to Hollywood. She's been the greatest inspiration in my career. She's the one."

"Bruce Willis wants to talk to you"

She's the one, in fact, who used to pull little Michael aside when he was just a boy and tell him, "You're going be a big star when you grow up."

Duncan shrugged off the prediction. As he grew, he used his immense size to fill lanes on the basketball courts in high school, and then at college at Alcorn State University in Mississippi. He majored in communications, but he didn't take things seriously then. He was the big athlete in the back of the class, cracking jokes. Duncan didn't graduate.

In his 20s, back in Chicago, he found work at Peoples Gas Company, taking a shovel to the ground for most of the day, then moonlighting as a bouncer at night. His co-workers at the gas company called him "Hollywood" because he'd watch television, remember what his mother told him about being a star, and say to anyone willing to listen, "Man, I can do that. I can act."

His co-workers weren't exactly supportive.

"I'd be digging a ditch and they'd say, 'Hey man, Bruce Willis wants to talk to you about a movie.' And they'd just crack up laughing," he says. Those co-workers had no way of knowing how that joke would turn on them.

"I found John Coffey"

Nine years ago, Duncan decided to stop listening to the laughter and live up to his nickname. He moved to Los Angeles to be a star. Of course, it never works out that way. You've heard this part of the story: struggling actor, down to his last buck, is ready to give up and move home. But he decides to go to one more audition.

For Duncan, his audition was for a beer commercial. He won the role as a drill sergeant.

Roles—stereotypically mindless ones, but paying roles—in television and movies eventually followed. He was a guard in *Back in Business* (1997), a bouncer in *A Night at the Roxbury* (1998), a bouncer for 2 Live Crew in *The Players Club* (1998), and a bouncer at a bar in the Warren Beatty film *Bulworth* (1998).

Then fate, in the form of a certain blockbuster movie hero, burst through the door. Duncan won a role opposite Bruce Willis in the box-office smash *Armageddon*. His role as Jayotis Bear Kurleenbear matched the depth of the movie.

But Willis and Duncan became fast friends. The pair has since filmed two other movies together, including *The Whole Nine Yards,* set for a spring release.

Willis, to his credit, saw the actor beneath Duncan's offensive lineman exterior during the filming of *Armageddon*. When Willis heard about *The Green Mile* and how they were casting for it, he told Duncan, "You have to audition for that movie as soon as we're done with this film."

Then Willis called *Green Mile* director Frank Darabont and said, "I found John Coffey."

Meeting with a King

The Green Mile is based on the serialized novel by Stephen King. Darabont wrote the screenplay and directed it, like he did with King's *The Shawshank Redemption,* the 1994 film nominated for seven Oscars. Set in a deep South penitentiary in 1935, *The Green Mile* delves into issues as daunting as the death penalty, racism, cancer. Hanks plays the head guard of a cell block known as *The Green Mile,* its clinically green floors marking the final walk for inmates sentenced to die in the electric chair.

James Cromwell plays the warden, whose wife is terminally ill; Michael Jeter warms hearts as a repentant Cajun inmate; Doug Hutchinson seethes as the sadistic nephew of the governor; Sam Rockwell gets comically dark as "Wild Bill," a walking nightmare.

And Duncan plays John Coffey, the giant black man convicted in the rapes and murders of two white girls. But Hanks' character knows there's something different about Coffey, and we soon learn that Coffey's hands, contrary to the murder charges, own the power to heal, even bring back the dead. A microcosm of faith, Coffey is a messenger of hope and lost hope (it's not lost on most film critics that Coffey's initials have a heavenly symbolism).

During the filming of *The Green Mile,* the actors and crew threw a birthday party for King. Duncan calls King a "genius," and says he was working up the nerve to ask the author a few questions about John Coffey. King moved first.

"He turned around and he looked at me and he said, 'You are exactly what I pictured in my mind that John Coffey looked like,'" Duncan says. "All my questions went away."

"Exhausted. Spent. Depleted."

The days spent on the set were a physical challenge, even for a guy used to digging ditches in eight-hour shifts, even for a guy who inherited the emotional gene from his mother. While some scenes breathed light air, including a few with a mouse named Mr. Jingles, the majority of Duncan's screen time is heavy. Many of the scenes directed under Darabont required several takes.

"Tired isn't even a good word" to describe what he felt at the end of each shooting day, Duncan says in his muddy baritone. "Exhausted. Spent. Depleted. Those are words you should use. You have to bring up this emotion, and you have to keep it up. It's like me asking you to cry this whole session, where everybody else talks, and he takes pictures. You're not supposed to concentrate on that. What you're supposed to concentrate on is crying, then I'll tell you to stop after 25 minutes.

"And that's being nice," he continues. "We actually went longer than that, because Frank Darabont is such a perfectionist and he has to have it just right. Everything has got to be perfect. So when you're crying, you may think, 'Oh, I'm doing a real good job.' He'll come over to you and say, 'I need just a little bit more.' You're like, 'Man, what do you want?'"

Darabont says casting an actor with Duncan's experience was a gamble, but the chips are still pouring from the slot machine.

"I should thank God or somebody for inventing Michael Clarke Duncan," Darabont recently said, "because he not only rose to the occasion, he exceeded my hopes. It was uncanny. He would *become* this person.

"I think Michael really brings the heart and the soul to this thing," Darabont says. "The character of Coffey has to be perfection. If that role isn't perfection, if it's not played to perfection by an actor who can be vul-

(continued)

(continued)

nerable and expose his heart, I think the movie fails."

"A moment I will never forget"

Duncan says Hanks was a tremendous help. During times when most stars are lounging with M&Ms in their trailer—not needed because their part is being read off-screen—Hanks was there for Duncan.

"Without him I would not have been able to bring that emotion up," Duncan says, "because when the camera's on me, he's on the other side of the camera and he's crying like a baby also. He's not the type of person that's going to feed you the lines. He's in his moment, too. When you look up and you see this great two-time Academy Award winner, and you're on the other end, man, you bring it up automatically and both of you guys are going at it. You're trying to keep each other going.

"We did one of those scenes where I take his hand and show him some things," Duncan says, "and I remember Frank saying, 'Cut,' and everybody was just silent for a couple of minutes. Everybody was kind of crying. Tom was still crying. I was still crying. Frank didn't even know what to say. That was a moment I will never forget."

Another moment Duncan would never forget, should it happen: winning the Oscar for best supporting actor. A recent article by the Associated Press deemed him one of the contenders for Academy consideration (official nominations won't come until February). The article also said Ving Rhames might earn an Oscar nod for his supporting role in the Martin Scorsese flick *Bringing Out the Dead.* The irony here is that Duncan, until now, has often been confused for the imposing, and bald, Rhames. That means those who are still confused about Duncan's identity could be seeing double on Oscar night.

Duncan says he's still not used to the talk about Academy honors. But he does have a pretty good line on that subject: "I've never slept with a man before in my life," he says, "but if I win

an Oscar, me and Oscar are sleeping together that night."

As with any film starring Hanks, there's been a good deal of attention given to *The Green Mile,* and Duncan is enjoying the perks. He recently spent time with the tabloid show *Access Hollywood* as its reporters drove him around his hometown of Chicago in a limo. It was all set up just right. Duncan says his limo pulled up to his old employer, the gas company, just as his former co-workers were punching out for the day.

When they saw Duncan stepping out of the stretch, those old jokes about Bruce Willis came flying in their face.

"Hollywood!" they shouted, and their sarcasm had been replaced by sincerity.

Here's another way to judge a guy: find out how willing he is to either take revenge on someone—say "I told you so"—or turn the other cheek.

"We started hugging each other, taking pictures," says Duncan of his old work buddies. "It couldn't have been better."

"If you feel something in your heart . . ."

"I have advice for people, period," Duncan says.

He's sitting up in his chair at the Ritz-Carlton. A reporter has asked him what counsel he could give young people, and Duncan is embracing the question. It turns out, like John Coffey, he has a message that he's bringing to the masses.

"If you feel something in your heart," he says, "and you really, truly believe in it, there is nothing on Earth that should make you quit. And I mean nothing. I mean family, friends, people in general—if you really believe it, man . . ."

Duncan pauses, takes a deep breath. This guy feels what he's saying. His eyes are turning red, tears just starting to form. But he doesn't hold back.

"Let me tell you something: Had I not believed in myself and what I was doing, I wouldn't be talking to you guys right now. I mean that from the bottom of my heart. I tell kids that. I say, 'Believe in something. Don't let people tell you, "Oh man, you can't be a writer, you can't be a doctor or lawyer." Who are they to tell you what you can do with your life? Why are you going to listen to somebody else to tell you what you can do?'

"People told me, 'Man, you ain't never going to be an actor. Act for me.' I said, 'Well, I don't know how.' They said, 'Well, you ain't no damn actor then.' I thought about it and said, 'Well maybe I'm not.' I listened to them. Don't ever give up. If you truly, honestly believe, please don't quit. If I had, I wouldn't be at this Ritz-Carlton. I'd be back in Chicago in them ditches."

The Green Mile *is a production of CNN Interactive sister company Castle Rock Entertainment, a Time Warner property.*

From CNN.com, Dec. 10, 1999.
Reprinted by permission.

A Day in the Life of...

Health Writer Shari Roan
Los Angeles Times

One of the things I've always loved about journalism is the freedom reporters often have to structure their days. This is perhaps most obvious between the hours of 7 a.m. and 10 a.m. in the newsroom of a daily paper. Except for the few people with specific shifts—such as the morning cops reporter—most reporters and editors arrive whenever they choose. Of course, their choices are based on what the day has in store for them.

As a writer for the weekly "Health" section of the *Times,* I tend to have three kinds of typical days. One type is when I am out of the office reporting a story. The second is what I think of as a writing day. On these days, I try to clear other tasks from my schedule so I can devote myself to writing with as few interruptions as possible. The third type of typical day is the one I'm going to describe in detail. It's a miscellaneous day. And it's one that, I think, is important to portray because it shows the multi-tasking, juggling and intense "working the

beat" effort that is at the core of being a successful reporter over a sustained period of time.

So, here we are: 7:30 a.m. at the *Los Angeles Times.* Large Starbucks decaf in hand, I turn on my computer and take a quick look for messages from within the newsroom, then switch to Lotus Notes to check outside e-mail. I commute by train from outside the city and like to arrive in the newsroom before the phones are ringing and tension starts filling the air. Since it's Monday, I track down the week's crop of medical journals to find out what stories will break this week. I find one article about a Chinese herbal remedy that shows good results in men with prostate cancer. Since the study is published in a respectable journal and the results are highly positive, I set the journal aside to discuss with my editor later. I don't see anything else today that I think will work for the "Health" section, which publishes each Monday. Next, I eye the yellow message-waiting button on my phone. Seventeen messages. Ugh. This is the worst part of my job, since few of the phone calls will be helpful to me. Most are story pitches from public relations professionals.

One call is from someone I need to talk to: the PR person for a doctor I want to interview. After three phone calls back and forth, we set a time for an interview later in the week. After finalizing the details for this interview, I have six more phone messages to collect from voice mail. I spend about an hour returning phone calls, often simply to turn down a request for a story on a particular subject. With that chore accomplished, I log off the *Times'* computer system and onto the Internet to search the topic I'm starting to report: refractive eye surgery, such as LASIK, in children. I click on Favorite Places for quick access to Grateful Med, a site that stores medical journal articles. I print some papers and pull out a manila folder, which will become my catch-all "LASIK/kids" folder.

It's mid-morning and the newsroom din grows. I pick up my mail, which I haven't collected for three days. The pile is about one-foot thick. I open each piece of mail, regardless of how dubious it looks from the outside. (I think I'm one of the few reporters who do this.) But I scan and toss most of the mail quickly. On this day, however, I find a surprising number of gems. I learn that a weight-loss diet drug will be studied in children as young as 12; that the Food and Drug Administration has approved the first non-surgical treatment for removing gallstones, and that a bill is pending in California that will allow optometrists to prescribe some medications. I send a computer message to my editor, David Olmos, asking to meet with him to discuss potential stories and to prioritize.

I meet with David for about an hour, discussing the LASIK/kids story and the other ideas. He asks me to check into the Chinese herb study and says he will farm out the other ideas to the staff to check into. I return to my desk, start a file on the potential herb story, and make a few phone calls about the diet drug and gallbladder stories to provide David with more information.

OK, it's not all work, work, work. I spend the next 15 minutes gossiping with a colleague. I then go downstairs to the cafeteria and take lunch back upstairs to my desk, where I eat my tuna sandwich while reading the *Archives of Pediatric and Adolescent Medicine*. That journal has several interesting stories that, while not yielding immediate stories, are noteworthy. I place Post-its on several of the pages and set it aside.

At this point, half my day is gone and I still haven't done much work on the story that is my immediate concern—the LASIK/kids story. I vow to start making phone calls on it but get a computer message from David asking me to read an

Summary

Feature writing differs from news writing in several significant ways, including less emphasis on timeliness, more emphasis on the entertainment value of the story, and the expectation that the reader will read the story to its end. These differences have an impact on how feature writers find their facts and how they structure their stories, with much less emphasis on the inverted pyramid form.

Feature writers may work for newspapers, magazines or online publications, and each medium has its particular demands. Freelancers quickly become aware of the competitive nature of their writing and of its relatively low pay.

e-mail from a reader who is critical of a story I wrote in today's "Health" section. I sigh, and call up the e-mail. It's from a cardiologist who disagrees over my decision to use the words *heart attack* instead of *myocardial infarction* in my story. (The story is on a decision by cardiologists to redefine how a heart attack is diagnosed.) I re-read my story and the journal paper announcing the new definition, then review my interview notes. I conclude again that *heart attack* is an acceptable lay term for *myocardial infarction*. Even the American College of Cardiology and the expert cardiologists I interviewed used the term. I e-mail my reply to the reader, explaining that we try to avoid dense medical terminology when writing for a lay audience. An hour has been wasted. Still, we are obligated to reply to our readers' questions and concerns whenever it's possible and reasonable to do so.

It's 3 p.m. Since I arrive in the newsroom early, I leave at 4 p.m. most days in order to arrive home by 6 p.m. and begin my "Hey, Mom" job. Glancing at the clock, I gamble that I may still be able to reach someone in the FDA press office, even though it's 6 p.m. in Atlanta. I'm lucky. My favorite press office at the FDA answers a question I have about doing LASIK in minors. I arrange to have the press officer fax me some pages from an FDA document on LASIK. Next, I go to a file cabinet containing manila folders of stories I've done over the past year or two. I've written on LASIK before. So I dig out the old file and sift through it to find contacts for this new story.

The day ends with some frantic organizing of my desk, opening more mail and reading faxes. No! On a day that has already had its share of compelling, possible stories to check out, I hold a press release describing a state program to provide medical insurance for high school students who want to participate in sports but can't afford the mandatory health insurance. I'll have to call about this tomorrow morning. As usual, I am never working on just one story at a time but am constantly sifting through tips and leads and thinking about what story will follow the one I'm working on now. I stuff my backpack with five pounds of files, papers and books and head for the train.   ■

Shari Roan is Health Writer for the Los Angeles Times. *Used by permission.*

Key Points

▶ Newspaper feature stories that are tied to the news are called "news features."

▶ Newspaper feature stories that are not tied to the news are called "independent features."

▶ Magazine features frequently display more of the writer's personal voice, while newspaper features frequently display the newspaper's institutional voice.

▶ Query letters are an important tool for freelance writers, who must compete for an editor's attention.

▶ The many different kinds of feature stories include profiles, how-tos, health and science stories, environmental stories and many others.

Web Links

Here are a few interesting sites on the Internet where you can find out more information or see examples of various kinds of feature writing.

http://www.newspapers.com
http://www.slate.com
http://ajr.newslink.org/
http://www.ajr.com
http://www.poynter.org
http://cnn.com

InfoTrac College Edition Readings

For additional readings, go to **www.infotrac-college.com**, enter your password, and search for the following articles by title or author's name.

- ▶ "Writing How-to Articles," Dennis E. Hensley and Holly G. Miller, *Writer*, May 1996 v109 n5 p14.

- ▶ "Specialized Journalists in Demand," Richard J. Roth, *Quill*, May 2000 v88 i4 p34.

- ▶ "Storytelling vs. Sticking to the Facts: 'It Was a Dark and Stormy Night' Doesn't Always Serve Readers" (Consider the source), *Quill*, April 2002 v90 i3 p22.

- ▶ "Reporting Differently: How to Come Back With a Notebook Full of Narrative" (Nieman Narrative Journalism Conference), Mark Kramer, *Nieman Reports*, Spring 2002 v56 i1 p13.

Exercises

Go to your CD-ROM to complete the following exercises:

- ▶ Exercise 7.1
- ▶ Exercise 7.2
- ▶ Exercise 7.3
- ▶ Exercise 7.4

Research and Writing Skills for Opinion Writing

Research for Opinion Writing

Leads and Structures for Opinion Writing

You've been editor-in-chief of your school newspaper now for almost two weeks, and the first issue will be coming out soon. Over the summer, the administration announced that tuition will stay the same, but fees have gone up $50 per semester. You and your managing editor think that's a bad idea, so you want to write an editorial about it.

Your sports editor, though, thinks otherwise. She says that half of the new fees will go to the athletic department to help support the volleyball team and the new women's soccer team, and that sounds like money well spent. Your feature editor, too, thinks maybe the new fees aren't that bad, since $10 of them will go to support the theater department's ambitious new program for producing plays by student and faculty playwrights.

How are you going to handle this diversity of opinion? Do you write the editorial and claim it as the newspaper's official opinion, although two of your top editors disagree? Do you publish two editorials with opposite opinions? Do you run personal columns instead, and let each editor have his or her opinion in print that way? Do you run the editorial and also a column which disagrees with it? Do you just back away from the issue entirely so you won't raise a ruckus on your staff?

Opinion writing is an important part of media writing, and

161

knowing how and where to express those opinions is what this chapter is all about. As you will see, there are several kinds of opinion writing and they can be found in newspapers, magazines, television and radio and in the new media. The basic kinds of opinion writing that can be found in today's media include editorials, columns, letters to the editor and reviews. Here's an overview that defines and discusses each of those.

Editorials

Editorials are the opinion of the newspaper, broadcast station, magazine or Web site as an institution. You are probably most familiar with newspaper editorials, which are the expressed opinion of the newspaper, usually arrived at by a group known as the paper's editorial board. In large newspapers there may be quite a few members of that editorial board. In small newspapers there may be just one person.

The (New London, Conn.) *Day,* for instance, is a mid-size daily serving New London and portions of eastern Connecticut. The paper has three people on its editorial board

When it comes time to write an editorial, says editorial page editor Morgan McGinley, the process usually begins with the paper's editorial board deciding which issues to write editorials about. While that issue might be something that occurred recently, it frequently is a topic that has been in the news for a while and under discussion by the editorial board. For instance, the editorial "A Woman's Place Is in the Pulpit," in the "Writers at Work: Media Samples" section at the end of this chapter, came about, says McGinley, because "The editorial board had been having conversations about women as priests and pastors for quite a while, so when the vote came up in the Southern Baptist Convention, it was a natural for us to write about."

Who gets to write a particular editorial? Usually it's the person who has the most knowledge on the topic at hand. At *The Day,* McGinley says, assignments are arrived at this way: "We don't have a formal editorial board discussion more than twice a week, but we have adjoining offices and a lot of interaction, so we discuss topics as we go along. Because the three of us have worked together as a group for 12 years, we generally know each other's thinking on major topics as we talk it through. If there's a more general topic, I usually assign the writer who has the strongest opinion to write the piece. That approach usually leads to the most lively and interesting writing."

At a large newspaper like *The Baltimore Sun,* the process is similar. Stephen Henderson, associate editor of the editorial page, says, "We meet every day at 9:30, but not everyone's there except perhaps on Monday, when we have our big meetings."

With six full-time writers and Henderson writing as well, *The Sun*'s staff is more than twice as large as that of *The Day,* but the general method of choosing which writer will write which editorial remains the same.

"It's almost like a newsroom with reporters and their beats," Henderson explains. "Each writer has areas he or she knows a lot about and is interested in, so it's a natural selection on who writes. On the occasional odd topic we'll have to discuss it and work things out, but for the most part, writers set their own agendas."

Henderson himself wrote the editorial "A Silence That Kills," reprinted in the "Writers at Work: Media Samples" section at the end of this chapter. As he explains, *The Sun* had been focusing editorially on Baltimore's homicide rate for more than a year with an ongoing series called "Getting Away With Murder."

When one particular case came up, it struck the editorial board as a prime example of what was wrong with Baltimore's criminal justice system. "These guys clearly murdered this person and then ended up walking," says Henderson. "There were screwups in the police department and prosecutorial screwups, too. It was a very clear outrage. We decided that our best response would be a piece that spoke to that outrage.

"A lot of what we write is intended to shape public policy, but this was different. This was telling people 'You don't have to take it anymore.'

"Why did I write it? Well, the publisher came storming down the hall and wanted something done, something said, and one of my niches is, I'm a pretty good outrage writer, so I took it on."

Broadcast Editorials

Broadcast editorials are rare in the modern broadcast media, but that hasn't always been the case. During the era of broadcast network dominance in television, local and national editorials were aired with some frequency, with local television stations often making editorials a regularly scheduled portion of the evening news, and in some markets, local television and radio stations still air editorials.

But in most markets, the editorials have disappeared. Until 1987, an FCC requirement called "the fairness doctrine" required stations to devote time to controversial issues of public importance and allow equal time for opposing viewpoints. The result was frequent editorials and equally frequent dissent aired on local stations. When the fairness doctrine was dropped in an era of deregulation, stations apparently no longer felt the need to challenge the opinions of viewers. Opinions remain important to both radio and television, as you'll see in a bit; but in a more personal form, especially in talk radio, a format that found a great deal of popularity during the 1980s and 1990s.

Columns

A newspaper, magazine or new-media column is the opinion of the person writing the column and not necessarily the opinion of the publication. In the newspaper business, in fact, the opinions of various columnists may be in direct disagreement with those of the newspaper's editorials and those of other columnists. Operating under the premise that a newspaper can be a marketplace of ideas, many editors consider it their duty to offer a variety of opinions on a given topic. This "marketplace of ideas" concept is less often found in magazines and new media, where publications are generally directed toward a specialized readership.

Newspaper columnists usually work for a particular newspaper, which pays their basic salary and, in return, expects one or more columns each week. Some columnists, in fact, write a daily column, a demanding task indeed.

A columnist typically specializes in a particular kind of column, ranging from politics to the highly personal. Some newspaper columnists are syndicated nationally, and their columns read by hundreds of thousands or even millions of readers. Many nationally syndicated columnists write about politics, and their work is usually found on the *op-ed page* of your daily newspaper. Other nationally syndicated columnists offer advice on relationships, parenting, business, sports, movies, books, arts and crafts—the list is a long one. To give you an idea of what column writing is about you can read a "A Day in the Life of . . . Newspaper Columnist Cragg Hines" in this chapter.

Letters to the Editor

A *letter to the editor* is the opinion of the letter writer and of no one else. Most daily newspapers make a point of publishing as many letters to the editor each day as possible. But, for larger papers especially, this means that many letters aren't published because there just isn't room.

The editor in charge of picking which letters to publish usually tries to find a diversity of opinions about a given topic, but also factors in items like length (the shorter, the better, usually), frequency of submission (some people send in letters every day, and so the editor may look for a fresh voice rather than printing yet another letter from that same reader), quality of writing, relevance to current issues, and reader interest in an issue.

Newspaper Reviews

Newspapers frequently review movies, television shows, books, plays, art exhibits, restaurants, classical and popular music, dance performances and the like.

Generally, most newspaper reviews are short, no more than 10 or 15 column inches in length, or about two double-spaced manuscript pages. In that length, newspaper reviewers usually try to summarize and then assess the good points and bad of a particular offerings. Most reviewers seem to adhere to three general guidelines.

Reviewers typically review something for what it's trying to be, not criticize it for not being something else. It is unfair, for instance, to criticize an Italian restaurant for not serving tacos or curried chicken. Similarly, it is unfair to criticize a pop artist for not performing jazz, or a romantic-comedy film for not being much of a thriller.

Reviewers don't give away important elements of whatever they are reviewing. In reviewing a new spy movie, for instance, a reviewer might summarize the basic plot but shouldn't ruin the movie's suspense for would-be viewers by giving away that surprise ending.

Reviewers know that they are informing as much as reviewing. For newspaper reviewers, especially, the review is likely to be read by readers who are thinking about going to see that play or film, or buy that book, or eat at that restaurant. This means that the reviewer has to meet the readers' information needs while also making value judgments about the item. How much does a typical dinner cost, for instance, at that Italian restaurant? At what theater is the play being performed? When will you be able to buy that new compact disk?

Steve Persall of the *St. Petersburg Times* says, "As a newspaper film critic, I know that a lot of readers are reading about the film for the first time, so I have to give them the basics of things like the plot and even what kind of film it is—a political thriller or a romantic comedy or whatever. We're expected to be something like *Consumer Reports* for the cinema, informing ticket buyers of the best ways to spend or save their dollars at the box office.

"At the same time, I want to tell them what I think of the film in several key areas: the acting, the writing, the directing, the cinematography and so on. There must be room for the concept of cinema art along with the commerce factors. Moviegoers can get trained to settle for less when it comes to quality. It's up to film critics to make them stretch their expectations. When consumers demand more quality, that's what filmmakers will supply."

Persall adds this cautionary note about the hectic pace of newspaper reviewing: "The nature of newspaper work is that I don't have a lot of time to make those decisions or write up the review. If I screen a movie one day I often have to turn in the review the next day. Some newspapers don't allow a lot of space either, for a review, so reviewers must learn to write tight."

In his review of the film *The Contender,* reprinted in the "Writers at Work: Media Samples" section at the end of this chapter, you can see how Persall blends information and value judgments into his story.

Magazine Reviews

Magazines, like newspapers, often review books, music, stage plays, film, television, food, nightlife and many more items. For monthly magazines, that used to mean that when a writer wrote a magazine review, he or she knew that the review couldn't be as timely as those in newspapers. The payoff for this lack of timeliness was that magazine reviews are often much longer and more thoughtful than newspaper reviews. Certain less timely subjects (fine art, books, restaurants and the like) worked better for magazine reviewers, and the time-dependent reviews, like those for a new movie, worked less well.

The emergence of online magazines has begun to change this mix. For many magazines, the online site has timely material that the monthly print version doesn't have. Similarly, those magazines that exist only online (and there are hundreds of them, with more emerging all the time) can be as timely as they choose to be about their reviews.

As a result, there is no reason that an online magazine reviewer can't be every bit as timely as his or her counterpart at a local newspaper, at least when it comes to reviewing movies, television, plays and the like. For book reviewers, the online publication doesn't have as many advantages.

Mark Kelly, editor of the online version of *Locus* magazine, which covers the science-fiction and fantasy fields, puts it this way: "For us, the big difference between Web site and magazine is (1) timeliness of news and (2) the ability to compile data over time, like the Locus Index to SF.

"Our Web site does run listings or notices of new books, usually weekly, and here the emphasis is on timeliness—but these are not reviews, just brief descriptions. I'd like to expand the amount of substantial reviews on the Web site, but the way reviews are written, depending on advance galleys from the publishers, it would be misleading to imply that Web sites can respond to book publications with immediate reviews in a way that magazines can't. At best, I'm making an effort to time the few reviews I do run (like the samples or reprints from *Locus* magazine) to correspond to the actual publication of the book, rather than running them in advance, but even this isn't always practical."

Locus, *an online niche publication, is marketed to writers.*

Research for Opinion Writing

As with any other kind of journalistic writing, the process of writing an opinion piece begins with solid reporting. Whether you're writing an editorial, a local column, a book or movie review, a sports column, or any other kind of opinion piece, the first thing you have to do (once you've decided what you're going to write about) is your research.

For editorials, Morgan McGinley's advice for research goes like this:

"The first thing is to talk to the beat reporters who cover the subject at your newspaper. Ask them all the pertinent questions. They'll often have much more information than they use in a story and can supply you with a much better informed position.

"The next thing is to assume that you need to check major facts even though your paper has filed the story. This is basic practice for reporters, and editorial writers need to be at least that thorough.

"You should seek information from print and electronic sources, particularly from reliable Web sites. But remember, you have an obligation to make sure the material is accurate. Just because it's on the Internet doesn't necessarily mean it's true.

"Finally, make sure you discuss the issue with the other editorial writers so that you get the benefit of their thinking. Strong opinion requires strong facts behind it."

McGinley's advice holds true for most kinds of opinion writing and can be summed up with this four-step process for reporting and research for opinion pieces.

Talk to the News Reporters

As McGinley points out, the reporters who routinely cover what you want to write about will be able to help you in several ways. First, they will be up to date on the current details. Also, they will have a list of sources you can call for even more information. Don't be afraid to solicit the reporter's opinions on the topic, by the way, and you can usually take that as a very well-informed opinion, indeed. But remember that you are forming your own opinion, and your perspective might be different from the reporter's for any number of reasons. In other words, listen and learn from an informed reporter, but remember always that you are building your own opinion.

Verify the Facts

It is your job to make sure the facts you get from any secondary source—even a reliable reporter—are verified before they are used. As you've read elsewhere in this book, you should never use single-source information in any event, and that's just as important for opinion writing as it is for newswriting. Getting a second source to verify your first source is standard research and reporting for a professional.

You certainly don't want to pass on incorrect information, for one thing. And if you are trying to sway (or bolster) your readership's opinion on something, you need to have reliable, double-checked facts backing up your opinion. If you're wrong on the facts very often—even just once or twice—your ability to persuade is compromised.

Get Additional Information

Once you've verified the facts that you have, the next step is to get *more* facts. You will find that the more research you do, the easier it becomes to marshal your arguments, simply because you have more arguments to marshal. Also, as with any writing, the more research you've done, the better the writing is likely to be, since you'll be able to pick the very best facts to use in any particular part of the story and not be stuck with whatever facts you've managed to come up with.

Finally, as you get additional facts you may find your opinion beginning to change—and that's a good thing. If additional facts begin to sway your opinion about something, then it's time to think about how valid your original opinion was. That leads us to the final part of the research process.

Discuss Your Opinion With Others

Most professionals willingly engage in discussions about their opinions. At a newspaper or broadcast station or at a magazine with a sizable staff, those discussions sometimes take place in regularly scheduled meetings, but just as often they occur outside the meeting rooms, over cups of coffee in the break room or at lunch. As Morgan McGinley notes, at a paper like *The* (New London) *Day,* "We don't have a formal Editorial Board discussion more than twice a week. But we have adjoining offices and a lot of interaction, so we discuss topics as we go along."

In some new-media offices, the situation is similar, with a mix of formal meetings and informal hallway conversations. But the emergence of Internet publications has meant that often the on-site staff is quite small and often the writers and editors are many miles apart and usually connected only by e-mail, fax or telephone. This same sort of isolation has always been the case for smaller, traditionally printed magazines, too.

This changes how you discuss your opinions, and no matter how frequently you're online, the lack of personal one-on-one conversation has an impact.

If you find yourself working alone in, say, a home office, communicating with your editor and other writers primarily by e-mail, you will probably find it useful to actively seek opinions that both support and challenge your own. Listservs are good for this, of course (see Chapter 5 for more information about listservs). But ongoing e-mail conversations with one or two trusted acquaintances may prove even more useful. The important point to remember is that unlike hallway conversations these opinions from others aren't likely to come your way unless you firmly seek them out. So do that.

Leads and Structures for Opinion Writing

Because they are intended to persuade at least as much as inform, most opinion stories—whether editorials, columns or reviews—follow a generally similar structure. While there are any number of variations, the need to persuade means that you will probably follow a pattern like the following in your story.

Begin by Stating Your Opinion

As with any media writing, the lead paragraph of an opinion piece is the key to the story's success. Like the leads in other kinds of media writing, the lead in an opinion story needs to entice the reader into continuing on with the story. And in opinion writing the lead typically accomplishes something else as well, letting let the reader know what topic is being discussed and just where the writer stands on the issue.

Occasionally, the writer may suspend the lead, hooking the reader with an interesting thought that keeps the reader going deeper into the story. As Cragg Hines from the *Houston Chronicle* says, "I try to follow generally a conversational approach that I hope will draw in readers."

But often the writer states his or her opinion right at the front of the story and then marshals the arguments as the story moves along.

Take a look at the opinion pieces reprinted in this chapter, and notice how each states its opinion at or very near the start of the story. Here are four examples:

Keep quiet, Baltimore.

Keep quiet about the 4,000 recidivists who run city streets, committing crimes with increasing bravado and little fear of punishment. Keep quiet when probable murderers slap hands and embrace in court after they walk free.

Say nothing about a police department that can't solve more than half the 300 city murders each year. Or homicide detectives who trash important evidence before trials. Or prosecutors and judges who can't or won't stop the delays that so often set criminals free.

The Baltimore Sun, March 19, 2000

The Southern Baptist Convention, in its infinite wisdom, has now joined the Roman Catholic and Orthodox churches in affirming a ban on women as pastors. The Baptists cited scripture as a reason for saying that women cannot be pastors. This is an argument that, like the argument of the Catholic Church against women priests, is certain to result in more defections from the church.

It's wrong, not for that reason, but for the larger reason that equally qualified, religious and faithful women have just as much to offer as priests and pastors as do their male counterparts.

The (New London, Conn.) *Day,*

The Democratic Party has leased—if not sold—its soul over the death penalty.

Twenty or 30 years ago, if the Republican presidential nominee had allowed the execution of an arguably retarded man, as occurred in Texas last Wednesday, I hope I'm not fooling myself to think there would have been a protest at a Democratic National Convention the following week.

But don't expect a ruckus over Texas' take-a-number death chamber (Wednesday was a double-execution day in Huntsville) from Democrats in the City of Angels. It's not in Al Gore's script.

The death penalty has become the third rail for many Democrats. Opposition to capital punishment made them look weak on law and order. It cost them elections. So they decided they weren't quite so opposed after all.

It was heartening to see the brief outcry from some Democrats in June as Texas executed Gary Graham.

Cragg Hines, *Houston Chronicle,* Aug. 15, 2000

This partisan drama doesn't hide its liberal bias, but moviegoers of any political stripe can enjoy its strong performances and compelling story.

It's the nature of American politics that someone will gripe about *The Contender,* a verbose potboiler that doesn't mind stamping bad guys with scarlet letters spelling out *GOP.*

After all, it's from Hollywood, the glitzy refuge of liberal thinkers seeking campaign donations, so what do you expect? Being a registered Democrat isn't necessary to enjoy Rod Lurie's film, but it would probably help.

Steve Persall,
St. Petersburg Times, Oct. 12, 2000

Next, Give Necessary Factual Background Information

Take a look at each of the reprinted stories in the "Writers at Work: Media Samples" section in this chapter. Notice how quickly background material is inserted into the story. It is this background material that gives the reader the necessary context to appreciate the writer's argument.

In *The Baltimore Sun* editorial ("A Silence That Kills"), for instance, the second and third paragraphs cite particular statistics to back up the editorial's plea: "the 4,000 recidivists who run city streets," and "a police department that can't solve more than half the 300 city murders each year."

Later, the editorial gets even more specific in its background information, giving exact names, monetary amounts, crimes, dates and more. These facts lend an air of believability to the editorial's plea. It's hard to deny there is a problem when the facts pointing to that problem are so clearly presented.

As *Houston Chronicle* columnist Cragg Hines points out, "Opinion without fact can too easily be prejudice. If you don't have the facts and can't marshal them effectively, why should a reader bother to consider your view—or read you consistently? Or, for that matter, why should a newspaper even carry your column?"

Frequently, there is a key fact or anecdote that brings the point you are making home with emphasis. You'll want to find that fact or anecdote and make sure it's used well in the story. Cragg Hines points to one particular such fact in his death-penalty column, "It's Politics, Not Principle, as Democrats Duck on Death Penalty," in the "Writers at Work: Media Samples" section at the end of this chapter. "The death penalty column was running long, and I was afraid I was going to have to cut what I considered a (pardon the expression) killer fact: That the convict whom Clinton refused to spare in 1992 was 'so retarded he left the pecan pie from his last meal to eat later.' [For a fixed-length column not wholly devoted to that particular case, the pie detail says in a phrase a lot more than an IQ figure and clinical diagnosis could in a couple of paragraphs.] An editor, thankfully, convinced me to find some place else to trim."

Finish Strong A strong ending ties in with the idea that your structure is unlikely to be the inverted pyramid, where the least important information comes at the end. As we noted earlier, this has to do with your readers' expectations. In an opinion piece, readers who begin the story are likely to finish it. Unlike the way they read news stories, they aren't grazing, reading the headline and first paragraph or two to glean the important news before moving on to the next story. In an opinion story, readers have an interest in the topic before they begin, or they're unlikely to have started the story in the first place. As a result, once they begin they will most likely read to the end. This puts pressure on you to end the story well. You'd like to leave the readers convinced that your opinion is the right one. If you can't persuade them, however, you should at least leave them thinking you had some good points to make.

Cragg Hines puts it this way: "I try to—and almost always do—make a final statement. Whether it is a strong one is another issue. It can be ironic, edgy or, even, merely a logical summation. Far more than in general news writing, an opinion writer is obligated to round off each piece in hopes of giving the reader a sense that a worthwhile journey has come to an end. Usually, it is a succession of paragraphs, a sort of coda, building to the final comment."

Hines adds, "Sometimes you can say it, sometimes you let others do the work for you. For example, at the end of a column about the wacky Reform Party convention ["Go, Pat, Go! . . . Far Away and Quickly," *Houston Chronicle,* Aug. 13, 2000], I let an unidentified reporter-wag have the next to last word: 'I cover mutants, misfits and the maladjusted.' Then I let Russell Verney, an old Perot lieutenant, close with a bit of gallows humor: 'I'm only manning the Kool-Aid stand.' Admittedly, I was taking the chance that readers would catch the allusion to the People's Temple mass suicide in Guyana in 1978 (in which the poison was not actually mixed into Kool-Aid but something called, I believe, Flav-R-Aid). But I think writers can waste a lot of time underestimating readers, and I find that objections to making copy too 'knowing' come primarily from editors who seem way too intent on dumbing down newspapers."

Writers at Work: Media Samples

A Woman's Place Is in the Pulpit

The Southern Baptist Convention, in its infinite wisdom, has now joined the Roman Catholic and Orthodox churches in affirming a ban on women as pastors. The Baptists cited scripture as a reason for saying that women cannot be pastors. This is an argument that, like the argument of the Catholic Church against women priests, is certain to result in more defections from the church.

It's wrong, not for that reason, but for the larger reason that equally qualified, religious and faithful women have just as much to offer as priests and pastors as do their male counterparts.

None of the major faiths that reject women as priests or pastors seems ruffled by alienating women, but they should.

Women are qualified to serve in the leadership of these respective faiths. Denying them those opportunities will only weaken the churches in the long term.

The Reform and Conservative branches of the Jewish religion have long realized that, and so there are female rabbis. There are female pastors and priests in other denominations, among them the Episcopal, Congregational, Presbyterian and Methodist churches.

The trouble with relying on one literal interpretation of scripture to deny women leadership in a religious organization is that the process fails to acknowledge both the richness of language and thought contained in the Bible. Can there be just one interpretation? Can that interpretation then be used to deny whole segments of a society equal opportunities as if one gender were inherently better or chosen as God's gender?

The argument does not make sense.

Women who feel a calling to serve their respective faiths as leaders cannot do so in full measure if they cannot ascend to the top posts in particular parishes and congregations. Those women who now dutifully follow the rules of whatever denomination do so of free will, of course. They can always choose other religions, provided they are willing to bear the emo-

(continued)

(continued)

tional trauma to their consciences and the confrontations that may result in their families.

The Southern Baptists continue to preach to an old, rigid line. Women in their church increasingly are becoming restive with that interpretation of scripture which denies them what they feel ought to be their rights as dedicated church members.

From *The* (New London, Conn.) *Day,* Reprinted with permission.

It's Politics, not Principle, as Democrats Duck on Death Penalty

By Cragg Hines

LOS ANGELES — The Democratic Party has leased—if not sold—its soul over the death penalty.

Twenty or 30 years ago, if the Republican presidential nominee had allowed the execution of an arguably retarded man, as occurred in Texas last Wednesday, I hope I'm not fooling myself to think there would have been a protest at a Democratic National Convention the following week.

But don't expect a ruckus over Texas' take-a-number death chamber (Wednesday was a double-execution day in Huntsville) from Democrats in the City of Angels. It's not in Al Gore's script.

The death penalty has become the third rail for many Democrats. Opposition to capital punishment made them look weak on law and order. It cost them elections. So they decided they weren't quite so opposed after all.

It was heartening to see the brief outcry from some Democrats in June as Texas executed Gary Graham. Unfortunately, the alarm was sounded by some who could barely find their voice when Democrat Bill Clinton left the campaign trail in 1992 to sign an Arkansas death warrant. The convict was so retarded he left the pecan pie from his last meal to eat later.

Al Gore supports the death penalty but squirmed when faced with pleas for a national moratorium. That movement arose after new evidence showed more than a dozen death row inmates in Illinois were innocent and Republican Gov. George Ryan called a temporary halt to executions.

There's no question Graham, as are most death row inmates, was a nasty piece of work. If their convictions are upheld, they should be locked up forever. Period.

The Democratic convention's silence aside, the death penalty is never far from the center of a political discussion in their host state of California, where the Democratic turnaround picked up steam.

Top California Democrats had a history of strong opposition to the death penalty, led by Govs. Edmund G. "Pat" Brown (1959–1967) and Edmund G. "Jerry" Brown Jr. (1975–1983).

But in 1986, the younger Brown's appointed state supreme court chief justice, Rose Bird, was ousted by voters, in large part because she had never voted to uphold a death sentence.

The message was obvious. At the 1990 Democratic State Convention, gubernatorial candidate Dianne Feinstein (now a U.S. senator) purposefully showcased her support for the death penalty. She won the nomination but lost to a bigger law-and-order candidate, Republican Pete Wilson.

In 1994, Wilson's Democratic opponent was Kathleen Brown, daughter and sister of the earlier Democratic governors. She said that even though opposed to the death penalty on moral grounds, she would carry out the law. That didn't wash, and she lost.

Two years ago, Democrat Gray Davis (who had been the younger Brown's chief of staff and whose marriage ceremony was performed by Rose Bird) made support for the death penalty central to his gubernatorial campaign. He won big.

Now Davis' prospective judicial appointees are quizzed closely about their views on the death penalty, and the governor (honorary chairman of his party's convention) has made clear that he expects his judges to resign if they change their mind on the issue.

Perhaps delegates will sleep better knowing the party is in such determined hands.

From the *Houston Chronicle*, Aug. 14, 2000. Reprinted with permission.

A Silence That Kills

Keep quiet, Baltimore.

Keep quiet about the 4,000 recidivists who run city streets, committing crimes with increasing bravado and little fear of punishment. Keep quiet when probable murderers slap hands and embrace in court after they walk free.

Say nothing about a police department that can't solve more than half the 300 city murders each year. Or homicide detectives who trash important evidence before trials. Or prosecutors and judges who can't or won't stop the delays that so often set criminals free.

Keep quiet, Baltimore, because you've got other things to think about. Like the upcoming baseball season. Or which weekends you'll spend in Ocean City this summer.

Keep quiet if you will, but know that your silence and your lack of outrage over the pathetic state of this city's criminal justice system make you an accomplice to the mayhem. Your silence kills.

These are your courts. They're your cops. They're your judges and your prosecutors. Until you stand up, tell them you've had enough and demand a system that works for citizens instead of criminals, the nonsense will continue. Thugs will walk the streets undeterred—maybe in your neighborhood. They'll rob and rape and kill— maybe they'll do it to people you know. And the slow rot that's eating at this city's core will become a ravenous decay, leaving no neighborhood untouched, no life unscarred.

How much more will it take for the city to raise its collective voice in protest?

When will Baltimoreans shout, like the television anchor in the 1976 movie *Network* suggested: "We're mad as hell and we're not going to take it anymore!"

At *The Sun,* we're already there. For more than a year, we've been writing (in editorials and news stories) about the continuing violence and how screwed up justice has become in Baltimore. We've pleaded with the governor, the mayor, the state's attorney, the chief judge of the Court of Appeals and others to fix it.

We've advocated changes in the city prosecutor's office, which is overworked and understaffed but also suffers from a lack of direction and an unacceptable level of incompetence.

We've pushed for reform at the city's Central Booking and Intake Center, where the absence of a judge to hear bail reviews has helped to clog the system with frivolous cases.

We've asked city and state officials to shelve their turf squabbles in favor of a unified approach to curbing the city's crime epidemic.

Some of what we've suggested has been enacted: The prosecutor's office will get more attorneys, prosecutors took over charging of criminals from the police department and the police department's rotation policy has ended, among other developments. A Criminal Justice Coordinating Council has been resurrected.

But much more has to be done. State's Attorney Patricia C. Jessamy still offers more excuses than answers or solutions to her office's pitiful per-

(continued)

(continued)

formance. Judges who make upwards of $103,000 (some as much as $110,000) a year still roll their eyes at the mere suggestion of weekend or holiday duty at the clogged Central Booking facility. And despite Mayor Martin O'Malley's election on a platform of "zero-tolerance" of criminals, thugs still know that justice is a joke in Baltimore.

Just ask Jay Anderson, William Harrison and Stacey Wilson. That trio walked last week—for the second time—on charges they murdered Shawn L. Suggs in 1995.

The case against them seemed promising when it was filed five years ago, but what happened in the intervening time made it easy for the defendants to beat the charges.

Prosecutors, judges and defense attorneys delayed the trial 12 times between 1995 and 1999, which violated the defendants' right to speedy justice. So in 1999, a Circuit Court judge threw out the charges.

An appellate court later reinstated the charges and ordered the defendants to stand trial. But by then one key witness was dead and another—a heroin addict—had changed her story. Moreover, homicide detectives admitted that they had destroyed key evidence against the defendants. (Just Friday, *The Sun* released details of a report on the homicide squad suggesting that lost evidence, incomplete case folders and other inexcusable dysfunctions may be the norm.) Not surprisingly, a jury returned not-guilty verdicts for all three in the Suggs case, and they walked out of court free men. But is that justice? Did the process fairly serve either the defendants or the victim's family?

These kinds of screwups should make Baltimore want to scream with anger and frustration. Judges' and prosecutors' phones should ring off the hooks, and the mayor should be bombarded with complaints. But do you think that happened? Want to bet that it didn't?

This week's judicial miscarriage was only the latest example of what goes on every day in Baltimore, the most recent in a long line of debacles that allow criminals to do whatever they want and not fear reprisal. But there's still no palpable outrage, no sense that city residents are gut-sick about what's going on. Something has to change. There must be a groundswell of public opinion that forces the important fixes we need in the criminal justice system. It would be no less important than was the civil rights struggle or the push for women's suffrage at the beginning of the early 20th century.

Anyone can lead this movement. Mayor O'Malley has a perfect platform from which to do so. Gov. Parris Glendening—an influential two-term governor with fewer than two years left in office—also has a position of advantage.

But you, Baltimore, must do your part. Your anger and persistence could be the fuel that feeds this effort. Phone your leaders. Pressure them to change. Do something.

No one in this city can afford to keep quiet any more.

Let them know

Call these people to demand change in Baltimore's criminal justice system:

State's Attorney Patricia C. Jessamy, 410-396-4996

Police Chief Ronald L. Daniel, 410-396-2020

Chief District Court Judge Martha F. Rasin, 410-260-1525

Circuit Court Judge David B. Mitchell (who heads the criminal docket), 410-396-5052

Mayor Martin O'Malley, 410-396-4900

Maryland Gov. Parris N. Glendening, 410-974-3901

From *The Baltimore Sun,* March 19, 2000.
© 2000 The Baltimore Sun.

A Vote for
The Contender

By Steve Persall

This partisan drama doesn't hide its liberal bias, but moviegoers of any political stripe can enjoy its strong performances and compelling story. It's the nature of American politics that someone will gripe about *The Contender,* a verbose potboiler that doesn't mind stamping bad guys with scarlet letters spelling out *GOP.*

After all, it's from Hollywood, the glitzy refuge of liberal thinkers seeking campaign donations, so what do you expect? Being a registered Democrat isn't necessary to enjoy Rod Lurie's film, but it would probably help.

However, Lurie's partisanship is one of the strengths of *The Contender,* creating a rare political drama naming names when possible, making transparent comparisons when needed. Beliefs about real issues and scandals give viewers personal links to the drama, to either swoon or scoff but always care about what's happening.

Slanted, yet stimulating.

Lurie's version of the perfect president is Jackson Evans (Jeff Bridges), a compassionate Democrat with Kennedy's charm and Clinton's appetite for food and a legacy. His swan song will be a vice presidential appointment, after the death of his former running mate. Evans wants the choice to matter, picking Sen. Laine Hanson (Joan Allen) as the first woman to serve in such a high position.

First, Hanson must pass through congressional confirmation hearings. Her appointment is immediately opposed by Sen. Shelly Runyon (Gary Oldman), who orders a private investigation into Hanson's personal life. It uncovers an alleged sexual indiscretion when Hanson was a college freshman, ripe material for a smear campaign.

How that defamation of character occurs is the core of *The Contender.* Runyon collects figurative knives for Hanson's back, then doles them out to others for slashing, publicly keeping his hands clean. Even his addressing Hanson as "the distinguished gentlelady" is a slap. Lurie makes him a hissable demagogue, with diplomatic insults and subtle grandstanding, a petty man with power. Republican, of course.

Hanson takes Runyon's blindside hits with more dignity than defiance. She refuses to dish back any dirt, even when Evans' aides set the table. Hanson claims, rightfully, that what may have happened when she was 18 is nobody's business now. Lurie gives her plenty of chances to eloquently express her political views—pro-choice, anti-gun, pro-people—while retaining her bipartisan sainthood.

But the sexual topic opens the door to other aspects of Hanson's personal life that threaten her confirmation. Her words get turned against her, her past political decisions misinterpreted, all under Runyon's shield of "a new birth of national honesty and decency."

The Contender is an engrossing battle of sound bites and cloakroom dealing, no matter how you vote. Lurie, a former film critic, has a good ear for credible dialogue tinted with research. Every character, even Runyon, gets at least one scene that humanizes them. Like TV's *The West Wing,* this film is a civics lesson disguised as melodrama, reassuring us that politicians are people, too. The film is a likely contender for Academy Awards (mostly California voters, you know), and three performances deserve that consideration.

Allen should be a front-runner for making Hanson an imposing victim, hard-shelled with a fragile soul beneath the decorum. The script and performance raise doubts about her character's ability to handle the job Evans proposes. Allen keeps Hanson on an even keel, never hysterical or angry, and always as curious about the outcome as Lurie wants the audience to be.

Oldman is nearly unrecognizable as Runyon, balding and devious, with Midwestern folksiness. This is a great addition to his gallery of film rogues, a

(continued)

(continued)

fearless twerp whom we demand to see brought down.

Bridges makes Evans the most electable movie president since Kevin Kline's Dave, mixing comic relief with left-wing righteousness. His sincere expressions are scene-stealers, whether forcing a power play or enjoying the perks of a White House chef.

The Contender never hides Lurie's respect for Democratic ideals and disdain for anyone across the aisle. Concerned parties demanding equal time should build their own movie studio.

The Contender
Grade: A–
Director: Rod Lurie
Cast: Joan Allen, Gary Oldman, Jeff Bridges, Christian Slater, Sam Elliott, William Petersen
Screenplay: Rod Lurie
Rating: R; profanity, sexual situations, brief nudity, mild violence
Running time: 126 min.

From the *St. Petersburg Times,* Oct. 12, 2000. Reprinted by permission.

A Day in the Life of...

Newspaper Columnist Cragg Hines
Houston Chronicle

It may not be typical for columnists, but many of my days seem to begin about 3, 4 or 5 a.m., when I sit bolt right up in bed with an idea for a column, a refinement of an idea for a column or a specific way for handling a column topic I've already settled on. The "bolt right up" part may be a bit of dramatic exaggeration, because I actually usually begin by remaining prone and wondering if this thought is actually worth turning on the light and writing down. For over the years, I've learned that there is little chance that I will remember some nocturnal bright idea in the morning unless I commit it to paper. Some colleagues admit to having a handheld memo recorder for the purpose, but I prefer a legal pad and can usually find one in a pile of books or files near the bed (at any rate, somewhere on the floor nearby).

Sometimes the pre-dawn hours will yield just the idea for a column, sometimes the lead and key paragraph(s) ("the nut") and some-times a pretty complete sketch of what eventually will appear in the newspaper. I also can make notes on sources to call, reports to check, other means of research, angles to explore. Once this narrative thread, etc., plays out, I almost always go soundly back to sleep. Sometimes the cold light of day reveals a less than successful concept, and the page of legal paper can be mercifully committed to the trash. More often, I think enough of the idea to at least explore it further.

The real start of the day is reading newspapers (although I will often have heard the news on National Public Radio while showering). *The Washington Post* and *The New York Times* are on my doorstep, one of the pleasures of living in the nation's capital. First thing at the office, I routinely plow through the *The Wall Street Journal, USA Today,* the *Financial Times, The Washington Times.* Later in the day arrive the *Houston Chronicle, The Dallas Morning News* and the *Los Angeles Times.* If I hear of or see a reference to a story in a paper not on my list, the Internet means the piece is probably just a click or two away. The same for the texts of government white papers, industry reports, court decisions from afar, etc.

Many of the major stories in the morning papers I sometimes have already read (often the

Summary

Opinion writers attempt to persuade others through their writing. Editorials, reviews and columns are three common types of opinion writing seen in today's media. But these forms require more than taking a stand on a question. Good opinion writers know that they are also reporters, who must research, verify facts and use interesting writing to attract readers.

Opinion writers use a structure that gets to the point quickly, backs up the opinion with facts, and then has a strong ending rather than an inverted pyramid fadeout.

night before) on the wires that pour into the *Chronicle*'s computer system (which I can access either at the office or by remote hookup through my traveling laptop. Sometimes before leaving the office at night (if I'm running late), I already have an idea of what will be on the front pages of *The New York Times* and *The Washington Post* the next morning, because their "play notes" are distributed to their subscribers. I can call up the stories themselves later at home—as well as seeing if there are any late-breaking exclusives.

Every now and then, even though I think I have settled on a topic (for my regular columns, which appear in the *Chronicle* on Sunday and Wednesday), an issue raised in one of the morning papers will strike my fancy enough (most often by triggering my low threshold for outrage) that I at least make a few calls or investigate/research further to determine if it's feasible to put aside the column I was working on and take up a new cause on deadline. After 30 years of daily news reporting, including plenty smack up against deadline, this is not as daunting as it may sound. Sometimes the shift to a new topic works easily; sometimes I decide to let the issue age a bit more or pass on it completely.

I have free range to decide on column topics. If I feel that an issue may be becoming overworked, I call the editor of the Editorial Page to discuss whether he's feeling burned out on a subject. Some general topics are more or less established by the political and government calendar, such as the primary season, national conventions, budget process, important foreign elections. Other topics are less immediately apparent, and I can turn to them out of personal interest or a belief that they need more attention than they have gotten. Sometimes I write about an issue because I believe it is so compelling that it would appear odd if I did not address it; for example, the stunning Mexican national election in July 2000. I was almost certain that I would want to comment on the outcome, and I did. ("Goodbye and good riddance" to the PRI, was my overall view. "Cause for Realistic Rejoicing in Mexico," *Houston Chronicle*, July 5, 2000).

On normal deadline days (Tuesday and Friday) when I need to deliver a column to the editor of the Editorial Page (I try to get it to him by early afternoon), the morning is usually taken up with finishing and polishing the column (assuming I've committed at least some words to the screen on the preceding day). I flesh out points, rephrase something—most often by making it simpler and shorter. If I squeeze this section, can I work in another subplot, a bit more detail? Is there a way I can make a point more crisply, with more edge, more stylishly, more tellingly? I also write a suggested headline (which not only can be used by the *Chronicle* but also serves as a caption for the column when it is moved as part of the report of Hearst newspapers to subscribers of *The New York Times* News Service. (I take it as a real compliment when an opinion-page editor of another newspaper breaks into the usual line-up of columnists to use one of my pieces.)

After the column is read by the editor of the Editorial Page, primarily for content/concept/readability (not point of view), one of the other editors on the page does the more hands-on copyediting, headline writing, checking for length and sees it into "type" (which in the Computer Age is a quick bit of coding and a series of key clicks). If the column is too long (I've never been told one is too short), I'm consulted on how it should be cut. Sometimes I will offer optional trims when I initially send in a column. I am cautious/caring/paranoid enough to almost always check back over a column when it has been finally set. These are mechanics, but I count them as important, because it's my name and my picture that will appear beside the column.

On non-deadline days, most of my time is taken up reading, reporting, thinking, writing, planning—in proportions that are difficult to assign and, at any rate, are ever-changing. Sometimes it's reading and reporting that I have to work in as time allows while focusing primarily on another issue. For instance, I had to review the record on the Vietnam War, in advance of President Clinton's historic end-of-term trip to Southeast Asia, in the final throes of the U.S. presidential election. (My Vietnam archive piled up near the bed, along with the legal pads.)

Sometimes the research is to make certain that my memory of an event (or string of events) is correct. I think providing historical context (short- and long-term) is one of the key responsibilities—as well as chief weapons—of an opinion writer. And the proliferation of data-bases on the Internet is a godsend to columnists (especially aging ones such as myself). Another great invention is the transcript wires, the services-for-hire that provide verbatim speeches/briefing/hearings/news conferences of the great and good. Also right up there with sliced bread is the Congressional Record online. But still, nothing beats being personally present at an event for the feel of the crowd (not to mention seeing colleagues, which is harder and harder in our far-flung, multinucleated media business. It may be "pack journalism" to some; I prefer to think of it as professional cross-pollination). One exception: If it's an opinion shaping event that the vast majority of the public will watch on television (such as an acceptance speech at a national political convention or a presidential debate), then that's how I, too, want to see it.

Given the abusive response to some columns, it's not evident that some members of the reading public appreciate (or would even acknowledge) that considerable thought—real cognitive weighing of evidence, alternatives, conclusions—goes into a column. The same can be said of writing—deliberate choice of words, phrases, styles to illuminate an idea which has to fit into a precise space and without illustration. A picture may be worth a thousand words, but I only get about 750 words and no art—except my half-column mug—twice a week.

Planning is required to determine if I can work in a trip, say, to see a candidate or to attend a seminar on a topic of potential interest for a future column, and still have time to fulfill my writing obligations. Even with writing only two columns a week, there are not many days limited to eight hours on the job.

If you have divined that there is no average day in the life of a national political columnist, then you are very perceptive and perhaps should consider opinion writing.

But now for the most amazing part: I get paid, and passably well, to do this amazingly fulfilling job.   ■

Cragg Hines is columnist for the Houston Chronicle *based in Washington, D.C. He has been a member of the newspaper's Washington bureau for almost 30 years, spending many of them as bureau chief as well as being the* Chronicle's *chief national political writer.*

Key Points

▶ Editorials are the opinion of the newspaper, broadcast station, magazine or Web site as an institution.

▶ A newspaper, magazine or new-media column is the opinion of the person writing the column and not necessarily the opinion of the publication.

▶ Reviews should criticize fairly (don't knock a country singer for not performing opera), not reveal endings, and inform the reader.

▶ Good opinion writing requires research; editorial writers should consult reporters and double-check facts.

▶ Opinion writing structures should begin with an opinion, follow with factual support for the opinion, and finish strong.

Web Links

Here are a few interesting sites on the Internet where you can find out or see examples of various kinds of opinion writing.

http://www.ncew.org
http://www.psu.edu/dept/comm/aope/aope.htm
http://www.slate.com
http://www.sportspages.com

InfoTrac College Edition Readings

For additional readings, go to **www.infotrac-college.com**, enter your password, and search for the following articles by title or author's name.

▶ "Make Your Opinions Count," Ron Beathard, *Writer,* Jan. 1996 v109 n1 p27.

▶ "Reading Editorials for a Living," Paul Hyde, *Masthead,* Fall 2000 v52 i3 p23.

▶ "The Pros and Cons of Writing Both Opinion Columns and News Stories," Dave Astor, *Editor & Publisher,* April 17, 2000 p33.

▶ "I Can Teach Any Student to Write Opinion," Laird B. Anderson, *Masthead,* Summer 1997 v49 n2 p5.

Exercises

Go to your CD-ROM to complete the following exercises:

▶ Exercise 8.1

▶ Exercise 8.2

9

Reporting and Writing for Broadcast

Until now, the focus in this book has been on helping you develop your writing skills through the printed word. The form and structure you have brought to your writing is based in part on the writing you have been doing most of your life. In many ways that writing style is about to change.

Whether you are writing copy for news, commercial advertisements or programs, preparing copy for broadcast is different than it is for print. It is based not on the written word, but on the spoken word. The focus is not on how your eye sees a series of words together, but on how your ear hears a series of words. Images conjured up by the spoken word may be just as profound, graphic and explanatory as the words you have set in print, but you reach the broadcast audience in different ways.

Before going further, take a moment to listen to what is going on around you. What do you hear? How are the sounds of the world moving around you? Close your book, sit back and close your eyes. Listen closely to the sounds around you. Is there singing? Try to listen to the lyrics. Are people talking? Try to distinguish how they talk to one another. Are their voices different? Does one person have a high-pitched voice, while another's is deeply resonant?

When you listen to people talk, when you hear their dialogue, you begin to understand that we do not speak the same way we write. For the broadcast writer, this presents both opportunities and problems.

For instance, punctuation for the broadcast writer conveys only sentence change and emphasis. It is used sparingly. Instead broadcasters use pitch, volume and cadence to keep their listeners involved in their story or presentation. Mood and tone are brought to your ears by the voice of an announcer who may be soothing or harsh, but who should always get (and keep) your attention.

Here's another point. While we rarely use contractions in writing for print, broadcast writers use contractions constantly because that is the way we talk. If you favor a less formal writing style, broadcast writing might be for you. On the other hand, while contractions are welcome, abbreviations are not. Trying to read abbreviated words aloud is both tedious and difficult. And often the reader will misinterpret the abbreviation and attempt to turn it into a word that does not exist.

Broadcasters have little time to present their message. Complex messages are difficult to convey in the easy style and shortened time frame of broadcasting. Because of that, most broadcast stories are written very tightly, with sparse use of adjectives or information that expands story elements beyond our basic understanding of the topic being presented.

There is another problem with broadcasting in general. It is transient. You have probably heard the old adage "In one ear and out the other." Well, for broadcast writing that is exactly the case. Sights and sounds whip by us at alarming speeds. Some people who listen to the radio or watch television are not deeply involved in that activity. Other noises and images from the rest of the world intrude on our attempts to listen to and watch the information being presented to us. It is the job of broadcast writers to cut through the clutter of the images and sounds of everyday living to present information that can be retained reliably.

To do this usually means that some information is repeated in a story, though often in different forms. There is also a tendency to focus on the most dramatic and consequently most attention-getting information. It takes extensive practice to become an excellent broadcast writer, but the best writers are always in demand.

Getting the News

Glen Selig is an investigative reporter for WTVR-TV in Saginaw, Michigan. Selig has been a broadcast news reporter for more than five years, and he has worked hard to hone his craft of writing for broadcasting. Selig must meet a number of challenges in preparing stories that are both interesting to people and easy to tell. Because he is dealing with investigative reporting, the information seldom comes to him in a form useful for broadcasters. Much of his reporting is done with the assistance of computerized records, an even bigger challenge for the broadcaster.

"The idea is to take a very detailed story and make it both recognizable and understandable to the casual viewer," said Selig. "I try to keep the use of numbers low, but often focus on the dramatic aspects of the story, and how it affects the people in the story. Even computer-based reporting must focus on people for them to understand the impact on their lives."

Selig doesn't have a specific formula for telling viewers about a story, but he always keeps in mind the fact that everybody is in a hurry today. And they want their news in a hurry too.

From the Beginning

So how do we go about the business of broadcast writing? There are guidelines and rules, though both are occasionally broken if the story dictates. Still, we do have a format that is relatively universal.

Because we are dealing in a medium that is transitory, we generally write all of our stories in present or present perfect tense. (See "Shifts in Person or Tense" in Chapter 3.) Writing in this way adds immediacy to the story and makes it appear as though the event is happening now, even though sometimes the story is several hours old. Here are two examples. The first is standard newspaper style. The second represents a relatively direct broadcast approach to the story's lead.

Newspaper Style

In a historic settlement that would cost cigarette makers $360 billion over 25 years, the tobacco industry surrendered Friday to unprecedented new rules that would strictly limit how tobacco is marketed and advertised in America.

(Associated Press)

Broadcast Style

Tobacco companies are bowing to pressure to pay some 360-billion dollars . . . over the next 25 years . . . to settle claims against them.

AND they will face history-making new rules in their quickly changing marketplace.

In the Associated Press newspaper example, the emphasis is on completeness and detail. In the second story the lead is aimed at immediacy. Broadcast writing thrives on the immediate. Wherever possible, writers should emphasize the story in a way that brings that immediacy to the forefront. But there are bad examples of trying to make old news look new.

Bad Example

The search is called off at dark for the body of a man believed thrown into a canal when his car overturned Thursday.

This is from an 11 p.m. Thursday newscast. Since (outside of Alaska) the United States is dark by 11 p.m., the story forces present tense. A better approach would be to use present, present perfect or future tense to emphasize some aspect of the search that could be happening either at the time of the newscast or the next morning.

Better Examples

Divers will resume their search at dawn for the body of a man believed thrown into a canal when his car overturned Thursday afternoon.

Police and volunteers are planning their next step in the search for a man believed thrown into a canal when his car overturned this afternoon.

In both of these examples—the first in future tense, the second in present tense—the writer changes the emphasis of the lead to maintain the idea that something is happening now or about to happen soon. This meets the broadcast standard of focusing on immediacy without forcing grammar into a box that doesn't make much sense (as in our bad example). Unfortunately, a number of "tabloid" television magazine shows seem to think that present tense means using *is* all the time. Instead, they are taking broadcast writing to a new low and confusing viewers in the process.

The point of these examples is to start you thinking about your sentence structure as both broadcast writer and listener. When sentences say something is happening now, but later show the event happened earlier or will happen later, the listener becomes confused and unable to follow. A straightforward approach is best because the listener will readily make sense of the message.

Keep It Simple

Since we are writing a temporary message, it is difficult for listeners to keep track of complex ideas. As you can see from the Associated Press example above (under "Newspaper Style"), at least three ideas are discussed in the lead sentence: the historic settlement, the amount of settlement, and the fact that new rules will be tougher on the tobacco industry. Reexamine the broadcast example. The lead sentence reduces the three ideas to two, and both ideas are tied closely together (the settlement and the amount of money in the settlement). A second sentence is used to convey both the historic nature of the settlement and the new rules.

In general, all broadcast copy should be written with an eye toward simplicity. One thought per sentence is always best. Two thoughts per sentence should be used only when the thoughts are closely related. This simple approach also helps guide us in constructing our broadcast stories. Since we can focus on only one or two ideas in a lead, the information that flows from those ideas must be linked together in such a way that the focus of the story remains clear and simple. In most instances, that means we will have room for only a few details about even the most complex story. And each of the selected details must be central to the story's main theme or lead.

Another way we keep our writing simple is to eliminate nearly all punctuation. Sentences still act as complete thoughts, but in some instances we find it much better to use ellipsis marks (. . .) as our punctuation form. Ellipses create the necessary pause, but allow the reader to interpret the length of the pause for appropriate message effect.

> Two people are dead . . . that after their twin-engine airplane crashed into a mountain this morning.

> The marriage of the century is over . . . Prince Charles and Princess Diana today officially called an end to their often stormy union.

While using ellipses allows writers to create pauses for readers, other punctuation marks should be avoided. Using a question mark or exclamation mark may make perfect sense in general writing, but either can be lethal when used in broadcast writing. The reason becomes obvious when you think about it. Punctuation marks appear at the *end* of sentences written in English. Someone reading a story aloud may not know that the required pitch is changing a statement sentence to a question until after the sentence is read. Avoid any sentence structure that requires the reader to read ahead. It is almost impossible to read copy aloud and read ahead

Attribution: Just "Say" It

One of the most frequent problems beginning writers run into is their "need" to use different words. This is a problem for both print and broadcast writers. Unfortunately, this desire to use an array of words also leads to the temptation to change attribution words. Attribution words specifically tell us who is speaking. In print, we often use *said*. In broadcast, we move to present tense with *says*. In journalism, the idea is stay as neutral as possible. When we veer off course with attribution, we too often veer into dangerous territory.

As with *said* in print writing, you cannot overuse *says* in broadcast writing. It is a simple way to clarify and send the message to listeners about a speaker's statements. Broadcasters seem particularly prone to wanting to beef up their language through more emphatic word choices. But these word choices also lead to adding a position or point of view to a story. Words like *charges, expects, feels, thinks, believes, alleges,* and *criticizes* change the focus of the story. Here's an example:

Poor
> Mayor John Jones is criticizing plans to build a thoroughfare through Hillsdale Park. He wants to see how development takes place in the area before acting.

Is the mayor really critical of the plan? There's a big difference in these two sentences. The mayor's wish to delay action (the wait-and-see about development) doesn't mean he does not agree with the plan.

Better
> Mayor John Jones says he wants to wait to see how development takes place before endorsing a plan to build a thoroughfare through Hillsdale Park.

The facts in both examples are essentially the same, but the positions and emphasis are different. Writers should be careful to work to reduce the confusion of a story. Of course, if the mayor is critical of the plan, why not let the speaker say it?

> Mayor John Jones says it's a bad idea to build a thoroughfare through Hillsdale Park.

This example brings us to another area of difficulty for broadcast writing: the use of quotes. Broadcasters generally avoid using quotes in stories. If a speaker says something that needs quoting, the best way to present that quote is through a sound bite or an actuality. An *actuality* is a video or audiotape of a speaker actually making a statement on some subject. And it works much better than trying to write quotes into broadcast copy.

Writing quotes in broadcast is always cumbersome and requires specific reference to the quote.

Mayor Jones says . . . and I'm quoting now . . . "That jerk of a Councilman will never get me to approve of a new thoroughfare."

Specifying that the next few words are a direct quote is essential if the quote is accurate. It is better to paraphrase, and better yet to get the quote on tape and use the sound bite in the story. The words of interviewees are often far more dramatic, poignant and telling than the words we writers bring to the page.

Basic Style Rules

So far, we have examined some of the general aspects of broadcast writing. Now it's time we can look closely at the rules and formatting that give broadcast news writing its own unique style.

Dealing with Numbers

How we deal with numbers is a two-edged sword. We must write numbers so that others read them aloud easily, and we must write so those listeners may easily understand what we are saying. At the same time we must ensure that we have a high degree of accuracy in reporting these numbers. This has led to some controversy among experts in broadcast news.

Some experts believe we should avoid the use of numbers, while others believe that when numbers are essential to explaining a story, they must be included. Our position is that some number usage is unavoidable, but that we must ensure that numbers are as accurately given as possible. So here are a few general guidelines.

Where possible, numbers should be rounded off. The larger the number, the more important it is to keep it simple. For example, 1,825,785, 282 in print form could appear as:

Nearly two billion

Over one-point-eight billion

Just over one-point-eight billion

About one billion 825-million

Each example is dependent upon the level of your need for accuracy in the story.

Numbers are written in numerals and words. Express a number in one of three ways:

▶ The numbers one through eleven should be written out in words.

▶ The numbers 12 through 999,999 should be written in figures (and be rounded).

▶ Numbers over one million should use a combination of both with the guideline aimed at readability.

Examples

Only 23 people showed up for the protest at the mayor's office.

Nearly three million 450-thousand people signed the petition.

There are 626, 352 registered voters in Douglasburg.

There were four people in the car as it careened over the cliff.

Where numbers involve money, spell out the monetary unit. Do not use dollar signs or cent signs.

Examples
The lunch bill was 16-dollars and 45-cents.

Taxes are going down by three cents a mill.

Numbers that show specific differences must remain exact. Specific differences include election results and athletic team scores, for instance.

Examples
The final score in tonight's game was 126 to 97.

Election returns for the state show the president beat his challenger one million 365-thousand 425 votes to one million and 62 votes.

For numbers that tell time, use words and numerals.

Examples
The alarm clock is set to sound at seven-23 P-M.

John said lightning struck his house about six o'clock last night.

Notice in these examples how characterizations of time change. The first reference is very specific about the time set on an alarm clock. The second example is vague, but still provides a general idea of when the lightning strike took place. We often use generalizations when discussing time, since it is difficult to be specific. A typical news story might use time this way:

> Police say the break-in took place between midnight and four A-M.

Use *midnight* for "12 A-M" and *noon* for "12 P-M" because they are readily understood and that is the way most people talk. Note that *A-M* and *P-M* are capitalized and hyphenated. That's to keep newscast readers from trying to make words of the time designation.

Use reasonable numerical examples. Many experts make a point of telling writers that numbers are difficult for people to conceive and understand. They will tell you to use examples rather than flat, uninviting numbers. In general, we agree with that philosophy. But writers also must ensure that those examples are not overly trite or insulting to your audience's intelligence.

One of the best examples we have ever seen came from an Associated Press story where the writer, rather than talk abstractly about the U.S. annual corn harvest in billions of bushels, reported that the corn crop would fill enough train cars to stretch around the world. Now that is a lot of corn. How would you like to be stopped at a railroad crossing with all of those cars rolling by?

On the other hand, there are very bad examples. During the administration of President Ronald Reagan, a network reporter attempted to talk about the budget in terms of jellybeans. Her focus was on the number of jellybean-filled rooms it would take to show just how large the budget had become. While the concept was good, jellybeans are still relatively small candies. You can get a lot of jellybeans into only a few rooms, so while the objective was to show the enormousness of the budget, the example failed to paint an adequate picture.

Numbers are important. We can not ignore them in broadcast writing, but we must use them sparingly, and when necessary we must define the numbers in terms that our audiences find understandable.

What Day Is It?

How to deal with days of the week is another subject where broadcast writers need to be careful. If an event is taking place tomorrow or took place yesterday, say "tomorrow" or "yesterday." Do not try to be formal in your approach to days. Some experts believe that writing in a way that explains when something is happening, like "day after tomor-row," is more explanatory than writing the specific day of the week. We believe that the key is flexibility and readability. So, if it reads better to write one way as opposed to another, do it.

In other instances, dealing with days is clearer cut. Saying "a week from Thursday" is better than giving a specific date of the month. Listeners will not need to run to the calendar to check when that date falls. If you do not need to be specific for activities that are taking place over a long period of time, write in general terms.

Names, Ages and Titles

Just as we treat numbers and attribution differently in print and broadcast, we also treat names, titles and ages somewhat differently. Remember, we are writing for the ear, not the eye. Understanding comes quickly when words flow together to form a cohesive whole.

When using names, titles and ages, you can improve understanding by delaying these details until the ear has "caught up" with the story. One of the difficulties the ear has is that it tends to need time to process detail information. We need to write stories that delay significant facts in order to give the audience time to warm up to the story.

The following is an example of a typical print story dealing with an individual.

> Microbank Industries Chief Executive Officer James Alexander Clements, 42, has been appointed director of the United States Information Agency, according to a news release issued today.

This lead would look significantly different in a broadcast format.

> There's a new director at the United States Information Agency. The chief executive officer of Microbank Industries . . . 42-year-old James Alexander Clements today was named head of the agency.

Notice how the construction changes from an emphasis on information to an emphasis on conversation. In the first story, as in much print newswriting, the lead packs the significant information into a single sentence. In the broadcast example, the information is spread over two sentences. Each sentence is used to give one or two specific details of the story.

Often we first focus on the "what" of an event or incident in broadcast because it is usually the most general information. We then become more specific as we write the story. We also tend to save one important detail for the end of the story.

Note the way in which age is represented in broadcast writing. In a typical broadcast sentence, the age is actually placed *ahead* of the subject's name. Much of this stems from crime stories. Here's another print example, followed by a broadcast example.

Print Style

Charles Johnson, 37, of 1612 Maybridge has been charged with murder in the Oct. 13 slaying of Willie Joe Ralston, 51, of 422 S. Bingham Rd. A neighbor found Ralston's body after he failed to pick up his newspaper for several days.

Broadcast Style

Police have charged 37-year-old Charles Johnson of 1612 Maybridge with murdering a west side man on October 13th. A neighbor found the body of 51-year-old Willie Joe Ralston in his home at 422 South Bingham Road.

In this story, while the print version is a bit more efficient, it would be difficult to read out loud. The story also would be difficult for a listener to understand since the numbers are crammed together. In the broadcast story we have rearranged the information in the lead paragraph to spread out the numbers. This makes the numbers less intrusive for listeners, who now have details given to them in such a way that the numbers are more easily processed. With the age rewritten, the address somewhat delayed, and the date written in a conversational style, the sentence can be read aloud easily, even by someone who has never seen the story.

Another area where we often change the order is with an individual's title. Briefly look back at the example sentence in the naming of a new director to the United States Information Agency. The print story places Clements' corporate title before his name and age, and before the significant action (his naming to USIA directorship).

In broadcast, the title is often separated from the name of the individual and used to describe the individual under discussion. This accomplishes two goals. First, it keeps us from being repetitive in the use of a name. Secondly, it again spreads out the details of a story for the ear to grab them in smaller doses. Here's another example with a well-known individual.

Donald Trump and Marla Maples have called it quits. The real estate developer and entrepreneur released a brief statement about the breakup of the marriage earlier today.

In this example, the identifier is not a corporate title, but the descriptive "real estate developer." This is often a preferred approach in broadcast writing since corporate titles may be misleading about what an individual actually does.

Putting It All Together

So far, our emphasis has been on understanding the differences between broadcast writing and print writing. Now it is time to bring the individual elements from the last several sections into a cohesive whole. It is time to write the story.

Most broadcast-story selection is based on the same criteria used by print journalists. Attributes of timeliness, proximity, conflict, prominence, human interest and general importance usually contribute to story selection. In television, however, another element becomes crucial. That is the visual component of a story.

It is important to understand that sometimes a story that is told through photography is better than a story that has been spoken by an anchor or a reporter. Most television news stories would be newspaper stories anyway, but occasionally the visual nature of the story makes it all the more suitable for television.

Whether writing for radio or for television the style is essentially the same, but there are some changes in the formatting. Radio tends to format its copy in much the same way that newspaper copy is formatted. Where newspapers generally "slug" a story, radio writers will insert a time as well. Here's an example:

> Runs: 16
>
> The space station Mir is in trouble. Neither the Russian cosmonauts nor the American astronaut aboard believe they can repair the damaged station. That could mean the ongoing space mission will finally come to an end.

For radio, it is important to know the length of a story, but less important to shift other components. For television, the writer must think both visually and aurally. A typical television news script would look like this:

> On-cam: The space station Mir is in trouble tonight. Neither the Russian cosmonauts nor the American astronaut aboard believe they can repair the damaged station.

Take VCR: runs 14   An unmanned supply shuttle damaged the Mir on Wednesday, ripping a hole in the testing laboratory and disabling one of the space station's solar panels. If repairs can't be made soon, it will likely mean an end to the ongoing space mission.

Television needs to format its copy in a manner that allows directors to immediately see how the story is scheduled to air. That includes details like the length of the story, the facts about any videotape accompanying the story and even who might read the story on air. This allows those involved in the production of a television newscast to make decisions that keep the news program running smoothly. In order to do this, television scripts are split into two sides with the right side containing the material that will be read on air and the left side of the page containing the technical information about the who, what and where of the mechanical side of the story.

Where to Begin

As in any news story, the lead is the most important part of a television or radio story. It is the lead that must grab the attention of listeners. In broadcasting as in print, a lead can make or break any story. For most stories, a *summary lead* that points out the strongest aspect of the story is appropriate. How should we construct that lead? The following is a list of facts from which we will build a story.

United Brotherhood of Electrical Workers Local 443 goes on strike at midnight tonight against National Widget Company. The union and the company had been bargaining over a new contract for six months.

Talks fell through this morning, and the union called for a walkout.

Approximately 16,000 workers are at the plant; 6,000 are members of UBEW.

Workers wanted higher wages including six percent raise now and five percent next year. Three year contract, third year wages reviewed in second year.

Tips and Tactics

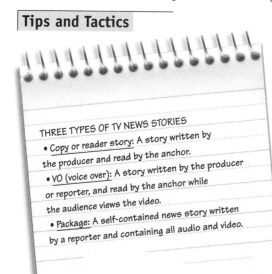

THREE TYPES OF TV NEWS STORIES
- Copy or reader story: A story written by the producer and read by the anchor.
- VO (voice over): A story written by the producer or reporter, and read by the anchor while the audience views the video.
- Package: A self-contained news story written by a reporter and containing all audio and video.

All workers will honor picket lines. Old contract ran out sixty days ago, but workers had stayed on the job while negotiations continued.

Our first priority is to discover the most immediate and important piece of information from the list we have developed. For purposes of this exercise, let's say we are writing the story for the 11 p.m. newscast. Our lead might go like this:

> In less than an hour . . . workers at the National Widget Company will walk off the job. Contract talks between the company and the United Brotherhood of Electrical Workers broke off earlier in the day, and union leaders called the strike.

This is a summary lead. It picks out the one dynamic aspect of the story and leads with that information. The remainder of the paragraph then goes on to explain the lead, as is typical of a summary broadcast news story. Additional information would then be conveyed in the story. An anchor might conclude the story with a statement that shows how the station will continue to cover the story as it unfolds and that full coverage of the strike will begin in the morning. If the story is important enough to the community, the station might resort to live coverage of the strike and ongoing information about how nonstriking workers affected by the strike should proceed.

The summary lead may reflect either a hard-news edge to the story, in which the details are quite specific, or it may take a softer approach. The softer approach is often used in broadcasting, where it is expected that listeners or viewers need time to get up to speed on the story. Here is an example:

> Officials are mulling their next step in the process to upgrade city services. That after voters today overwhelmingly rejected a proposed tax increase to add police and firefighters to the community.

This softer lead is meant to give the story a more immediate time frame and push it into a future position. It is often called a "setup" or "throwaway" lead because it doesn't contribute specifically to the facts of the story at hand. The fact that the tax increase was voted down is delayed to give the audience a newer perspective on the story and push back the hard facts.

Whether to use a hard lead or a soft lead depends on a variety of factors including how many times you have reported the story, the expected effects of the story and the probability that future stories will give rise to information on the issue. In general, the hard lead is the first choice, but experience with your audience also becomes a factor in writing leads later on.

Leads can be approached in many ways, but the hard and soft lead approaches are probably best for new or inexperienced writers. Nevertheless, several other leads deserve discussion.

Question Lead

The *question lead* can be constructed in such a way that it is quite compelling, but most new writers fail to understand that questions asked should not be questions with ready or silly answers. It is dangerous in the hands of many writers, yet most everyone seems to think they write them well. Here's a bad example:

> How would you rate your nail polish? Does it dry quickly? Does the color last?

Since few men wear nail polish, it is likely that half the audience just tuned out on this story. Other audience members might answer simply by replying "Who cares?" Someone also might ask if this is only a bad lead, or is it a bad story idea altogether? That may be the better question.

A better example of a question lead might go like this:

> Have you ever wished you could change something about your life?

The quick answer here might be "Who hasn't!" But it will get attention. The lead is very general, and realistically there are very few people who haven't wished that some aspect of their lives was different. That fact makes this a good setup for whatever the story is about, and the story could take a number of different directions.

Still, the question lead is fraught with problems. In general, avoid using this style.

Well-Known-Expression Lead

The *well-known-expression lead* uses everyday expressions to set up a story. Benjamin Franklin left a strong imprint on the nation's expressions. A few of his enduring expressions include:

"A penny saved is a penny earned."

"...nothing can be said to be certain except death and taxes."

"Remember that time is money."

"...for want of a nail the shoe was lost; for want of a shoe the horse was lost, for want of a horse the rider was lost."

Gertrude Stein provided a more recent source for familiar expressions.

"Rose is a rose is a rose is a rose."

"You are all a lost generation."

"What is the answer? . . . In that case, what is the question?"

Writers often take some license with these and other familiar expressions to develop a lead that is both interesting and somewhat timeless. The effect is to keep people listening. Here's an example:

> If a rose is a rose, then Jim Williams ought to know a bit about them. He is the newly crowned king of roses. His new rose variety won best of show at the Kansas State Fair today.

Familiar expressions can provide excellent leads; however, be careful, some familiar expressions are really clichés and need to be left out of your writing. Nevertheless, in general this is a form that most writers can use quickly and well.

Metaphor and Simile Leads

Metaphors and *similes* as leads focus on aspects of the language that allow the use of a word or phrase in a sentence to conjure up an image. Metaphors may offer a fresh approach to writing. They create imagery by using a word or phrase to figuratively represent something else. Consequently, the listener does not need much time to visualize the action. Metaphors often involve *personification* giving a person some nonhuman quality or giving some inanimate object human qualities. Like metaphors, similes substitute well-known actions for less understood actions to create the image. Similes are apparent by their use of *like* and *as* in the writing.

These leads are used often in both print and broadcast, but writers should be careful in their selection. Many have worn out their welcome and are now only cumbersome clichés. Here are some broadcasting examples.

Simile
> As surely as spring drives off the last of old man winter's frost, Uncle Sam will be after you with his outstretched hand. It's tax time once again.

Metaphor
Jones cowered wolfishly while the judge read the verdict.

Again, the word here is caution. Inexperienced writers often try to force this writing style. Some phrases to avoid include *head over heels, clean as a whistle, nick of time, smell a rat,* and *pearls of wisdom.* These have been much overused. Give them a rest today, and perhaps they can be dusted off and used again in mid-21st century.

These are just a few of the lead styles we use in broadcast writing. When in doubt, stick to the least difficult and most straightforward hard and soft lead styles.

Beyond the News Story: The Newscast

Television and radio newscasts are not randomly conceived, but require a great deal of knowledge by broadcast writers. For new writers, it is important to understand that all newscasts have a "flow." Regardless of how you feel the story you are writing to be, it will be placed in some order with several other news stories. The art of arranging these stories into a cohesive whole is the job of a newscast producer.

In radio, the producer for a regular newscast is frequently the announcer who has prepared the material for airing. Writing and announcing on radio generally go hand in hand. This makes sense. The writer understands his or her own cadence, pitch and delivery style. The newscast is made to flow around that style. Except at all-news radio stations, the newscast is usually brief, three to seven minutes without commercial time. The radio producer will arrange stories for flow and then usually break for a commercial, returning with sports, weather, traffic reports and any other incidental information that is specific to that station's format.

Television producers look at flow in much the same way as radio producers, but they are generally dealing with a greater diversity in individual reports, a longer newscast period and, most importantly, video.

The term *flow* is important to both radio and television producers. It refers to the act of arranging the aspects of a newscast into a cohesive whole that makes sense to viewers and listeners. It is both art and science.

Blocking

The most common method of producing a newscast is called *blocking.* In this fashion, the producer looks at the available stories and arranges them in blocks that fit together. One "block" might contain three crime stories and another block several government stories, both local and national.

Another way to block stories is to place them in categories. This is generally done with local, state, regional and national news stories relegated to individual groups (blocks) within a newscast. Nearly all newscasts, whether radio or television, will lead with the strongest local story before moving into a true blocking mode. This occasionally changes when a regional or national story—such as that of the September 11 tragedies—is so overwhelming that it needs to lead the newscast. The producers may decide to do a local angle on the story to ensure that a local story is included in the block, but that is not always possible. At any rate, the remainder of the newscast returns to the blocking method after the off-story is aired.

Counterblocking

An interesting outgrowth of producing techniques today has been the use of *counterblocking*. In this production method, a top hard-news story will often be followed by a soft-news story. This approach tends to spread hard news stories through the newscast and allows viewers a breather between strong and often visually emotional stories. It is based on audience research in the early 1990s that showed that viewers and listeners often were overburdened with information. If viewers get a break, it is thought they may keep watching the station and not get turned off by heavy graphics or serious news.

In counterblocking, only one or two of the hardest-hitting stories appear before the first set of commercials, and often a strong investigative story is held until the end of news block. This leads to some controversy, however, with reporters occasionally complaining that their stories have been "buried."

Mini-Casts

Another method of producing is a to parcel out the top stories across the top of each news segment. This, in effect, creates several mini-newscasts. As in counterblocking, this approach spreads the heaviest information around and gives the viewer or listener a break. Each segment of the news has a top story, and the lesser stories flow out of that mini-lead.

In some instances the mini-casts use the blocking technique of arranging stories along a local, state, regional, national format. The two forms then become nearly indistinguishable from one another.

Tim Bajkiewicz

WFLA-TV anchor/reporter Byron Brown writes on deadline.

Arranging Stories

Let's take a set of stories and show how they might be arranged differently in each broadcast producing form. Understand that if the story is for television and has video and an actuality or a radio actuality, it will become more important because it adds to story's ability to be told. We will assume that there are three time blocks (the periods between commercials) for news and that the newscast can also have a kicker. A *kicker* is a closing story for a newscast, generally with a light, humorous or "feel good" quality about it. This sample will be produced for an 11 p.m. television newscast.

Story List

A: Three gunmen rob local convenient market . . . *clerk* killed

B: Governor signs legislation that opens 22 new *parks* . . . cost $360 million

C: City police crack down on drunk drivers . . . 50 *roadblocks* planned

D: Mayor says city's *roads* are crumbling, money needed fast . . . $62 million

E: Outbreak of *measles* at local schools costing students and school districts

F: Medical Examiner says recent *suicide* was really a homicide . . . three people sought

G: 14 people hospitalized from bad *shrimp* at local restaurant

H: Federal government forces new standards for auto *emissions* . . . cost of cars will rise

I: Victim's rights group stages protest over state *parole* board policies

J: Three people indicted for fraud in *roof* repair scam against elderly

All of these stories have strong news components and, depending on your audience, might lead at least a news segment. Here are three ways those stories could be ordered in blocking, counterblocking, and mini-cast formats.

Blocking	Counterblocking	Mini-Cast
E (measles)	E (measles)	A (clerk)
G (shrimp)	G (shrimp)	F (suicide)
A (clerk)	B (parks)	C (roadblocks)
F (suicide)		J (roof scam)
C (roadblocks)	A (clerk)	
	F (suicide)	E (measles)
D (roads)	C (roadblocks)	G (shrimp)
J (roof scam)	D (roads)	I (parole)
I (parole)		
	I (parole)	B (parks)
B (parks)	J (roof scam)	D (roads)
H (emissions)	H (emissions)	H (emissions)

A Day in the Life of...

Robin Guess
Investigative Reporter
WFTS-TV, Tampa Bay

Investigative reporting is one of the most challenging and also one of the most rewarding aspects of journalism you can pursue.

My workdays as an investigative reporter at WFTS-TV in Tampa, a Top 15 market, are long. It is not unusual for me to put in 18 hours on any given day, and there are countless occasions when a story dictates working on weekends.

I also spend an inordinate amount of time in various government buildings digging through documents. And long hours sitting in undercover vans observing individuals and documenting their activities.

It is difficult, demanding work and my dream job.

No two days are alike for broadcast reporters.

The only daily routine I attempt to stick to is making a gargantuan effort to begin each day listening to and reading the staggering number of phone calls, e-mails and letters I get. So I devote a lot of my day to cultivating sources and reaching out to a wide variety of people.

Frankly, the majority of tips don't pan out for a variety of reasons. But every now and then, you get a terrific tip. To get to the terrific tips, however, you must sift through a lot of letters and e-mails or listen to a lot of drivel left on the tip line or on your office phone message recorder.

Also, I try to attend the daily editorial meetings and pass along stories for the pool of general assignment reporters to pursue. A lot of solid daily stories come to investigative reporters, but unless they are critical follow-up stories from our investigations, I pass those on.

After that, I get to the business of my stories. At any one time, I am juggling about a dozen or so investigative stories. Each of these stories is in a different stage of development. I prefer pursuing stories about political corruption and government waste. So naturally, a day rarely

Notice that the blocking newscast is typically the inverted pyramid with the most important stories running first. While it's true that closely related story topics are placed near one another, the newscast still tends to flow downward to the least important story.

In the counterblocking segments, each segment has a probable lead story. The second story is closely related, but stories following that lighten up significantly. The emphasis is not on keeping together stories that are closely related, but on spreading out information.

In the mini-cast, the emphasis changes dramatically by grouping the stories into categories. We could call the first segment the "crime" segment, the second segment the "disease" segment, and the last segment the "government" segment. But each segment has a strong lead story.

These newscast producing methods change from city to city and from station to station. Some stations use adaptations of the above methods. Other stations create their own production values. However, regardless of a station's production style, it is likely that the station will maintain a consistent approach across all its newscasts. This is an important aspect of understanding how broadcast news works. The decisions are not made in a vacuum; some method is utilized in producing every newscast.

---

passes when I have not written an FOIA (Freedom of Information Act) request or used a state's public records law to get government records.

These types of stories demand this research because there is almost always a paper trail—or better yet a money trail—to be followed. Once I request and receive the volumes of documents I ask for, I must read every word and study every line.

Everyday, I conduct interviews, interviews and more interviews. Many are on-the-record. But there are also many people who have and will share information, but they don't want to be on television. And then there are those who wish to remain anonymous and will tell you exactly where the body is buried, but you have to work out many details to protect their anonymity.

I work very closely with my photographer and producer. On average, I would guess, we shoot about a dozen videotapes 30 to 60 minutes in length to document our story. Every one of those tapes must be logged. Logging is one of the most tedious tasks we face, but it must be done (and, no, we don't have loggers who protect reporters from such chores).

Writing the story is one of the things I love most about my job. But the script process can be grueling. Once I complete it, my executive producer reads it and may suggest changes. Then the script must go to the assistant news director for approval. Next, the news director reads and approves the script, and he may ask for changes. When we are collectively satisfied with the script, it must then be blessed by our attorneys. Since I am an investigative reporter, all of my stories are read by the attorneys before they go to air. The attorneys' role is to point out possible problems or courses of action that may be taken if the subject of a story decides to sue.

General assignment reporters often complete basic stories within a day, but it may take weeks or months from inception to completion to get any one story of mine on the air. I get very little sleep and eat irregularly—and there is no job I could love more.   ■

Robin Guess' award-winning investigative report, "A Sweetheart Deal," can be found on the Investigative Reporters and Editors Web site.

Summary

Writing for broadcast differs in significant ways from writing for print, starting with the reality that broadcast writing depends on the spoken word, not the written word. As a result, for instance, broadcast writers find that contractions are much more common but abbreviations are to be avoided. Broadcasters also must be aware of the short amount of time available to present their message. This time constraint, together with the transient nature of the broadcast media, means most stories are simple and very tightly constructed.

The structure of newscasts has a major impact on how broadcast news is written, and *flow* is an important term to remember. The two most common techniques for structuring a newscast are blocking and counterblocking. Both terms refer to the placement of stories.

Key Points

▶ Broadcast style differs from print style.

▶ Broadcast writers have little time in which to present the news.

▶ Broadcast leads focus on immediacy.

▶ Keep it simple.

▶ Just "say" it.

▶ Be careful with numbers.

▶ Block or counterblock for newscasts.

Web Links

Here are a few interesting sites on the Internet where you can find out more information or see how broadcasters handle the news.

http://www.rtndf.org
http://web.missouri.edu/~jourvs/careerww.html
http://www.pbs.org/newshour/
http://www.ap.org/pages/history/broadcast.htm

InfoTrac College Edition Readings

For additional readings, go to www.infotrac-college.com, enter your password, and search for the following articles by title or author's name.

- ▶ "Writing the Words We Hear," Herb Brubaker, *Quill*, Jan. 2001 v89 i1 p55.

- ▶ "A Conversation With Fred Friendly," Fred Friendly, *Nieman Reports*, Winter 1999 v53 i4 p162.

- ▶ "Forget Walter Cronkite, Try Max Headroom: Venerable ABC News Veteran Sam Donaldson Is the Latest to Hear New Media's Call" (Company business and marketing), Kenneth Li, *Network World*, Oct. 4, 1999.

- ▶ "Pseudo-News Destroys Broadcast News Credibility" (Brief Article), Joe Saltzman. *USA Today* magazine, July 2001 v130 i2674 p75.

Exercises

Go to your CD-ROM to complete the following exercises:

- ▶ Exercise 9.1

- ▶ Exercise 9.2

This chapter is written by Ken Killebrew, assistant professor in telecommunications at the University of South Florida. Killebrew spent more than a decade in broadcast news in Illinois, winning four awards for reporting including two for investigative reporting. He now actively produces research and teaching materials for converged media environments, the next wave of journalism.

Writing for the Web

The manager seems impressed as the interview session comes to a close. You've presented yourself well, and your portfolio of traditional media work is solid—you know you certainly spent time in building those skills in college.

Then the manager says: "Listen, you definitely have the skills to work here, but there is a slight problem—we aren't going to have anything open in your area for at least six months."

You feel the sigh rising from your chest.

"But," the manager adds after a long pause, "we do have an opening right now for someone to write on our Web page. I didn't see any work in your portfolio for the Web. Do you think you can handle this position? Are you familiar with HTML? Can you get all the linking done for us?"

Think. Think. You covered this topic in your introductory media writing class, but you're foggy about that now, since it didn't really seem all that important. What did your professor tell you about writing for the Web? *Linking,* what does she mean by that? And what does *HTML* mean? "*Hey, Tomorrow, Maybe Later?*" "*Have Tuna, Make Lunch*"?

206

A few minutes later, as you walk out the door, still jobless, you sure wish you could find some alternate universe where you had paid more attention to the workbook assignments in that intro class.

Good Journalism Is Still Good Journalism

With the advent of a new medium like the Internet, it certainly seemed reasonable a few years ago for media writers and editors to assume that a brand-new, fresh writing style might develop that catered to the millions who get their news and information from this new technology. But what writers who work in new media have found is that while writing for the Internet can make special demands, especially in terms of reporting skills, it also relies heavily on the same fundamentals of good writing that you've seen throughout this text. You can see this for yourself by performing a simple Web search through a search engine such as Google. Look for writing advice for Web writers, and you'll see site after site offering advice on how to best communicate in this new medium. The advice looks something like this:

- ▶ Write concisely.

- ▶ Abandon fluff and overblown adjectives.

- ▶ Expect readers to scan your material.

- ▶ Get the important part into the story first because readers are unlikely to scroll through a long story to get to the ending.

- ▶ Use headlines, subheads and lists.

In other words, write like a journalist. Employ the inverted pyramid format. Avoid repetition. Write with clarity.

Much of the advice you'll find is aimed at a large Web constituency: businesses. The business world has become encumbered with a dense, jargon-laden form of communication that does very little actual communicating, but makes the writer seem very intelligent. That is, if you measure intelligence by the number of syllables and unfamiliar words that can be crammed into a business report.

We argue that this form of communication doesn't work well in any business situation, but especially not on the Web. It seeks to impress rather than express.

Reading on the Web

It certainly seems clear that nonfiction Internet writing relies on the basics of good journalism. This becomes even clearer when you exam-

Use the Web's Strengths in Stories

University of South Florida professor Marie Curkan-Flanagan advised a Top 100 station in the North to incorporate the Web into its stories rather than using it only in between-stories promotions. When a reporter held up an affidavit in the middle of a story and told viewers they could read it themselves on the station's Web site, the site's hits jumped from the usual 5,000 to 16,000.

▶ *Use interviews:* If your organization is going to run a long series, why not interview the reporter about what he or she learned? You might find an increase of Web site hits.

Or why not include an audiotape or video-tape of the actual interview?

▶ *Use the computer:* Instead of creating a static map, Web designers often take advantage of the computer's mouse to create an interactive map that brings content up when the mouse crosses certain locations on the map.

▶ *Use blogs:* The *blog,* or *Web log,* is an idiosyncratic journal that can be compiled by anyone—perhaps you've already read several yourself. Some journalists are learning that the blog is a way to increase their audience by creating links to their work while expounding on any number of topics—some of which do not fit the traditional definition of newsworthiness. ∎

ine the results of Web readership studies. Two of the leading researchers in Web readership, Jakob Nielsen and John Morkes, have found that Web readers are less dedicated than readers of other media and thus are more likely to abandon a page.

This finding isn't that surprising when you consider actual media usage. When most readers pick up a daily newspaper, they turn immediately to their favorite sections. Some may scan the front page, but others will turn immediately to international news or sports news or the comics. Many readers never turn to some sections of the paper at all, or only read through them on occasion.

Similarly, most magazine readers buy a particular magazine that caters to their interests, and once they have established their favorites, they don't often change.

Even in television, while many viewers have the ability to explore dozens or hundreds of cable or satellite channels, they usually tune in to a favorite program and have just a few favorite channels.

In short, Internet users, like any media consumers, return most often to familiar Web pages, where they browse quickly to find information. If they can't find the information they want there, then they'll go to another Web page.

Because of these habits, Nielsen and Morkes offer the following important advice to media writers writing for the Internet:

- ▶ Web pages should employ *scannable text*—text that is easy to browse.

- ▶ Web pages should use highlighted *keywords,* with hypertext links serving as one form of highlighting and typeface variations and color as another.

- ▶ Web pages should use meaningful *subheadings* (not "clever" ones).

- ▶ Web pages should use *bulleted lists.*

- ▶ Web pages should have *one idea* per paragraph (users will skip over any additional ideas if they are not caught by the first few words in the paragraph).

- ▶ Web pages should use the inverted pyramid structure.

- ▶ Web pages should have *half the word count* (or less) of stories found in more conventional print forms.

Nielsen and Morkes also found that credibility is important for Web users, since it is often unclear who is behind information on the Web and whether a page can be trusted. Credibility can be increased by high-quality graphics, good writing, and use of outbound hypertext links. (Nielsen, "How Users Read on the Web," Alertbox, Oct. 1, 1997, www.useit.com/alertbox/9710a.html).

Finally, say Nielsen and Morkes, Web readers are not impressed by "marketese," the phony sales language that promises this product is the neatest, keenest and swellest to ever be foisted on the public. Marketese virtually never works with great effect in any form of persuasive writing from editorials to advertising to public relations—and Nielsen and Morkes found readers actively avoided any Web site that smacked of it and ranked sites that used it very low in credibility.

Media Convergence

For years, newspaper and television journalists considered each other with suspicion and disdain. Indeed in some journalistic circles, newspaper types were known as ink-stained wretches, pathetically out of date and miserable, while television types were called "talking dogs," because the moment Fido could read a teleprompter, they were all out of work. Then add to the mix, the Webheads, those Internet specialists of the 1990s, and you had a new gang on the newsroom turf.

Occasionally, one side would drift into the other's territory, particularly with newspaper columnists pontificating on those political argument roundtables, but generally there was a real, if invisible, barrier.

But a recent trend in journalism has changed the scene within a few newsrooms in the last few years, and may well soon affect numerous others. This trend is known as *convergence* and can be defined as a news operation that brings together the elements of print, broadcast and Internet journalism. And, while it is still in the experimental stages, convergence has the potential to become an accepted standard throughout journalism.

First, the Federal Communication Commission is expected to further relax rules that used to prevent one owner from running a television station and a newspaper within the same market. This will allow more news companies to attempt a converged newsroom.

Second, the converged newsroom is a response to what many expect will be the future of mass communication, a linking of television and the Internet. By joining forces with these two media, newspaper companies are able to expand a shrinking audience. Television, on the other hand, benefits from a large newspaper staff (many big-market stations function with about 10 reporters) to get to more stories as well as access to an electronic library far beyond the typical news operation.

The Growth of Convergence

One of the oldest convergence efforts began at the *Sarasota Herald-Tribune* in 1995 when *The New York Times*-owned newspaper launched SNN (Six News Now), a local, 24-hour, cable news production that featured a repeated 30-minute newscast. It was the first disk-based cable news channel and the first to be completely integrated within its partner–owner news station.

The SNN and *Herald-Tribune* staffs frequently collaborate on stories, and *Herald-Tribune* reporters often appear as on-air reporters.

More recently, SNN and the *Herald-Tribune* have joined with the Internet site Newscoast.com to provide an Internet presence as well. Other newspapers have approached convergence by creating partnerships with existing television stations. Among them are the *Denver Post* and KUSA-TV; *The Virginian-Pilot* and WVEC-TV; the *Winston-Salem Journal* and WGHP-TV; and the *Bay Insider* and KTVU-TV in San Francisco.

Denver Post multimedia editor Howard Saltz has watched convergence grow since the mid-1990s.

"The partnership [between the *Post* and KUSA-TV] has existed for many years and predates what has come to be known as convergence," he says. "Originally our reporters would appear on newscasts as experts in the areas they cover.

"It was originally cross-promotional, but now it is seen as having value to journalists in both organizations and as the stepping stone to where we'll be in a couple of years from now. Promotion is not nearly as important anymore."

The partnership has thrived even though the *Post* and KUSA-TV have different corporate ownership.

"We are partnered with the No. 1 station in town, and because of that, it doesn't need us as badly as the No. 3 or No. 5 stations might," Saltz explains. "The advantage is that when we do something on air, it's seen by a lot more people."

Convergence Partnerships

Convergence partnerships may include a strong Internet presence beyond those links leading to the station or newspaper home page. Some of these are the Web site AZ Central, *The Arizona Republic* and KPNX-TV; and MySanAntonio.com, the *San Antonio Express-News*, KENS-TV and WVEC-TV.

The *Orlando Sentinel* goes yet a step further. Reporters there may, within any day, file stories for the newspaper, for television (Central Florida News 13), online and for one of six local radio stations. The Tribune Company owns all of the media outlets, and *Sentinel* reporters may find themselves on any of them on a given day.

Perhaps the most ambitious experiment in convergence is taking place at the Newscenter, where *The Tampa Tribune*, WFLA-TV and Tampa Bay Online—all owned by the Media General chain—share a large newsroom that opened in 2000. The television and Internet offices are found on the second floor above the studios while the newspaper reporters and editors work on the third floor. But a spacious atrium, shown on page 215, serves to emphasize the convergence rather than the separation of departments.

Even at the Newscenter, though, executives are still adjusting to a new way of telling the news. "The state of convergence at the Newscenter is in constant flux and our definition changes almost daily," says copy editor Deb Halpern. "When we first started this process several years ago, we considered it a huge breakthrough when we began sharing story ideas. Now, the flow of story information is a part of our daily routine."

Impact on Journalists

"Convergence is a lot harder than it looks. When we originally started down this path, we told ourselves and our co-workers that convergence wouldn't mean more work; it would just mean working smarter. Wrong! Convergence is more work, but if you got into the business of journalism to tell stories, convergence should let you tell them better and to more people. That's why we have so many journalists on staff who are willing to put in the extra hours and extra effort to make convergence work," Halpern says.

Halpern and others at the Newscenter have found that convergence has forced them to consider different alternatives to finding the news.

"Our latest effort is to explore and exploit points of intersection among the print, TV and online partners. We define *points of intersection* as those content areas that matter most to our customers. For example, research shows us medical reporting is of strong interest for customers across all three media platforms. We have recently started targeting medical stories as a place to converge. We look for ways to expand the reach and depth of our medical stories with online, print and broadcast components that we hope will complement each other."

In converged newsrooms, reporters may be asked to tell stories in each of the three media. The added responsibility translates into more deadlines to meet and more skills to develop.

Television reporters may be asked to compose weekly columns on subjects they cover as beats, such as consumer reporting.

But television reporters write every day. Newspaper reporters, on the other hand, face the task of learning how to appear on camera and use broadcast reporting techniques to tell stories. The idea of having to appear live on the air is fear-inducing for some reporters, but not for as many as you might suspect.

"Actually the reporters are probably much more comfortable as a group with the arrangement than the editors are," the *Post*'s Saltz explains. "It could be explained by the age factor—reporters tend to be younger than the editors—or by the time factor where editors are responsible for the time that reporters allocate to various things."

Still, some reporters say convergence complements their print stories and they like the opportunity to use an on-air appearance to hook viewers into reading tomorrow's story.

Criticism of Convergence

Convergence critics worry that the blending of media eliminates the number of voices telling the news. Some newspaper reporters worry that the print newsroom will discard those not photogenic enough for television standards. Some television reporters worry that their work will be judged on strictly print-based standards rather than on their ability to weave words with pictures.

Both sides worry about the question of pay. If newspaper reporters are doing the work of television reporters, shouldn't they receive equal compensation? (In some markets, the pay differential is not huge and beginning newspaper reporters often make considerably more than beginning producers and reporters.) And what about those high-priced anchors?

But the synergy of convergence can also change newsroom cultures in positive ways.

At the *Orlando Sentinel*, the newsroom now features "The Bridge," an elevated command desk where editors from various departments work near one another and discuss upcoming stories. News meetings have changed from closed-door, management-only affairs to open meetings at the bridge.

You can read more about this elsewhere in this book, including the "A Day in the Life" feature on CNN.com feature writer Jamie Allen in this chapter and in Appendix C in the back of the book. For now, it's enough to remember that Internet writers have the powerful ability to link their stories with other sites on the Web. This means that Web writers need to always consider how and when to link to those other sites. For example, if an online story refers to a particular column by *The Boston Globe*'s Ellen Goodman, the journalist can link directly to *The Globe* site or directly to the very column mentioned. (This will depend on your source's archiving practices—that is, does the other Web site maintain a copy of the column?) Similarly, an online story about a merger with another company can easily include a link to that company's Web site and financial information. For a great example of how this linking can be done, see the stories by *Detroit Free Press* columnist Mike Wendland, in "Writer at Work: Media Samples," in this chapter.

Do It Yourself

The Internet also enables any person with access to a computer and Web-page software to become his or her own publisher. This is one of the greatest strengths of the World Wide Web and also one of its major weaknesses. It used to be said that freedom of the press truly existed for only those who owned the press, but the Internet makes cyberspace available to anyone with access to a computer and a modem. For those who find the mainstream media unable or unwilling to cover a particular story or a particular viewpoint, the Internet provides an alternative medium in which to see the news. A range of Web sites can be found for readers of almost any political persuasion, for example. For those who feel disenfranchised by the mainstream media, the Internet offers a place where their views are taken seriously.

It's important for you to remember, though, that this ease of publication means that much of what you find on the Internet is untrustworthy, since it may not have been professionally reported, written, or edited. Since anyone can publish almost anything on the Internet, the wary Web writer knows better than to trust what he or she finds unless either the site where it is found is trustworthy or, better still, the information can be verified somewhere else that is trustworthy. You can read more about this in Chapter 5 on research skills for media writers. You should know, too, that some critics worry about the Internet's effect on its audience, especially in a democratic society. Because it allows for such easy access, the Internet also allows for further fragmentation of the audience, making it more difficult to reach people with the shared information so necessary to keeping a democratic society functioning.

Inside a Newspaper Web Site

Not all newspaper Web sites are created equal. Some, like Nando-times.com or the *San Jose Mercury News* site, are quite ambitious with a staff of several reporters who work for the online service.

More typical is the Web site operation at *The Virginian-Pilot* in Norfolk. Web journalist Chris Brownlow is one of the editors who puts out the Web edition daily. Brownlow says most of her colleagues are much more like copy editors and page designers than news reporters.

"Staff reporters pretty much do most of the reporting for us. We do occasionally write stories, but we also do some shovel work," Brownlow said. *Shovel work* refers to the act of taking a newspaper story and putting it onto the Web page. At its most basic, some Web sites simply take all elements of the newspaper story—headline, cutline, photos—and just paste them onto a Web page.

The Virginian-Pilot, like many, does make some changes before the product goes online.

"What we will spend most of our writing time doing is composing different headlines and nut graphs," Brownlow says. "Because of the nature of Web pages, we have to do more teasing of stories, and the headlines and nut graphs that we produce have to be more compelling because there isn't a big block of type directly underneath them. Ours have to lead the reader to click to the story."

And those headlines aren't as static as traditional newspaper headlines. Breaking news means that the Web staff has to adjust on the fly.

"In the event of a major news event, such as the [Sept. 11, 2001] terrorist attacks on America, we were constantly working to update our pages to try and have information that you couldn't get on television," Brownlow said. "That meant lots of changes almost minute by minute during the heaviest part of the story."

Allyn DiVito, *The Tampa Tribune.*

An atrium symbolizes the cooperation among media at the Newscenter in Tampa. The WFLA-TV and TBO.com newsrooms are downstairs from The Tampa Tribune *newsroom.*

Adapting to the New Technology

The Virginian-Pilot keeps one full-time reporter in the Web department.

"Our department does have someone whose main responsibility is to write, and she came to us with a newspaper background," Brownlow says. "She says the main thing you have to adapt to is 'getting past the technology.' " For online journalists that means adapting to a world where deadline pressure is constant.

"When she is dealing with her sources, they don't understand that you are not still playing by the traditional 5 p.m. newspaper deadline," Brownlow says. "As soon as we get a story done, it goes on the Web page."

The Web journalist does need some writing ability, however. Brownlow says Web journalists at *The Virginian-Pilot* will write and construct packages that are designed to last beyond the news cycle. Her work in the entertainment department, for example, led her to create a series of Web stories on historical landmarks in Virginia.

"First, you have to do your research on the landmarks, gather information and write, but you are also creating interactivity with everything you do," Brownlow says.

"You put together an interactive map that gives you information about a specific landmark when you roll a mouse over it. You look for ways to use audio and video.

"I also worked on putting together talknets, online interview sessions with, say, the person at one landmark who portrays Thomas Jefferson and has become knowledgeable about him. That's the sort of thing you can't get through the newspaper."

Writing Code and Other Pieces of Cake

Not long ago, novice Web journalists would have had to learn basic HTML (*h*ypertext *m*arkup *l*anguage) in order to build a rudimentary Web page. Those days are gone. Learning HTML is still a fine idea, much like eating all of your vegetables, but it's not the necessity it was as little as four years ago.

"We're not HTML programmers," Brownlow says of her colleagues at *The Virginian-Pilot.* "But we do know enough to put together the elements on our Web page. We use a software package that does some of this, but it would be a good idea to learn some basic HTML." Fortunately, a quick search on any search engine can lead you to plenty of pages devoted to learning basic HTML.

It's more likely that Web journalists either buy an HTML editing package or download an HTML editor directly from Internet sites for free. There are numerous packages out there, and many of them are designed for beginners. Few of them require users to write HTML code; instead they have pull-down menus that enable editors to build buttons onto pages or choose a wide variety of JavaScript libraries. (JavaScript is a programming language that allows Web page designers to do such things as automatically change a formatted date on a Web page, or cause a linked-to page to appear in a pop-up window, or cause text or a graphic image to change during a mouse rollover.)

As a result of these new software packages, most Web journalists can worry less about HTML code and much more about constructing good Web pages. Some basic problems that can be avoided easily are:

- ▶ *Orphan pages.* Every page should include a back button or a way to get to some other page.

- ▶ *Lack of archives.* Especially in Web journalism, there should be a way to get to older information.

- ▶ *Poorly constructed headlines.* As opposed to traditional news headlines, Web headlines must be clear and precise. Newspaper sites often use the same headline that appears in print, but these can be confusing when taken out of context.

- ▶ *Looping animation.* This effect can really slow down a Web page and send users away with a scream.

- ▶ *Broken links.* Fixing broken links is the scut work for Web journalists, but readers become frustrated when a link doesn't lead anywhere. This tends to reflect poorly on the Web designer, who should provide better site maintenance.

Current Limits and the Wide-Open Future

Jakob Nielsen says the World Wide Web is still too slow for high-end and low-end computer users alike. He thinks that by 2003, bandwidth will be expanded enough to meet high-end users' needs and that low-end users will be cruising by 2008. And, he says, we certainly expect that at some point in the future the Web will become much more video-friendly.

We expect that the Web will continue to evolve, and Web journalism will evolve along with it. It is not unreasonable to expect, for example, that Web journalists of the future will be required to write a brief version of a story as well as a longer version of the story, with links embedded in the copy to an electronic library as well as to other Web pages. In addition, the Web journalist may well make available a tape recording of the entire interview for those readers curious enough to seek that.

It is unlikely that traditional print media will be able to incorporate these links in a paper product. A 2000 experiment by *The Dallas Morning News* with Cuecat, a device designed to read embedded links on newsprint, failed miserably. Readers did not want to take a device and run it over a bar code for linklike information. But readers are trained to follow links while reading Web pages.

Web journalists of the future may well become the equivalent of a one-person television news crew. Those journalists will be able to gather sound and video information to accompany or drive a written story.

The traditional boundaries of mass media may very well vanish into cyberspace as we go farther into the 21st century. It may become the responsibility and necessity of future Web journalists as well as future journalism professors and students to think and prepare beyond the boxes of print, video and sound. The ones who are able to do that, unlike the unfortunate young media writer whose story opened this chapter, will help define the future of media communication.

Writers at Work: Media Samples

Rocky the Squirrel

Editor's Note: *When it comes to engaging readers or viewers, it's tough to beat a good animal story. Few papers have developed a finer appreciation of such stories over the years than the* Detroit Free Press. *The paper's technology columnist, Mike Wendland, who is also a Fellow at Poynter, added a new dimension to the genre with a video sidebar to a column about a pesky squirrel. "In more than 25 years of journalism experience in print, broadcast and the Net,"* Mike says, *"I have never received such an immediate, warm, supportive response from the public."* [From Poynter.org:]

By Mike Wendland
Poynter Fellow

The column was meant to be fun—a look at the frustration I experienced in trying to use technology to thwart a persistent little Pine Squirrel I call Rocky, who has bested every attempt I've made over the past couple of years to keep him out of my bird feeder. [See "Squirrel Tops Contraption in Nutty Duel Over Bird Feeder," below.]

But in describing for print Rocky's hilarious and never-say-die antics as he beat the latest high-tech bird feeder I installed, I really wanted more than just words and a still picture to tell the story.

So I shot some video on a home digital camcorder and then used the iMovie editing software on a new G4 733Mhx PowerMac I was testing to produce a two-minute video I call "Persistence."

I had to post the video on my own Web site, www.pcmike.com, because the Freep's ["Freep" is the nickname for the *Free Press*] Web site, for a bunch of technical and policy reasons, wasn't able to accommodate the files I needed to upload to their server.

No problem, I thought.

I had no idea how huge a hit the video would be. In the first 24 hours, some 10,000 people tried to access the video, first posted in the RealVideo format. I normally buy about 8 gigs of bandwidth a month, plenty to handle the 3,500 daily visitors my site gets. But the extra demands of the streaming video and the massive interest soon exhausted that, and the site went down until I contacted the hosting company and shelled out another $80 for more bandwidth.

But after lots of reader feedback asking me why the video wasn't in Apple's proprietary QuickTime streaming format, I found a free service Apple offers that allows its customers to store streaming video on an Apple server. It took me ten minutes to transfer the video over.

You can see the QuickTime version of the video by clicking here.

I'd send you to look at the Real version on my site, but I can't afford the extra hits. But trust me, there is no comparison to the quality. QuickTime is faster, cleaner and plays back in a larger box than RealVideo. And setting up the page on Apple's servers was a breeze. As was editing the piece in iMovie.

I really like the way using the Net and video to enhance a print story completes the reporting process. So did the readers, who went to the Net to watch the video, and then e-mailed me their reaction. In turn, I posted e-mail summaries on my online e-journal, even including pictures of some of the weird contraptions people suggested I use on Rocky. Before becoming the technology columnist at the Freep, I spent most of my news career as an investigative reporter. My stories have sent people to jail, sparked governmental reforms and exposed corruption and wrongdoing. But in more than 25 years of journalism experience in print, broadcast and the Net, I have never received such an immediate, warm, supportive response from the public.

Besides the 10,000 Web site video visits, I have received more than 300 e-mails from people all across the country and even England and Australia. Many said they forwarded the column and video link to friends. And several dozen urged me to keep making Web videos available to accompany my columns.

I really like that idea. Think of Web videos as sidebars. They're a terrific way to add more depth to our journalism, drive traffic to our Web sites and then back to the newspapers. And, most importantly, the whole process creates a strong bond to the reader as it develops a sense of converged community.

I owe this newfound appreciation for multimedia to Rocky who, last I saw him this morning, was clinging to the feeder contentedly munching away, oblivious to his new-found celebrity.

I just hope he doesn't invite his relatives over to dinner.

From Poynter.org, Aug. 15, 2001,
Reprinted by permission.

Squirrel Tops Contraption in Nutty Duel Over Bird Feeder

By Mike Wendland

This technology is for the birds.

But I know a squirrel that figured a way around it.

In fact, this never-say-die little pine squirrel who has brilliantly thwarted every attempt I've made at keeping him out of my bird feeder for the past couple of years, took all of three days to beat the Yankee Flipper (www.yankeeflipper.com), a high-tech bird-seed dispenser advertised as "squirrel proof."

What it does is toss the squirrels off the feeder by twirling them around and around. A motor-driven, weight-sensitive perch ring at the bottom of the feeder activates when anything over feather weight lands on it.

"Brilliant, Innovative, Frustratingly Funny, Wickedly Clever," reads the

(continued)

(continued)

manufacturer's hype.

It's expensive. Just over $100. But I was desperate.

I've been waging war with this 6-inch-long demon for three years.

First, I mounted the bird feeder on a pole that stretched way over my back deck. Rocky can jump 10 feet. That was easy for him.

Then I installed one of those squirrel-guard contraptions between the pole and the feeder. It was child's play for Rocky, who hung upside down from the guard to dine.

There was another feeder that had a metal grate that shut when anything heavier than a bird landed on the perch. Rocky bent the guard back far enough that he could reach in to get at the seed.

Last year, I really thought I had him. I bought a feeder that delivered a small electrical charge from a 9-volt battery whenever a squirrel touched the metal feeder post and a perch area.

But Rocky never gives up. Patiently, persistently, over several months, he actually chewed his way through the thick green plastic covering at the top of the feeder. Then, he just dropped into the feeder itself to lie atop the seeds and eat to his contentment.

The Yankee Flipper was my last hope. I set up a video camera to record the happenings. Since I'm testing out an Apple G4 with movie editing capabilities, I edited it into a movie you can watch yourself online, at www.pcmike.com.

Rocky did not take kindly to the Yankee Flipper. For three days, over and over, he was twirled around and flipped off. He jumped on it. He gingerly tried to grab it. He hung upside down and tried to approach it from the top.

But every time his little squirrel feet hit that perch ring, the motor would activate and start spinning him.

The video shows it all.

But Rocky is persistent.

He beat it.

He somehow figured out how to squeeze his body between the perch ring and the feeder, supporting most of his weight by clinging to parts of the feeder not connected to the weight-activated mechanism.

So much for technology. As you read this, Rocky is no doubt gorging himself on gourmet black oiler sunflower seeds meant for the birds.

The one satisfaction I have is at the rate this squirrel is eating, he's going to get too fat to fit through the ring and activate the motor again.

I'm still hoping for technology to win the war.

From the *Detroit Free Press*, Aug. 14, 2001. Reprinted by permission.

RELATED STORIES, SITES
In this story:
A 9-foot-tall bad guy
"Blew me away"

Actor Brings Hubbard's *Battlefield Earth* to the Big Screen

By Jamie Allen
Senior Writer

ATLANTA (CNN)—Much has been written about John Travolta's involvement in Scientology, the spiritual and philosophical organization founded by sci-fi author L. Ron Hubbard.

But Travolta was first introduced to Hubbard by a book, not his teachings, when he read the author's 1982 fiction bestseller *Battlefield Earth*. Like the book's 6 million other readers, Travolta says, he loved the story of how humanity, led by hero Jonnie Goodboy Tyler, overcomes an alien race that has enslaved them and the planet at the turn of the year 3000.

Unlike other readers, Travolta was, you know, *John Travolta,* someone who could actually turn it into a movie.

But even for the man who was the disco king of the '70s, the where-is-he-now poster child of the '80s and the silver-screen comeback of the '90s, it took until the year 2000 for him to produce Hubbard's vision at the multiplex.

A 9-foot-tall bad guy

"I could never get a script right," Travolta says in a recent visit here to promote the film. "Cut to years later and I have this comeback, and I'm too old to play Jonnie, and it's time to play the villain."

Along with his producing duties, Travolta portrays Terl, a 9-foot-tall alien and chief of security for Earth. Terl, Travolta says, is a "comic villain" who is bent on a blind revenge against just about everyone he encounters when he finds out that his promotion off Earth has been denied.

"My character is always blackmailing, leveraging, taking advantage of others," he says.

Battlefield Earth is based on the first half of Hubbard's novel. It's the kind of special-effects, eardrum-blowing bonanza that has come to characterize summer fare. The Warner Bros. release doesn't hit theaters until Friday, and already there's talk of a sequel using the second half of the book.

It was directed by Roger Christian, who came recommended to Travolta by George Lucas. Christian worked with Lucas on the original *Star Wars* as a set decorator, and on *Star Wars: Episode I—The Phantom Menace* as a second unit director.

"Blew me away"

When he saw the finished product, Travolta says, "it blew me away. We hit every note the reader loved, almost by survey."

So, are there any Scientology references in the movie?

Travolta, traditionally reluctant to discuss his Scientology beliefs, shrugs off the question. But he points to a theme that is prevalent throughout the action-adventure, and it sounds like one of Hubbard's guiding principles.

"Jonnie's tribe (is) led to believe that every star in the sky is kind of a god or something," Travolta says. "And Jonnie is saying, 'Look, that may not be the case here. We may have to do something ourselves to fix this situation, because right now nothing's helping us.' That was one of the middle themes, you know."

The release of the film comes at a busy time for Travolta. Though the project has been his "baby" for 18 years, his wife, actress Kelly Preston, last month gave birth to Ella Bleu, the couple's second child and first daughter.

"We're a pretty happy household right now," he says.

Battlefield Earth *is a production of CNN Interactive sister company Warner Bros., a Time Warner property.*

CNN.com, May 11, 2000.
Reprinted by permission.

A Day in the Life of...

Feature Writer
Jamie Allen
CNN.com

If you look in the journalism want ads, under "Reporter," you'll often see in the job description "must be flexible." They don't mean that you should practice yoga, though it might help relieve tension. Instead, a flexible mind and schedule is required.

If you're a reporter, your job is different every day. Some days, you'll be on the run from morning till night. Others, you'll spend eight bleary-eyed hours in front of your computer, waiting for five people to return your calls while trying to meet a deadline. Still other days, you'll mix writing and planning.

Good reporters crave new challenges and variations in schedule. It keeps the job fresh and exciting.

That said, on this day—a cloudy, breezy Tuesday—I arrive to work at CNN Center in Atlanta a little after 9 a.m., purchase a large coffee (a rare but necessary constant in my day) from the Dunkin' Donuts in the building. This will be one of those writing and planning days.

My desk is on the tenth floor in a room of dozens of other desks. The term *prairie-dogging* might have been invented here. The room is long, wide, flat, like a prairie, with computers lining row after row of desks. When something big happens—when news breaks or someone tells a funny joke—workers pop up from behind their computers, resembling prairie dogs coming out of their holes. Right now, they are sitting quietly, shying away from the fluorescent lights shining down.

I sit at my work station, make a mental note to organize my desk; it's cluttered with press releases, books, and payola sent by publicists. I will burn the payola in a ritualistic ceremony at a later date. I check voice mail while logging on to my computer. I have a couple of messages waiting from publicists who are hounding me about stories that I don't really want to cover. Soon, they will reach me on the phone, and I'll be forced to tell them the truth: "My editor says I can't do it, though I really think it's a great story."

I check e-mail. I have one from a publicist for The Glands, a band I've been wanting to interview. They're from Athens, Ga., following in the footsteps of so many other groups from that college town. But they have an original sound, they're getting strong reviews and they're starting a new tour next week.

I e-mail the publicist, asking for an interview on Thursday, two days from now. I want to drive to Athens to meet the lead singer-songwriter in person, and I suggest to the publicist that we meet at his favorite hangout. I want a nice backdrop to this feature piece. Also, anytime I can get out of the building, rather than talk to a subject on the phone, I do it. I mean, there are only so many ways you can write in an article, ". . . he said over the phone."

I log on to CNN.com and read through the top stories. I turn on the TV sitting next to my desk, tuning it to CNN. As a reporter, you must be a news junkie. It's all around you and you can't help but consume it morning and night. Even though I write about entertainment and books, I follow closely the daily news events, from international news to local politics. You never know when they're going to merge with what you're doing.

Also, while watching the news, it's healthy to join my co-workers in a round-robin session of making fun of our television anchors. We can make fun of them because we are not on camera, and thus are safe from people like us.

My editors for the "Books" and "Entertainment" sections hand me their daily rundowns that list the stories for today. Good news. I have two stories that have already been posted on the site—one on "Doonesbury" cartoonist Garry Trudeau and a review of a book that I didn't particularly like.

It's a good feeling to have work published, no matter how often it happens. I read through

Summary

Media writers certainly need to understand the special reporting and writing needs for writing for the Internet. But they also need to know that good journalism is still good journalism, and the basics taught by classroom instructors and found in this text remain valuable tools for Web writers.

The convergence of broadcast and print media is beginning now in several places around the country, and the trend will certainly expand. While traditional media will continue to prosper, knowing how to meet the needs of a converged newsroom will be useful for future media writers.

the stories to make sure they are free from the journalistic menace known as "typos." No, that's not true. I read through the stories to relive my favorite parts. Although most reporters won't admit it in print, writers like to read what they've written, over and over and over.

Another good feeling—I have a story that I completed yesterday that will be posted sometime this week. I am ahead of the game. I check my list of upcoming stories and ideas that I keep on my computer. It ranges in length from 10 to 20 items at any given time. I have several coming up that need attention—interviews planned, etc.

By mid-morning, I'm transcribing an interview I did with James Atlas, the author of a new biography on [the novelist] Saul Bellow. I spoke with him on the phone a few days earlier. My deadline for the story is Friday. Since I have a few days, I'll print out the quotes, read them, highlight the good ones to get an idea of where I want the story to go and what kind of original angle I can take.

I'll start writing it by the end of the day. I don't plan to finish it today, but I like to get ideas down while they're fresh. I'll also take the book home tonight and choose the parts I want to highlight in the article.

Lunchtime arrives. I head down to CNN Center's atrium, which features a plethora of fast-food restaurants and tourists. It's good to get away from the computer. Along with lunch, I try to take walks at least a couple of times to stretch my limbs and rest my eyes. I buy an unhealthy lunch and take it back to my desk. While eating, I read through my favorite sites, including our own and the sites of competitors. It's always good to see what the competition is doing. Something might spark a story idea, and nothing gets you motivated like the sight of another media outlet doing a story that you were meaning to do, but hadn't gotten around to yet.

Today, the sites have nothing interesting. In fact, one site is featuring—perhaps in reaction to my article?—an archived article on Garry Trudeau. We rule.

Someone tells a joke a few computers over. Prairie-dogging ensues.

Throughout the day, I'm fed a steady stream of story possibilities. Publicists send e-mails for upcoming movie screenings. I mark them on my schedule. A publicist calls and says a big celebrity is coming in town to promote his film. Would I like to interview him? Sure, I say. I mark it on my schedule.

I spend the last portion of my day working on the Saul Bellow story. This is my favorite part of the job, writing. It's why I became a reporter. To the outsider, it looks awfully boring. For the purpose of this article describing my day, I sit in front of my computer for two hours before realizing it is past time to go home.

I make a mental note to clean off my desk tomorrow; I grab my book on Bellow and my Glands CD. I will listen to the CD several times in the next two days leading to the interview. It helps to be prepared, because, as they say here in Atlanta, Ga., tomorrow is another day. ∎

Key Points

▶ The basics skills for good reporting and writing remain important to Internet media writers.

▶ Learning HTML skills probably isn't necessary for most media writers.

▶ Tight, concise writing is important.

▶ Web writers need to be able to pull together elements of a story from broadcast and print sources.

▶ Web writers need to be able to link to other sites throughout a story.

Web Links

Here are a few interesting sites on the Internet where you can find out more about writing for the Web.

http://search.yahoo.com/bin/search?p=writing+for+the+web
www.msnbc.com/news/op_/front.asp?0dm=Ø10TØ [See the Web logs, especially Eric Alterman's exemplary "Alteration."]

InfoTrac College Edition Readings

For additional readings, go to **www.infotrac-college.com**, enter your password, and search for the following articles by title or author's name.

▶ "Be an Online Expert: Host a Topic-Specific Web Site and Gain Writing Clips and Exposure," Moira Allen, *Writer*, March 2002 v115 i3 p17.

▶ "Why Online Journalism Is a Great Career Choice," Steve Outing, *Editor & Publisher*, May 1, 1999 p49.

▶ "So You Want to Be an Online Journalist?" J. D. Lasica, *American Journalism Review*, Nov. 1997 v19 n9 p48.

Exercises

Go to your CD-ROM to complete the following exercises:

▶ Exercise 10.1

▶ Exercise 10.2

11

Reporting and Writing for Public Relations

Your old professor from three years ago asked you to stop by his media writing class and tell the current crop of beginning media writers about your successes in public relations.

Sitting there in the front row while he introduces you, you recall how it felt when you first walked into that class yourself and how surprised you were to find out that public relations—in your professor's mind, at least—mostly seemed to boil down to writing.

You did your assignments, passed your style and grammar tests, and got on with your academic career, graduating a year later. The writing never came easy to you, but you got better and better at it from that first writing class right up to the last one that final semester before graduation.

Then came your first public relations job, working for a local hospital's media relations department. Now, a couple of years later, you're the assistant director, and boy, do you have some insights to share with these students about how things really are.

The old prof introduces you, and you walk up to the front of the room.

"My job," you say to them, "requires me to do a lot of different things, from taking part in management decisions to working on the hospital's annual fund drive.

"But we're not a big hospital, and there are only three of us in the media relations department, so most of what I do most of the time," and you pause dramatically before saying it, "comes down to writing."

And you begin to explain to them what the real world is all about.

Practicing Good Public Relations

Public relations practitioners have to analyze trends and public opinions, counsel executives, understand all aspects of their institution and be able to craft messages to various audiences.

Journalists in the print and broadcast media generally write for one audience and one medium, with any difference appearing only in the type of story written. When you work in public relations, you will have to write—and write effectively—messages intended to communicate with a wide variety of different audiences. It will be up to you to use the style appropriate for each purpose.

Most of this chapter is concerned with helping you learn to write news releases for print and broadcast; but public relations practitioners must write effective brochure copy, speeches, background information and position papers for company executives, in addition to writing and editing copy for several different kinds of corporate magazines.

All these various kinds of writing come down to material that is primarily *internal* (written to be read by those connected to your company) or *external* (written to be read by a wider public). Occasionally, as in the case of corporate magazines, they can be both.

Internal Writing

When you write for internal publications, you are likely to find yourself, in effect, doing the work of a magazine editor, a newspaper reporter, a copy-desk editor, a magazine fact checker, a magazine feature writer, a news and feature photographer, a newspaper or magazine (or both) page designer, and more. Sometimes you will be expected to be all of these things during the same workday.

Internal writing in public relations refers to all the publications you may write that are read by those who work for or have a close connection to your company (or, if you are working for a public relations agency, the company you are doing the work for). Among the most common things you will write for internal readers are the employee newsletter, the corporate magazine, company brochures, and the annual report.

Employee Newsletter

You may very well find yourself writing and editing the employee newsletter. Most corporations have such a publication, and it is usually read closely by virtually every employee. The newsletter typically tries to accomplish two things at once:

The newsletter is meant to boost employee morale. To this end, the employee newsletter is commonly filled with the results of the company bowling team, softball team, and the like. There will also be a great deal of coverage of the company picnic and other special outings, and frequent profiles on employees (or their family members) who have done something newsworthy, from developing a new labor-saving device for their job, for instance, all the way to winning the lottery or traveling to Paris for their 20th anniversary.

The employee newsletter is usually filled with as many employee pictures and names as you can reasonably fit in, in an effort to maximize your readers' interest.

The newsletter is used by management as an important communications tool. The employee newsletter is frequently the place where management talks to staff. When there are changes, for instance, in the employee health care package, the employee newsletter is likely to carry the news about those changes. And if the company is in the middle of a corporate crisis (a merger, perhaps, or layoffs, or a weak position in the market), it will be your job to give management's perspective on these events through the employee newsletter.

Corporate Magazine

Most corporations have a magazine (occasionally it's a newspaper) that is read by everyone connected in one way or another to the company: management, staff, stockholders, subcontractors—anyone, really, who wants to know what's happening with the company. Although the magazine is an internal publication, in many companies it is external, as well, being sent out to a wide variety of people in an effort to showcase the corporation.

This corporate magazine is frequently a highly professional publication, one as well-written and well-designed as any magazine you might buy at your local bookstore's magazine rack. To work for this magazine, you need all the skills of any professional magazine writer, editor or designer.

Courtesy Duke University Health System. Cover photo: Will McIntyre

A corporate magazine is meant for an audience composed of people associated with the institution or company.

There are literally thousands of these corporate magazines, each with a definite mission and audience in mind. Here is the cover of one such magazine. *Duke Medical Perspectives* is published by the Office of Creative Services and Publications in conjunction with the Medical Center Office of Development and Alumni Affairs and has a readership composed of alumni, current staff, patients and their families, and others interested in the successes of the medical center.

Company Brochures and Booklets

Company brochures and booklets come in a wide variety of different types. Some are very expensively produced, others more modest. They are often meant to communicate with an internal audience (a particular kind of employee, for instance) but are also frequently meant to communicate with an external audience (potential customers, for instance). Take a look at the cover and inside copy of a brochure from the Finger Lakes (N.Y.) Blue Cross and Blue Shield, shown on the next page.

These brochures are frequently produced in house, but occasionally farmed out to freelance writers. In either case, the idea behind a brochure is to inform, but it doesn't hurt to find ways here and there to make them enjoyable to read, as well. Freelance writer Nick DiChario, who wrote the "Navigating Medicare" brochure says: "You can really make your work stand out if you find ways to entertain as well as inform, whether you're writing brochures, manuals, or laundry lists. People will remember work that is engaging as opposed to strictly factual and informative. You want your readers to learn, after all. And most people tend to learn much better if they are captivated not just by the topic, but by the creativity of the writer as well. The *Dummies* books are perfect examples of this. If you were to look at just the information in those books, you'd find it as dry as a 4-day-old doughnut. The style, language, graphics, and self-deprecating jokes have made them a multimillion dollar industry. It's not all about text. Presentation counts."

Annual Report

The annual report is a regular part of public relations writing, and one of the most demanding forms you'll encounter, since the annual report

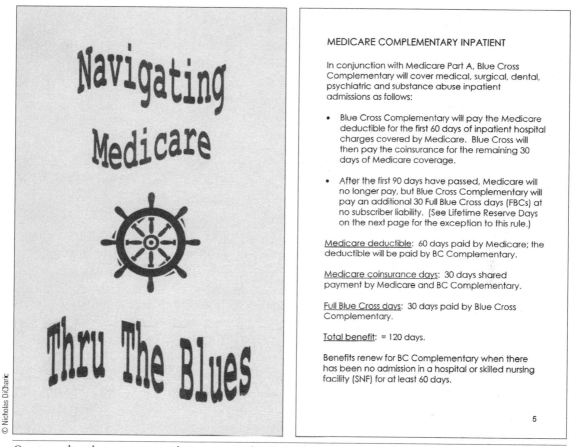

Company brochures can provide important, detailed information to employees and clients.

is usually an expensive, time-consuming effort on your part, and it is filled with detailed information that absolutely *must* be correct.

A typical annual report's contents might include an introduction (perhaps with some corporate history); a letter to the stockholders from the chairman of the board or the chief executive officer (or both); a breakdown of all the corporation's various holdings with descriptive material about each; a detailed financial review including information on stock prices, net sales, debt and the like; balance sheets for each of the holdings and for the corporation as a whole; statements of stockholder's equity; statements of cash flows; the auditor's report; and a directory of key personnel, perhaps with biographical information on the top people. All of this is packaged in a slick, expensively produced publication. The front covers from two annual reports are reproduced here.

Photo by Leo Holub

A full-color photo graces the front of this biological preserve's annual report.

External Writing—The News Release

If you work in public relations, you will almost certainly find yourself spending a considerable amount of time writing new releases for the media. For many of these releases, you will have the facts right in front of you and will be able to work with the people you want to quote, so the releases are sometimes easier to write than a story for a newspaper or magazine. That's the good news.

However, in some cases you will have to do as much, or even a lot more, reporting and interviewing than a newspaper or magazine reporter would do before you can write the release. And then you may have to go through a chain of command to get your story approved before you send it out.

And then, all too often, all that hard work is wasted because your release quickly finds its way into a reporter's trash can at the local newspaper, or local television or radio stations. That's the bad news.

A reporter may receive anywhere from two dozen to two hundred news releases in a day. When faced with mountains of paper, the reporter isn't going to be impressed with advertising or by a flashy logo or a nifty, themed press kit.

The reporter wants news, but is typically leery of the value of a news release. Still, there's a news hole

Reprinted with permission of St. Joseph's-Baptist Health Care.

This company's annual report features high-quality production values.

to fill. In smaller papers, if the release is newsworthy and seems ready to go into print, it may be published as is or with minor editing. At larger papers, the release may have enough merit to convince the reporter to follow up with a story. This will only happen, though, if the news in the release is accurately and compellingly portrayed.

On the other hand, a release that doesn't conform to news style and has basic errors like misspellings is much more likely to end up in the trash can. Take a look at this actual bad example (with some details changed to protect the guilty) and do not imitate it:

PRESS RELEASE

WEBSTER FOOD BANK CHARITY AUCTION

No dateline ▶

WOW! Excitement is building, as the donations are received for our fourth annual charity auction, on **Unprofessional lead** ▶ Saturday, April 26th, 2001. Many have responded to our need once again, with amazing generosity. The **Incorrect style** ▶ **throughout** items and money donated will go to helping support our mission.

Still needed are sponsors, program advertisers and items for the auction **Inappropriate** ▶ **capitalization for Hungry Herbert's** itself. The success of our annual event depends on the support from local businesses and private citizens.

The Webster Food Bank is a not-for-profit charitable corporation, serving Webster and Kirkood Counties. Our mission is soliciting donated and low-cost food items to be distributed through its 74 charitable agencies, feeding the needy, the ill, the elderly and children.

No regular funding is received by the Food Bank from the government or any religious organizations. We fulfill our mission through tile generous donations of private citizens, area businesses, sales from our community thrift store and fund raising events, such as the charity auction.

The auction will be held at the FOP Lodge, Shelbyville, April 26th. The silent auction begins at 6pm with dinner and the live auction to follow at 7pm The food will be catered by "THE FAMOUS BANQUET CHEF" Hungry Herbert's. Tickets are $20.00 per person, or corporate tables are available. General admission for the auction only, is $5.00 at the door.

For more information about this event or to make a contribution please call Danielle Ruth at the Food Bank, (000) 555-1212, Joyce Miller (000) 555-1212 or Cindy Halloran (000) 555-1212. Pickup of donated items is available.

As a practitioner, you not only have to write the release, but you will have to function as a reporter as well. You start with an understanding of news and then pursue the information you need within the organization. Research and interviewing skills don't lose their importance. If a news release is supposed to answer a reporter's questions, then you have to ask the right questions to perform your job.

That doesn't mean that some releases aren't light features. When done well, this kind of news release can be effective. Take a look at this example, from an Internet release:

Subj: **IMPORTANT ANNOUNCEMENT**

Date: 12/29/98 5:14:40 PM
        Eastern Standard Time

From: bwilber5@concentric.net
        (Bob Wilber)

To: Interested parties

An important announcement to media, team associates, and friends—

FOR IMMEDIATE RELEASE

Del Worsham Takes Steps to Commit to New Full-Time Team Member

DEC. 29, 1998—COSTA MESA, CALIF. — Del Worsham, driver of the Checker-Schuck's-Kragen Pontiac Firebird Funny Car on the NHRA Winston Drag Racing circuit, has announced a plan to add a critical new member to the Worsham & Fink racing program, as well as to all aspects of his life. Del recently made a formal proposal to the engaging individual, one Connie Medina of Costa Mesa, Calif., and his offer was accepted at once.

As part of the Worsham program, Ms. Medina will take on the role of Connie Worsham, as she becomes the wife of the popular Funny Car driver. Terms of the engagement were not announced with the exception of the fact that the agreement is a lifetime contract.

An intimate ceremony designed to take this commitment "to the next step" is scheduled for February.

And, in related news, such mergers must be contagious in the Worsham & Fink camp, as Marc Denner, crew member on the team, engaged in a similar proposal 2,000 miles away in Wichita, Kansas, within 24 hours of his driver's announcement. Krysta Batten was offered a lifetime contract by young Mr. Denner and, like Ms. Medina, she accepted at once.

E-mail messages to Del Worsham, Connie Medina, Marc Denner, and Krysta Batten may be sent by simply replying to this e-mail. They will be automatically forwarded to the appropriate parties.

Congratulations to our very dear friends!

Bob Wilber, team manager for the Del Worsham team which competes in the NHRA's Funny Car division, says that when Worsham told him of his marriage plans, "Del wanted me to do a press release because he's so shy he doesn't like telling anyone. So I tried eight different versions of a standard release 'Del Worsham is pleased to announce . . .'—and hated them all. Then, this just came to me. I wrote it in about five minutes and hit send before I could change my mind."

Renee Buchanan has worked as a public information officer for the University of North Carolina at Wilmington and currently is coordinator of advancement and alumni affairs for the University of Florida Health Science Center. She thinks that a lot of news releases should never see the light of day: "You should ask whether this communication raises a public interest or concern. Because if it doesn't, then you shouldn't spend your time on it. This means you have to educate your bosses who don't understand that a newspaper is not going to run a story just because they gave a dozen plaques to people."

Feature Approaches

Getting the news across is the primary purpose of a news release, but using a feature approach can also hook the reporter just as a feature lead may hook the reader.

Press Release

For Further Information Contact:

Honeywell Communications:
Shari Phillips

(602) 561-3746 or e-mail
info-fl51@space.honeywell.com

Space Shuttle *Atlantis* Equipped with Honeywell's "Glass Cockpit"

PHOENIX, ARIZONA, JUNE 14, 1999 — NASA's Space Shuttle *Atlantis* cockpit has a new look. A Honeywell "glass cockpit" look. Honeywell Space Systems in Phoenix designed and built the Multifunction Electronic Display Subsystem (MEDS) now installed in Atlantis.

The new liquid crystal displays, which replace the orbiter's electro-mechanical and cathode ray tube (CRT) displays, operate with the convenience and control of the most advanced commercial and military flat-panel display technology available today.

MEDS is a space-qualified adaptation of the display technology used on the Boeing 777. Using MEDS, shuttle crews have easy access to vital information through the two- and three-dimensional color graphic and video capabilities. Information also is interchangeable between screens, allowing crews to select the display format that best suits the needs of their particular mission.

There are nine MEDS displays in the forward flight deck and two MEDS units in the aft flight deck of *Atlantis*, which is scheduled to make its debut launch with the new displays in December.

Honeywell is under contract with Boeing North American to provide MEDS for all four Shuttle orbiters.

The practitioner here hoped to catch a reporter's attention with a first line that teases the news here. Then she has to explain a complex subject in terms that a journalist with long-forgotten classes in science can understand. The writer does a good enough job translating aerospace engineering jargon that some newspapers may well run the release verbatim—but only because it's clearly written.

"I cannot emphasize the writing enough,' Buchanan says. "I work for very educated people, but I have to write for them. In public relations, no matter who your bosses are, you are their voice to the public."

Include Other Important Information

Professional news releases include some important information not found on a standard news report. Reporters need to have a contact person for the news, especially if they choose to follow up on your release.

The practitioner may often be the contact, but it may also be an executive within a company. The contact information usually lists name, title, and phone numbers, and should include an e-mail address as well as a work address.

The release should also include a release date. Some releases are designed to go out on a certain date and are, in news lingo, *embargoed* for that time. Usually a release includes the phrase *FOR IMMEDIATE RELEASE*, but it might also say *NOT FOR RELEASE BEFORE SAT. SEPT. 1*. Unfortunately, reporters and editors may resist your embargo if they deem a release highly newsworthy.

The release date can also affect the newsworthiness of the piece. If an editor doesn't receive a release marked *NOT FOR USE AFTER OCT. 11* until the 13th, you probably not only miss getting your story in that issue, but the editor is less likely to trust you again.

One of the great advantages in writing news releases is that you get to create your own quotes. You then get approval for the quote from the person for whom you have, literally, put words in her or his mouth.

There's a warning here, though. Many seasoned reporters will cut most hyperbole. Don't have the president of Werner's Widgets saying, "Our widget is unquestionably THE technological advance of the 20th century, and it's all because we are the most caring, industrious and profitable corporation in the world." You can try to sneak this hype past an editor, but it's not a good idea. Instead, you will want your quotes to convey a message, but not sound bombastic or even forced. You will want to make the words sound as if someone actually did speak them.

"You want to have credibility with the news media," Bartell cautions. "You want them to know that they can rely on your information."

Meet the Deadline

You will want to understand the needs of reporters as far as deadline. It doesn't do your organization any good to send out a wonderful news release for Saturday's news at 6:50 p.m. that Friday. The release is not going to be seen until Monday unless it contains earth-shattering news. "We recently had a major transplant—the first of its kind—and the operation wasn't finished until 8 p.m. Eastern time," Buchanan said. "My local media were shut down for the evening, but I could still get the news out to the West Coast folks."

She adds, "Deadlines are crucial. You need to know when it's too late to help. If a reporter needs to talk to a researcher, but the interview can't happen until after 5 p.m.—and that's when the reporter is on the air—then you have to call back the reporter and try to approach the story differently."

Length and Locality

You really believe in your company's new program, and to prove it, you spend several pages telling about some of the strategic minutiae (the trivia of the trivial) of the program. Unfortunately, reporters don't need several pages of information, and if the release is too long, it will lose out to another release from the stack of mail.

Marilyn Bartell, public information officer for the city of Roseville, Calif., says, "In our media market [Sacramento] a television station will receive anywhere from 200 to 300 news releases a day. You have to hook them with the headline or the first sentence, or it's going into the round file immediately."

Important news can be included in releases of more than 200 words or so, but it really needs to be justified by the circumstances. If the release stretches past two pages, then the justification becomes more important. Generally, be as concise as possible while answering the questions a reporter will need answered.

"Keep it simple and short," Bartell says. "Just write a great headline and a great first paragraph and, preferably, keep it to one page if you can."

Take a look at this release from Bartell's office.

Contact:

Marilyn J. Bartell

Public Information Officer

(916) 774-5201 or 536~245 (pager)

No. 97-36

June 13, 1997

FOR IMMEDIATE RELEASE

ROSEVILLE CITY COUNCIL BEGINS BUDGET WORKSHOPS

The Roseville City Council will focus on the FY 1997–98 budget at three budget workshops on Thursday, June 19; Monday, June 23; and Tuesday, June 24. Budget adoption is expected after the Wednesday, June 26, public hearing. All budget meetings begin at 4:30 p.m. in the City Council Chambers, 311 Vernon Street.

The proposed $175 million budget is 14 percent larger than the $153 million budget that was adopted last year. The increase is primarily for capital improvements including:

- Construction of the Hardrock and Pleasant Grove electric substations.

- Park renovations, construction of a new park next to Quail Glen School, Diamond Oaks green renovation and completion of *the* Maidu Park sports court facility.

- Widening of Atlantic Street, improving the Sunrise/Douglas intersection, and beginning design and environmental work for the Roseville Parkway/I-8O overcrossing.

- Water system expansion projects.

- Pleasant Grove wastewater treatment plant design.

The City budget's normal 10 percent reserve will be maintained, and the

(continued)

(continued)

City's full-time equivalent staff will increase less than one percent—from 833 to 839 employees. Roseville's proposed $46 million General Fund supports police, fire, library, parks and recreation, and general government services. Major project proposals include:

- Moving the police department to its new facility.

- Implementing a new records, mobile data and dispatch system that links Roseville with other agencies to quickly obtain criminal history information.

- Establishing a geographic information system (GIS) and permit tracking system.

- Setting aside $1 million for flood control improvements.

Roseville's strong economic growth, use of technology to minimize staff increases and long-range planning continue to provide the resources the City needs to invest in programs, services and facilities that meet the needs of the community. For budget details, please contact Finance Director Phil Ezell at 774-5319.

***

Find the Angle

Finding a local angle is important to the story. The business editor of a San Diego newspaper probably doesn't have any interest in a Wisconsin woman being general manager of a company's franchise in Oshkosh. But if that woman grew up a member of a prominent San Diego family (or other newsworthy tag), then the release has some local interest and might—though probably not—get some attention. A Sacramento editor would toss it with a curse. But the Oshkosh area newspapers probably would include it. A news release is more likely to be accepted by local media if it includes a tie-in with a local business.

Proximity remains an important news value, and public relations practitioners should remember its importance. The armed services and many universities contain a "hometown news" program within their public affairs units. If a serviceman from Ottumwa, Iowa, wins a promotion, then the hometown news unit will write an appropriate announcement and send it to the Ottumwa news media. Hometown-boy or hometown-girl stories are news to local newspapers and broadcasters—and, as we'll see next, even more so in some media outlets.

Other Avenues

Small Dailies and Weeklies

It would be unusual for your press release to be printed word for word in a large metropolitan newspaper, even if it is meticulously crafted and is filled with news. But in many smaller newspapers, you might well expect to see your release printed almost exactly as is. Editors seek to fill space in their papers, and smaller newspapers are not likely to have access to a wire service like the Associated Press to help fill that space. With limited staff at those editors' command, well-written press releases can be a blessing to them.

One author of this text spent some time working for a nondaily newspaper and particularly appreciated the state parks and wildlife department's well-written and timely news releases. The department kept him stocked with news about hunting, fishing and conservation efforts, and as a result, the department's releases were a regular staple in the newspaper. Wise practitioners generally follow the same philosophy of presenting newsworthy releases to the broadcast media.

External Writing—*Broadcast*

Broadcast material should conform to the sights and sounds needed by television and radio, respectively. Because broadcast writing is generally tighter and more limited by time than print writing, you'll have to make that adjustment in your writing.

The video news release (VNR) has become extremely popular as corporations have acquired video equipment or hired production companies in order to produce broadcast-quality video releases. Rare until the latter half of the 1980s, VNRs now enable a company to present "usable" news for broadcast. If, for example, your company makes plastic contact lenses, a VNR about a new lens can include video of your company's products and interviews with your company's executives.

The broadcast news hole has increased with the growth of cable television, and VNRs are one tool that organizations of all kinds use to get their message across. Some news operations may choose to broadcast the VNR as is, and others may just use clips or video footage from it, but it does serve as another means to get your message across.

In radio, practitioners may use a minidocumentary, a three-minute report on an important issue for your organization, to get a message across. The minidoc is usually written to allow the radio news reporter to write the lead-in and the ending. Such scripts may be provided.

Another common practice for radio releases is an audiotape of sound bites and a script that can be used for several different approaches, allowing the reporter to choose which angle will be used.

External Writing—Other Forms
Backgrounders

Recently a major airline was embarrassed when its CEO had to admit that he hadn't heard of a plan that would reduce the cost of children's tickets on his airline, thus raising the question of an airplane filled with pre-teens. The public relations practitioners for the airline needed to provide the CEO with a *backgrounder,* a well-researched document that states the issue, gives a historical perspective and examines the consequences of alternative positions. It's more likely to feature documentation and facts than opinion.

Position Papers

Position papers detail where a company stands on an issue and explain why. They should take into consideration current legislative information or the latest scientific data. They require practitioners to research a subject extensively. Even more important, they require practitioners to address the issue.

For example, a position paper addressing the environmental effects of pesticide spray for agricultural pests shouldn't merely state that bugs are bad for vegetables, but should address the issue of the environment. Position papers are not misdirection ploys.

Speeches

Executives may ask you to write speeches for them. You may normally fall asleep during these, but they can represent potential disaster for your company's image if you adopt the wrong tone for your audience.

Speeches are opportunities to state a company position. They need to be appropriate for the situation and need to complement the executive's speaking skills. For example, it's not a good idea for the executive to tell a graduation audience that the most important thing the graduates learned in college was how to make a collect call home for money. The parents who spent thousands of dollars on tuition, the students who invested a great deal of study time and the faculty who consider education to be important probably won't appreciate the humor. In another setting, they might. But not at a graduation ceremony.

Speechwriters not only need to understand company policy and the issues to be addressed, but also need to work with the speaker to understand speaking patterns. It would be humiliating to your boss to include words in a speech that the executive didn't know. It would be humiliating to write long sentences when the executive tends to talk in short bursts. And it would be humiliating when you got called in on the carpet the following day.

In most cases, the speechwriter's work is edited, in effect, by the person giving the speech, who will look it over closely (perhaps in early drafts) and then give it a final polish before delivering the speech.

Memoranda and More

Practitioners may also have to master the ability to write memoranda and business letters. Unfortunately, this may well require you to develop the ability to communicate in bureaucratese. It's important to remember to keep the business jargon in the memoranda and not in your news releases. You may also, in some instances, have to compose the copy for an institutional advertising campaign—one in which you help sell the company's image rather than a product.

Public relations combines a journalist's writing and editing skill with a solid understanding of news and the ability to communicate the organization's position in the context of the audience and its needs and interests. You have the responsibility of presenting the organization's story and information in a form appropriate to its intended purpose. It's not about folding napkins and shaking hands—though maybe once in a while you'll get to do both. To see the different responsibilities of the field, see "A Day in the Life of . . . Public Relations Practitioner Nancy Reynolds," in this chapter.

Vonette McCauley

A Day in the Life of...

Public Relations Practitioner Marilyn Bartell

When massive floods hit the Sacramento area in 1995, Marilyn Bartell found herself, er, hip-deep in the work. As the city of Roseville's public information officer, she found herself putting in 24-hour days as reporters and the public kept asking questions about evacuations, road closings, sandbag locations and the like.

Then the president and three White House staffers decided to fly in to inspect the damage.

It had just become deeper for Bartell.

"We had to work practically around the clock for three or four days and then we got a call from the president [Bill Clinton]," she remembers. "I had to handle the media credentialing for 120 organizations from high schools to CNN and Reuters [the world wire service]. I was involved in putting together printed information, putting together a media area because only a few reporters got to go on the inspection. At one point, the president gave a speech, and then I had to put together one-on-one interviews with the other Cabinet members—Cisneros, Panetta and Peña."

And she had to keep on top of the dissemination of information about the flood.

In that kind of crisis situation, you might expect that dealing with the reporters might be a tough job, but Bartell had a powerful tool on her side: her reputation.

"In a disaster, news coverage can be a real disaster, but I had developed a good relationship with the local reporters and that gave me credibility," Bartell says.

She earned her credibility through hard work, delivering timely, professional releases to the broadcast and print media over time. And at a time when it mattered, her credibility led to coverage that wasn't a disaster for the city of Roseville.

As a professional who worked for California Department of Education before taking the Roseville job, Bartell had learned how to craft her messages to the appropriate audience.

"I think the first thing is to consider just who's most likely to read the story," Bartell says. "The audience determines how simple or complex your writing has to be. A lot of terms we use are technical and not understood by everybody. By simplifying the language, using analogies and using a conversational tone, your agency gets its message across."

That doesn't mean everyone will like the message. Bartell recently handled releases about the city's plan to increase utility rates. The citizenry of Roseville was not exactly thrilled to know that basic electricity and water service would cost more.

"You have to try to educate people about the changes and the reasons for them," Bartell said. "Nobody likes a rate increase, but the utility industry is charging more to remain competitive and there are things you need to do now that will save money later."

Bartell estimates she spends about 50 percent of her time as a writer, mostly for newsletters, "but I do a lot of different things as well."

Professional communication skills remain at the core, though.

"It's very important to write well—people are in a hurry and don't take time to read a lengthy report. If you aren't writing accurately and concisely, then you don't get your message across."

The communication industry will make good writing even more valuable, especially in an age where a lot of traditional assumptions about mass communication may not apply.

"The communication industries are changing so fast, and I would recommend that anyone looking at public relations be prepared to have those writing and editing skills for whatever changes do happen."

She has some suggestions about what sorts of skills will help in the workplace. Ideally, she says, practitioners will have:

► Writing and editing skills.

► Public relations experience from internships and entry-level jobs.

► Design skills.

► Photography skills.

► The ability to work with the Internet, the World Wide Web, or whatever replaces them.

► A sense of deadline, both for others and of their own.

"You might use those skills differently for a corporate job than for nonprofits and the government, but you will need them," Bartell says. "Corporate offices tend to have a lot of regional coordinators, and they tend to have a lot more money to spend on a campaign."

But that takes more than skills, she added. Succeeding in public relations also takes a special kind of person.

"They need to be curious and interested in a lot of different things," Bartell says. "They should be open-minded, enthusiastic and a bit of a risk taker, which you need to be in order to get the best stories."

Bartell says the most jarring problem for those in public relations is the most basic communication problem for any professional.

"The worst thing you can put in a release is incomplete information and have poor grammar, spelling and punctuation," she says.

"It doesn't give you any kind of credibility if you make those kind of mistakes." ■

Marilyn Bartell is public information officer for the city of Roseville, CA.

A Day in the Life of...

Public Relations Practitioner Nancy Reynolds

It's no "9 to 5" job. Depending on the day, you may or may not love that about public relations. When you're running late getting the kids off to school in the morning, you're grateful for the flex time. For the most part, you alone manage the demands on your schedule while others simply notice if you miss your deadlines. Who cares if you're writing the final pieces for your monthly newsletter during the traditional workday or at home in the middle of the night? No one watches your clock if you're keeping track of time.

On the other hand, when you get a phone call from a reporter just as you shut down your computer at the end of the business day, you better have backup to get the kids from day care. You're not going anywhere until you research an answer to this latest query and perhaps write and get approval for a quote for the appropriate company representative.

So goes a day in the life of a corporate public relations professional.

I show up for work about 8:30 a.m. planning to finish my last two feature stories for the monthly employee newsletter. The printer expects it tomorrow. No problem. I can turn those stories out in two hours, leaving plenty of time to coordinate reviews with the story owners while I begin layout and design.

As I settle into my chair with my morning java, the phone rings. It's the president's administrative assistant. Our company sponsored the building of a Habitat for Humanity house, and he's just agreed to speak at the home dedication this afternoon. Although he likes to speak off the cuff, he needs talking points, including details about our employees' efforts toward the home's construction.

What did I do before the Internet? I easily find all the information I need about Habitat for Humanity online and then contact the local chapter for an accuracy check. I track down our company's Habitat coordinator for details about our employees who helped make this event possible and then contact a few of them, so I can inject their side of the story. (Plus I can kill two birds with one stone, since I was planning a Habitat article for next month's employee newsletter.) I deliver the goods to the president along with directions to the event and the name of a Habitat point of contact who will meet him there.

Whew! Now I can get back to the pending edition. I'm barely back in my chair when the alarm sounds on my Palm Pilot. I almost forgot about my 11 a.m. United Way committee meeting. Together with volunteers from all areas of the business, I roll up my sleeves and throw ideas onto a white board. We need a theme, a kick-off event, incentive prizes . . . an entire campaign strategy. What can we do to position the company as a good corporate citizen and convince our employees to share a portion of their salaries with our neighbors in need?

I take time for a quick lunch. When I return to my desk, my head is still spinning with ideas for United Way. I'm excited about our plans and prefer to focus on the campaign, but my newsletter is more pressing. I have to force myself to shift gears (kind of like going from 4th to 2nd on the interstate). If I don't finish these stories today, I'll have to write them at home tonight after I get the kids off to bed. The pressure energizes me, and the words start to flow. I rebound from a few more distractions in the afternoon (a media query, a call from a local charity looking for a corporate contribution, a request for a last-minute memo to announce an organizational change).

Finally, I've finished my features. I've got time to e-mail drafts to the story owners before I leave, so I'll have their comments first thing in the morning in case I need to make changes. I back up everything to a diskette, which I store safely in my briefcase along with my digital camera.

I stop by the Habitat dedication on the way home in case the media want to interview our president about our company's commitment to affordable housing for the economically depressed. I snap a few photos for my own Habitat story and interview the happy new homeowner, who is most grateful to my company for its financial assistance. She automatically likes me because I represent this wonderful company that just handed her a new future. It feels really good.

Later that evening, after dinner, baths, homework and bedtime stories, I boot up my home computer, open PageMaker and retrieve my diskette from my briefcase. Three hours later, I finish layout and design. I allow myself a moment for pride in accomplishment. It's a great issue.

When I get to work, I'll proofread for typos and make any last minute changes to the stories I wrote today. Correction . . . it's after midnight now, so technically I wrote those stories *yesterday*. Oh well . . . I set my alarm and drift off to sleep.

When I arrive at the office again, I review my task list as I reach for my coffee. The phone rings. It's one of my story owners. "You did a great job on the story, but I have some bad news," he says. "The program you wrote about has been postponed indefinitely due to yesterday's organizational change. We can't run the story."

Time to shift gears again, only this time it's more like going from 4th gear to reverse! Good thing I have my Habitat story in my hip pocket—photo and all. I'll improvise.

So goes a day in the life of a corporate communications professional. ■

Nancy Reynolds left the military to earn a bachelor's degree in public relations and then entered the field of corporate communications.

Summary

Public relations practitioners seek to effectively communicate with a number of audiences. Effective communication usually comes down to effective writing. When you examine some of the Web sites given in "Key Links" below, you will notice that many of the pages lead to sites about research, better writing and news.

Practitioners must especially learn the craft of meeting the needs of different audiences, internal and external. You should learn how to communicate effectively with those connected with your company or client as well as those outside of your company. Your messages should meet the needs of your audience, be it internal or external. Your newsletter should be understandable to the employees, your speeches should fit the occasion and the speaking ability of the presenter, and your news releases should meet the newsworthiness and deadline requirements of reporters.

Key Points

▶ The practitioner analyzes trends and public opinion, counsels executives, understands his or her institution or client, and can deliver effective messages to different audiences.

▶ The internal audience includes those connected with the company and is reached through company newsletters and magazines, brochures and annual reports.

▶ The external audience includes those outside of the company. These audiences may be reached through news releases, backgrounders, position papers, speeches.

▶ A news release is not advertising or hyperbole. It relates newsworthy information to the media and other audiences in a form that fulfills the public's needs.

▶ News releases should always include a contact person and his or her telephone number.

▶ Practitioners should understand media deadline requirements and ensure that releases are timed to fit within those deadlines.

Web Links

Also, here are a few interesting sites on the Internet where you can find out more information or see examples of various kinds of public relations writing.

http://www.prsa.org
http://www.iabc.com
http://www.prnewswire.com
http://www.niri.org
http://www.newslink.org

InfoTrac College Edition Readings

For additional readings, go to **www.infotrac-college.com**, enter your password, and search for the following articles by title or author's name.

▶ "Baum's *Wizard of Oz* as Gilded Age Public Relations," Tim Ziaukas, *Public Relations Quarterly,* Fall 1998 v43 i3 p7.

▶ "Foot in Mouth Disease" (Humorous public relations gaffes) (Brief Article), Melanie Wells, *Forbes,* Aug. 20, 2001 p42.

▶ "Writer's Notebook," Richard E. Eaton, *Public Relations Quarterly,* Summer 2000 v45 i2 p47.

Exercises

Go to your CD-ROM to complete the following exercises:

▶ Exercise 11.1

▶ Exercise 11.2

▶ Exercise 11.3

▶ Exercise 11.4

▶ Exercise 11.5

12

Research and Writing for Advertising Copywriting

For much of the semester, you've been tapping your fingers against the desktop wondering just what all of this news stuff has to do with your intended major: advertising. You don't plan to ever conduct an interview and write a 16-inch story on deadline. You don't ever want to stand before the camera and deliver the news. You certainly don't want to write public relations copy for anyone.

You want to work in advertising.

You're not sure whether you want to be a copywriter or an account executive (or both), but you like the excitement of the advertising world, you like the creativity of it, and you're quite sure you don't want to find yourself sitting at a keyboard late in the day trying to meet a tough deadline.

Well, even if that's the case, there are some very good reasons for you to learn what you've learned so far from this book. For one thing, as your instructor will tell you, salespeople need to understand and practice good communication. Many of the things you've learned here are going to serve you well even if you wind up writing memoranda, proposals and letters.

For another thing, it can't possibly hurt you in your advertising career to know what media writers are going through on a daily basis—and it just might help you when you're making a decision to place an ad in a newspaper, in a magazine, on the radio or on television.

Finally, if you find yourself on the creative side of advertising, guess where you're likely to find yourself from time to time? That's right, sitting at the keyboard, trying to be creative and persuasive and informative all at once while a big deadline looms.

So, let's take a look at copywriting, where you'll see that many of the key principles of mass communication writing that you've already learned will apply to the advertising world as well.

It's Not Just Creativity

The stereotypical view of copywriting usually includes a team of, shall we say, nonconformist creative types guzzling Jolt cola (if not Jack Daniels) by the barrel. The copywriters are flighty and unconventional and come up with wacky ideas to sell a product.

Well, we're not saying that never happens; but the truth of the matter is that the stereotype doesn't necessarily hold true. It is important to be creative, but—we hate to let the secret out—even those zany copywriters are following a format and style just like any other writer.

In large advertising agencies, a copywriter is usually teamed with an artist to come up with ideas based on a creative brief or a creative strategy statement, a document that details the generalities of the campaign, the product, the purpose and the audience. The copywriter and artist then conform to that plan before coming up with an approach (if they're wise, they will read James Marra's *Advertising Creativity: Techniques for Generating Ideas* for developing ideas). Think of it as creativity harnessed to practicality—which, come to think of it, is pretty much what any professional writer faces. Here are examples of two creative briefs. Notice how they help define the copywriter's job.

TU Electric

Target audience: All adults in TU Electric's service area. The most critical segment of customers is young families with children, mid-to-low household income.

Objectives

1. To improve name recognition and build positive awareness of the newly established TU Electric name and logo.

2. To reinforce positive customer attitudes toward the company, its personnel and its services.

3. To re-establish employee identity and company unity following the recent consolidation.

Key customer benefit and support:

Benefit: The electric company provides dependable power, and when a storm, high winds, or any other occurrence interrupts electrical service, the company responds promptly. *Support:* Electric company employees are on duty 24 hours a day, 365 days a year to make sure power is available. A call to the emergency repair service number will promptly bring a crew to restore power as quickly as possible.

Tone and manner: The personality and image of TU Electric to be projected through the advertising is that of a dependable, dedicated, professional friend. The ads should convey that employees, although they are ordinary folks, are experienced and serious. In addition, the ads should project determination, honesty and strength.

Bermuda

Target audiences: *Primary*—Adults 45 and over, household income $75,000+, attended or graduated from college, live in northeastern region of the United States. *Secondary*—Adults in same age, income and education category who live Chicago, Dallas, Houston, Atlanta, San Francisco and Los Angeles.

Objectives

1. To reinforce awareness that Bermuda is a class destination with great weather where the vacationer can relax and unwind.

2. To increase knowledge that in addition to sun, sea and sand, it offers a variety of good restaurants, sightseeing and sports facilities.

3. To change the targets' attitudes regarding Bermuda's value-for-the-money as a tourist destination.

4. To stimulate a stronger, immediate, do-it-now attitude toward requesting information (action).

Key consumer benefit and support:

Benefit: Bermuda is a warm, beautiful island for upscale vacationing year-round. It is populated by friendly, English-speaking people and offers a range of accommodations and a wide variety of vacation experiences that give visitors their money's worth.

Support: Bermuda, a British Crown Colony, is semitropical and has an ideal resort climate with two seasons—spring and summer. The average seasonal temperature is 72 degrees with rain during only 10 percent of the days. There are more than 100 places to stay on the island ranging from large resorts through cottage colonies to guest houses. Ministry of Tourism activity lists indicate a complete range of events each month. Past airport and cruise studies among visitors document Bermuda's high rating on key considerations that influence the selection of a vacation destination plus Bermuda's high perceived value vis-à-vis the Bahamas and the Caribbean islands.

Tone and manner: The personality and image of the island to be projected is that of a class destination. Bermuda's personality reflected in the advertising should key around the island's British heritage and style—the place is a little foreign but friendly. The tone of the advertising must be upscale and sophisticated and border on being snobbish.

Writing for Your Audience

Copywriters need to focus on the potential audience for an advertisement. Many factors may play a role in crafting a particular advertisement, and more than a few have to do with the target audience. Who are the likely consumers of the product? What do they know about the product? What is the goal of the campaign, and how can that be conveyed to the audience?

Remember advertising usually refers to purchased space in a medium in which you place your message. Publicity, on the other hand, almost always deals with unpaid space in media. Though some agencies have advertising and public relations wings, they're usually separate. (Occasionally, some public relations personnel will be asked to construct image advertising.)

Advertising, therefore, is subject to a good deal of control by the people who create individual ads. You determine the headline, the message, the artwork, the design, and the tone of the piece. In some cases, you may even determine where the advertisement appears in a newspaper or on a television program (it's more likely that a media department or media buying service will do this). You may even use a medium not used by other mass communicators, like billboards or direct mail.

Usually the copywriter has a good idea about the audience based on the product. The market research industry has thrived in the 20th century and can describe a potential audience in a number of interesting ways. Some marketers can generalize about your product choices on the basis of your ZIP code. Others can measure the general characteristics of an audience fragment using demographics or psychographic studies.

"All of the market research—focus groups, statistics, surveys—helps tremendously," says copywriter Debra Jason of Boulder, Colo. "You probably wouldn't write the same letter to a 17-year-old male as you would to a 35-year-old single mother. If the client doesn't have that kind of research, I'll ask my neighbor if she'd buy this product. Or go into a chat room on the Internet and ask. That's not scientific, but it is something."

Since Jason specializes in direct marketing, she composes letters to bring about some sort of behavior. If a particular client isn't sure about the composition of the audience, she will ask for the mailing list that the client intends to use. "If the list is *Cosmopolitan* [magazine] readers, I'll have *Cosmopolitan* send a reader profile," she says. "Then I know who's in the audience and how to structure the message."

What sorts of interests and knowledge base does a typical *Cosmopolitan* reader have? The magazine's research staff knows. Publications have to understand the composition of their target audience. It is not difficult for journalism educators, among others, to scorn the tabloid *National Enquirer* for its celebrity gossip and its titillating news. But did you know the *Enquirer* has won national awards from health reporting groups for its coverage of arthritis? The tabloid knows, through readership studies, that a large portion of its readership base suffers from or is interested in knowing more about arthritis.

If you understand the general age, income and education level of your audience, your copywriting should reflect that knowledge. Write with that reader or viewer in mind.

Never Underestimate Your Audience

One of the biggest dangers anyone working in advertising faces is not giving the audience enough credit. This results in shoddy advertising and leads to problems with the public and eventually with your client. You see this in campaigns that insult the audience's intelligence and campaigns that make promises the company only nominally meets (offering a bonus "sports watch" that runs for about eight days, for example).

Stan Freberg told how he approached the audience during the beginnings of his long, successful career in the advertising world. Freberg had been a popular recording artist in the 1950s with a string of comedic satires of songs, television shows and the like. He branched into humorous advertising, a field that probably needed a shakeup. After a few successes, he was called by a big-time advertising agency to serve as a consultant. It seems they had presented a series of advertisements to a man named Jeno Paulucci, who owned Chun King, a manufacturer of canned Chinese food.

Freberg wrote in his autobiography, *It Only Hurts When I Laugh,* "As the spots played, I sunk down into my chair in the dark. Each one, it turned out, was worse than the one before. Hard sell, followed by stupid sell. In an embarrassing attempt at humor, an animated announcer leaned over an animated baby in a baby carriage. He asked him what he thought of Chun King. The baby raised up and gave him a loud raspberry in the face, spraying animated saliva all over the announcer's face. The lights came up . . . "

> Paulucci asked for his opinion, as the advertising agency stared daggers through Freberg.
>
> "You want the truth?" I asked him. . . . I paused for just a second, then I told him the truth. "Those are without a doubt some of the worst commercials I've ever seen." Jeno slapped the table. 'What did I tell you?' he yelled, endearing me to his agency.
>
> I told him why they didn't work. Especially the feeble attempts at humor. 'First of all, the baby joke doesn't work because canned chow mein is not something you feed to babies. Humor has to be based somewhat in reality. An announcer just wouldn't ask a baby how he liked your product, so you've lost the audience immediately. And having the baby spit at the announcer was an instant turnoff. Do you guys think that spot is funny?" I asked the agency.
>
> One of them said to me, "Well, no, I don't personally think it's all that funny, but they might think it's funny."
>
> "No good!" I told him. "That's the attitude that's responsible for all the advertising that doesn't work. You can't act like your tastes are one thing and the audience's tastes are another. If you don't like an ad, why should anybody else? And who are "they"? We're all consumers.

We are them and they are us! That's why I always create commercials for myself first of all. I am the consumer I know the best. If I think it's a great commercial, I figure the rest of the people might think so too . . . . "

Stay Aware

David Ogilvy, the respected head of the Ogilvy & Mather agency, and author of *Ogilvy on Advertising,* laments in his book that many in advertising agencies are not well read about their own craft. "I asked an indifferent copywriter what books he had read about advertising. He told me he had not read any; he preferred to rely on his own intuition," Ogilvy said. He then asked whether the copywriter would be willing to have his gall bladder removed by a surgeon who relied on intuition.

"Advertising agencies waste their client's money repeating the same mistakes," Ogilvy writes. "I recently counted 49 advertisements set in reverse (white type on black background) in one issue of a magazine, long years after research demonstrated that reverse is difficult to read."

Copywriters should be also aware of the world outside the agency. If you're going to conduct up-to-the-minute, cutting-edge campaigns, you need to understand how today's situation can affect your message. When you consider that a large percentage of advertising is business-to-business, a wise copywriter reads voraciously about world affairs and financial matters in order to avoid embarrassing errors in representing a client.

Got Milk ® California Milk Processor Board

The "Got Milk?" campaign exploded from being a regional ad to being a nationally recognized one.

Writing the Ad

Psssst, writing good ad copy means more than putting out a great slogan.

Remember the "Got Milk?" campaign? It is one of the more universally acclaimed advertising series in recent years, featuring, for instance, a chocolate chip cookie with a bite out of it, and it's mostly visual. Copywriters, you see, need to be able to think visually as well as verbally.

Some television commercials, in fact, have no script at all except for a superimposed logo at the end. And if some critic were to ask cautiously just what the message is in such an advertising campaign, then the answer would be simply that the ad sells. If the audience remembers it, and makes the right associations with that memory (healthy, economical, high-quality, durable—whatever), then the ad has worked, and that doesn't always take much in the way of words.

Actually, it sometimes seems that television advertising has become little more than a battle of special effects designed to keep your attention focused so you won't zap to another station. And that is, in fact, an important element of television advertising in these days of remote control and dozens, or even hundreds, of stations.

So, while a great slogan never hurts, it's the content of the advertisement that works. The ad should take fullest advantage of its particular medium—television, radio, newspaper, magazine, outdoor—but it should also be well-written, even if very few words actually appear.

Advantages and Liabilities

Remember that each medium has its own advantages and liabilities. For most advertisers most of the time, the reach of the ad is balanced against the cost. Usually, advertisers think in terms of cost-per-thousand when it comes to spending their money; that is, how much money does it cost to reach 1,000 audience members?

But there are plenty of complications with that basic idea, most of them having to do with the kind of 1,000 audience members that the ad is reaching. An expensive television ad might reach many millions for a relatively low cost-per-thousand; but if most of those TV viewers are not potential customers, then the money may have been wasted. A magazine ad that has a relatively high cost-per-thousand might be more effective ultimately because its audience is composed of potential buyers.

A surfboard company, for instance, would waste most of its TV ad money if it ran its ads during the evening news. How many of those viewers are potential surfboard buyers? The same company knows that buying an ad in a surfing magazine, while that has a higher cost-per-thousand, is actually much more effective.

Nevertheless, each medium has its advantages and liabilities.

Newspapers

In newspapers, your advertisement is tangible. It doesn't disappear into the airwaves. It can't be wiped out by a remote control. It can be saved, clipped or carried, and customers can refer back to the advertisement

ALTON SMITH has always loved cars. He first turned his backyard hobby into a full-time occupation in 1964, when he took a job on the line inspecting brake drums, fittings and gears. He remembers being gung-ho "because the guys depended on you." After nineteen years on the line business, Alton talks about being gung-ho again. This time as a tool and die maker, building a brand new car called Saturn in Spring Hill, Tennessee.

"...My best buddies in high school were twins. A couple of guys named Hugh and Hugo. We all had cars. And every Saturday we'd tear something down and put it back together just for the fun of it. So it's no big surprise that we all ended up in the car business.

But those guys wouldn't ever believe I just picked up and went to work for a car company that's never built a car before.

Well, what I'm doing now here at Saturn is something completely different.

Here, we don't have management and we don't have labor. We have teams. And we have what you call consensus. Everything's a group decision. **In the last seven months, I've only had a few days off here and there. But this is where I want to be. This is living heaven.**

You work through breaks and you work through lunch. You're here all hours and even sometimes Saturdays. And you don't mind. Because no one's making you do it. It's just that here you can build cars the way you know they ought to be built.

I know the competition's stiff. I was out in California for a family reunion and everything was an import. Hondas, Toyotas. Well, now we're going to give people something else to buy.

I wouldn't be working all these hours if I didn't think we could...."

A DIFFERENT KIND of COMPANY. A DIFFERENT KIND of CAR.

If you'd like to know more about Saturn, and our new sedan and coupe, please call us at 1-800-522-5000.

Saturn Corporation

Tight writing is the key to this Saturn car magazine ad.

for more information. Think of your own experience with newspapers. Haven't you clipped a coupon out of your student newspaper for a 2-for-1 deal on pizzas?

Newspapers also offer display and classified advertising that is usually much cheaper than advertising on television, and is similar to the cost of advertising on radio or in magazines.

On the other hand, newspaper advertisements are discarded by the consumer usually after one reading and almost always after one day. Newspaper ads also must compete with other ads on the page and with the news copy for attention.

Magazines

In magazines, you may well deal with an audience that understands a specialty product. In *WaterSki* magazine, for example, a boat advertisement might well contain some detailed facts about engine specifications that wouldn't be understood or necessary in a general-circulation newspaper.

Like newspapers, magazine ad copy must compete for the reader's attention with other ads on the page or, if it's a full-page ad, with other ads in the magazine. Similarly to newspapers, as well, magazine ads must compete with the editorial matter of the magazine for the reader's attention, though with magazines the ads and the magazine's editorial matter are usually complementary and not in conflict.

Radio

In radio advertising, you have a medium in which you can't actually show your product. That seems like a liability, but Freberg turned it into an advantage when designing a spot for the radio advertising industry. Through sound effects and good writing, Freberg was able to "drain" Lake Michigan, "fill" it with ice cream and hot fudge, "cover" it in whipped cream and have a giant maraschino cherry "dropped" onto it by the Royal Canadian Air Force. "Try doing THAT on television," he intoned. The ad was a notable success.

Another of radio's liabilities is its ephemeral nature. If the listener doesn't hear the ad, it's gone, and until it comes on the air again, there is no opportunity for it to work. And in many cases the ad must compete with a string of ads, the effectiveness of each blurred as it competes not just for the listener's immediate attention, but for the listener's memory. If there are four ads in a row, which ones does the listener remember? Studies show that the first and last ad are remembered best, and the ads in the middle remembered least. But a number of factors can change that, including your writing an ad which, while buried in the middle, is better and more memorable than the others.

Among radio's great advantages are that ads are relatively inexpensive, especially when compared with television ads, and that radio's intimacy (with the announcer talking directly to the listener) is an excellent, and effective, way to communicate.

Finally, radio, like magazines, is usually tightly tied to a certain set of listener demographics, so advertisers can target specific audiences with ads on specific radio stations, and even on specific programs on those stations that reach a very particular listenership.

Television

Television allows great flexibility to its advertisers, who are able to take advantage of television's visual storytelling skills. In the early days of television, advertisers used animation to create memorable characters like Sharpy the Parrot, who hawked Gillette razor blades; Tony the Tiger, who told audiences that Sugar Frosted Flakes were Grrrrrreat!, and the Old Pro, who extolled the virtues of Falstaff beer to baseball fans. Today, cartoon characters still exist, but have been joined by more technologically sophisticated creations like the Claymation California Raisins and Budweiser's croaking frogs and jealous lizards.

Television also allows the identification of a product with an identifiable spokesperson. Celebrities like Bill Cosby may endorse products, or advertisers may create characters like Madge, the hairdresser who was forever dousing her customers' nails in Palmolive dishwashing detergent; the lonely Maytag repairman; or Spuds McKenzie, a comfortable canine used as a trademark for Budweiser.

Advertisers are able to use television's intimacy to create characters who maximize their target audience. Eighteen-year-old males probably weren't very comfortable with Madge, and older viewers probably wondered just what a scruffy Spuds had to do with beer; but the target audiences responded enthusiastically to these characters. Those who create commercials are able to match the spokesperson with the qualities deemed important for a particular product.

Internet

With the Internet, advertising appears to have come full circle. Words and graphics become animated through computer programming.

As with so much else about the Net, advertising is still in a developmental stage at this point. But Net advertising has progressed tremendously in the few years since Prodigy featured ad messages in glaring colors with nearly unreadable typefaces.

Internet advertisements are often linked to a site that features a company's product line and information about the company itself. It also appears that computer-oriented advertisement lends itself to companies that rely heavily on catalogs. The Internet's ability to categorize information has helped a number of advertisers in creating online catalogs, complete with order forms.

When and if encryption of credit information becomes safer, then you might well expect more companies to offer goods and services via the Internet.

Other

Direct-mail campaigns remain popular with certain advertisers. Mailing allows an advertiser either to blanket an area or to focus its efforts within a certain physical location.

Advertisers and marketers already know what the consumer preferences are within a given ZIP code, for example. When one author of this text lived in an apartment near the University of South Florida campus, he received a constant flood of mail from pizza delivery establishments. When he moved further from campus, the mailings slowed to a trickle. (When he went on a diet, they virtually stopped.)

Billboards can be effective as well. An entire industry exists to craft visual messages that draw the attention of drivers and passengers along freeways and on heavily traveled streets.

HUBBA, HUBBA

To write good ad copy, you might bear in mind the following hints. We've organized them as HUBBA (Heads matter, Use brand names, Be visual, Be brief, and Always make a promise).

Heads Matter

The place where strength comes from.

Put it where you want to be kissed.

Please DON'T FEED the animals
(but feel free to play with them)

Before people read a single word of your incredibly creative body copy, they've already scanned the headline above the smaller print and decided whether to invest a few seconds in reading on. The three headlines above, for example, attract attention to a sporting apparel shop (Lady Foot Locker), cosmetics (Ici), and a touring attraction (The Robot Zoo.)

Copywriters invest plenty of creative energy in making just the right headline to draw readers into the copy. This principle should sound familiar from the news chapters. The equivalent to a great lead in copywriting is the headline, and some of the rules that apply to newspaper headlines also apply to advertising headlines. The message must be clear and must fit into the allotted space. If, for example, the headline requires four words with no more than 22 letters, a 27-letter headline won't be accepted, no matter how poignant or inspiring.

One of the most successful advertisements in the 20th century was graphically unappealing, with large blocks of text underneath an unimposing drawing of a piano. But the headline made it a classic remembered by advertising professionals today.

"They laughed when I sat down at the piano, but when I started to play . . . "

A great lead in copywriting is the headline or the *lead-in*. "In direct mail, you generally have five seconds where the reader will look at the headline, maybe the subheads and decide whether to read it or not," Debra Jason said. "In an advertisement, you have maybe three seconds. You'd better have something that will catch their attention."

Use Brand Names

Well, isn't this obvious? Not quite. Many poor advertising campaigns fail to link the brand name of the product with the attributes of a successful product. In fact, Ogilvy, the copy guru, recommends that you put the brand name in the headline. If the brand name isn't actually a part of the main headline, it should still stand out apart from the copy.

Advertisers hope that a product will actually advance past brand-name recognition to a point where it is used interchangeably with the product itself. If you don't believe it, just take out a Kleenex to wipe your glasses and then make a Xerox of this chapter. Then settle back with a Coke, as we Southerners like to say.

Advertisers hope that a product will actually advance past brand-name recognition. They ant the public to think of their product as the only one that fits the bill, not just one among many. So the Coca-Cola company, for example, wants people to think only of Coke when they want a beverage to drink.

Despite this goal, advertisers must take care to safeguard the trade-marked brand names they are advertising. They do this by making sure that the brand name is used only as an adjective, never as a noun. They will not say "A Kleenex will take care of it"; they will be careful to say "A Kleenex tissue will take care of it." Allowing a brand name to be used as a common noun runs the risk of depriving the name of its trademark protection.

Be Visual

In many advertisements, the visual image is the message.

Copywriters learn early that people tend to remember visual images and that the copy must fit the tone and premise of the artwork—when, of course, such copy exists. You can pore through numerous magazines and find plenty of advertisements that use captivating photography or other art with the only copy being a brand name included in large letters.

Advertising researchers can tell agency personnel just how effective various elements of an advertisement are. People remember vivid visual images. The trick for advertisers is to tie those to the brand and the copy.

Be Brief

If you think news writers have to use words sparingly and accurately, you haven't even seen the beginning. When you have to get a persuasive message across in 20 seconds, you'd better not waste any words whatsoever. You will need to make every word in the advertisement count.

"When I do a presentation, I emphasize being clear," Jason says. "How do I make myself clear? By writing short sentences. If I see a brochure and the copy goes on in one paragraph for more than five or six lines, I'll stop reading.

"You can break the rules of grammar we all learned back in junior high school," she added. "The idea that one paragraph is one complete thought? Forget it. I'll break that paragraph into two or three paragraphs. I try never to have more than five lines before a paragraph—and a lot of times I'll have one-line paragraphs."

Keep sentences short. (Gee, that sounds familiar, maybe you read that in a newswriting chapter.)

In particular, watch out for wordy phrases that don't enhance your message. Prepositional phrases ("of the [noun]," especially) can often be tightened by changing word order and eliminating the preposition: *Leader of the industry* becomes *industry leader*; *advantage of the product* becomes *the product's advantage*, and so on.

Always Make a Promise

Some promises grab you by the throat: Use our product and you won't have icky dandruff. Some promises sneak past while you're being entertained. But almost every ad ought to promise something, either directly or implicitly.

Consider, for example, a series of Budweiser beer advertisements featuring Louie the lizard and his buddy watching from a distance as the Budweiser frogs croak out "Bud-Weis-Er." Louie is quite upset and notes that it's entirely possible that an "accident" might befall the frogs. "They might eat a tainted fly," he suggests.

Those ads barely mention the product, but imply that a lowly lizard could elevate his status by serving as a spokesperson for Budweiser and, by the way, the viewer could also elevate his or her status by drinking Budweiser. In this case, the audience member is required to make these unspoken leaps, but the promise does exist.

In the "Got Milk?" advertisements, people are deprived of milk. A rude businessman finds himself in a gleaming white room with a plate of gigantic chocolate chip cookies and a refrigerator filled with empty milk cartons. "Where am I?" he intones. And as the image fades on the screen, flaming letters spell out "got milk?" The implication is, of course, that milk will refresh you.

Substance Over Format

As a copywriter, you can design advertisements that use all kinds of illustrative tricks and special camera effects. You can spend millions on a campaign featuring expensive celebrities at scenic locations. You can commission the design of Claymation wombats or virtual-reality llamas as corporate spokesfigures. But despite what one advertising campaign tried to tell you, image isn't everything (in fact, Sprite advertisers created a campaign mocking that campaign). Substance matters more than format.

In order to create a memorable advertisement, you will need to deal in specifics. What, specifically, makes a Wardrip Widget such a wonderful device? Is it the craftsmanship? The utility? The price? The availability? All have been used as the focus in series of advertisements.

But remember that the point of the campaign is to sell. And features—even unique features—don't always sell the product. When an advertising agency recruited Stan Freberg to help with a campaign for Kaiser aluminum foil, the previous campaign had focused on how Kaiser "quilted" its foil, making it crimp easier than other brands. Unfortunately, that unique proposition didn't sell the foil, mainly because its competitors had virtually all the shelf space for their foils. When Freberg focused on the problem in his campaign (an animated foil salesman struggling to get shelf space), distribution and, later, sales increased.

Specific benefits usually beat features. The single most important question a copywriter faces is "What is the benefit to this specific audience?" When you reach the point where you can figure this out, then you will have a successful career in advertising, direct marketing or any of the other areas dealing with persuasive copy.

That fickle audience we talked about really wants to know "What's in it for me? You want to sell me this widget? What do I get out of it?"

Beginning copywriters too often think in terms of nonspecific benefits. A Gateway 2000 computer advertisement put the benefit right into the headline where it couldn't possibly be missed: "A great computer, a monitor and a printer for $1,499."

Motivation

Advertising is designed to motivate people to some sort of action. In the case of *image* advertising, it may ask people to consider the corporation as a respectable enterprise rather than a major polluter or a weapons manufacturer. Most usually, though, advertising asks consumers to make a purchase decision of some sort.

Please understand that an advertisement is not a magic bullet, as unfortunately, some students seem to believe. In this dream world, consumers are helpless in the face of sophisticated techniques of persuasion and manipulation that drive the economies of multinational corporations. (This dream is usually followed by the conspiracy theorists' best friend—the subliminal advertisement that can't be escaped.)

What sorts of psychological appeals make people want to buy your product or consider your organization in a better light? Some would say you should consider appeals to fear, greed, guilt and exclusiveness.

Afraid of stinking like a horse on that big date?
Use this deodorant.

Want to make thousands in 30 days? Buy this product.

Your kids are falling behind in school? Buy this computer.

Want something special? Our product is special.

You've seen those ads. However, most advertisers believe that positive appeals lead to higher sales than negative appeals do. Appeals to love, honor, charity, popularity and fellowship with others work far better for many companies than do those more negative appeals. And sometimes a negative appeal for a product relating to health or safety isn't so negative at all. Certainly many organizations are concerned not only with selling products, but with selling an image through their advertisements. An advertisement showing a Down's syndrome employee at a McDonald's restaurant may not result in higher sales of hamburgers, but it does result in a more positive image for this large corporate entity. Image advertising has grown steadily in recent years. If you, as a copywriter, can persuade me that your client possesses attractive qualities, then I am much more likely to think highly of that client.

Remember, the goal of some advertisements is to increase name recognition or to *position* a product line.

It's Not Just Super Bowl Ads

You probably began to think of advertising after watching television. You can even understand that radio and print media use advertising as well. But you've only scratched the surface of what talented copywriters can be expected to write. Copywriters are also expected to write—and write with some success—direct-mail letters, fund-raising letters, and copy for catalogs.

Those ubiquitous credit-card letters, promising low rates and great service? Some copywriter had to write those. Those fund-raising letters from groups as diverse as the National Rifle Association and Greenpeace? Assembled by copywriters. And just as copywriters for those familiar television commercials hope to influence a purchase decision, so too do these copywriters hope to persuade their audiences to send a check.

Tight writing is just as important here, but so is the concept of compelling writing. If you write a direct-mail advertisement well enough, some readers may skate through five pages of it. If it doesn't appeal, then readers may toss it after a glance.

As in other forms of advertising—and in news writing—specifics work better than generalities. What, specifically, do you want your audience to do? What, specifically, do you have to offer that others can't?

Advertorials

Finally, let's mention one more area where the rest of the textbook may well help you. A form of advertising known as the advertorial has become a popular development. *Advertorials* are written in news style and are presented in story format with a headline and 13.3-pica columns just like news stories, but they are clearly efforts to sell or promote a product.

An ethical news operation tries to make certain that the advertorial cannot be mistaken for the magazine's or newspaper's own news stories. The advertorial may well be printed in a different font with a different headline font and should be clearly marked as advertising. The copy should be written by advertising staffers, not by reporters and editors.

This distinction isn't strong enough for some purists, who think any such imitation news story dilutes the news product. And, traditionally, most news operations of any size try to keep the advertising and news departments separate. In some daily newspapers, these are referred as the "first floor" (where the advertising offices usually may be found), and the "second floor" (where the newsroom may be located.) Essentially, it still remains a good idea for each department to avoid influences on the other. Advertising staffers should not suggest that reporters write favorable stories about advertisers, and reporters shouldn't meddle with the advertising department's decisions either.

Photo by Chuck Thompson

A Day in the Life of...

**Advertising Copywriter
Ray Straub**

Wake up. Get out of bed. Drag a comb across my head. Go to class. Oh wait, that must have been a previous life. This time around I'm *Ray Straub, advertising copywriter.*

7:00 a.m.: The radio alarm blasts me into semiconsciousness. I stumble toward the hallowed hot tub and clamber in. Like a gentle, downward-sloping path toward sentience, the 104-degree water eases me into the day.

I visualize my day's workload as the sole copywriter at a 15-person agency in Clearwater, Florida: meetings, deadlines, headlines, ads. Within 10 minutes the idea that I may create greatness today has me raring to go.

8:10 a.m.: By now I'm hitting the road. I've got a fast car and I love to drive, but I loathe those . . . who . . . drive . . . slow . . . in the fast lane. I actually sold my house and bought a new one, doubling my mortgage, just to shorten my commute. It's worth it.

8:30 a.m.: I enter the office, fire up the Mac, check the e-mail and phone messages, then examine the day's work orders: some radio spots, a direct-mail piece and . . . ugh . . . a holiday card for a car salesman. He sends these to customers and prospects every chance he gets. It's my job to carry on 15 years of tradition, which means cheeseball poems that say, "Happy Whatever, now buy a car."

I throw that file in the corner, knowing I'll knock it out in 10 minutes this afternoon. No sense in wasting prime early-morning brainpower on such schlock. I dig further into the pile and find a copywriter's joy: a television spot. As usual, there's no money in the budget and it needs to be on the air in a week, but it's another chance at greatness. I break out the yellow pad and begin to pour out ideas.

9:30 a.m.: I visit my creative director to discuss the projects I've been working on recently and to catch up on office scuttlebutt. I'm really lucky because my CD has been through wars of all kinds and, as a result, can warn me about the various traps and pitfalls a writer must avoid in order to survive in this business. If you find a good, well-seasoned creative director, stick with him.

Sometimes, with unsophisticated clients, it's a matter of walking a fine line between what they want and what they need. It seems bizarre that they'd hire an ad agency, then dictate exactly what the work should look like and precisely what it should contain.

You wouldn't tell your doctor how to treat you, or your lawyer how to defend you. Why not? Because they're experts who know what they're doing. So are we.

Some would say of such clients: "They bought a dog so they could do some barking" or that they make "sow's ears out of silk purses."

10:00 a.m.: I'm finding talent and negotiating on stock footage for an upcoming spot. (Since I work at a smallish agency, I not only write ads for television and radio, but also produce them.)

10:30 a.m.: I'm throwing down more concepts for the TV spot. Most oft-repeated phrase: "What if?" The best thing you can do in concept is just to get it all out and worry about what works and doesn't work later. No rules, just write. (I invented that. It's fun to twist words and things around, like "Pre-Madonna.") I usually end up with 50 or so headlines for each ad I work on.

11:30 a.m. I'm out of the office, directing voice talent and editing a radio commercial that I wrote for a major pizza chain. The good part about producing your own spots is that you can personally keep your vision alive.

12:30 p.m.: Back at the Mac, I'm chowing down junk food while doing a bit of work. Usually I do company jobs during lunch, but sometimes I'll spend my "break" on side jobs.

My freelance jobs are always more free than lance, like the *pro bono* brochure I'm writing for the Greyhound Pets of America group, or the occasional project for beloved old professors.

1:30 p.m.: I'm proofreading a new business pitch. Just as the office computer expert gets hit

Summary

The skills that make good reporters and public relations practitioners apply to good advertisers: the ability to write persuasively and tightly, the ability to quickly research a subject, the willingness to revise a piece until it improves. Though advertisers employ creativity, they learn to harness that creativity to meet the client's needs. And though an advertiser may be a wizard at video, print or Web design, the substance of the ad outweighs the format.

up constantly to fix crashes and bugs, the copywriter is frequently barraged with questions on grammar and usage. I get recruited for proofing of all kinds; the office calls me "Raydar" because errors jump out at me. With all modesty, I am far superior to those spelling and grammar checkers on the computer.

I thank Kim Golombisky, who taught the Mass Media Grammar Slammer class in college. She hammered grammar so deep into my brain that I dream in Associated Press style.

2:30 p.m.: With double vision from scrutinizing 30 pages of copy and indents on my hand from heavy use of red pens, I hand back the pitch, previously assumed to be perfect. Work hard and pay attention in your writing and grammar classes, and you, too, can acquire radar.

2:40 p.m.: I just cranked out the silly poem for that holiday card. It's brilliant in its own horrid way.

3:00 p.m.: You caught me. I'm not just reading a magazine; I'm catching up on the advertising industry by flipping through the trade pubs. Crucial.

3:30 p.m.: I'm back to the TV spot ideas. Time is tight, so now is when I start crossing the clichéd, mundane, senseless and stupid ideas off my list (you always hope there aren't *too* many of them). Then I wipe out the good ideas that would be problematic to produce. I'm left with 10 ideas, five of them good and two potentially great.

3:55 p.m.: Got to go. The suits are calling for me.

4:15 p.m.: Great. I was called into a meeting where I had to sing, for the clients, the jingle/stinger that I wrote for their radio campaign, and do the announcing for the copy bits. It could have been demeaning . . . except that the clients ate it up. Totally.

I was fortunate enough to come up with some great headlines for the client's billboards and a new slogan, which then led to tie-in print and radio work. I took it upon myself to research the proposed media buy, concocted a strategy and nailed the creative. If you work and if you're lucky, it comes to you easily. I think it helps to see things from a million different angles. Then you can combine previously unrelated items into original ideas. That's creativity.

5:29 p.m.: A small herd makes a dash for the door. At last, I can get some work done. I dive headfirst into a pile of direct mail, newspaper and magazine ads that need copy.

7:00 p.m.: My two art director friends and I blow off some steam by blowing the heads off of various mutants and monsters, courtesy of our networked Macs and the wonderful world of 3-D video gaming.

8:00 p.m.: I'm driving back across the bridge to Tampa, where I tune in to the Lightning hockey game and hope we're not getting crushed again.

Life is good in the fast lane.   ■

Ray Straub is currently Senior Copywriter at Zimmerman Partners Advertising in Ft. Lauderdale, the largest ad agency in the Southeast.

Key Points

► Advertising isn't just random creativity, but the harnessing of creative ideas to specific goals that are related to customer needs.

► Copywriters must learn how to write to varied audiences and to respect those audiences instead of underestimating them.

► Copywriters would do well to remember Ogilvy's advice on producing advertisements that stay on target.

- ▶ Being able to produce a persuasive message means being able to give that message in as few words as possible.

- ▶ Copywriters seek to match motivations to the audience in order to reach customers.

- ▶ The purpose of an advertising campaign is not to produce really slick ads, but to sell—and to do so without lying.

Web Links

http://www.aaaa.org
http://www.aaf.org

InfoTrac College Edition Readings

For additional readings, go to **www.infotrac-college.com**, enter your password, and search for the following articles by title or author's name.

- ▶ "Why Would Anyone Want to Write Advertising?" (Brief Article), Linda Westphal, *Direct Marketing*, May 2000 v63 i1 p37.

- ▶ "Heads Up!" (Effective headlines in advertising), Jerry Fisher, *Entrepreneur*, Oct. 1996 v24 n10 p108.

- ▶ "Relaxed Attitude Should Help You to Write Proper" (Writing advertising copy), Drayton Bird, *Marketing*, May 9, 1996 p16.

Exercises

Go to your CD-ROM to complete the following exercises:

- ▶ Exercise 12.1

- ▶ Exercise 12.2

- ▶ Exercise 12.3

- ▶ Exercise 12.4

- ▶ Exercise 12.5

13

Editing and Revision for Media Writers

How Editing Happens

Get TRICI

A Sample Revision

I t's 2 a.m., and your media-writing class is at 8 a.m.; but as you type the last line of the 10-inch campus news story, you feel good about yourself. The story has two sources and some good quotes mixed with solid facts to back them up, and best of all, the story seemed to flow right onto the screen as you worked on it. From start to finish, the writing of the piece couldn't have taken more than 30 minutes. After a few hours of sleep, you turn the story into your professor with a confident smile on your face.

A week later, though, when you get the story back, that smile turns into a worried frown. There's a large red *C* at the top of your story, and this comment from your professor: "Nice reporting, but poorly organized, and with some very sloppy writing. See me."

Ulp. What went wrong?

Well, as your professor will point out to you when you go for that meeting to discuss the story, a number of things went wrong, most of them having to do with your ability to edit and revise your own stories.

Successful media writing, you see, requires more from you than a rushed, one-draft story. To do professional work as a media writer, you need to learn that the hard work of reporting, organizing and writing your story is only the beginning. Before the story gets into print (or gets put into the mail, if you are writing a news release in public relations), you must polish the story, editing and revising it until it is as perfect as you can make it.

Then, as you will quickly discover once you're a professional in the field, even *after* you've done a good job of editing yourself, there will be more editing and revision before the story is published.

How Editing Happens

While the essentials of editing and revision remain the same for all media writers, there are differences in the process for each medium. Here's how the editing and revision process works for writers in various kinds of media.

Newspapers

At a newspaper, you will often be pressed for time. Nevertheless, you will be expected to turn in clean copy, with no misspellings, no obvious grammatical errors (like those noun–pronoun and noun–verb agreement problems discussed back in Chapter 3), and a structure that quickly and cleanly conveys the news in the story.

Once your story leaves your hands, it will go to a copy desk, where several editors will read it and make corrections, sometimes in consultation with you. The copy editor will correct any misspellings, fix any obvious grammatical or style errors, and then give a quick few minutes of time to considering the story's structure and even its reporting.

For any major changes, the copy editor will probably consult you. For minor changes, he or she will simply make the corrections for you and the story will appear in the next day's paper.

A major lament for newspaper reporters is that the copy desk changes their stories, "ruining" the stories in the process. From the editors' perspective, of course, those changed stories have been "saved." If you don't want the copy desk to make changes, you need to turn in clean copy, which probably means learning how to do an excellent job of editing your own material.

On every copy desk of every newspaper, the paper's writers have a reputation that to one level or another affects the kind of editing the copy desk performs on a story. If your writing has the reputation of being sloppy, then the editors know they must actively look to make corrections and you are likely to be more heavily edited. If you turn in sloppy copy, then, you have no cause for complaint when the desk does a lot of editing on your work.

However, if you have the reputation as a writer who turns in clean copy, the editors learn to trust you and your work will be much more lightly edited. If you'd rather be trusted, and have the copy desk leave your material alone, then learn to do a good job of editing and revising your own story *before* you turn it in.

Magazines

As we've noted elsewhere, in magazine writing you are in competition with other writers for the editor's attention, so you have little room for sloppy copy. As Kathleen Stauffer, managing editor for *Catholic Digest* notes, "Repeated misspellings, things like using *to* when you meant to use *too*, or especially things like *it's* when you should have used *its* are definitely red flags for me."

But if your copy is clean and the story well organized, this is how it gets into print.

If you are a staffer, the process of editing and revision is similar to the one that takes place at a newspaper, with the editors talking directly to you about any major changes.

If you are a freelancer, the story must first compete successfully against dozens or hundreds of others for the editor's attention. If the story passes that test (and remember that sloppy copy is one of the first things to ruin a story's chances with an editor) and is purchased by the editor, then he or she will work with the story, making the changes the editor thinks the story needs, and then fax or mail you the changes.

"We work extensively with writers," says Stauffer at *Catholic Digest*. "Sometimes I will assign an assistant to work with a rough manuscript and its author and I will oversee the process, checking on the story's progress. Sometimes, on the other hand, I handle it myself. I prefer to do it over the phone," after, she notes, the writer has received the edited manuscript back in the mail.

Once you receive the changes, you are expected to make them if they are matters of grammar and style, or of fact or accuracy. If, though, the changes are more in the nature of writing style, you should feel free to discuss them with the editor and, occasionally, argue the point, trying to keep things the way you have them. Too much argument, of course, will work against you.

For both staffers and freelancers there is an additional factor in magazine editing and revision: the fact checker. *Fact checking* is usually done by editorial assistants in their first job at the magazine (they are often just called "fact checkers"), and it is their job to double-check every fact in your story: every statistic, every phone number, every date, every quote, the spelling of every name and job title—everything they can think of to check.

When your story is bought (or received by the editor, if you're a staffer), the fact checkers get to work on it immediately. They then mail you all their questions (usually in the same envelope as the editor's

Tips and Tactics

Two Newspaper Editors Discuss the Editing Process

© Newsday, Inc.

Phil Mintz,
*feature editor
at (Long Island)*
Newsday

"There are some writers here at *Newsday* who I know will need a very light edit, but few staffers whose copy I would put in the dirty category. The best writers at the paper are excellent reporters and stylists. Since a key element to clean writing is a thorough understanding of your subject, those are the stories that generally need only a few touch-ups.

"The hard work comes when the writer hasn't put enough effort into reporting a story and the time needed to write it clearly—and I see that in a lot of freelancers. Since, in my section at least, we can pick which writers we want to use, we won't go back to those people.

"As a writer, I found that most problems with stories arise with miscommunication between writers and assigning editors resulting in stories that don't match expectations. So as an editor, I try to make sure the writers I work with are on the same page as I am before they start working on a story. As for copydesk editing, I didn't have much of a problem with the process. Sure, there were a lot of stupid questions, but there were also the good ones that helped the stories or kept me from making a mistake. (There's one longtime editor here who has a reputation for asking a ton of questions, but I'd rather *he* read my copy than worry if someone on the desk was letting something get by.) In the 16 years I've been at the paper, there's only a handful of stories that I can honestly say were harmed by editors. I think part of this attitude was shaped by a decade or so as a rewrite man, where I worked more closely with editors than most writers. Now, as an editor, I'm trying to take the same approach (but without the stupid questions). I'm still too new at this not to respect writers and what it takes to turn a good idea into a story that will grab readers." ∎

Photo by Robert Seals

Tom Seals,
*copy editor on
the sports desk
at* The Kansas
City Star

"Ever watch reruns of the TV show *M*A*S*H*? (Some editors would argue that a reference to a 1970s program is too obscure for college-age readers in the 21st century.) It was about the zany-but-dedicated characters who worked at a surgical unit near the front line during the Korean War. (Some editors would argue that it should be called the Korean Conflict.) The hero, Hawkeye, (some editors would argue he was an anti-hero) and his fellow surgeons performed what was termed "meatball surgery" to patch up the seriously wounded (some editors would argue that there's no such thing as a nonserious wound), hoping to keep them alive long enough to reach a real hospital. In times of crisis—when there were too many patients and too few doctors—the medical staff would throw quick bandages on the injuries of the less seriously wounded soldiers and devote their full attention to saving the critical patients, all the while hoping they hadn't misdiagnosed the patients they'd decided to push aside. It was thankless work, performed under less than ideal circumstances, and though the doctors saved most of the patients, they sometimes sadly wondered what they could have done with more time and better conditions.

"Being a copy editor at a daily newspaper is often similar to being a surgeon in a M*A*S*H* unit—minus the life-saving and the blood. When I have four stories to edit in the final half hour before deadline, I throw quick headlines on the stories in stable condition, then try to stop the bleeding on the ones in critical condition, all the while hoping I didn't read right past a glaring fact error in the stories I already shipped off. I save most of the patients, but at the end of the night I sometimes sadly wonder what I could have done with more time and fewer stories to edit.

"During a typical day I edit any number of wire-service stories, plus four or five staff-written stories. The local copy is the meat and potatoes, the bread and butter (if the preceding eight words made you wince, you might be an editor) of a daily newspaper, and as such get added editing attention. And since we're always hoping to get the latest information into the paper, the final hour before deadline is always far more hectic than the four or five leading up to it. Fortunately, when there are questions in local stories, you can talk to the writer, either face-to-face or by phone, and sort through the problems. It's sometimes one of the hardest things for an editor to do. Most editors don't relish telling a writer a story isn't good enough, and most writers would rather not hear it. But both editor and writer have to remember that a discussion of the story before it goes into the paper is far less embarrassing than a published story that is confusing—or worse, wrong.

"Example A: I recently edited a sidebar from a football game about a punter who had struggled early in the season, then finally had a great game. Before his great game, the punter had been unwilling to admit that he'd been struggling. It was a perfectly acceptable story with no real problems, except that its lede seemed to foreshadow something that was never delivered:

> *The secret is out now that Todd Sauerbrun has ended his season-opening slump and punted the way the Chiefs expected him to when they signed him as a free agent during the off-season.*
> *He was trying so hard to make a good first impression on the Chiefs that he was pressing.*

"Um, what secret? He had a broken leg? He'd been arrested? He'd been exchanging sensitive military documents? Well, no. He was trying too hard, but that's hardly a secret. Rather than rewrite it myself, I got the reporter on the phone and told him the hardest thing for a writer to hear: The lede doesn't work. I read it to him. His response? 'Yeah, that's not right. Make it . . . um . . . "He has a confession to make." Does that work better?' Much.

> *Todd Sauerbrun has a confession to make now that he has ended his season-opening*

slump and punted the way the Chiefs expected him to when they signed him as a free agent during the off-season.
He was trying so hard to make a good first impression on the Chiefs that he was pressing.

"Now, instead of reading the story feeling as if you've missed the secret, you roll right through it. That's what the writer wants, and that's one of the things an editor looks for. I didn't make a Nobel Prize winner out of junk. I pointed out a flaw, and the writer happily fixed it. That's why writers love editors.

"Example B: I edited a feature about a gymnast competing at the Olympic Trials. I found the lede long and hard to follow. I double-checked with the person in the slot that night to make sure I wasn't missing the point, then chopped out half the words in the lede and basically removed all the confusion and attempts at creativity. That's a last-resort editing technique used on deadline, but I made this editing decision two hours before dead-line. When the writer dutifully called to see if there were any questions, I replied, "Naw, we're cool." He called again after midnight, angry. He'd just looked at his story on the newspaper's Web site, and didn't recognize his lede. What happened? My lame reply, "Well, your lede didn't work," seemed indefensible. It was a busy night. I was in a hurry. But he'd done his job, calling to see if there were questions. By not telling him about my problem with his story, I'd failed to do my job. That's why writers hate editors.

"I've been an editor for 20 years, in news and sports, at four newspapers— I've been in the business so long that I actually worked for a paper that published in the afternoon (honest, lots of them used to do that). So much has changed in that time, the competition, the tools of the trade, the world. But one thing has remained constant: Every writer needs to be edited. Even the best of them occasionally misspells, misuses and drops words. Even the best of them sometimes gets a fact wrong. Even the best of them sometimes writes a paragraph that just doesn't work. And interestingly, the best of them are usually the most grateful when an editor helps improve a story." ∎

broader comments on the story), and you are expected to make the changes or explain why the changes don't need to be made.

Public Relations

In public relations, you may be writing as part of an internal or external magazine or newspaper, in which case the editing procedure is the same as (or very similar to) the one you've just read for those kinds of publications.

For news releases, you will be expected to produce a release that is faultless in terms of grammar and style, but you can expect your boss, and his or her bosses, to take a good hard look at the release before it goes out. They will frequently make changes.

It is not uncommon in public relations work for top management to approve news releases before they are sent out to the media. In many cases, these top managers are not writers; they're businesspeople. So their main interest in your writing will be in the content of the release; that is, did you get the facts right? But you can expect them to notice grammar and style problems, too. And the last person you want noticing that you're shaky in those basic areas is the top boss in the firm.

Finally, in public relations you may often be working where you *won't* have anyone editing your copy. In many businesses, the media relations department (by whatever name it goes—media relations, public relations, or something similar) is so small as to consist of one overworked person, or maybe just two or three. In that case, it is entirely possible that the only edit your story will get will be your own; so the ability to self-edit becomes crucial.

In other cases, you may be freelancing public relations material (an occurrence that is increasingly common, as you can see in Appendix C). Again, the ability to self-edit becomes crucially important, along with the ability to negotiate, as you can see in the "Tips and Tactics" feature in this chapter by talented novelist, short-story writer and public-relations writer Nick DeChario.

Editing for Broadcast

Unlike copy for newspapers and magazines, which goes through very formal editing procedures, the copy written for broadcasting is often viewed by only one or two people before it is aired.

The process is different depending upon the size of the market and the complexity of the station's operations. Generally, in smaller markets the reporter writes and edits the story to ensure that it adheres to the time allocations given by a producer. It may or may not be read by the producer before airtime. In a larger market, the reporter may give the details of the story to a writer or assistant producer. Those individuals then write the copy, which is reviewed by the producer of the newscast. If the producer has confidence in the writer, the copy may simply go to the computer to be called up on the teleprompter.

In broadcasting, there is a great deal of responsibility on the shoulders of reporters and writers since little review of their copy takes place. Accuracy is the responsibility of the few. Anchors, who are reading the stories, sometimes become involved in the copy they read, but their interest is usually directed more towards readability than accuracy. If the story is a self-contained package, there is little review beyond discussions between a reporter and producer or anchor.

Reporters recently hired by a station often have their copy reviewed by assignment editors to ensure that it meets the station's standards for quality and appropriateness. Once the station is comfortable with the reporter, the copy gets little more than a quick review for placement in the newscast.

Tips and Tactics

Editing and Revision for Public Relations

By Nick DiChario

When you're writing newsletters, brochures or public relations material, revising and polishing is absolutely crucial. Nothing is perfect the first time through. Get used to it. You'll be working with people whose responsibility it is to give input, suggestions and criticism, regardless of how well you've done your job.

I have a friend who intentionally puts "sinkers" into every first draft she writes, because she'd rather bait a client with something that is obviously awkward than have the client object to something good.

Part of the skill of editing, and often part of your success as a public relations writer, is in how you balance your talent, instincts and know-how with the demands of your customers. In this way, public relations writing may be more challenging and far more frustrating than, say, journalism or fiction.

What do you do, for example, when a client prefers a brochure that is grammatically incorrect because a comma or capitalization in the proper place looks awkward? You might point to the exact page in your stylebook that proves you right, but you'll soon discover that the workplace is not a court of law. You would never stumble over this in your own short story or an article for a newspaper. The important thing for you is to know the right way and constantly reinforce it. The process of fine-tuning your work is not just to hone your natural genius, but to keep the people who think they're experts at bay and teach them a thing or two about good writing along the way.

You also need to be comfortable with the "committee process." I've written a number of brochures that have gone through several levels of management and more than 48 people before final approval. Every word was scrutinized, and I had to respond to all suggestions before I was allowed to proceed. A 500-word brochure might take months to complete for no other reason than that you can't get your committee to agree on *insure* or *ensure*. ∎

Get TRICI

The major difficulty with editing your own stories is one of recognition. It's hard to recognize the mistakes you've made, even the obvious ones. After all, you made the mistake in the first place, so it's not surprising that you have a hard time recognizing it when you come back to edit your own story.

There are some things you can do, though, that will help you see the errors you made in your first draft. Here are five techniques for self-editing. You might think of these as the TRICI ("tricky") Edit Plan, where you *T*ake some time, then *R*ead the story aloud, *I*solate your lines, *C*hange your context, and *I*solate your paragraphs.

Take Some Time

For the same reasons you change your context, you should also put as much time between the first draft and the revision as you can. For newspaper and broadcast reporters, that often isn't much time at all; but even taking the time to walk to the break room and sip on a cola or a cup of coffee will help.

For magazine, public relations and advertising media writers, you will often have time to wait a day or two before editing the story. You'll be pleasantly surprised at how many of your own mistakes you can catch when you've had a little time (and that change of context) to help make the material look fresher to you.

Read the Story Aloud

The best way of all to slow down and concentrate on your story when you're revising is to read it aloud. Many writers do this, and with most media stories (with the exception of a rare, long magazine piece) the reading process will take only a few minutes.

In fact, when you're pressed for time (to meet a newspaper deadline, for instance), reading aloud is frequently the quickest way to get the kind of accuracy you need.

Isolate Your Lines

Another good way to slow down as you edit your own material is to take a piece of paper and cover everything on the page from the bottom except for the line you are editing. This helps keep you focused on just the material in that one line.

As a reminder to slow down and take your time, line by line, put a checkmark or a dot at the end of each line when you finish looking at it closely. And only then, after you're read it and checked it off, should you move the paper down to the next line. This technique is also very useful for looking at how your story is structured, as you'll soon see.

Change Your Context

As you are probably starting to discover in your writing, when things are going well, you can get lost in the act of writing; your creative mind goes into a kind of fugue state, a state of mind where you look up and an hour has passed and the entire three-page feature story you have due is done.

Trouble is, the creative mind that does such a good job of writing that first draft is often not a very good speller, and frequently has other style and grammar problems, as well.

What you will discover is that when you are editing and when you are writing you are in two very different frames of mind. In both cases you are tightly focused on the task at hand. But while you can comfortably get lost in the process of writing, in the case of editing you have to go much, much more slowly, concentrating on each word. If you start to speed up, and slip back into that creative mindset that produced the story, then you most probably won't catch your own mistakes.

To avoid that, the first thing you should do is change your context. If you wrote the story on a computer screen, then edit it on hard copy (and transfer the corrections in later). If you wrote the piece in the living room, on a laptop, then move into the kitchen to edit it. If you wrote it late at night, edit it first thing in the morning.

However you do it, make sure that the context in which you do the editing is different from the context in which you did the writing. If it is, you'll better be able to look at the story fresh, almost as if it were written by someone else. That fresh look will allow you to see mistakes that you might otherwise miss.

Isolate Your Paragraphs

Using that same piece of scratch paper, place it at the end of the first paragraph of your story. Read that paragraph; then ask yourself what should logically come next.

Now take a look to see what you actually wrote. Is that what you expected? All too often it won't be, or it will be close, but not quite what you now know you should have written.

Do this same technique paragraph by paragraph, and you'll likely find yourself moving some paragraphs around, rewriting others, and writing a new one here and there as well. And your story will be much better as a result.

A Sample Revision

The Baltimore Sun's *Del Q. Wilber discovered early on that rewriting was "as important as the actual writing."*

To see how a story goes from first draft to published piece, take a look at the following feature from reporter Del Wilber of *The Baltimore Sun*. Wilber, in his first few months at *The Sun*, learned that revising is the hard work that turns an ordinary story into an excellent, front-page piece.

"This story was one of my first substantial feature stories at *The Sun*," he says, "and it further solidified my belief that the rewriting process is as important as the actual writing. I wrote one draft, then another, then another before showing it to a friend, who took a whack at it. Then, I showed the story to my immediate editor who reworked the story some more. Finally, I got some advice from my paper's managing editor, William K. Marimow, who made further suggestions that really strengthened the story. He suggested I lead with more drama and tension. That, I think, made the story a much more compelling read.

"In the end, I was fairly happy with the story, though I think it could have used many more improvements. I also now wish that I hadn't written the story. The charges against the suspect were eventually dropped when a Howard County grand jury refused to indict him. Never trust that the cops have the right man. Wait until a jury convicts the defendant or the suspect pleads guilty before writing a story about a cop who did good police work. I still haven't figured out exactly what went wrong in that case."

Det. Nathan Retting drove by a shallow stream in a nondescript woods hundreds of times while working patrol for the Howard County Police.

Then one June day in 1995, the stream, only yards from Route 99 in Woodstock, revealed a 10-year-old mystery: the bones of an Ellicott City woman who vanished New Year's Day, 1985.

From his first days on the force, only months after **Taylor's** disappearance, Rettig says he followed the case's twists and turns.

This May, two years after the body was found, Retting was given the task of solving his first homicide. Seven months later, on Nov. 24, Retting arrested the man long suspected in the slaying.

Many credit Rettig's determination, his discipline for tracking down witnesses, for linking crucial pieces of evidence, for finding a **suspects'** friend whose statements helped Rettig get the two-year-old autopsy results changed to homicide.

Charged in the alleged murder is Kenneth Allen White, 47, an unemployed mechanic from Lebanon, Pa.

White vigorously denies involvement in Taylor's death.

"I didn't do it," White said at a recent bail hearing. "I could have gone behind the **iron curtain** if I wanted to. I turned myself in to face these charges . . . to clear my name."

Legal experts cautioned that White is innocent until proven guilty, that the age of the case and the lack of forensic evidence could make it difficult to prosecute.

"This will definitely be a challenge," said **Garry** Deise, a professor at the University of Maryland School of Law who has arguments for the defense to make. "The (**prosecution**) will have to navigate through a mine field to satisfy a jury."

But that doesn't mean much to Stephen Gover, Taylor's brother, who said the detective's determination assuaged his pain.

"The arrest gives me a little closure," said Gover, **46**. "I didn't think they had enough to catch the guy."

For his part, Rettig says he never took the case personally, never get too close, worked his eight-hour days and then went home to his wife and kids.

On a cold December afternoon, Rettig, his gray-white speckled hair **flayed** from the bitter wind, sat in his unmarked cruiser, only a quarter mile from Taylor's temporary grave.

"When I'm here," said Rettig, who's been a detective for two years, "I think about all the times I drove by that place as a patrolman and never knew."

Adjusting his tan overcoat and nudging his large glasses up his nose, Rettig spoke carefully about the case, pondering every question and answer, wary that a single slip could ruin years of police work.

The former Marine, former **Hoosier**, who never dreamed he'd be a detective investigating a murder, said during several interviews that building this case was like building a home, that other detectives built the foundation and walls, that he only "finished" it up.

Many others disagreed, they said Rettig took a carefully planned blueprint by others and then built a solid home, that his job took a lot of determination.

"On this case you needed a bit of a bulldog, a dog who won't let the bone go," said **State's Attorney** Bernard Tay-

lor, who will be prosecuting the suspect. "Nathan did that; he was persistent."

Rettig's sergeant agreed. "Nathan did a fantastic job bringing all the information together into a workable case," said Sgt. Greg Marshall, who heads the violent crime unit. "It got solved because nobody gave up on it from 1985 through 1997, everybody involved did their part, particularly Nathan."

In May, Marshall called Rettig into his office and handed him a box of papers and a three-ring binder with all the information relating to Taylor's slaying.

Rettig pored through **the documents, the notes, the reports and organized the file, thought of a game plan.**

He read about how Taylor visited the **Valley View Inn** on New Year's Eve, how she left with a man she didn't know, how the 31-year-old mother was never seen again.

He knew that Taylor was a recent stroke victim, that she was on medication, that she was a good person who loved her kids and was on welfare.

He understood that pure chance spelled Taylor's demise, the suspect needed to cash a check and had met another man who recommended the Valley View Inn.

For months, Rettig's work on the case consisted of making phone calls and organizing the file while sitting at his small desk, decorated with a Semper Fi bumper sticker, Marine Corps and American **flag,** a small teddy bear hanging from a thumb tack.

In the **detectives'** large office, a board lists all the active cases, blue marker with red marks stating the case was closed. Rettig doesn't think Taylor's slaying is even on the board, the case is that old.

Rettig began to see some holes in the old reports, learned that the uncle of the suspect had seen his nephew kissing Taylor at the bar. He said he remembered seeing Taylor leave with the suspect.

Rettig soon discovered that uncle and suspect hadn't spoken in **ten years,**

(continued)

(continued)

that they were related by marriage, that there were several inconsistencies with the suspect's statements.

Rettig traveled to Lebanon and interviewed White at city police headquarters, in a large room, around a large table with a couple of chairs.

Rettig said he sat at the corner, at a right angle to the suspect, and started offering "softball questions" to the suspect, who told his story.

The man denied going to the Valley View Inn with a local man, a direct contradiction to his 1985 statements, according to Rettig and the records charging White with the crime.

Then Rettig showed the suspect a picture of the Valley View Inn as it appeared in 1985. As the alleged murderer studied the picture, Rettig placed a photograph of Taylor on the table.

According to the charging documents, "White recoiled away from the table and refused to look at the picture."

The court documents then state that Rettig said: "Why did you kill her, Kenny, why did you hill her?"

Rettig didn't want the suspect to doubt that he was under a microscope. "I was firm in the way I said," Rettig recalled.

Later that day, Rettig received another break in the case when he interviewed the suspect's **friend Dennis** Herman of Lebanon.

It was a sunny day, recalled Rettig, who met Herman in the living room of his yellow mobile home. Rettig said Herman sat in a reclining chair and appeared calm. After a few moments, Herman began speaking freely, Rettig said.

"There was no pressure there," Rettig said. "Just two people talking."

Herman could not be reached for comment.

According to court records, Herman told Rettig that the suspect had told him several details about the death of Taylor: "1) that the girl in Maryland had been raped and murdered, 2) the girl had been strangled and had her neck broke, 3) her body had been in the shallow grave 20 feet off the road and 4) she had been buried with ropes and shovels."

Herman then said that the suspect had provided a detailed description of the wooded area where Taylor's remains were found, according to the charging documents.

Rettig then checked newspaper clippings about Taylor and realized that those details weren't available to the public.

But Rettig didn't seek to arrest White right away; the detective and prosecutors needed more, they needed the 1995 autopsy changed from "undetermined" to "homicide."

So, Rettig brought **Herman** statements and other **lead** to Donald G. Wright, the deputy medical examiner, who re-evaluated the autopsy and changed the cause of death.

Wright, Rettig and prosecutors refused to discuss the details of the autopsy change.

"This is not all that unusual," said Taylor, the prosecutor. "It has been done before. They take a lot of things into consideration. It's not all just science."

Those familiar with the case say it's unusual that a detective, or anybody for that matter, would put so much effort into a case that nobody seemed to remember.

"They built a good case," said Lebanon Police Sgt. Greg Holler who assisted in the investigation. "The tenacity of the detectives working the case, those investigating the original missing person's report, that solved it. You don't see too many 12-year-old cases like this getting solved.

"It could have easily fallen through the cracks."

Del Wilber

That's a solid story. But Wilber's editors thought it could be even better and helped him work on it through several drafts over the next few days. This, ultimately, was the published story.

Detective Ties Up Loose Ends to Make Case in '85 Killing

Suspect charged 13 years after woman disappears

by Del Quentin Wilber
Sun Staff

On June 16, Howard County Detective Nathan Rettig slid a woman's photograph toward Kenneth Allen White.

The smiling face in the picture belonged to Sandra Lee Taylor, an Ellicott City mother of two young children who vanished Jan. 1, 1985, after a night of New Year's revelry.

White "recoiled," Rettig said. Then, in a Pennsylvania police station, the detective looked White in the eye and asked: "Why did you kill her, Kenny, why did you kill her?"

White, 47, of Lebanon, Pa., an unemployed mechanic and father of a 9-year-old girl, is charged with first-degree murder. He vigorously denies involvement in Taylor's death.

"I didn't do it," White said at a Dec. 9 bail hearing. "I could have gone behind the Iron Curtain [in 1985] if I wanted to. I turned myself in to face these charges to clear my name."

Investigators long suspected White, who was seen kissing Taylor and then leaving with her from an Oella bar on New Year's Day, but the case moved slowly, from detective to detective, remaining one of 15 unsolved homicides in Howard County since 1975.

Even when environmental workers stumbled across Taylor's skeletal remains in June 1995, there was little real progress. Then, last May, the mystery was placed in Rettig's hands.

Rettig joined the Howard County Police Department four months after Taylor disappeared. As a patrol officer, he drove daily along Route 99 in Woodstock, only a few yards from the shallow stream where Taylor's bones would be found 10 years later. Rettig became a detective two years ago.

Veteran detectives, prosecutors and the victim's family credit Rettig's discipline in tracking down witnesses, linking crucial pieces of evidence and finding a suspect's friend whose statements helped change the two-year-old autopsy results from "undetermined" to "homicide."

But legal experts say the case will be difficult to prosecute because of its age and its near-total reliance on circumstantial evidence.

"This will definitely be a challenge," said Jerome E. Deise, a professor at the University of Maryland School of Law who has defended numerous murder suspects. "There is virtually no forensic evidence, it's all circumstantial."

However, Deise said that he has only seen the documents charging White with the slaying—all written by the prosecution—and a newspaper account.

Whatever the outcome, Stephen Gover, Taylor's brother, said Rettig's determination eased the pain of not knowing.

"The arrest gives me a little closure," said Gover, 47. "I didn't think they had enough to catch [a suspect]."

For his part, Rettig said he never took the case personally, never got too close, worked his eight-hour days and then went home to his wife and kids.

Building a case

On a cold afternoon recently, Rettig—his gray- and white-speckled hair scattered by the bitter wind—sat in his unmarked cruiser, only a quarter-mile from the stream where Taylor's remains were found.

Adjusting his tan overcoat and nudging his eyeglasses up on his nose, Rettig spoke carefully about the case, pondering every question and answer, wary that a single slip could ruin years of work.

The former Marine—raised by an office manager and a school librarian in the small Indiana town of Geneva—never dreamed when he graduated from South Adams High School in 1981 that he'd someday investigate a murder.

(continued)

(continued)

During several interviews, Rettig emphasized that building this case was like building a home—others laid the foundation and he did the finishing work. He said that the original work on the missing person's report and that of other detectives over the years were the crucial building blocks.

But colleagues say that Rettig did far more than put on the final touches—he built the house.

"On this case you needed a bit of a bulldog, a dog who won't let the bone go," said Assistant State's Attorney Bernard Taylor, who will prosecute the case. "Nathan did that—he was persistent."

Rettig's sergeant agreed. "Nate did a fantastic job bringing all the information together into a workable case," said Sgt. Greg Marshall, who heads the violent crime unit. "It got solved because nobody gave up on it from 1985 through 1997. Everybody involved did their part, particularly Nathan."

After Marshall handed Retting a box of papers and a three-ring binder with all the information about Taylor's slaying, the detective spent several weeks making phone calls and organizing the file.

Working from his small desk, decorated with a Semper Fi bumper sticker, American and Marine Corps flags and a small teddy bear, Rettig read how Taylor visited an Oella bar—then known as the Valley View Inn—on New Year's Eve, how she left with a man she didn't know, and how the 31-year-old mother of two made a brief stop at her nearby home and was never heard from again.

He learned that Taylor was a stroke victim and that she was on medication. He understood when friends said that Taylor, who suffered the stroke when she was 23, controlled her symptoms, but would be easy prey if someone noticed how her right arm moved awkwardly.

Court documents charging White with the slaying said White was in Howard County that New Year's Eve in 1984 with his wife's uncle. White needed to cash a check that night. At a bar in Sykesville, White met a man who recommended the Valley View Inn. It was there he met Taylor.

Rettig examined the old reports. He learned that White's wife's uncle had seen White kissing Taylor at the bar. The uncle said he saw White leave with the woman.

Taylor's brother said he saw her for the last time around 7 a.m. New Year's Day. She got out of a reddish-orange car and walked quickly into the three-story home they shared. A few minutes later, Taylor's brother saw her get back into the same car, vanishing from friends and family.

The car matched the description of White's Chevrolet Vega station wagon.

White was a suspect from the beginning. But without a body, the investigation stalled. Even with the body, there was little to go on.

The interview

On a warm, sunny day in June, Rettig traveled to Lebanon, Pa., and interviewed White at city police headquarters.

Rettig sat at a table with White and asked the suspect his name, address and general questions that White could easily answer. Then he let White tell his story, Rettig said.

Rettig said White denied traveling from the bar in Sykesville to the Valley View Inn with a local man, something he had admitted doing in 1985, according to court records.

Rettig placed a picture of the Valley View Inn as it appeared in 1985 before White. Then he put the picture of Taylor on the table. White jerked backward, Rettig said.

Later that day, Rettig sat in the living room of the mobile home of the suspect's friend, Dennis Herman of Lebanon.

Herman sat in a reclining chair. After a few moments, he began speaking freely, Rettig said.

"There was no pressure there," Rettig said. "Just two people talking."

According to court records, Herman told Rettig that White had revealed several details about Taylor's death: "1) that the girl in Maryland had been raped and murdered, 2) the girl had been strangled and had her neck broke, 3) her body had been in the shallow grave 20 feet off the road and 4) she had been buried with ropes and shovels."

Herman also said that the suspect had provided a detailed description of the wooded area where Taylor's remains were found.

Rettig checked newspaper clippings about Taylor and realized that those details weren't available to the public.

Rettig didn't seek an immediate arrest. The detective and prosecutors needed the cause of death on the 1995 autopsy changed from "undetermined" to "homicide."

Rettig brought Herman's statements and other information to Donald G. Wright, the deputy medical examiner, who re-evaluated the autopsy. He made the change.

On Nov. 24, Rettig and detectives from Lebanon City and other Pennsylvania authorities tried to arrest White at his apartment. White wasn't there. He had learned of his impending arrest after receiving a solicitation letter from a Columbia lawyer who used a computer service to comb arrest warrants.

White turned himself in that evening.

Those familiar with the case say it's unusual that a detective, or anybody for that matter, would put so much effort into a case that nobody seemed to remember. "They built a good case," said Lebanon Police Sgt. Greg Holler who assisted in the investigation.

"The tenacity of the detectives working the case, those investigating the original missing person's report, that solved it. You don't see too many 12-year-old cases like this getting solved."

Rettig, returning to the small wooded area where Taylor's remains were found two years ago, is reflective. The slow, meandering stream, strewn with leaves from naked trees, seems peaceful on this brisk December afternoon.

"Whenever I'm here," Rettig said, "I think about all the times I drove by here as a patrol officer and never knew."

From *The Baltimore Sun*, Dec. 31, 1997.
© 1997 The Baltimore Sun.
Reprinted with permission.

It would be worthwhile for you to look over the two versions of the story and note the changes, some of them small and several of them quite large.

Was all the hard work of editing worthwhile? Well, as Wilber says, the story *did* run on Page 1A of *The Baltimore Sun*.

A Day in the Life of...

**Magazine Editor
Nan Woitas**

It's 6:30 a.m., and as soon as my eyes open, I roll out of bed and head to work. It's not like the old days, when I'd hit "Snooze" several times, dreading the moment when I simply *had* to put on a business suit and fight traffic on the way to a chaotic newsroom.

Now, I'm eager to start my workday as an editor for a popular women's magazine. That's because the earlier I get going and the more efficiently I work, the more time I'll have to do non-work activities. And though I love my job and work hard to craft the best stories possible, that's the real motivator—deciding how *I* want to spend my day.

So long before my Manhattan colleagues begin dodging commuters and fumbling for subway passes, I pad to my living room, still in my pajamas, and flip open the notebook computer on my desk. Last night, I pulled my work for the day onto my desktop so I could get started right away. With my husband and baby still asleep, and no office chitchat to distract me, I can work faster, more efficiently, getting what's considered a day's work done in half the time, more than a thousand miles away in Florida.

Okay, today I'll be rewriting a piece for Issue 47—one that came in from a new freelancer who didn't quite understand our dramatic, emotion-laden style of storytelling. I'll need to bang that out in a hurry. Though it's only September, we're up against deadline for the magazine that hits newsstands on November 14.

On my cordless, headset telephone—one that makes me look more like a pop star than a stay-at-home, working mom—I leave a quick voice mail message for a colleague in the office who keeps track of what the telecommuting editors are doing. While I'm summarizing my tentative plans for the day, I'm preparing a quick breakfast. But she doesn't have to know

that. I try to keep the clattering of plates to a minimum—it's not the most professional background noise.

By 8:15, I've gotten that new writer's story in shape and e-mailed it to my supervisor. I've attached to that message three suggestions for short sidebars that would complement the piece. And I've sent in a sheet with my ideas for a headline and summary paragraph to introduce the story. Later, my boss will read the story and fax back a copy with her notes in the margins detailing what she'd like tweaked a bit. She'll also fax back the sidebar suggestions with one circled by the editor-in-chief. That's the one I'll flesh out. But they won't be in the office for more than an hour, so now's the perfect time to go out for a morning stroll with my husband and the baby, who are just waking up. Just to be sure I don't miss a call from someone who needs to talk to me before we return home, I'll forward my calls to my cellular telephone and take it with me.

Just before 10 a.m., the cell phone trills. It's our copy chief. He needs me to look over the

Summary

Editing and revising are an important part of the writing process. Though the way you edit differs from medium to medium, in each case you will be expected to edit your own stories carefully and also to work with editors to improve your stories.

One technique for self-editing is to get TRICI, Take some time, Read the story aloud, Isolate your lines, Change your context, and Isolate your paragraphs.

Freelance writers find it especially important to be able to edit and revise their own stories.

Key Points

- ▶ Get TRICI.
- ▶ Develop good editor–writer relationships.
- ▶ Clean copy is important.

final layout—what we call the "galley"—of the story I worked on for Issue 46. Now! He wants to know if I've received the fax. "I'll check my machine and call you right back," I promise, jogging home ahead of my family.

At home, I pull up my e-mail program. Yep, the eFax is there in my inbox. Reading it carefully line by line, I find a misspelled name and a major fact error that was inadvertently written in when the piece had to be shortened by 50 words at the last minute. I call the copy chief and explain the changes he needs to make before sending the pages to be printed. Good thing we caught the problems before sending the story out to 3 million readers!

My e-mail notification alarm bings once, then a second time, then a third. Suddenly, three things need my attention—fast! Another editor called in sick this morning. So I have to call the subject in her Issue 46 story to do a readback [of the story to check for errors] before the copy desk "dumps" [finalizes] the finished galley. If the subject demands changes to our story, I'll need to get them in quickly. Also, I need to recraft the sidebar for my own story for that issue. In looking over the final version, our editor-in-chief decided the topic—survival tips you can teach children in case they're ever lost in the woods—is too scary for our readers. Searching the Internet, I turn up a Web site that details tips on how to make sure kids never get lost in the first place. I call the expert listed on that site, do a 10-minute interview, and turn in a sidebar that's still service-oriented, but unlikely to cause too much worry.

By now, it's almost noon and I'm finally getting to that third item in my inbox. It's the Issue 47 story with the "fixes" my boss wants. After making a few changes and struggling to tighten it by 100 more words, I e-mail it back to her. With all my work for the day behind me, I flip my notebook computer closed. Time to fix lunch, and decide how I want to spend the *rest* of my day. ∎

Nan Woltas worked as a student journalist with her college paper and at the St. Petersburg Times. *She was a reporter with* The Tampa Tribune *before becoming a freelance editor.*

▶ Edit for grammar and style, but also for larger issues like logic and flow.

▶ Learn from your editing mistakes and don't repeat them.

Web Links

http://owl.english.purdue.edu/handouts/general/gl_/sedit.html
http://www.writingcenter.pdx.edu/resources/revising.html
http://www.ltcc.net/modules/lect_/swriting/revising/
http://www.mc.maricopa.edu/users/masseyjo/eng217/
    Class/Lectures/Editing.htm

InfoTrac College Edition Readings

For additional readings, go to **www.infotrac-college.com**, enter your password, and search for the following articles by title or author's name.

▶ "Clean Up Your Copy," Michael Bugeja, *Quill*, Jan. 2001 v89 i1 p56.

▶ "Retired Editor Finds Plenty of Work Correcting Media's Minor Mistakes," Jim Fox, *St. Louis Journalism Review*, Feb. 2001 v31 i233 p24.

▶ "Clichés to Live By" (Tired phrases turn newspaper readers away), Jack Hart, *Editor & Publisher*, Feb. 10, 1996 v129 n6 p3.

▶ "Speaking Up" (Role of copy editors), L. Carol Christopher, *Quill*, July-August 1999 v87 i5 p27.

Exercises

Go to your CD-ROM to complete the following exercises:

▶ Exercise 13.1

▶ Exercise 13.2

▶ Exercise 13.3

▶ Exercise 13.4

▶ Exercise 13.5

14

Legal and Ethical Concerns

You never expected to see the inside of a courtroom as a participant. Oh, you figured that maybe you'd have to fulfill your duties as a citizen and serve on a jury, and you've dreamed every now and then of suing that annoying neighbor.

But today, you're a defendant taking an oath in the front of the judge. You lower your hand and brace yourself on the witness stand. That attorney doesn't exactly resemble friendly, homespun Ben Matlock; instead, you seem to notice a startling resemblance to Vlad the Impaler.

"Would you please tell the court," the attorney snarls viciously, "just exactly how long you have been a liar?"

Uh, that's not exactly the kind of treatment you had in mind when you entered the communication business.

"Then, would you please tell the court how your untruthful work here doesn't violate libel laws? Or that your behavior conforms with any known ethical code in your field?"

"Well," you venture, wishing you'd paid a whole lot more attention to those lectures in journalism school, "so, all right, I wrote that stuff about your client and it turns out it *isn't* true. But it's a free country, isn't it? And whatever happened to freedom of the press?"

If that's the best defense you have, frankly, you're in big trouble. And that's the kind of trouble you'll want to avoid in your media career. This chapter can't tell you everything you need to know about libel, ethics and copyright. But it will give you a basic understanding of what you can and cannot (or should not) write. For the sake of your career—and maybe your pocketbook—this information is worth knowing.

Freedom of Speech

If you're an American, you have probably heard the phrase "freedom of the press" bandied about in conversation, with many people seeming to think that our Constitution protects anything they'd like to say about anyone at any time.

Of course, it's not quite that simple. While our political system does protect certain freedoms to say certain things, the media aren't completely free to make any statement. There are laws that govern published or broadcast materials. Also, while the law tells communicators what they *can* do, good communicators also need to know what they *should* do, how they should behave, even when the law doesn't address the situation. These codes of behavior are called "ethics."

Libel

When journalists and public relations practitioners think about legal concerns in their respective fields, they're usually worried about conforming to civil libel law. *Libel*, at its most basic, is published defamation (as opposed to *slander*, which is spoken defamation). *Defamation*, in turn, may be defined as words that harm or injure one's reputation (either personal reputation or business reputation).

Published, in this case, usually means information that appears before more than one person, usually (but not always limited to) appearance in a newspaper, magazine, news release, or television broadcast. In essence, it's not libelous for you to scrawl a defamatory comment about your seatmate (have you taken a close look at that seatmate?) and show it to him. But, when you show that comment to others in the class, the possibility of libel emerges.

The Big Chill

Media executives tend to be extremely concerned about libel suits. Such suits not only serve as an embarrassment to the company but may also lead to monetary damages from juries, and even a *frivolous* libel suit (one where the person filing suit has no chance to win) costs the media outlet time, effort and considerable expense to defeat in court.

As a result of those worries, some critics think, media executives no longer follow up on stories the way they used to, and still should. This hesitance to take on potentially libelous stories is called "the chilling effect" by media critics and is, no doubt, quite real. It's an especially important worry when it pervades a media outlet enough that the outlet no longer serves as a good watchdog on the actions of businesses, government and politicians, athletes or other public figures.

However, while there are concerns about the chilling effect, it's worth noting that most news organizations defame somebody almost every day, and you are likely to be part of that during your career in the media. After all, when reporters write about how the governor violated campaign laws or that a local man was arrested on criminal charges, you would think those would harm their respective reputations, and perhaps they do. But the same aspects of libel law that protect the people that the media talk about also, in turn, protect the media. Among these are the following:

Truth, No Consequences

You are protected against libel if the story is provably true. In 1735, journalist John Peter Zenger was hauled into court on charges of seditious libel by the colonial governor of New York. Zenger's lawyer, Andrew Hamilton, argued successfully that punishment should be withheld because the stories were factual. The jury agreed.

While that was in Colonial days, and didn't set a legal precedent, it did, nevertheless, bring out the idea that the truth of a statement matters. That idea, coupled with the idea of the Founding Fathers that government should make "no law . . . abridging the freedom of speech, or of the press," became a cornerstone of our press freedoms. The truth, today, always serves as a defense in libel suits.

Public Officials and Public Figures

Starting with a libel case from the late 1950s and early 1960s, the U. S. Supreme Court has offered the media certain protections when it comes to writing about public figures.

This defense for libel, frequently referred to as the *"New York Times* rule," goes back to an advertisement in *The New York Times* during the time of civil rights protests in the late 1950s and early 1960s. A group concerned with eliminating the racism that gripped the South published a full-page ad in *The Times* about the actions of Montgomery, Alabama, officials in breaking up a protest rally.

The advertisement contained some statements that were shown to be in error. L. B. Sullivan, a Montgomery city commissioner who also was in charge of the police department, sued *The Times* under Alabama's libel laws. The case eventually reached the U.S. Supreme Court, which overturned earlier decisions and held that writers could err in the coverage of public officials, as long as such errors were made of haste and not from malice. The courts define *actual malice* as the reckless disregard of whether information is factual. The law later widened to include not only public officials, who are governmental figures but also most public figures, from football coaches and actors and anyone else who has willingly entered the public spotlight.

Over the years since that case, this defense has been occasionally strengthened and occasionally weakened by subsequent court cases, but it essentially remains the same. As a media writer, you are better protected when you write about public figures than you are when writing about private individuals.

Privilege

The courts have granted *absolute privilege* to government officials. In a democracy, the courts argue, officials must be able to discuss the issues of the day without fear of slander or libel laws. Thus, speeches and comments made in the performance of one's duties in government are protected.

Journalists are granted privilege—though not absolute privilege—in reporting about those speeches and comments. Thus, reported statements made in a courtroom, city council meeting room or senate chamber, during the course of public meetings, are generally protected from the libel laws. Absolute privilege does not always extend beyond the borders of legal meetings and court hearings, so the general rule is to be prudent and well informed on the facts of an issue.

This protection extends to public records, the documentation that records official government activities. For reporters, this allows careful examination of court transcripts, real estate records and automobile registrations—and that any information gleaned from the records protects the information from a libel suit.

Fair Comment

Every time a sportswriter criticizes a coach's decision, or talks about a pitcher's inability to get a curveball over the plate, that writer has caused harm to the coach or the ballplayer, perhaps even affecting his or her livelihood. And yet the writer is free to say those things.

Similarly, every time a critic blasts a new play or movie, or rips an artist's new CD, harm has been caused. But the critic is free to speak his or her mind.

Every time that a writer or broadcaster makes vicious, nasty comments about public figures in editorials or opinion columns, the same damage has been done.

And yet the coach, the pitcher, the actors, the musicians, the public figures from any walk of life can't get a dollar from the court, because the *fair comment* defense states that those who willingly thrust themselves into the vortex of public opinion open themselves to fair comment and criticism. You wanna be in show biz? Swell, but you lose the rights granted to private citizens: Reviewers are allowed to savage your heartfelt performance on stage or film, and sportswriters are free to refer to your splendid play at shortstop as not too bad, considering your glove must be made of concrete.

Of course, even columnists and reviewers are open to libel laws if their comments stray from the boundaries of fair comment. It is important that your comments be related to the reason the person, or business, is in the public eye. For example, consider a review of Randy's Haggis and Spam Restaurant. The reviewer remains perfectly within rights to note the sloppy service, the limited wine list, the poor presentation and the flavorless cuisine. But the threat of libel awaits if the reviewer were to say: "And Randy, the owner, is an obvious drug addict with no cooking sense at all." Now the reviewer has left the realm of opinion and attacked Randy personally instead. For that, the restaurant owner is within the law to sue.

Please understand that this protection of criticism doesn't exist everywhere. In Australia, for example, sports journalists routinely use "code words" to imply that an athlete performed poorly. One publication paid handsomely when an athlete was described as "fat and slow," even though the comments were exceedingly accurate. Thus, Australian athletes who miss easy goals are referred to by the media Down Under as "unlucky" or "off their form."

Privacy

Communicators must be also wary of violating privacy. The right to privacy often clashes with the so-called right to know. Generally, if a private citizen makes news, that outweighs the right to privacy. Still, there are at least four areas of concern.

Appropriation

Advertisers and public relations practitioners need to be wary of privacy rights, since newsworthiness is no longer a consideration. Generally, someone's name or image cannot be used to make money without that person's permission.

Consider, for example, a photograph of a female student walking across campus. If a local photo studio were to use that picture in an advertisement called "Co-Ed of the Week" (you laugh, but this wasn't unusual 40 years ago), then the student could sue, provided she hadn't signed a permission waiver. However, that same photograph used as a news feature photo would be protected as newsworthy.

A broadcast station was found guilty of violating this privacy rule some years ago when it filmed the entire act of a circus performer who worked as a "human cannonball." Because the station showed his entire act, rather than just showing him entering the cannon, he argued it had appropriated his act for profit, and the courts agreed.

Intrusion

This rule protects people from overzealous media pursuit. Our student walking across campus, for example, is protected when in her home or office. Many photographers, in fact, will ask people photographed in a home or office setting to sign a release form.

This also means that reporters cannot use electronic eavesdropping devices to gather information from people in their homes or offices, even though such technology does exist. It also means that a real-life reporter using the standard Hollywood device of breaking into a house to gather information would be subject to legal action (not to mention breaking-and-entering statutes).

Embarrassing Personal Facts

You would think that discussions of embarrassing personal facts would be completely free in an era when descriptions of an American president's private parts have been made public. However, private citizens still have protection under this law. The classic case is quite old, but dates back to a time when a major magazine showed a photograph of a hospitalized woman suffering from a rare disease. "The Starving Glutton," it said, of a woman who lost weight no matter how many calories she consumed. She sued the publication over this embarrassing information and won.

False Light

People who believe that what a journalist implies about them is incorrect (even if the portrayal is positive) can sue under *false light* protection.

A woman successfully sued when a reporter's story implied that he had interviewed her when he had, instead, only interviewed her children. A broadcast station that used a videotape of a woman walking down a street during a story about prostitution was also found to have violated the false light law.

Copyright Law

Copyright law is intended to protect writers from having their work stolen. Generally, if you wrote it, according to current copyright law in the United States, it's yours, and no one else can use those words without your permission.

But there are a number of exceptions to that general standard. For instance, if you are on the staff of a newspaper or magazine, or working for a corporation or public relations agency, or working for an advertising agency, then the words you write on the job, will, with rare exception, belong to the company that hired you.

Similarly, if you are a freelancer and you sign a contract that says your words belong to a publication or business that has hired you to write a story, then the words are no longer yours. Perhaps this is fine with you. On the other hand, if that story winds up in a number of reprints and is much more widely disseminated than you'd thought it would be, you might regret not having hung on to the rights.

Work for Hire

The sort of contractual arrangement in which the words no longer belong to you is called "work for hire," and it is, in essence, what most staffers do when they write for their publications. Many freelancers do the same thing, especially in public relations work, where the corporation wants to keep tight control of its printed material.

First Serial Rights

If you are *not* on the staff, but sell your work to a publication for its use, then you typically retain most of the rights to those words. You have simply given the publication the right to use your story one time, after which all the other rights revert back to you. This right is called "first serial rights" (or "first North American serial rights"). This use of nonstaffers for production of stories is most common in the magazine industry, where it has been standard policy for most magazines for many years. In recent years, many newspapers have also begun buying a great deal more freelance material. Recent changes in copyright law mean that you (and your heirs) own the rights to your words for your lifetime plus 70 years.

Second Serial Rights

Second serial rights (sometimes called "reprint rights") means that the story has been previously published and the writer is granting permission to the media outlet to publish the story a second time. Again, after one-time publication the remaining rights revert to the writer.

All Rights

All rights means that the writer is selling the story forever. Selling all rights is similar to doing work for hire: The words become the property of the publication. Should any reprint rights be sold, the money goes to the publication rather than the writer.

These rights may not sound particularly important if the writer thinks the story is a one-shot article, but should a Hollywood producer decide to buy the rights for a motion picture, the writer doesn't get a dime.

Electronic Rights

In this evolving area, copyright law basically follows the standard policy that once you have created a work in "fixed form" (the term used by the Copyright Office), it is automatically copyrighted in your name, unless you create it under someone else's copyright (as part of an online service or online publication, for instance).

Fair Use

Fair use is the limited use of part of a copyrighted work without the expressed (written) permission of the copyright holder. This is a tricky area, but the law generally says that, especially for educational purposes or for criticism (a book review, for instance), you may use excerpts. If there are any doubts about having used too much material, you should seek permission.

How to Copyright Your Words

Do nothing. That's right, under normal circumstances, current copyright law protects your words as soon as they are created.

Problem is, you don't have any proof of just when you created them. So, if it comes to a court case to prove that your words belong to you, your best protection is to have registered your copyright with the Copyright Office of the Library of Congress.

This is a simple, and relatively inexpensive, procedure. The easiest way to go about registering your copyright is to call the Copyright Office, at (202) 707-9100 in Washington, D.C. When you make that call, a voice mail program will direct you through a process that will end with the proper forms mailed to you. Fill them out, attach your words, pay the $30 fee, and that's it. You can also reach the copyright office through the Internet, at www.loc.gov/copyright.

Corporate Speech

For many years, corporate speech was generally unprotected by the First Amendment. Corporate speech, usually misidentified as advertising, is often much more and may have implications regarding issues of tremendous public interest. The U.S. Supreme Court has spent more than 30 years coming to grips with whether advertising and issue-oriented (but paid for) speech should be protected just as other speech. The outcome is still uncertain.

Public relations and advertising students must understand that the courts still have jurisdiction for corporate speech, and its level of protection under the First Amendment may vary greatly depending on the nature of the speech. However, corporate speech can receive First Amendment protection if it meets what has come to be known as the Hudson test. The speech must advertise a legal issue or product and it must not mislead in order to pass the Hudson test.

Public relations practitioners must worry about First Amendment concerns for publications that reach the public and also may be liable for withholding information from the public if they should issue false and misleading news releases. Practitioners at publicly held companies, in particular, are required to show responsibility to their company and to the public.

Besides dealing with the courts, practitioners also must be aware of the Federal Trade Commission (FTC) that oversees deceptive advertising practices and may fine advertisers who choose to disobey FTC regulations. The Securities and Exchange Commission and the Food and Drug Administration also have some regulatory power toward corporate speech.

Access

The public in the United States has a right to certain information accumulated by its governments in the course of working on its behalf. But this right did not originate from the First Amendment. It evolved from the process of several concepts, primarily the public's "right to know." This implied "right" led to the passage of the federal Freedom of Information Act (FOIA) in 1966. The federal act was not the first—several states had FOI laws in place—but it quickly became the blueprint for state laws where none had previously existed.

The federal law pertains only to the access of records that are deemed to be part of an administrative public agency. In passing the law, Congress exempted itself, the federal judiciary and the U.S. president and president's staff. Still, Congress opens a great deal of material to public view.

There are nine exemptions to the federal law aimed at keeping some functions of government business out of the public view. Included are exemptions that forbid the opening of government personnel and medical records, exemptions for a variety of records from corporate and financial institutions where disclosure could cause competitive harm, and of course the well-known national security exemption. Some police agency material in ongoing cases and internal staff memos are also exempt. Many states have created similar exemptions to their laws to maintain consistency with federal law.

This area of law is generally referred to as "access to information," and while it includes access to public documents, access generally includes your ability to attend public meetings. It is an important area of interest for all mass communications students. Most states have separate laws dealing with opening public records and opening meetings. The extent of these laws and their various levels of openness vary greatly from state to state.

Government has generally been held accountable to the public to do its job in the "light" of public review. However, it has only been in recent decades that most states and the courts have recognized the public's right to view most records and attend meetings. Public records laws and open meetings laws are now in place in all states. Taken collectively, these laws are referred to as government in the "sunshine" or "sunshine laws."

Broadcast Regulations

Media writers working for television and radio must take into account the copyright, libel law and ethical issues their print counterparts do, as well as be aware of the variety of regulations that government issues over the broadcast media. So, not only must broadcasters face First Amendment questions, they must also contend with the rules established by the Federal Communications Commission (FCC). The FCC has overseen the public airwaves since 1934. Restrictions on broadcast content, cable rates and equal-time provisions for political candidates are within the FCC's regulatory area, and the commission has the power to take broadcasting licenses away from those who violate those regulations.

The premise behind the regulatory control exercised by the FCC (a level of control that has, in recent years, been on the decline in an era of deregulation) is that the airwaves for both the television and radio media are limited and so organizational control is necessary. The public's interest is the other basic premise behind the FCC's regulatory control.

While the media currently exist in an environment that is generally deregulating, rather than regulating, there are still a very large number of regulations controlling everything from on-the-air obscenity to the kinds and amount of broadcast stations a person can own. A good way to keep up with these issues is on the Internet, at the FCC site at http://www.fcc.gov/ or at other sites, including the site of the National Association of Broadcasters at http://www.nab.org/.

Ethics

Be ethical.

The sentiment addressed above may be perfectly lovely, and you may be ready to swear your allegiance to the ethical standards of your particular field. However, the problem with ethics will come when you begin your career. That's when we leave the field of hypothetical situations and enter the realm of reality.

For example, journalists should not accept "freebies," gifts of value dangled before them. You, of course, would never touch such a vile proposition. Your ethical behavior would prevent you from accepting anything like, um, front-row tickets to your favorite band's concert.

But you really, really, really like that band. And, what would it hurt to take the tickets? You might not even be asked to review that concert.

And when your editor tells you that the tickets can't be taken, you wonder long and hard about the fairness of it all. Those vows you made in journalism school have been washed away in a sea of freebies.

Every mass communication field has its own ethical standards, and some behaviors—taking free lunches, for example—are acceptable in some fields and not acceptable in others. A thorough discussion of these fields could add dozens of pages to this textbook, so we're going to focus on some general practices that apply across the board. For a more thorough—and ongoing—look at issues of media ethics, you can visit http://www.poynter.org, the site of the Poynter Institute for Media Studies. Poynter offers a wide range of seminars and workshops throughout the year, including a number of them specifically directed toward ethics issues.

Ethics Codes

Every field has at least one generally accepted code of ethics, and some mass communication organizations have their own personalized ethics code. The biggest problem with most ethics codes can be explained this way: If an attorney violates the American Bar Association's ethical standards, he or she can be disbarred (lose the license to practice law); if a mass communication professional violates an ethics code, only rarely does that cause the loss of a job. In fact, many ethics code violations are not punished by even a rap on the knuckles.

Some violations, strangely, even seem to be approved by management. When Disney threw an anniversary celebration at its Disney World park in the dead of winter, hundreds of journalists accepted a free trip to the Magic Kingdom and most received approval from their employers to do so, though journalism ethics codes state that journalists should not take gifts of value and, clearly, a junket to sunny Florida qualifies as a gift of value.

Even if the journalists were to turn around and report negative news on Disney in the future, they have elected to present *the appearance* of a conflict of interest.

If you are going to practice ethically in your field, ultimately you—and you alone—will determine whether you follow those standards or not. Because mass communication professionals aren't licensed, usually no board will remove your credentials if you break an ethics code (though some organizations with their own codes might fire you).

A good ethics code tells you not only what you shouldn't do, but what you should do as well. You can see the ethics codes of several organizations in Appendix A, including the Statement of Principles of Radio and Television Broadcasters of the National Association of Broadcasters (NAB), at http://www.nab.org; the codes for the Society of Professional Journalists (SPJ), http://spj.org/ethics: at the Standards of Practice of the American Association of Advertising Agencies (AAAA) at http://www.aaaa.org; and the Code of Ethics 2000 of the Public Relations Society of America (PRSA), at http://www.prsa.org/.

Following the death of Diana, Princess of Wales, in 1997, the British Press Complaint Commission formulated the Code of Practice for British journalists. You can read about the commission at http://www.pcc.org.uk/.

Telling the Truth

You learned about this back in elementary school, right? Never tell a lie.

But what happens if you're working in public relations and your bosses tell you that your corporation's headquarters intends to move out of town in three months, costing hundreds of citizens their jobs? And, oh, you know, don't breathe a word of this to anybody, your bosses say.

Two weeks later, your phone rings and a reporter asks you if the corporation intends to leave town.

What do you say?

Do you lie to the reporter? Do you violate your bosses' trust? Do you pretend that the phone line has static and that you can't hear a word on the other end?

A simple lie seems to be the easy way out. But understand that you lose the reporter's trust with the lie (and if you're found out, you may wind up embarrassed in the story).

So, don't lie. Reporters who practice deceit in order to get a story invite deceit from their sources. Advertisers who lie about a product can face charges from the Federal Trade Commission or scorn from consumers who learn that your detergent doesn't remove all stains. Public relations practitioners who lie to their public can cause more damage to their cause than they can imagine.

Your best bet in this kind of case in public relations is to have built the sort of relationship with your bosses that allows you to work with them as part of the management team and include truthful contact with the media as part of the corporate package.

Remember, a lot of mass communication work depends on trust. And how you can practice trust with someone who has lied to you?

Plagiarism

Your audience should also trust that your work is your own.

Plagiarism is the use of writing of others without their permission. This has become increasingly common for a variety of reasons, including the large amount of public relations material available to writers and the vast amount of research material available through online sources (including those term-paper-for-sale creeps).

Attribution usually takes care of this problem.

Every public relations practitioner can tell you that some journalists never even rewrite a news release—and though practitioners are perfectly content to have a release in print, they usually tell those stories with a note of scorn in their voices. Most journalists rewrite news releases or attribute them to the source.

The biggest danger with plagiarism is that plagiarists never stop with one theft. If you start down this road, you will find that dozens of stories need to be plagiarized. Eventually, your bosses will catch on and—unlike with other ethics code violations—you will be dismissed.

The availability of information through electronic bulletin board services makes plagiarism a strong temptation. But remember that information ought to be double-checked for accuracy and then attributed to its source.

The safest policy: Don't plagiarize.

Words of Warning

In our examples under "The Big Chill" above, the governor and the local man could not successfully sue for libel if the story were shown to be true. The reporters would have been careful to keep notes or to be able to show information like an arrest report to demonstrate the article's truth. But notes based on false statements would not serve as protection. Suppose, for example, you used a quote from a source named Lynn Liar. It's important to understand that Liar is not guilty of libel. You are. Liar merely told you a fib—you and your newspaper or broadcast outlet or public relations agency published it.

In the same vein, accuracy of quotation is not a defense. If you quote someone who says something libelous, *you* are responsible for the libel, not the person you quoted. Quoting them accurately does not protect you in any way.

Deception

Some familiar examples of questionable ethical behavior involve deception. The law holds reporters, advertisers and public relations practitioners to certain standards of truth, but ethics may be applied where the law stops.

For example, the authors of this text live in the Tampa Bay area, which has mild winters, great beaches and numerous golf courses. It is also home to the sweepstakes industry, the folks who send mass mailings that seem to claim that you—yes, you—have won millions of dollars. Many of us realize that these packages are gimmicks designed to get you to subscribe to magazines or some other tricks. And we know that they usually include some form of small print that says that you *may* have won, not that you have *actually* won. As such, most of these companies were legally protected.

But that didn't stop several folks recently—all financially strapped retirees—from buying a plane ticket to Tampa with the "winning" entry in hand. They were driven to the sweepstakes office where someone had to enlighten them that they had just spent their meager savings for nothing, despite the bold headlines and exuberant promises in the advertisement.

Is it ethically acceptable for sweepstakes companies to make these claims? Don't confuse the question with the legal viewpoint. At the time, it was perfectly legal for these companies to send these mailings out, but some would argue that these packages strained the concept of ethics in advertising.

Journalists can also fall prey to the deception bug. Some have taken false identities in order to get stories. The *Chicago Sun-Times* once operated a bar deliberately loaded with code violations in order to find out about bribe-hungry inspectors.

Others can't resist the urge to sweeten a story with an embellishment here, a fictional take there. Some photographers fall to the temptation of digital manipulation or even old-fashioned darkroom tricks, like burning in a blur to represent a baseball. Some writers wish that a source had actually said something or had a different background—and then make it so in print. The lure is often a really great sounding quote that will eventually become a habit.

Former *Boston Globe* columnist Patricia Smith, for example, lost her job after *The Globe* determined that she had fabricated quotes in columns. Some columnists have manufactured quotes for years—but usually to some clearly fictional character. But Smith used real names of real people and put words in their mouths.

Smith was the first of three *Globe* columnists to fall under the ethical spotlight. Two others received sanctions after questions of the originality of their work surfaced. Mike Barnicle was suspended after he used verbatim jokes from comedian George Carlin in his column. In July 2000, columnist Jeff Jacoby was suspended for "journalistic misconduct" in using material from an e-mail about the founders of the Declaration of Independence (even though he did note in an e-mail note prior to publication that he was trying to correct some of the mistruths in the original e-mail).

Good journalists read voraciously. They may see so many pieces of information in a month that they may forget where they saw an anecdote. But they need to remember. It's acceptable to use the anecdote—with attribution.

As you work in mass communication fields, you should strive to avoid deception and to make your product your own.

Dilemma

A dilemma is a situation in which a person faces two decisions, each with unpleasant consequences. The fire or the frying pan, for example.

Sometimes in communication fields, you may face dilemmas. Reporters may have to choose between alienating an important source or leaving out a part of the story. By adhering to ethical principles, you may sometimes reason out your decision, but an ethical dilemma can still leave you perplexed.

Consider this public relations situation: You are working as the chief information officer for the region's largest public hospital, one that handles any number of specialized areas and is the place where most poor people wind up getting treatment. Because the hospital is funded by the government, contentious board meetings are often spotlighted in the media.

The government has now hired a new director to oversee the hospital, and he tells you and other important personnel that he has decided that the hospital must be made private. He certainly does not want this information released until he has lined up support throughout the community. He is your client, and you must present his ideas in the best possible light.

As the plans lurch forward, he now wants you to create a media event, a community meeting in which the public will enthusiastically greet the change in the hospital. And he would like you to arrange for a busload of off-duty hospital employees to be transported to the event to play the role of members of the general public.

Should you release this information to the news media, or should you go along because you have a responsibility to your client and cannot betray his plans?

How can you find an answer?

If you model your behavior on established ethical principles, then you can more easily come to a difficult decision. If you have not modeled your behavior on these principles, then you may wind up making your decision based on your client's hairstyle.

Summary

The First Amendment to the Constitution provides for freedom of speech, but there are a number of limitations on just how free a media writer's speech can actually be. Libel laws, broadcast regulations, and copyright law all involve limitations of one sort or another on a writer's freedom to publish material. Libel laws are meant to protect someone from being defamed through the media. Broadcast regulations are meant to help achieve fairness and accuracy on the limited number of frequencies available to the media. Copyright law is meant to protect a writer from having his or her words stolen by someone else.

Ethics are also an important concern to a media writer. What is considered ethical or unethical behavior varies from medium to medium and is different for advertisers and public relations practitioners than for newspaper or broadcast journalists.

Key Points

▶ Media writers should know the First Amendment.

▶ You must have a strong legal defense if you defame someone.

► Truth, privilege, public and private persons, and fair comment are important defenses.

► Corporate speech has a different level of First Amendment protections.

► Many ethical issues revolve around the appearance of the writer's having a conflict of interest.

► Copyright protections are automatic, but your copyright can be registered with the Copyright Office.

Web Links

http://www.loc.gov/copyright
http://www.journalism.sfsu.edu/www/ethics.html
http://www.journalism.indiana.edu/Ethics/
http://www.uta.fi/ethicnet/
http://www.poynter.org/dj/projects/newmedethics/jvnm2.htm
http://www.fcc.gov/
http://www.nab.org/
http://spj.org/ethics
http://www.prsa.org/
http://www.aaaa.org
http://www.pcc.org.uk/

InfoTrac College Edition Readings

For additional readings, go to **www.infotrac-college.com**, enter your password, and search for the following articles by title or author's name.

► "Taking Ethics to the Net" (Online journalism), J. D. Lascia, *Quill,* July 2001 v89 i6 p42.

► "Privacy and Speech" (Publication of illegally obtained information), Paul Gewirtz, *Supreme Court Review Annual 2001,* p139.

► "Freedom of Information Under Attack: In the Name of `Homeland Security,' the Work of Journalists Is Made Harder (Watchdog Journalism Conference), Charles Lewis, *Nieman Reports,* Summer 2002 v56 i2 p84.

Exercises

Go to your CD-ROM to complete the following exercises:

▶ Exercise 14.1

▶ Exercise 14.2

▶ Exercise 14.3

▶ Exercise 14.4

Codes of Ethics

Statement of Principles of Radio and Television Broadcasters Issued by the Board of Directors of the National Association of Broadcasters

Preface

The following Statement of Principles of radio and television broadcasting was adopted by the Board of Directors of the National Association of Broadcasters on behalf of the Association and commercial radio and television stations it represents.

America's free over-the-air radio and television broadcasters have a long and proud tradition of universal, local broadcast service to the American people. These broadcasters, large and small, representing diverse localities and perspectives, have striven to present programming of the highest quality to their local communities pursuant to standards of excellence and responsibility. They have done so and continue to do so out of respect for their status as daily guests in the homes and lives of a majority of Americans and with a sense of pride in their profession, in their product and in their public service.

The Board issues this statement of principles to record and reflect what it believes to be the generally accepted standards of America's radio and television broadcasters. The Board feels that such a statement will be particularly useful at this time, given public concern about certain serious societal problems, notably violence and drug abuse.

The Board believes that broadcasters will continue to earn public trust and confidence by following the same principles that have served them well for so long. Many broadcasters now have written standards of their own. All have their own programming policies. NAB would hope that all broadcasters would set down in writing their general programming principles and policies, as the Board hereby sets down the following principles.

Principles Concerning Program Content

Responsibly Exercised Artistic Freedom

The challenge to the broadcaster often is to determine how suitably to present the complexities of human behavior without compromising or reducing the range of subject matter, artistic expression or dramatic presentation desired by the broadcaster and its audience. For television and for radio, this requires exceptional awareness of considerations peculiar to each medium and of the composition and preferences of particular communities and audiences.

Each broadcaster should exercise responsible and careful judgment in the selection of material for broadcast. At the same time each broadcast licensee must be vigilant in exercising and defending its rights to program according to its own judgments and to the programming choices of its audiences. This often may include the presentation of sensitive or controversial material.

In selecting program subjects and themes of particular sensitivity, great care should be paid to treatment and presentation, so as to avoid presentations purely for the purpose of sensationalism or to appeal to prurient interest or morbid curiosity.

In scheduling programs of particular sensitivity, broadcasters should take account of the composition and the listening or viewing habits of their specific audiences. Scheduling generally should consider audience expectations and composition in various time periods.

Responsibility in Children's Programming

Programs designed primarily for children should take into account the range of interests and needs of children from informational material to the wide variety of entertainment material. Children's programs should attempt to contribute to the sound, balanced development of children and to help them achieve a sense of the world at large.

Special Program Principles

1. Violence.

Violence, physical or psychological, should only be portrayed in a responsible manner and should not be used exploitatively. Where consistent with the creative intent, programs involving violence should present the consequences of violence to its victims and perpetrators.

Presentation of the details of violence should avoid the excessive, the gratuitous and the instructional.

The use of violence for its own sake and the detailed dwelling upon brutality or physical agony, by sight or by sound, should be avoided.

Particular care should be exercised where children are involved in the depiction of violent behavior.

2. Drugs and Substance Abuse.

The use of illegal drugs or other substance abuse should not be encouraged or shown as socially desirable.

Portrayal of drug or substance abuse should be reasonably related to plot, theme or character development. Where consistent with the creative intent, the adverse consequences of drug or substance abuse should be depicted.

Glamorization of drug and substance abuse should be avoided.

3. Sexually Oriented Material.

In evaluating programming dealing with human sexuality, broadcasters should consider the composition and expectations of the audience likely to be viewing or listening to their stations and/or to a particular program, the context in which sensitive material is presented and its scheduling.

Creativity and diversity in programming that deals with human sexuality should be encouraged. Programming that purely panders to prurient or morbid interests should be avoided.

Where a significant child audience can be expected, particular care should be exercised when addressing sexual themes.

Obscenity is not constitutionally protected speech and is at all times unacceptable for broadcast.

All programming decisions should take into account current federal requirements limiting the broadcast of indecent matter.

Used by permission.

Endnote

This statement of principles is of necessity general and advisory rather than specific and restrictive. There will be no interpretation or enforcement of these principles by NAB or others. They are not intended to establish new criteria for programming decisions, but rather to reflect generally accepted practices of America's radio and television programmers. They similarly are not in any way intended to inhibit creativity in or programming of controversial, diverse or sensitive subjects.

Specific standards and their applications and interpretations remain within the sole discretion of the individual television or radio licensee. Both NAB and the stations it represents respect and defend the individual broadcast's First Amendment rights to select and present programming according to its individual assessment of the desires and expectations of its audiences and of the public interests.

Society of Professional Journalists Code of Ethics

Preamble

Members of the Society of Professional Journalists believe that public enlightenment is the forerunner of justice and the foundation of democracy. The duty of the journalist is to further those ends by seeking truth and providing a fair and comprehensive account of events and issues. Conscientious journalists from all media and specialties strive to serve the public with thoroughness and honesty. Professional integrity is the cornerstone of a journalist's credibility. Members of the Society share a dedication to ethical behavior and adopt this code to declare the Society's principles and standards of practice.

Seek Truth and Report It

Journalists should be honest, fair and courageous in gathering, reporting and interpreting information.

Journalists should:

- ▶ Test the accuracy of information from all sources and exercise care to avoid inadvertent error. Deliberate distortion is never permissible.

- ▶ Diligently seek out subjects of news stories to give them the opportunity to respond to allegations of wrongdoing.

- ▶ Identify sources whenever feasible. The public is entitled to as much information as possible on sources' reliability.

- ▶ Always question sources' motives before promising anonymity. Clarify conditions attached to any promise made in exchange for information. Keep promises.

► Make certain that headlines, news teases and promotional material, photos, video, audio, graphics, sound bites and quotations do not misrepresent. They should not oversimplify or highlight incidents out of context.

► Never distort the content of news photos or video. Image enhancement for technical clarity is always permissible. Label montages and photo illustrations.

► Avoid misleading re-enactments or staged news events. If re-enactment is necessary to tell a story, label it.

► Avoid undercover or other surreptitious methods of gathering information except when traditional open methods will not yield information vital to the public. Use of such methods should be explained as part of the story.

► Never plagiarize.

► Tell the story of the diversity and magnitude of the human experience boldly, even when it is unpopular to do so.

► Examine their own cultural values and avoid imposing those values on others.

► Avoid stereotyping by race, gender, age, religion, ethnicity, geography, sexual orientation, disability, physical appearance or social status.

► Support the open exchange of views, even views they find repugnant.

► Give voice to the voiceless; official and unofficial sources of information can be equally valid.

► Distinguish between advocacy and news reporting. Analysis and commentary should be labeled and not misrepresent fact or context.

► Distinguish news from advertising and shun hybrids that blur the lines between the two.

► Recognize a special obligation to ensure that the public's business is conducted in the open and that government records are open to inspection.

Minimize Harm

Ethical journalists treat sources, subjects and colleagues as human beings deserving of respect.

Journalists should:

- ▶ Show compassion for those who may be affected adversely by news coverage. Use special sensitivity when dealing with children and inexperienced sources or subjects.

- ▶ Be sensitive when seeking or using interviews or photographs of those affected by tragedy or grief.

- ▶ Recognize that gathering and reporting information may cause harm or discomfort. Pursuit of the news is not a license for arrogance.

- ▶ Recognize that private people have a greater right to control information about themselves than do public officials and others who seek power, influence or attention. Only an overriding public need can justify intrusion into anyone's privacy.

- ▶ Show good taste. Avoid pandering to lurid curiosity.

- ▶ Be cautious about identifying juvenile suspects or victims of sex crimes.

- ▶ Be judicious about naming criminal suspects before the formal filing of charges.

- ▶ Balance a criminal suspect's fair trial rights with the public's right to be informed.

Act Independently

Journalists should be free of obligation to any interest other than the public's right to know.

Journalists should:

- ▶ Avoid conflicts of interest, real or perceived.

- ▶ Remain free of associations and activities that may compromise integrity or damage credibility.

- ▶ Refuse gifts, favors, fees, free travel and special treatment, and shun secondary employment, political involvement, public office and service in community organizations if they compromise journalistic integrity.

- ▶ Disclose unavoidable conflicts.

- ▶ Be vigilant and courageous about holding those with power accountable.

▶ Deny favored treatment to advertisers and special interests and resist their pressure to influence news coverage.

▶ Be wary of sources offering information for favors or money; avoid bidding for news.

Be Accountable

Journalists are accountable to their readers, listeners, viewers and each other.

Journalists should:

▶ Clarify and explain news coverage and invite dialogue with the public over journalistic conduct.

▶ Encourage the public to voice grievances against the news media.

▶ Admit mistakes and correct them promptly.

▶ Expose unethical practices of journalists and the news media.

▶ Abide by the same high standards to which they hold others.

Sigma Delta Chi's first Code of Ethics was borrowed from the American Society of Newspaper Editors in 1926. In 1973, Sigma Delta Chi wrote its own code, which was revised in 1984 and 1987. The present version of the Society of Professional Journalists' Code of Ethics was adopted in September 1996.

Standards of Practice of the American Association of Advertising Agencies

We hold that a responsibility of advertising agencies is to be a constructive force in business.

We hold that, to discharge this responsibility, advertising agencies must recognize an obligation, not only to their clients, but to the public, the media they employ, and to each other. As a business, the advertising agency must operate within the framework of competition. It is recognized that keen and vigorous competition, honestly conducted, is necessary to the growth and the health of American business. However, unethical competitive practices in the advertising agency business lead to financial waste, dilution of service, diversion of manpower, loss of prestige, and tend to weaken public confidence both in advertisements and in the institution of advertising.

We hold that the advertising agency should compete on merit and not by attempts at discrediting or disparaging a competitor agency, or its work, directly or by inference, or by circulating harmful rumors about another agency, or by making unwarranted claims of particular skill in judging or prejudging advertising copy.

To these ends, the American Association of Advertising Agencies has adopted the following Creative Code as being in the best interests of the public, the advertisers, the media, and the agencies themselves. The AAAA believes the Code's provisions serve as a guide to the kind of agency conduct that experience has shown to be wise, foresighted, and constructive. In accepting membership, an agency agrees to follow it.

Creative Code

We, the members of the American Association of Advertising Agencies, in addition to supporting and obeying the laws and legal regulations pertaining to advertising, undertake to extend and broaden the application of high ethical standards. Specifically, we will not knowingly create advertising that contains:

a. False or misleading statements or exaggerations, visual or verbal testimonials that do not reflect the real opinion of the individual(s) involved, price claims that are misleading

b. Claims insufficiently supported or that distort the true meaning or practicable application of statements made by professional or scientific authority

c. Statements, suggestions, or pictures offensive to public decency or minority segments of the population.

We recognize that there are areas that are subject to honestly different interpretations and judgment. Nevertheless, we agree not to recommend to an advertiser, and to discourage the use of, advertising that is in poor or questionable taste or that is deliberately irritating through aural or visual content or presentation.

Comparative advertising shall be governed by the same standards of truthfulness, claim substantiation, tastefulness, etc., as apply to other types of advertising.

These Standards of Practice of the American Association of Advertising Agencies come from the belief that sound and ethical practice is good business. Confidence and respect are indispensable to success in a business embracing the many intangibles of agency service and involving relationships so dependent upon good faith.

Clear and willful violations of these Standards of Practice may be referred to the Board of Directors of the American Association of Advertising Agencies for appropriate action, including possible annulment of membership as provided by Article IV, Section 5, of the Constitution and By-Laws.

First adopted October 16, 1924. Most recently revised September 18, 1990.

Member Code of Ethics 2000
Approved by the PRSA Assembly
October, 2000

The PRSA Assembly adopted this Code of Ethics in 2000. It replaces the Code of Professional Standards (previously referred to as the Code of Ethics) that was last revised in 1988. For further information on the Code, please contact the chair of the Board of Ethics through PRSA headquarters.

Preamble

Public Relations Society of America Member Code of Ethics 2000

- ► Professional Values
- ► Principles of Conduct
- ► Commitment and Compliance

This Code applies to PRSA members. The Code is designed to be a useful guide for PRSA members as they carry out their ethical responsibilities. This document is designed to anticipate and accommodate, by precedent, ethical challenges that may arise. The scenarios outlined in the Code provision are actual examples of misconduct. More will be added as experience with the Code occurs.

The Public Relations Society of America (PRSA) is committed to ethical practices. The level of public trust PRSA members seek, as we serve the public good, means we have taken on a special obligation to operate ethically.

The value of member reputation depends upon the ethical conduct of everyone affiliated with the Public Relations Society of America.

Each of us sets an example for each other—as well as other professionals—by our pursuit of excellence with powerful standards of performance, professionalism, and ethical conduct.

Emphasis on enforcement of the Code has been eliminated. But, the PRSA Board of Directors retains the right to bar from membership or expel from the Society any individual who has been or is sanctioned by a government agency or convicted in a court of law of an action that is in violation of this Code.

Ethical practice is the most important obligation of a PRSA member. We view the Member Code of Ethics as a model for other professions, organizations, and professionals.

PRSA Member Statement of Professional Values

This statement presents the core values of PRSA members and, more broadly, of the public relations profession. These values provide the foundation for the Member Code of Ethics and set the industry standard for the professional practice of public relations. These values are the fundamental beliefs that guide our behaviors and decision-making process. We believe our professional values are vital to the integrity of the profession as a whole.

Advocacy

▶ We serve the public interest by acting as responsible advocates for those we represent.

▶ We provide a voice in the marketplace of ideas, facts, and viewpoints to aid informed public debate.

Honesty

▶ We adhere to the highest standards of accuracy and truth in advancing the interests of those we represent and in communicating with the public.

Expertise

▶ We acquire and responsibly use specialized knowledge and experience.

▶ We advance the profession through continued professional development, research, and education.

▶ We build mutual understanding, credibility, and relationships among a wide array of institutions and audiences.

Independence

- ▶ We provide objective counsel to those we represent.

- ▶ We are accountable for our actions.

Loyalty

- ▶ We are faithful to those we represent, while honoring our obligation to serve the public interest.

Fairness

- ▶ We deal fairly with clients, employers, competitors, peers, vendors, the media, and the general public.

- ▶ We respect all opinions and support the right of free expression.

PRSA Code Provisions

Free Flow of Information

Core Principle

Protecting and advancing the free flow of accurate and truthful information is essential to serving the public interest and contributing to informed decision making in a democratic society.

Intent

- ▶ To maintain the integrity of relationships with the media, government officials, and the public.

- ▶ To aid informed decision making.

Guidelines

A member shall:

- ▶ Preserve the integrity of the process of communication.

- ▶ Be honest and accurate in all communications.

- ▶ Act promptly to correct erroneous communications for which the practitioner is responsible.

- ▶ Preserve the free flow of unprejudiced information when giving or receiving gifts by ensuring that gifts are nominal, legal, and infrequent.

Examples of Improper Conduct Under this Provision:

- ► A member representing a ski manufacturer gives a pair of expensive racing skis to a sports magazine columnist, to influence the columnist to write favorable articles about the product.

- ► A member entertains a government official beyond legal limits and/or in violation of government reporting requirements.

Competition
Core Principle
Promoting healthy and fair competition among professionals preserves an ethical climate while fostering a robust business environment.

Intent

- ► To promote respect and fair competition among public relations professionals.

- ► To serve the public interest by providing the widest choice of practitioner options.

Guidelines
A member shall:

- ► Follow ethical hiring practices designed to respect free and open competition without deliberately undermining a competitor.

- ► Preserve intellectual property rights in the marketplace.

Examples of Improper Conduct Under This Provision:

- ► A member employed by a "client organization" shares helpful information with a counseling firm that is competing with others for the organization's business.

- ► A member spreads malicious and unfounded rumors about a competitor in order to alienate the competitor's clients and employees in a ploy to recruit people and business.

Disclosure of Information
Core Principle
Open communication fosters informed decision making in a democratic society.

Intent

► To build trust with the public by revealing all information needed for responsible decision making.

Guidelines

A member shall:

► Be honest and accurate in all communications.

► Act promptly to correct erroneous communications for which the member is responsible.

► Investigate the truthfulness and accuracy of information released on behalf of those represented.

► Reveal the sponsors for causes and interests represented.

► Disclose financial interest (such as stock ownership) in a client's organization.

► Avoid deceptive practices.

Examples of Improper Conduct Under this Provision:

► Front groups: A member implements "grass roots" campaigns or letter-writing campaigns to legislators on behalf of undisclosed interest groups.

► Lying by omission: A practitioner for a corporation knowingly fails to release financial information, giving a misleading impression of the corporation's performance.

► A member discovers inaccurate information disseminated via a Web site or media kit and does not correct the information.

► A member deceives the public by employing people to pose as volunteers to speak at public hearings and participate in "grassroots" campaigns.

Safeguarding Confidences

Core Principle

Client trust requires appropriate protection of confidential and private information.

Intent

► To protect the privacy rights of clients, organizations, and individuals by safeguarding confidential information.

Guidelines

A member shall:

- ▶ Safeguard the confidences and privacy rights of present, former, and prospective clients and employees.

- ▶ Protect privileged, confidential, or insider information gained from a client or organization.

- ▶ Immediately advise an appropriate authority if a member discovers that confidential information is being divulged by an employee of a client company or organization.

Examples of Improper Conduct Under This Provision:

- ▶ A member changes jobs, takes confidential information, and uses that information in the new position to the detriment of the former employer.

- ▶ A member intentionally leaks proprietary information to the detriment of some other party.

Conflicts of Interest

Core Principle

Avoiding real, potential or perceived conflicts of interest builds the trust of clients, employers, and the public.

Intent

- ▶ To earn trust and mutual respect with clients or employers.

- ▶ To build trust with the public by avoiding or ending situations that put one's personal or professional interests in conflict with society's interests.

Guidelines

A member shall:

- ▶ Act in the best interests of the client or employer, even subordinating the member's personal interests.

- ▶ Avoid actions and circumstances that may appear to compromise good business judgment or create a conflict between personal and professional interests.

- ▶ Disclose promptly any existing or potential conflict of interest to affected clients or organizations.

► Encourage clients and customers to determine if a conflict exists after notifying all affected parties.

Examples of Improper Conduct Under This Provision

► The member fails to disclose that he or she has a strong financial interest in a client's chief competitor.

► The member represents a "competitor company" or a "conflicting interest" without informing a prospective client.

Enhancing the Profession

Core Principle

Public relations professionals work constantly to strengthen the public's trust in the profession.

Intent

► To build respect and credibility with the public for the profession of public relations.

► To improve, adapt and expand professional practices.

Guidelines

A member shall:

► Acknowledge that there is an obligation to protect and enhance the profession.

► Keep informed and educated about practices in the profession to ensure ethical conduct.

► Actively pursue personal professional development.

► Decline representation of clients or organizations that urge or require actions contrary to this Code.

► Accurately define what public relations activities can accomplish.

► Counsel subordinates in proper ethical decision making.

► Require that subordinates adhere to the ethical requirements of the Code.

► Report ethical violations, whether committed by PRSA members or not, to the appropriate authority.

Examples of Improper Conduct Under This Provision:

> ▶ A PRSA member declares publicly that a product the client sells is safe, without disclosing evidence to the contrary.

> ▶ A member initially assigns some questionable client work to a nonmember practitioner to avoid the ethical obligation of PRSA membership.

Resources

Rules and Guidelines

The following PRSA documents, available online at www.prsa.org, provide detailed rules and guidelines to help guide your professional behavior. If, after reviewing them, you still have a question or issue, contact PRSA headquarters as noted below.

> ▶ PRSA Bylaws

> ▶ PRSA Administrative Rules

> ▶ Member Code of Ethics

Questions

The PRSA is here to help. If you have a serious concern or simply need clarification, please contact (212) 460-1404.

PRSA Member Code of Ethics Pledge

I pledge:

To conduct myself professionally, with truth, accuracy, fairness, and responsibility to the public; To improve my individual competence and advance the knowledge and proficiency of the profession through continuing research and education; And to adhere to the articles of the Member Code of Ethics 2000 for the practice of public relations as adopted by the governing Assembly of the Public Relations Society of America.

I understand and accept that there is a consequence for misconduct, up to and including membership revocation.

And, I understand that those who have been or are sanctioned by a government agency or convicted in a court of law of an action that is in violation of this Code may be barred from membership or expelled from the Society.

B

Spelling, Capitalization and Punctuation

I t's your first day on the new job at Smith and Jones Media Relations, Inc., and you're pretty darn pleased with yourself. Here it is five o'clock, and you've met your deadline and turned in that press release on the opening of the new corporate headquarters building.

It was a long day, and you're ready to celebrate a little. You start to walk down the long hallway that leads from the boss's office to the exit door when you hear from behind a loud roar.

It's the boss, and she's *not* happy.

You wonder what went wrong. You got the facts straight, you're sure of that, and the story seems well organized. What could be the problem?

Cautiously, you knock. There's a growl for you to enter. You open the door to the boss' office. She looks up at you and frowns. "Chris," she asks, "how do you spell *accommodate*?"

You gulp.

"And since when do we capitalize the seasons of the year around here?"

You gulp again. You're beginning to get the drift.

The boss holds up your story and asks, coldly, "Chris, exactly when did the rules of grammar change to allow you to use *hopefully* when you meant to say 'we hope'? And just when did collective nouns start taking the plural pronoun?"

"I don't know," you mumble, and suddenly you know you're in for a rough time. You passed that grammar test in college, darn it, but that was more than two years ago, and somehow it all seems to have slipped away from you. You never really thought it would matter all that much anyway. Isn't that what spell checkers and grammar checkers were for?

"Chris," the boss says, handing you a couple of books. "Take a look at this. It's the *Associated Press Stylebook*, and when your college instructors told you that you had to know it and use it, they were right. The AP *Stylebook* is the standard tool for almost all media writers when it comes to matters of style and usage.

"And here," she adds, "is another book. Take a good look at Chapter 3 in this one, and then read closely Appendix B. Tomorrow, when you get in, you're going to take an editing test. If you pass it, then we'll let you try one more story."

The AP *Stylebook* is on every good media writer's desk. Many publications issue their own stylebooks, but they are inevitably based on the AP *Stylebook* and use it as the starting point for discussing local style concerns (how do you correctly spell the name of that bridge, for instance) or particular differences between AP and the editors' decisions on other matters of style (the use of italics, for instance). You simply must have, and use, *The Associated Press Stylebook and Briefing on Media Law*.

And if this was the other book that the boss handed you, then this appendix and the trouble spots found in Chapter 3 are the things she wanted you to learn. The truth of the matter is that for many jobs in public relations, newspapers, magazines or other media, you'd be taking that test before you were hired in the first place, and you might very well not be hired if you didn't pass it.

Why are editors so sensitive about these basic issues of spelling, capitalization and punctuation? Because these are the basic building blocks for all of your writing in the media. You cannot begin to construct professionally acceptable stories in any medium unless you have the basics under firm control.

Think of it this way. Each story that you write is like a house built of bricks, and the bricks are made up of your nouns, verbs, modifiers, phrases, clauses, sentences and paragraphs. If you build your house with bad bricks—if you don't know what is meant by noun–pronoun agreement and you wouldn't recognize a dangling participle if it thumped you on the head—then the house you build is not likely to be a good one. In terms of your writing, your story will fall apart under the scrutiny of a good editor, as happened at the start of this chapter with our mythical Chris during the first day on the job.

Perhaps more importantly, your story will very likely be one that can't communicate the way you'd like it to with your reader, and communication is what media writing ultimately is all about.

Whether you work in newspapers, magazines, public relations, broadcast news, advertising or anywhere else in the media, your future success begins right here.

Let's get started.

Spelling

Your ability to spell is crucial to your success in media writing. Certainly you will have access to a dictionary, and probably to a spellchecker, as well; but if you have to look up too many words, your writing will go slowly indeed. And if your spelling is poor, in most cases you won't recognize that the spelling of a word even *needs* to be looked up.

Commonly Misspelled Words

The rules for spelling sometimes seem confusing and contradictory to the beginning writer, and so we haven't included them here. Instead, here is a list of commonly misspelled words. These are words that you are likely to encounter often in your media writing, so you need to know them.

aberration	appellate	catastrophe
accede	aquarium	cavalry/Calvary
accelerator	assassinate	censor/censure/censer
accept/except	auxiliary	champagne
access/excess	bail/bale	changeable
accommodation	bailiff	chargeable
accessibility	bankruptcy	chauvinist
accustomed	battalion	cite/sight/site
advantageous	belief	collision
aerial	believable	commemorate
aerobic	belligerent	committed
aesthetic	bolder/boulder	compliment/complement
affect/effect	border/boarder	concise
align	born/borne	continuous
all right	break/brake	controlled
allotment	brochure	copyright
allusion/illusion	bulletin	correspondence
altar/alter	bureau	counselor
aluminum	bureaucracy	coup
amnesia	camouflage	courageous
analyze	canon/cannon	crochet
anecdote	cantaloupe	dependent
anonymous	canvas/canvass	descendant
antidote	capitol/capital	desirous
anxious	Caribbean	disseminate
appalling	catalyst	drunkenness

dyeing
dying
efficient
eighth
emigrate/immigrate
eminent/imminent
emphysema
essential
exceed
excessive
excitable
exercise
exhilarate
eyeing
Fahrenheit
fictitious
fluoridation
foreign
foresee
fortieth
freight
fulfilled
fundamental
further
generous
gnawing
goddess
government
governor
gruesome
gubernatorial
guest
handsome
harebrained
hereditary
hundredths
icicle
idiosyncrasies
impromptu
incidentally
indictment
inexhaustible
inferred

infinite
infinitely
innocence
interfere
interpret
kaleidoscope
knowledge
labeled
leukemia
lilies
livelihood
maintenance
malfeasance
malign
meanness
mileage
momentous
monsignor
mortgage
mosquitoes
movable
mustache
neutral
notable
obscene
occasionally
occur
omnipotent
outrageous
overrun
pageant
parentheses (pl)
pasteurization
persistent
pharmaceutical
pique
plaintiff
possess
profession
professor
promissory
propelled
prosperous

psalm
Qantas
quarantine
recede
recurrence
reminiscent
remittance
repentance
rescind
reservoir
restaurant
rheumatic
sacrilegious
sandwich
satellites
scarcely
serviceable
solemn
souvenir
specifically
succession
suddenness
suspicious
temperament
temperature
thousandth
traceable
tyrannical
unconscious
unnecessary
usable
veterinarian
virtuous
weather
whether
wintry
wreath
xenophobia
yield
you're/your
zealot
zoology

You'll note there are a number of words where the spelling depends on how you use the word. These words are common trouble spots for beginning media writers (and, let's admit it, for some veterans). Here's their correct spelling tied to their use.

accept/except

To *accept* something is to receive or embrace it, as in "He was willing to accept the bribe."

Except means to be excluded, as in "Everyone accepted the bribe except Senator Jones."

access/excess

To have *access* to something means to be able to approach or enter, as in "He had access to the library's special collections."

If something is in *excess*, it is beyond the ordinary limits, as in "The library's funding was in excess of its needs."

affect/effect

Affect is a verb, as in "The common cold affects your breathing," and *effect* is a noun, as in "The effect of the legislation was higher taxes."

However, *effect* is also a verb that means "to bring about," as in "They were hoping to effect a change in the system."

allusion/illusion

To make an *allusion* is to make an indirect reference to something, as in "He made an allusion to the previous performance."

To create an *illusion* is to create an unreal image, a trick, as in "He created the illusion of sawing Jane in half."

altar/alter

An *altar* is a religious table used for ceremonies, as in "They worshipped at the cathedral's main altar."

To *alter* something is to change it, as in "They wanted to alter the ceremony in some way."

bail/bale

To *bail* is to dip water from a boat or to jump from an airplane, as in "They had to bail out the rowboat or it would have sunk," or "He had to bail out of the plane before it crashed."

A *bale* is a large packet of something, as in "He loaded the wagon with five bales of hay."

bite/byte

Bite something or someone is either a verb meaning to grab something with the teeth, as in "The dog would bite him at every opportunity," or a noun meaning the act of biting as in "The dog had a ferocious bite."

Byte is a computer term referring to one unit of binary digits, usually used as part of a term referring to thousands or millions of bytes, as in "His hard drive had 16 gigabytes of memory."

bloc/block

A *bloc* is a group or coalition, as in "The conservative bloc wanted to stop the bill's passage."

Block describes a neighborhood unit, as in "They live in that block," or a solid piece of material, frequently wood or metal, as in "The child played all day with that one block."

As a verb, *block* means to get in the way of, as in "They tried to block the bill's passage."

bolder/boulder

To be *bolder* is to be more daring, as in "John was much bolder than Robert as they climbed the tree."

A *boulder* is a large stone, as in "They shoved the boulder aside and then continued on their way."

border/boarder

The *border* is the line between two states or countries, and is also the line marking the edge of something, as in "He crossed the border into Canada" or "He drew a border around the picture."

A *boarder* is someone paying to live with someone else, as in "She took in a boarder to help pay the rent."

born/borne

To be *born* is what happens on your day of birth, as in "He was born on July 1."

To be *borne* is to be carried, as in "The body was borne to the cemetery."

break/brake

A *break* is the space left when something comes apart, as in "They found a break in the handle," or it is the space between two things, as in "They took a break between workshops."

A *brake* is a device to stop something, as in "Samantha quickly learned how to use the brakes on her new bicycle."

canon/cannon

A *canon* is a basic rule or law, especially religious, as in "He studied the ancient canons while in the seminary."

A *cannon* is a weapon, as in "They fired the cannons until the barrels melted."

canvas/canvass

Canvas is a cloth material, as in "The sails were made of canvas."

To *canvass* is to poll a group on its beliefs, as in "They had to canvass the neighborhood about the election results."

capitol/capital

The *capitol* is the government building, as in "They met at the Capitol."

Capital is a financial word for a basic sum of money, as in "He kept the capital, though he didn't get much interest," or it is the city where government resides, as in "Springfield is the state capital." As an adjective, it means "best" or "excellent," as in "It was a capital idea."

cavalry/Calvary

The *cavalry* is the mounted military unit, as in "The cavalry came to the rescue."

Calvary is where Jesus Christ was crucified.

censor/censure/censer

A *censor* is one who prohibits, as in "The censor wouldn't allow our school newspaper to print the article."

To *censure* is to reprimand, as in "For committing the ethical breach, he was censured by his colleagues."

A *censer* is a ceremonial religious device in which you burn incense, as in "The altar boy held the censer."

cite/sight/site

To *cite* something is to refer to it, as in "He was able to cite four articles that proved his point."

To *sight* something is to see it, as in "He was able to sight the ship in the distance."

A *site* is a place where something exists, as in "Our school will be the site of the new exhibit."

climactic/climatic

Climactic says something is at its peak, as in "After four days of peace talks, this was the climactic proposal."

Climatic refers to climate, as in "Scientists worry about climatic change."

compliment/complement

To *compliment* someone is to praise the person, as in "She offered him a very nice compliment on his tie."

To *complement* is to mix with well, as in "Salsa is a perfect complement to tortilla chips."

Note: To offer something for free is to make it *complimentary.*

counsel/council

A *counsel* is a lawyer or other advisor, as in "He listened to his legal counsel before answering the question."

A *council* is a group, as in "The council met to decide the issue once and for all."

discrete/discreet

To be *discreet* is to show restraint, as in "He was discreet about his dealings with the media."

Something *discrete* is separated out by distinct items, as in "There were five discrete elements to the proposal."

dual/duel

Dual means two similar items of something, as in "There were dual proposals presented."

A *duel* is a kind of combat, as in "The teams were locked in a tight duel for the championship."

emigrate/immigrate

To *emigrate* is to leave a country which has been your home; and to *immigrate* is to enter a country as your new home, as in "He emigrated from Ireland in 1845" and "He immigrated to America in 1845."

eminent/imminent

To be *eminent* is to be thought of highly, as in "He is an eminent poet in his own land."

To be *imminent* is to be about to occur, as in "The hurricane's arrival seemed imminent."

faint/feint

To *faint* is to temporarily lose consciousness, as in "He fainted when he heard the news."

To *feint* is to fake, as in "Nick made a feint to the left, then went to his right to score."

Both of these are also nouns, as in "He lay on the bed in a faint" and "He made a feint left, then went right."

fiscal/physical

Fiscal refers to financial and accounting matters, as in "Your vacation time begins on July 1, with the start of the company's fiscal year."

Physical refers to your body, as in "He's a very physical player" or "We all had to take a physical before being admitted."

forth/fourth

To go *forth* is to move forward, as in "They moved forth from the castle."

Fourth is the number, as in "They were the fourth group to leave."

foul/fowl

A *foul* is an offensive or unfair act, as in "He was guilty of the foul." It's also an adjective, as in "His breath smelled foul."

A *fowl* is a chicken or other bird, as in "On their farm they raised beef and fowl."

gorilla/guerrilla

A *gorilla* is the animal, as in "He studied the gorilla for more than three months."

A *guerrilla* is an irregular soldier, a partisan, as in "The regular army fought the guerrillas for almost ten years."

grate/great

A *grate* is a protective framework of bars, as in "A grate covered the opening." As a verb, it is something you do to food or other items to break them into smaller units, as in "Emily asked Uncle Randy to grate the cheese."

To be *great* is to be outstanding, as in "He was one of the game's truly great hitters."

hangar/hanger

A *hangar* is a place where airplanes are kept, as in "They worked in the hangar all night to repair the landing gear."

A *hanger* is used to hang clothes, as in "He put his pants on the hanger."

hearty/hardy

To be *hearty* is to be jovial, as in "He's a hearty fellow."

To be *hardy* is to be physically fit, as in "She's so hardy she runs in any weather."

hoard/horde

To *hoard* something is to keep it, usually hidden, as in "He tried to hoard the extra food." It's also a noun, as in "He kept his hoard hidden."

A *horde* is an unruly group, as in "The whole horde of them descended on the town like a plague of locusts."

incidents/incidence

Incidents is the plural of *incident*, which is an occurrence of something, as in "There were twelve such incidents in just one month."

Incidence is the rate at which incidents occur, as in "There was a high incidence of crime in that particular month."

incite/insight

To *incite* is to promote or instigate, as in "He tried to incite the crowd to riot."

To have *insight* is to have special understanding of something, as in "He has real insight into the background of the issue."

it's/its

It's is the contraction for *it is*, as in "It's high time you understood the difference."

Its is the possessive, as in "The team won its game."

let's/lets

Let's is the contraction for *let us*, as in "Let's go to the opera tonight."

Lets means "allows," as in "The umpire lets the game continue."

libel/liable

Libel is the legal term for written defamation, as in "He sued the newspaper for libel, but lost."

Liable means "possible" or "likely," as in "He is liable to play tomorrow."

lightening/lightning

To be *lightening* something is to be making it lighter, as in "They were lightening the plane before they took off."

Lightning is the weather phenomenon, as in "The golfers were struck by lightning."

One of this book's authors still has a copy of a small-town newspaper with the headline: "Beth the mule killed by lightening." This should strike you as an unlikely death for a mule.

martial/marshal

Martial is a military term, as in "The president invoked martial law in the city."

To be a *marshal* is to be an officer in the military, or police or fire department, as in "He's the town fire marshal."

meddle/metal/mettle

To *meddle* in something is to get involved, as in "He knew better than to meddle with that issue."

Metal is the class of elements, as in "He used a metal rake because it was sturdier."

Mettle is courage or character, as in "She tested his mettle with that midterm."

minor/miner

To be a *minor* is to be legally not an adult, as in "He's a minor in this state."

A *miner* is one who works in a mine, as in "My dad was a miner for forty years."

ordinance/ordnance

An *ordinance* is a law, as in "The city council passed the new ordinance."

Ordnance is a military term for weapons and ammunition, as in "The brigade had plenty of ordnance."

palate/palette/pallet

Your *palate* is the roof of your mouth. *Palate* is also used as a synonym for taste, as in "He has a palate for fine wine."

A *palette* is a board used by a painter, as in "She mixes her paints on her palette."

A *pallet* is a board or platform used to carry things, as in "They placed the altar on a pallet and then moved it across the cathedral to the new spot."

peak/peek/pique

A *peak* is the topmost point or highest achievement, as in "She climbed to the peak in only five hours" or "The victory was her peak athletic achievement."

To *peek* is to look covertly or quickly at something, as in "She took a quick peek at the top-ten list."

To *pique* someone's interest is to arouse it, as in "His performance piqued the critic's interest."

plaintive/plaintiff

To be *plaintive* is to be mournful, as in "He was in a plaintive mood."

The *plaintiff* is the one who sues someone else, as in "The plaintiff demanded restitution."

poor/pour/pore

To be *poor* is to have little money or to be lacking in something, as in "The Dodgers were poor in pitching."

To *pour* is to make a liquid flow into or out of a container, as in "He poured the wine."

To *pore* is to read closely, as in "He pored over the reports, looking for something unusual."

A *pore* is also an opening on your skin.

premiere/premier

A *premiere* is the opening performance of something, as in "The play's premiere was a success."

A *premier* is a political leader, as in "He used to be the premier of Moravia."

Premier also means "best," as in "It was the premier event of the season."

principle/principal

A *principle* is a guiding truth, as in "He always places his principles first."

A *principal* runs a school, as in "The principal gave the students the afternoon off," or may mean first in rank, as in "She is the principal performer this evening."

prostate/prostrate

The *prostate* is a gland found in males, as in "He tested negative for cancer of the prostate."

To be *prostrate* is to be prone, as in "He was prostrate for five minutes after the knockout."

right/rite/write/wright

To be *right* is to be correct, as in "She's right on this one." *Right* is also a direction.

A *rite* is a religious ceremony, as in "They performed the rite at seven in the evening."

To *write* is to create using the written word, as in "They write the rules."

A *wright* is one who works, as in "He's a wheelwright" or "He's a boatwright" or "He's a playwright."

straight/strait

To be *straight* is to be without curves, as in "The road runs straight for the next ten miles" or "He's a straight shooter."

A *strait* is a narrow passage of water, as in "The ship passed the Straits of Hormuz."

taught/taut

To be *taught* is to learn from a teacher, as in "He was taught the rules."

To be *taut* is to be tight or firm, as in "She pulled the rope taut."

team/teem

A *team* is a group of individuals working together (and the word takes the singular pronoun, see Chapter 3), as in "The team won its game in the final minute."

To *teem* is to abound, as in "The waters teemed with fish."

threw/through

Threw is the past tense of *throw*, as in "He threw the first pitch."

Through means "finished," as in "He's through for the day." You can also *go through* something, as in "She traveled through the country in just two days."

vain/vane/vein

To be *vain* is to be egotistical or to be useless, as in "He's terribly vain about his talents" or "He tried in vain to win the prize."

A *vane* is a device indicating wind direction, as in "The weather vane indicated the wind was from the west."

A *vein* carries blood back to the heart, as in "The veins in his neck stood out from the stress."

vial/vile

A *vial* carries a liquid, as in "He brought the vial of blood to the laboratory."

To be *vile* is to be mean, despicable, as in "He's a vile character."

weather/whether

The *weather* is the condition of the atmosphere, as in "The weather looks like rain."

Whether introduces a clause with two choices, as in "They'll play whether it rains or not."

we're/were

We're is the contraction for *we are*, as in "We're going to the play."

Were is the past tense of *are*, as in "We were there when the play started."

wet/whet

To *wet* is to moisten, as in "They wet the field before the game."
To *whet* is to sharpen, as in "The smell whet his appetite."

who's/whose

Who's is the contraction for *who is*, as in "Who's there?"
Whose is the possessive pronoun, as in "Whose doll is it?"

you're/your

You're is the contraction for *you are*, as in "You're the one who finished the contest."
Your is the possessive pronoun, as in "It's your game to win."

Spell-checkers

Professionals will tell you not to count on your software's spell-checker catching your mistakes for you. Take a look at this sentence:

Where you're blew suite too knight.

Your spell-checker won't catch any of those words, because each word is spelled correctly. But you can see that a story composed of very many sentences like that will be unintelligible.

So, you have to know the difference between *wear/where* and *your/you're* and *blue/blew* and *suit/suite* and *to/too/two* and *night/knight*.

A Few Final Thoughts on Spelling

How do you learn to spell correctly? It begins with reading. As you'll hear in many places in this text, reading is the second most important overall thing you can do to improve your writing generally (writing, and writing regularly, is the first), and your spelling in particular. Read anything that's been published, and you're most likely going to encounter writing that a professional writer produced and a professional editor (and perhaps one or more additional copy editors) worked on to polish and correct.

In the act of reading, your spelling skills will benefit in two significant ways:

> ► **You'll see the words spelled correctly.** This will make it much easier for you to notice a word spelled incorrectly in your own stories. You may not always recognize why a word looks odd,

but because you have seen it spelled correctly countless times, you will notice that it doesn't seem right. That's the first step toward improving your spelling.

▶ **You'll see the words used in their correct context.** This should help you get past the kind of problem words you can see earlier in this appendix. Again, you may not always recognize why the word you've used is incorrect in that spot, but because you have seen it used correctly many times, you will recognize that it just doesn't look right.

Finally, remember that bad spelling, like bad eyesight, is not a crime. Still, you wouldn't want to ride to work with a driver who'd forgotten his eyeglasses. If you know your spelling isn't strong, you'll have to plan on spending extra time on revisions.

And if you're a good speller, but a lousy typist, you'll need to copy-edit carefully as well. You will probably learn quickly which typos you tend to make often: *univeristy* for *university* or *teh* for *the*. If you know your problem words ahead of time, you have a better chance of catching them.

Capitalization

Capitalization is another area of trouble for the beginning media writer. There are, unfortunately, a number of areas where media writing's rules on capitalization are different from the rules you may have learned in your English classes. In fact, there are even differences between the various media and even individual differences between publications or agencies.

There are, however, some general rules that most editors agree on, beginning with capitalizing proper nouns and lowercasing common nouns. Here are 10 additional basic rules for capitalization.

Do capitalize a formal job title that directly precedes a name.

> When she reached the scene, Sergeant Jones immediately took action.

But do not capitalize a job title that is generic or one that stands alone:

> When she reached the scene, police officer Jones took action.

> The sergeant took action as soon as she reached the scene.

Do capitalize the specific formal names of things.

> The Bible story of David and Goliath is a favorite of mine.

> The Legislature meets for two months starting today.

But do not capitalize the informal or generic names of things:

> The baseball yearbook is my bible when it comes to batting averages.

> Many state legislatures meet for more than two months at a time.

Do capitalize specific regions of the country.

> He grew up in the South.

> He spent ten years in the West.

But do not capitalize directions:

> He's heading south for the winter.

> I'm heading west for the holidays."

Do capitalize ethnic designations.

> She is an African-American.

> She is Hispanic.

But do not capitalize color descriptions:

> She is a black woman.

Do capitalize the first word in a quote when that quote is a complete sentence.

> John said, "This winter may be a snowy one."

But do not capitalize the first word in a partial quote when that quote is not a complete sentence:

> John said the coming winter "may be a snowy one."

Do capitalize academic departments where the word is already a proper noun.

> The Spanish department held a meeting yesterday.

But do not capitalize academic departments where the word is not already a proper noun:

> The mass communication department held a meeting yesterday.

Do capitalize specific governmental bodies.

> The Police Department offered a new program.

Also, do capitalize government committees when the title is specific and formal:

> The Senate Ethics Committee met on Tuesday.

But do not capitalize government committees when the title seems generic:

> The ethics committee met yesterday.

Do capitalize the days of the week and the months of the year.

> They first met on a Tuesday in May.

But do not capitalize the seasons of the year:

> They met in the spring.

Do capitalize the names of political parties.

> The Democratic candidate won that district.

But do not capitalize the names of political philosophies:

> He used to believe in communism, but now he claims to be democratic.

Do capitalize trade names.

> He drank a Coca-Cola after the victory lap.

> They played Nintendo until nearly midnight.

But do not capitalize generic terms that are similar to trade names:

> He drank a cola after the victory lap.

> They played video games until nearly midnight.

Remember that many of these rules have variations from publication to publication, so make sure you learn the specific capitalization rules for whatever publication or agency you are writing for. Most media publications, for instance, lowercase both *pope* and *president*, but some particular publications (say, a Roman Catholic magazine) might very well capitalize one or the other, even when used alone.

Abbreviations

The general rule on abbreviations is that those formal groups whose abbreviations have become well known are written capitalized and without periods, as in *NATO, FBI, CIA, OSHA, DEA, NOW, GOP*. Those common nouns whose abbreviations have become well known are abbreviated, but in lowercase, as in *mph, aka, dpi*. Those common nouns whose abbreviations are just two letters long usually are abbreviated in lowercase, and with periods, as in *a.m.* and *p.m.*

Here are three additional basic rules on abbreviations.

Titles for people are usually used, and abbreviated where common, only on the first reference. After the first reference, titles are not used before the name:

> Lt. Gov. Jane Doe attended the luncheon. Doe then proposed the new policy in an afternoon press conference.

State names that stand alone are not abbreviated. But states that follow cities are abbreviated.

> (He lives in Alabama) He lives in Selma, Ala.

Media editors still use the old style for state abbreviations and do not follow the newer post office style. Here's the list of state abbreviations:

Ala.	Fla.	Md.	Neb.	N.D.	Tenn.
Ariz.	Ga.	Mass.	Nev.	Okla.	Vt.
Ark.	Ill.	Mich.	N.H.	Ore.	Va.
Calif.	Ind.	Minn.	N.J.	Pa.	Wash.
Colo.	Kan.	Miss.	N.M.	R.I.	W.Va.
Conn.	Ky.	Mo.	N.Y.	S.C.	Wis.
Del.	La.	Mont.	N.C.	S.D.	Wyo.

You will notice that eight state names are not abbreviated at all. These are *Alaska*, *Hawaii*, *Idaho*, *Iowa*, *Maine*, *Ohio*, *Texas*, and *Utah*.

Do not abbreviate the names of streets. But do not abbreviate street names in a specific address:

> He lives on Main Street.

> He lives at 222 Main St.

Punctuation

Just like spelling and abbreviation, punctuation for media writers has a number of areas where there are differences from what you may have learned in English classes.

Generally, media editors try for clarity and simplicity in writing, which means a minimum of long, complex sentences. As a result, you will use semicolons and colons less often, and find yourself writing shorter sentences. This simplifies punctuation, at least to a certain extent.

When in doubt about punctuation in a long sentence, you will almost always be safe turning that long sentence into two or more shorter ones.

Still, even in shorter sentences there are certain basic rules you can follow that will usually have you placing your commas, semicolons, colons, dashes and parentheses in the right spot.

Commas

Here are some of the times you need to use a comma or commas, and some of the times that you should not use a comma or commas:

Always use a comma after *said* in a sentence, where *said* is followed by a direct quote.

> Tom walked up to Alice and said, "Let's go to the ballgame."

But do not use a comma when a paraphrase is used:

> Tom walked up to Alice and said he'd like to go to the ballgame.

Always use a comma between the city and the state, and also between the year and the date.

> Tom Seals lives in Springfield, Mo., now.

> Tom Seals won the contest on July 17, 1998, against talented competition.

Always use a comma between items in a list.
But do not use a comma before the final item when there is a conjunction (*and,* for instance):

> George, Alice, Ralph and Julie all went South for the winter.

Note: The exception to this rule is when you must use the final comma to avoid confusion: Patrick attended Yale, Princeton, and William and Mary.

Always use a comma after introductory words, phrases or clauses.

Introductory word
> *However,* she was unable to attend.

Introductory phrase
> *Taking the final shot,* Michael Jordan won the game.

Introductory clause
> *The committee passed the resolution,* but only after a lengthy debate had been held.

But a gerund or infinitive that is the subject of the sentence does not take a comma:

> *Playing* basketball is something at which Michael Jordan excels. (The gerund *Playing* has been used as the subject.)

> *To win* the game is important. (The infinitive *to win* has been used as the subject.)

Always use commas around nonessential words, phrases or clauses in a sentence.

> John Smith, who plays violin, was awarded the tuition scholarship by the orchestra's board of directors.

> *Spartacus,* starring Kirk Douglas, was a big hit.

In both examples, you could leave out the words inside the commas and the sentence would still make sense.
Do not use commas around essential words, phrases or clauses in a sentence:

> Violinist John Smith was awarded the tuition scholarship by the orchestra's board of directors.

> Actor Kirk Douglas was the star of *Spartacus.*

Always use commas to set off the transition words called "conjunctive adverbs."

Some common conjunctive adverbs are *accordingly, although, at the same time, besides, consequently, for example, furthermore, however, in addition, instead, meanwhile, namely, nevertheless, on the other hand, therefore, thus.*

So, a sentence using a conjunctive adverb looks like this:

> *However,* he was unable to reach his final destination.
> She was, *in addition,* unhappy about the situation.

Always use commas inside quotation marks.

> "I'm not going," said John.

> They played Ellington's "In My Solitude," a jazz classic.

Always use a comma when a conjunction joins two independent clauses in a sentence.

> The factory workers went on strike, and they promised
> it would be a long one.

But do not use a comma when an independent clause is joined by a conjunction to a dependent clause or a phrase:

> The factory workers went on strike and promised
> it would be a long one.

Never use a comma after an exclamation point or question mark that ends a quotation inside a sentence.

> "I love this game!" said the umpire.

> "What problem?" she asked.

Never use a comma around the abbreviations *Jr.* and *Sr.* after a name.

> Tom Williams Jr. was introduced next.

Note: This is another place where journalistic style may differ from what you may have learned in English classes.

Never use a comma after the first adjective when two adjectives modify a noun and the second one is tied closely to the noun.

> A bright blue sky welcomed the morning.

Note: If the adjectives are equal (try reversing them and putting an *and* between them), then use the comma between the two adjectives:

> The long, thin yardstick reached the switch.

There are, of course, a number of other rules about when to use commas (as in setting off *of course,* as we just did); but the preceding rules cover the basics that you'll need for media writing.

Semicolons

In media writing, you won't use the semicolon very often. As we've said before, it is generally better to break long sentences apart into shorter ones rather than use a semicolon or colon. But, there is one common use for the semicolon and one less common use.

Use semicolons to clarify a complicated list.

It is common in media writing to list things in a series. When you do that, use a semicolon between items if any of the items already has a comma.

> When it comes to comparing the three states, California has mountains, deserts and beaches; Florida has sunshine, warm weather and the Everglades; and Illinois has corn, corn and more corn.

Note that you must use the semicolon before the final conjunction, *and.*

Less commonly, use a semicolon before a conjunctive adverb that connects two independent clauses.

> The Bruins looked great in the first half; however, they played terribly for the rest of the game.

Note: Many editors might change that into two sentences.

> The Bruins looked great in the first half. However, they played terribly for the rest of the game.

Colons

Like semicolons, colons are used infrequently in media writing. However, there are several spots where they remain common

Use a colon to introduce a list of items. The items will usually be set off with a bullet.

> The wise traveler will include three basic items on a trip to Ireland:
> • Comfortable walking shoes
> • A rain jacket
> • A sense of patience

Use a colon to show time.

> They arrived at 7:45 p.m.

Note: when the time is on the hour, drop the colon and the double zero.

> They arrived at 7 p.m.

You may also use a colon in the subtitle of a book, play or movie.

> He read *Moonrise: A Tale of Adventure* to his students.

Colons also separate chapter and verse in the Bible, and sometimes are used to indicate a dramatic pause.

> The officer looked to the sky, sighed, and said: "Never again."

Dashes

Dashes are used to set off parenthetical expressions; that is, expressions that are dropped into the middle of a sentence for explanation but that otherwise wouldn't belong there.

> Brown spent much of the 1970s traveling through Europe—usually hitchhiking, but occasionally by train— but never found his way to Rome.

Note: While many editors frown on such sentence interruptions, they are usually more willing to see them set off by dashes than by parentheses.

Dashes are also occasionally used in the place of bullets (see "colons" above) and sometimes used when a dramatic pause is called for, in much the same way that a colon might be used.

Parentheses

Generally, most media writers and editors prefer to avoid using parentheses, since they complicate the sentence structure. As we've noted, if you need to put a bit of explanation into a sentence where it otherwise doesn't fit, dashes are usually the most acceptable way.

A common mistake is to think that you can accomplish with commas what you might otherwise do with parentheses, and that usually won't work.

Poor
> Johnson (back after missing three games with a sprained ankle), who started the game before leaving with four fouls in the third quarter, returned to score three key baskets in the final five minutes.

You can see the writer has tried to cram too much background information into this one sentence, and the parentheses don't help. The sentence needs to be rewritten.

Better
> Johnson returned to the lineup after missing three games with a sprained ankle and played well. He got into foul trouble in the third quarter, however, and had to sit out until late in the game, when he scored three key baskets in the final five minutes.

And those two sentences might be tightened and turned into three sentences by some editors.

Frequently, parentheses are also used to fix quotes that don't make grammatical sense inside the sentence where they are being used. Let's says the person you interviewed said, "They should win the game easily, I think."

As you write the story, you realize you need to explain who the *They* stands for, so you write it this way:

> Jones said, "They (the Bulls) should win the game easily."

The rewrite works, but most editors will prefer you find another way to fix the problem, perhaps through rewriting the story like this:

> Jones said the Bulls "should win the game easily."

By changing the troublesome part of the quote into a bit of paraphrase, you've avoided the confusion and still managed to get the rest of the quote into the story.

Summary

Editors and teachers focus on the basic issues of spelling, capitalization and punctuation because these are the basic building blocks for all of your writing in the media. As we noted at the start of Chapter 3, you cannot begin to construct professionally acceptable stories in any medium unless you have the basics under firm control.

Those basics include spelling, capitalization and punctuation, as well as an understanding of the elements of a sentence. When spelling, you must take into account that some words can be pronounced the same (or nearly so) and yet have different meanings and different spellings. In capitalization and abbreviations, media writers usually follow the *Associated Press Stylebook*'s rules, which occasionally differ from rules you may have learned in an English composition course. In matters of punctuation, media writers tend to use shorter sentences and fewer semicolons and colons.

Key Points

▶ Spelling matters to editors (and instructors!). Certain common mistakes, in particular, can get you into real trouble.

▶ Capitalization and abbreviation rules for media writers may differ from those for other fields of study.

▶ Media writers generally try to use shorter sentences and so less punctuation.

Web Links

Here are a few interesting sites on the Internet where you can find out more information about the basics of grammar and style.

http://www.andromeda.rutgers.edu/~jlynch/Writing/
http://www.wsu.edu:8080/~brians/errors/
http://www.copyeditor.com/default.asp?id=3
http://www.well.com/user/mmcadams/copy.editing.html
http://www.wisc.edu/writing/Handbook/index.html
http://writing-program.uchicago.edu/resources/grammar.htm

Exercises

On the CD-ROM that accompanies this text, *CD-ROM for Modern Media Writing,* are electronic study resources for this chapter:

- ▶ Exercises for Appendix B.
- ▶ Quick access to the **World Wide Web.**
- ▶ A demo of *Web Tutor* for *Modern Media Writing.*
- ▶ The **Modern Media Writing Web Site** at the Wadsworth Communication Café, which offers activities for this chapter at http://www.wadsworth.com/modernmedia_a.

Appendix C

Media Careers: Ready for Anything

You punch the alarm button and rise to your first glorious day as a college graduate. As you take the first jolt of caffeine and butter the toast, you begin scanning the employment ads.

That's curious, you think. Where are the mass media jobs?

You see plenty of jobs like the ones that kept you financially solvent through your years of education: telephone sales, waiting on tables, tending bar. But you have a diploma now in mass media, and you want a job that will put those skills to work.

Then you spot one buried among those other ads. You have the grades, and you belonged to several clubs on campus. Hopeful, even a little confident, you send out a cover letter and a résumé.

After some time, the rejection letter comes. It seems the company hired someone with more experience. That hardly seems fair. After all, you did have to work part-time jobs in order to continue your education. You didn't have the luxury of time to spend at a campus media outlet where you could get some clips or an audition tape. Isn't a diploma enough anymore?

Job Skills

In this appendix, we want to introduce you to the job market and to talk about some of the skills you will need in order to succeed in the mass media. We can't cover every job possibility, and we're not going to cover every job strategy. But here's basic information you ought to know.

The working world is better when you're doing something you love. There's something particularly sad about seeing talented people trapped in jobs they don't want to be doing. Imagine the frustration of a park ranger trapped in a warehouse job or a concert musician selling insurance. Imagine waking up every morning and realizing that you have to put in another day of drudgery. People stuck in this kind of employment may be making a living, but they often aren't particularly happy about their lives.

If you have the desire and the talent to be a writer, it's worse than frustrating when you can't find employment that lets you pursue that desire and talent. And since this is a writing textbook and you're reading it, you're probably interested in working at a job that pays you a decent wage to write.

Pay Scales

You're not in the media business to get rich, are you?

Good, because many media jobs are notoriously low-paying for entry-level folks. And though some entry-level positions may pay in the $30,000 range, others will pay below minimum wage. The salary depends on the market for a particular area and a company's policy toward hires. The chart "Salaries Compared" shows the results of the 1999 Annual Survey of Journalism & Mass Communication graduates conducted by The Grady College of Journalism & Mass Communication at the University of Georgia in Athens. (You can read the entire report at http://www.grady.uga.edu/annualsurveys/grd99/gr99rptd.fin.htm.)

Salary also depends on the type of entry-level position in a particular area. In newspapers, a major metropolitan newspaper is going to pay more money than a weekly newspaper in a rural area. In public

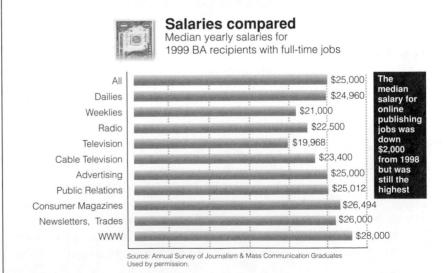

Salaries compared
Median yearly salaries for
1999 BA recipients with full-time jobs

All	$25,000
Dailies	$24,960
Weeklies	$21,000
Radio	$22,500
Television	$19,968
Cable Television	$23,400
Advertising	$25,000
Public Relations	$25,012
Consumer Magazines	$26,494
Newsletters, Trades	$26,000
WWW	$28,000

The median salary for online publishing jobs was down $2,000 from 1998 but was still the highest

Source: Annual Survey of Journalism & Mass Communication Graduates
Used by permission.

relations, an entry-level position in a large corporate setting may pay more than a position with a local not-for-profit. In broadcasting, an entry-level job in a large market will pay more than an entry-level job in a small market.

But it's easier to get a position in the smaller markets. And some large-market media outlets don't hire anybody without prior professional experience.

A few media jobs pay very well. An anchor for a Top 15 market will probably make at least $300,000 a year, and a star reporter for a network news operation will do well also. (Ah, but some anchors have held their jobs for 20 years or more.) Some news reporters with gaudy résumés can make six figures at a large newspaper. Some public relations stars in the corporate and agency settings make six-figure salaries, too.

More often, mid-career media employees may not get rich, but will earn a decent salary for a particular market. And some, frankly, don't ever do really well as far as salary goes. But these folks are usually happy to perform public service using those talents and skills they have.

Still, if a massive salary is at the top of your agenda, we heartily recommend business or engineering school or computer science.

Start Preparing

What should I do now in order to get a job when I graduate?

Begin sharpening your skills immediately by working in your particular area. You should work for the campus newspaper or broadcast stations, and that advice is also for public relations majors. Some clips from your student daily will help you get a job in public relations, especially when you mix them in with the part-time work you did for the campus media relations office or the internship you did for the local hospital's media relations department.

Remember, your experience is reflected through a collection of your work. Those wishing to work in broadcast will want to assemble a tape of their best work. Writers will want to assemble published clips of their stories, headlines or page designs. Advertising copywriters and designers will want to show their published work. Photographers will assemble their best work.

Media managers expect that these works will be in some sort of published form. You may have done some wonderful work in mass media classes, but they expect to see that work prepared in a professional manner. They do not give much credit to a class assignment with a shiny *A* in red.

The diploma just isn't enough. This reality can be a problem in an era where college becomes more expensive and some rent-making jobs pay very well but don't relate well to mass media. If you're serious about working in mass media, you will find a way to get published.

Is college media experience enough?

Well, maybe, depending on how ambitious your student-run media are. If your school paper is a daily that wins national awards and recognition, then those clips weigh more heavily than if the paper was a not-very-ambitious weekly.

Even then, though, remember that you'll be competing against students who not only have spent considerable time working for campus media outlets, but also have spent time in internships or working part-time in professional media outlets.

Many journalism schools offer credit for supervised internships or part-time work experience. And some have set arrangements with media outlets to supply these outlets with student workers. But the credit hours are less important than the opportunity to gain real-life professional experience and to make professional contacts. Often, mass media job openings are not published, but discussed among a grapevine of professionals. If a professional were to know you and respected your work habits, you could well be tipped to job opportunities before any advertisements appear.

"It's not possible to fully understand the profession and all of its nuances without face-to-face experience in a newsroom," says sports reporter Roger Mills of the *St. Petersburg Times*. Mills worked for his campus paper as well as working as a stringer (a writer not affiliated with the paper who writes stories for that paper) before landing a job in one of the *Times'* bureaus and eventually becoming a major league baseball writer.

Job Possibilities

The first warning we'll give you is to not be trapped into thinking that employers believe that students who concentrate in, say, broadcasting are the only candidates for a given job. Too often, students think majors and degree programs are somehow binding on employers and that, say, a newspaper is only going to hire journalism graduates.

That's often not the case. Employers are more concerned with skills and attitudes. It has happened that print journalism majors have been hired as public relations practitioners, broadcasting majors hired for the ad department, and so on.

There are some media practitioners, in fact, who look for majors outside of the journalism schools. Though we believe in journalism schools, we also think you should have a well-rounded education with a concentration in some other area that complements your mass media degree. Employers like to see someone who knows business or history or political science, in particular, and in this rapidly evolving area of new media, a computer science or information science minor (or even a few classes) can be an important boost toward your getting a great first job.

Broadcast Jobs

In broadcast, television jobs are often described as on-camera or behind-the-camera. You're familiar with reporters and anchors, but many broadcast journalists toil behind the camera working as producers, assistant producers or assignment editors. They help mold a newscast by arranging the order of presentation and by helping reporters to assemble stories. An entry-level assistant producer isn't expected to have much of an audition tape, but stations will expect you to perform well on a writing test.

You might be assigned to work on the assignment desk, which supervises and coordinates coverage. An assistant assignment editor would help make sure that the station's reporters and equipment are not required to be in too many locations at the same time.

Some people enter broadcast journalism in the production area. They become camera operators, sound technicians, or control room workers who handle TelePrompTers, character generators and other equipment. Those who operate cameras in the field, sometimes called "news photographers" and sometimes "videographers," usually specialize in that role, but most production people wind up handling several production responsibilities at once. News photographers tend to do much of their own editing and may reach a top salary of $40,000, and even higher in the largest markets. That's better pay than the studio camera operators, who make in the $6 per hour range.

After beginning your career, you might eventually wind up running a station's news operation as a news director, the person responsible for the overall news operation. Other management positions include the executive producer, who is responsible for what appears in the newscast, and the assistant news director, who may coordinate newsroom activities. Some stations include a managing editor, who handles coordination of news facilities.

Remember that in some stations, the job titles and roles may switch.

Many students break into the broadcast business after obtaining an internship. (It should be noted that broadcast outlets are likely to require students to work for no or little pay as interns; the law of supply and demand has failed to disappoint the broadcasters yet.)

And internships can lead to employment, even if it comes in another medium. University of Texas alumnus Brian Mylar, for example, earned an internship at KVET radio in Austin before beginning work as a reporter at two Austin television stations. He later moved to KXAS-TV in Fort Worth before moving to Fort Wayne, Ind., as an anchor at WANE-TV. Because Mylar wanted to become an anchor, he made a move to a smaller market.

In some outlets, an internship can lead to an anchor position. University of Southwestern Louisiana alumna Bernadette Lee worked as an intern with KPEL-AM in Lafayette, La., but was later hired as a news anchor for the talk-radio station.

One of the best online sites for anyone interested in the broadcast industry is "Shoptalk," a daily online newsletter documenting news, issues and job opportunities in broadcast news. Don Fitzpatrick Associates, an agency that represents some on-air broadcasters, puts out this popular product, and it is distributed by e-mail by the S.I. Newhouse School of Public Communications at Syracuse University.

Print Media

In newspapers, you're mostly familiar with reporters and columnists. However, you might also consider working behind the scenes as a copy editor or a page designer. Not that long ago, copy editors were expected to have spent some time working as reporters, but many newspapers now hire copy editors fresh from college. Copy editors double-check reporters' stories for style errors and factual errors and generally try to improve those stories.

In the old days, copy editors sat around a horseshoe-shaped desk. The editors who sat on the outside were called "rimmers," and were responsible for editing and trimming stories as well as writing headlines and outlines. The editor who sat inside the horseshoe handed out assignments and designed pages and was known as the "slot." Those terms still exist in the news business.

Beat reporters traditionally work within a beat system and report to an editor in charge of a desk. At a large metropolitan newspaper like the *Los Angeles Times*, there may be reporters working for the international desk, the national desk, the state desk, the city desk, the metro area desk and various desks within sections like business, features and sports. Each of these desks will include a group of copy editors to handle the stories from those reporters. Those desks will also feature managers, also called editors, who assign stories and supervise the work. An assistant city editor, for example, may assign stories and keep tabs on the day's local news output.

Reporters usually either cover a beat or work as a general-assignment reporter. Beat reporters are responsible for a specific area like city hall, education, police or the courts. Even reporters within specialty areas may well have beats. In the business section, for example, beats may include the economy, real estate, retail, banking and local industry. General-assignment reporters handle no particular beat, but rather are generalists, able to report on any number of areas.

Traditionally, the larger newspapers tend to pay higher salaries, but also tend not to hire very many novice reporters. Smaller newspapers are more likely to take a chance on someone directly out of school. However, as in any mass communication field, these rules are not set in stone.

"The easiest way onto a newspaper is still through the copy desk," says Nancy Waclawek, who helps supervise the internship process at the *St. Petersburg Times*. "It seems like there's a higher turnover rate there than with reporters."

Mark Lewis

Tips and Tactics

How to Get Your Foot in the Door in Magazines

By Lisa Costantini

All my life I knew I wanted to be a writer. Growing up, I devoured magazines. When I was the only member in my family to need glasses at 13, I figured I was being punished for reading books all those years under my covers. In high school, I joined my school's newspaper staff and interned at some local magazines. In college at the University of South Florida, I majored in mass communication, emphasizing magazine writing.

Senior year I did what every other journalism student did . . . I sent out what then seemed like a thousand cover letters in the hopes of hyping up my next-to-nothing résumé and landing my dream job in magazines. I spent hours copying clips I'd gleaned from my days on the high school newspaper and in internships. I worded and reworded my cover letter and résumé until I thought they were just right (or at least would slip past some assistant's desk and land on the editor in chief's chair!). Then I waited patiently by the mailbox. (Translation: I slept next to it so I could make sure the mailman didn't lose anything when he took it from his bag to my box.) Needless to say, I was very disappointed when nothing with a New York return address ever came my way.

However, all was not lost and I eventually did get my big break. As a final assignment upon graduating from college, my journalism professor had me interview someone who was working in my field of interest. He put me in touch with a former student of his who at the time was an editorial assistant at *Parenting* magazine in New York. We corresponded through e-mail, and she began to answer my never-ending flow of questions about her job. Within the next couple of weeks, she informed me that at the time I would be graduating, *Parenting* would be in need of a new intern. It was minimum wage and started immediately. I talked my parents into driving me to New York, and shortly thereafter I had a full-time job doing what I had always dreamed about.

Now for various reasons not every story turns out quite so great. Some writers are afraid to take the next step and move to New York, some don't know where to start so they just don't, and some might even think that they're not good enough to make it. I, at one time or another, thought I fit into every single category, but I got over it, and so will you.

Over the past couple of years, I've learned what not to do when it comes to getting a job in magazines and just as importantly, what *to* do.

As I explained earlier, sending out my résumé to every magazine that I was slightly interested in was not only a waste of my time but also a waste of theirs (not to mention a waste of paper and money spent in stamps). For me, not one phone call or job offer ever came from blindly sending out my résumé. Now, I'm not saying this is the case with everyone, but in my experience the best reason to send out your résumé while you're still in college would be if you were interested in an internship (whether it be for school credit or immediately after graduating, you can intern and will typically receive minimum wage).

The other thing that I learned was that no matter who you are, a fresh-faced editorial assistant or the editor in chief, no one likes to be inundated with phone calls from some stranger begging for a job. If you want to call and follow up to make sure someone received your résumé or to ask any questions, call Human Resources (but not every other hour). The truth of the matter is, if you send your résumé directly to the magazine, everything that goes in there gets read first by an editorial assistant whose job it is to decide whether to trash it or pass it.

Now, I don't want it to seem as if I'm saying you can't *ever* send your résumé directly to someone at the magazine, but the best way to get your résumé read is by knowing someone at the magazine.

How, you ask? Well, for starters, college is your best chance to make contacts. You're constantly interacting with other students and teachers. And believe it or not, your school assignments are a huge help when it comes to making contacts.

For instance, say your journalism teacher gives you the assignment of having to interview someone, anyone. Since you have to do the assignment, why not make a contact while you're at it? Pick a magazine that you're interested in, get online and research everything you can about it.

Then look at the masthead (the column near the front of the magazine that lists everyone who works there), pick a department, and choose someone (the lower the name, the better; an intern or editorial assistant would be your best bet). Now give that person a call and *briefly* let him or her know that you're doing an assignment for college and were wondering if you could do an interview over the phone in the subject's free time. Or, if it's better for your interviewer, you can send some questions via e-mail. Most likely, the person will be flattered you asked.

Now that you've made a contact, keep in touch. Hey, why not send them your story when it's done? Your subject could be so impressed with your writing abilities you might get a job offer before you even graduate.

Another way to know someone at a magazine is to keep checking out alumni who have graduated from your college. Most universities have Web sites where they continuously update the information on former graduates. Who knows? Someone who went to your college could have your dream job. Drop that person a line. It couldn't hurt! Good luck. ■

And some writers exit college with the background to begin a reporting career at a large newspaper. Mi-ai Ahern, the travel editor at the *Chicago Sun-Times*, began as an intern for a Norfolk, Va., newspaper and did so well that the paper offered the University of Maryland graduate a job after the internship ended.

Del Wilber of Northwestern University gained experience at two internships and chose to accept a two-year internship with *The Baltimore Sun*, where he works as a general-assignment reporter in the Howard County bureau, a specialized circulation area within *The Sun*'s distribution area. *The Sun* competes for circulation in Howard County with *The Washington Post*.

"The Howard bureau is exciting because we have daily competition with *The Post* and our editors keep a lot of their best young talent there, as they will tell you," Wilber says.

Most internships, it must be said, don't lead to job offers. When Deborah O'Neil of the University of South Florida completed one summer internship, she was offered a clerk's job with that newspaper, but instead used her clips from that summer and from the school daily paper *The Oracle* to get a reporting job in a *St. Petersburg Times* bureau.

Many newspapers will start new reporters in bureaus. These are smaller and less intimidating than the large newsroom, but the reporting standards are still high. Wilber, for example, was working for the city desk when he dug up some information about a plane crash story and was sent out to cover it. While he was in the field, a health story about a disease that killed thousands of fish and caused human illness broke, and because Wilber was already there, he covered a front-page story for a month. After proving himself, he was assigned to a bureau. To see what a day in the bureau can be like, see "A Day in the Life of . . . Bureau Reporter John Wing" in the appendix.

Newspaper jobs often lead to positions in other print media: magazines and newsletters. Magazine staffs include many journalists who began their careers in newspapers, but a stint with a paper is by no means a requirement for a position. Some larger magazines have a staff of writers, editors and other support personnel. Some smaller magazines depend on freelance writers to fill the space between the advertisements. Though many magazine writing jobs are contracted to freelancers, some staff positions do exist. Freelance writers, in turn, usually begin to work on earning book contracts, since the money is much better for books than for magazine articles.

The freelance writing business is a competitive one. It is relatively easy for a talented beginner to sell feature stories to local or regional magazines. But then it is considerably more difficult to sell to the top national magazines, and the book business is, again, even more difficult.

It does happen, though, and serves as a typical career path for a talented writer.

Internships and the willingness to work for low pay in large cities like New York can lead to jobs. It's likely that entry-level magazine candidates will work as fact checkers, who double-check every fact and quote in a story before it's published. Others will work as reporters, who gather information for senior staff writers.

But most magazines aren't nearly so ambitious in size. In the trade magazine field, a small staff will put out a monthly magazine. Editors for these publications not only have journalism skills, but also must quickly become experts in whatever field the magazine serves.

Freelance writing requires enormous discipline, energy and the ability to find well-paying markets. Though magazines like *Playboy*, *Esquire*, *The Atlantic Monthly*, *The New Yorker* and other national magazines pay well for freelance work, many magazines pay a few hundred dollars (or less) for a 1,000–3,000 word story.

That is why many freelance writers quickly work toward book contracts, which pay enough to make a living. In the book business, publishers typically pay upwards of $5,000–$10,000 as an advance against future royalties for a first book. The writer then makes 10–15 percent of the cover price of the book in royalties once the book is in the bookstores.

The newsletter industry is a fast-growing option for print media majors. The pay is good, and the job allows writers the opportunity to develop their writing and reporting skills in a specialty area.

Public Relations

Practitioners in this field are usually considered generalists, who can do a number of tasks well, or specialists, who are experts in one particular area of public relations.

Public relations jobs tend to be grouped into four areas: firm, corporate, nonprofit and government information.

Firm

In a public relations firm, practitioners work with clients who engage the staff. It may be that the firm assigns one practitioner for a specific function—for example, to serve as a publicist for an individual—or it may be that a firm assigns a team to conduct a detailed campaign for a group.

Counseling firms succeed when they meet client needs; therefore, they tend to hire practitioners who have proven skills in the public relations area. It is not unusual for a large agency to require at least five years' experience from its prospective employees.

Corporate

Practitioners who work in the corporate setting handle most or all public relations duties for the company. These jobs entail a variety of skills, ranging from press release writing to representing the corporation at public meetings. Many corporations that once included public relations practitioners with specialties have chosen to retain only generalists who can handle a number of tasks. When they have need of a specialist, they will engage a firm with an expertise in that area.

"You need to be flexible in corporate communication; the specialists are quickly headed the way of the dinosaur," says Joan Hammond, who works in public relations at Electronic Data Systems in Plano, Texas, and is president of the IABC/Dallas chapter. "I've never had two days alike since I've been here."

Hammond says students should take a number of mass communication courses to enter public relations as well as taking some management courses. But preparation shouldn't be limited to the university schedule book.

"They also should definitely work on their personal presentation skills," she adds. "They ought to think about joining Toastmasters [a group devoted to the improvement of public speaking] to improve those skills. They should understand how diplomacy works in a corporate setting."

Some corporate jobs pay extremely well, but the pay may not be enough when the corporation is the subject of negative media coverage. If the practitioner has developed managerial skills, the corporation's officers may well avoid action that would lead to negative publicity. But, it should be noted, not every corporation has such wise officers, and in such cases, the practitioner winds up trying to explain to an angry public why that corporation is, for instance, dumping chemicals into the river. It should be noted that many such corporations have little respect for the public relations process and may well have a history of firing practitioners at the first sign of financial downturn.

A good corporate practitioner not only represents the corporation to the public, but also represents the public to the corporation in its decision making.

Other practitioners work for industry associations. These people also receive good pay and benefits.

Nonprofit

Practitioners in the nonprofit field rarely have to worry about corporate decisions that stain an image. These practitioners represent fund-raising groups like the American Cancer Society or local outreach programs that do good works. The drawback to nonprofit jobs is the pay, which is low at the local level, especially when compared with pay in the agency and corporate areas. Nationally, groups like the American Cancer Society pay competitively.

The nonprofit (or not-for-profit) arena also includes practitioners who work in health care and education. They handle news releases and produce magazines as well as performing other responsibilities. These jobs pay respectably well and usually involve generalists.

Students considering nonprofit jobs should remember that some nonprofit organizations consider public relations an important function of fund-raising, which is necessary and not guaranteed. Every brochure, magazine or news release can affect the flow of donations.

Public Information

Practitioners in public information usually work for the government or some other public agency. They handle public relations responsibilities ranging from news releases to magazine editing to image building for any number of government agencies, including the military and law enforcement. They serve a liaison between the organization and the public.

Advertising

Specialists aren't dead in advertising.

Advertising agencies expect students to be able to handle several tasks. But the agencies often will then allow these generalist employees to develop in some area in which they demonstrate their talent.

It's not unusual for an agency novice to work as an assistant in several areas—media buying, media planning, copywriting, maybe even account management—before developing skills in one of those areas. After spending some years becoming an expert in one of those areas, the agency employee may well enter management, at which point, the employee will have become a generalist again.

A student with writing skills will probably enter the agency as an assistant copywriter, assigned small, specific tasks while learning how the agency writers function and how they develop advertising messages to fit the plan developed by the research staff. Some talented students who have shown their talent while still in college may be hired right out of school as full-fledged copywriters. That's not the usual scenario, but it can happen. When it does happen, it almost always happens to someone who has gained experience working in college advertising media and in internships.

Account executives serve as a liaison between the client and the team assigned to handle the client's advertising needs.

Media buyers and planners work to find the optimal medium or media for a particular advertiser, recommending among radio, television, newspapers, magazines, billboards.

Researchers examine the product's potential marketability and how well an advertising campaign works. As we emphasized in an earlier chapter, research drives creativity in most advertising campaigns.

Art directors provide visual messages. They work closely with the other "creatives," the copywriters.

In advertising, internships provide important experience to novices. And if you're good enough, an agency will hire you. University of Southwestern Louisiana student Tiffany Ringe received enthusiastic recommendations from her professors and was hired immediately after a one-semester internship with Davis Partners as an account executive.

Other Necessary Ingredients

The Internet

Employers not only want to see as much experience on your résumé as possible, but also would like to see skills that many of their employees don't have. For many of them, this means they would like to hire someone who doesn't blanch at the thought of going onto the Internet or the World Wide Web.

And not only are traditional mass communication companies looking for these skills, but also entire new online companies have sprouted and they also seek communicators with Net skills. Digital City, for example, is described as an online community available to those with America Online accounts. It hires editors to work in more than 30 communities by gathering information ranging from news stories to advertisements and presenting the material in graphic orientations.

One needs but a quick online journey to see that most news organizations now have an online presence. The Abcnews.com site, for example, features updated news with sound bites and a ticker that relates news of the day. Nando, the shorthand for the *Raleigh News and Observer* site, was an early standard setter for newspapers online. And, of course, it seems as if every corporation has its own Web site, and some of the sites are intended to help perform public relations and advertising functions.

A good candidate for online communication doesn't shrink from new technology. But lots of computer-literate folks can barely order dinner, much less communicate effectively with others. Mass communication students who can combine solid writing and editing skills with online expertise are highly marketable. Students who can design Web sites, can surf the Net effectively and are flexible enough to adapt to the changing cyberspace world will not have many problems finding employment.

"We have five people assigned full-time as section editors on an electronic newsletter," Joan Hammond of EDS says. "Fortunately, we have plenty of people who understand the Internet and intranets." In 1997, corporate communicators predicted a 500 percent increase in corporate presence on the Net by 1999.

Visual Literacy

In this textbook, we've focused on developing writing skills, but with the advent of the Internet, you will also want to work on visual literacy. You can't work in television or some advertising positions without a keen ability to combine words with pictures. But even the most traditional wordsmiths should be able to add a visual dimension to their writing.

Writers should be able to see visual angles to stories that can be expressed with photographs, infographics and other visual representations. Ever since *USA Today* moved newspaper graphics into a new era when it emphasized a colorful combination of art and information in its graphics, newspapers have increased their awareness of visual communication.

You need to be able to see how you can tell a story with words and graphics. Would a map explain the bank robbers' getaway route? Can a bar graph explain a city hall budget story? Writers usually don't actually compose the graphics, but they gather the information for artists to develop.

As online journalism continues to develop in the 21st century, it seems clear that journalism students will need to be able to tell the story not only in words and pictures and graphics, but also in sound bites, moving pictures, hypertext, links, and more. If you haven't taken your university or colleges courses in these computer skills, you'll want to.

A Passion for Your Work

Fresh out of college, Del Wilber wrote a succinct cover letter to *The Baltimore Sun* when he applied for a job: "I love newspapering. Please consider me."

It worked. Employers in mass communications want students who are skilled, but they also want students who demonstrate that they care about the field.

They want desperately to see some passion.

This doesn't mean that introverts need not apply, but even the shyest people can show that they care. Earlier in this appendix, we talked about how you'll want experience while earning a degree. Employers expect to see this kind of line on your résumé. If you, like many students, have to work at a nonmedia job to pay tuition, employers understand.

They won't hire you, but they will understand. They'll understand that someone else has the passion for writing.

If you have the passion, you'll find some way to gain experience even if you have to wait tables to pay the rent. Employers in journalism will look for internships and part-time work in media outlets. They want to see some work on the college newspaper, a college magazine, or a college broadcast outlet.

In advertising and public relations, the passion may be reflected in internships and in student contests such as the Bateman competition for public relations students or the American Advertising Federation's

World Series for college students, or the Hearst Foundation's contests in writing, photography and broadcast news. Many universities compete in these contests and winning entries have helped smooth the path to that first job.

You can also show passion through extracurricular involvement in mass communication organizations. Many professional organizations—the Public Relations Society of America, the International Association of Business Communicators, the Society of Professional Journalists, The Association for Women in Communication, the Asian American Journalists Association, the National Association of Black Journalists and others—actively seek student involvement and set up student chapters at some universities. And other student organizations form groups on their own.

When students become involved with a professional organization, they gain access to national and regional meetings where they can meet professionals. In mass communication, personal contact is always important. As mentioned earlier, job openings may well filter through the grapevine instead of the classified ad section. Some organizations will offer job bulletin boards or phone lines that list recent openings to their members. Students ought to take advantage of these groups in order to network and build up professional contacts.

It may well be true that no one ever got hired because his or her résumé listed membership in a professional organization, but it is also true that plenty of students have received job tips through those memberships.

Rachael Coleman

A Day in the Life of...

Bureau Reporter
John Wing
The Tampa Tribune

There is not a profession I can imagine with as many possible uncertainties as daily newspaper journalism. Even if you're relegated to one beat, say, federal courts or public health, the dynamic flow of not only events, but also the organization you work for, leads to unpredictable days on the job.

Thankfully, I have three semi-set beats—city government in Zephyrhills, a small but growing municipality of about 20,000 in the summer and 40,000 when the Northern "snowbirds" migrate

down here in the winter, cops and courts in Zephyrhills and Dade City, the county seat of Pasco County, and environmental issues.

It's intense and filled with pressure, but I can't call it work. It's too captivating and flat out fun to get slapped with that label.

Today is an example of why I focused so intently on becoming a newspaper reporter/writer. I got my hands on a great little story. That feeling is worth living for.

I get to my little bureau office at around 8:30 a.m. Mornings are my quiet, reflective, mental warm-up time on the beat. I start by reading the competition, the *St. Petersburg Times*, particularly the Pasco section and any stories related to the environment published in the main run.

I then do the same with *The Tampa Tribune*, comparing how we measure up with our stories compared to the same stories the competition covered. Which facts and angles did each publication focus on? What stories do we have that the Times doesn't have? Vice-versa.

I then scan online about four other newspapers, just for fun mostly, to see what's happening. This takes from 45 minutes to an hour, and serves as a real focus period for my day. Unless of course I've been beat on a story I should have had.

This has only happened a handful of times so far, and though it's not fun, it serves a higher purpose—as a sharp reminder to stay alert and to never slacken for a single day. That's what weekends are for.

The feeling of getting beat is about the same as getting punched hard in the stomach. I hate that feeling and fight each day to make sure it doesn't happen.

Toward this end, I make my morning police and fire/emergency response checks after reading the papers—better in person, but if I've got a full schedule, I'll do it over the phone.

It's important to build a relationship with the contacts, as rehashed and overworked as that phrase sounds. I have at least three people in the city government I check in with everyday. Gotten a few stories from them not even related to their jobs.

Shoot the breeze a little bit. Don't be afraid to show them you are a regular guy or gal, that you're not out to burn the town down with one big story. Impart to them in whatever way you can that you'll be there for a while, you'll be back and you're not just after that one day's story.

You're a part of the town you cover. If you can pull this off—and admittedly, it takes time, and a measure of patience with some folks who

simply hate the media—you'll be the reporter who gets a whisper in the ear when the other guy is being pompous and full of self-importance.

Today, I was busy. I had a story I'd been following for two days, about some folks who had a condemned well out in Land O' Lakes and were being jerked around by state bureaucrats, and today was the day I would deliver. I worked hard the previous two days to get everything I needed, but it took a little longer than I liked. Turns out the story is better for it because I tied it all together, but to do that you need understanding editors and the ability to turn around quick-hit daily stories while digging for the bigger nuggets.

It's a juggling act, part of the fun. Basically, these folks had been assured their water was safe for drinking and bathing after a high-tech filtration system was installed at their home.

Turns out the contaminants were actually becoming more concentrated as the vein containing some nasty chemicals opened wider, spilling into their well at a faster rate than the filters could block.

The family's three-year-old toddler suffered chemical burns on his hands and feet from bathing in the stuff. Three layers of his skin burned off. So my task was getting all the information verified. I had to get the parents to release medical records on the kid. I had to get the state Department of Health and state Department of Environmental Protection to provide records of their activities concerning the testing and filtration installations. I had to match up what the homeowners were saying with what the bureaucrats were saying.

Guess who was fibbing?

Summary

Experience is the key to finding a job in mass communication fields. If you haven't already begun to gather material for your portfolio, the time to begin is now. Take advantage of campus publications or their equivalents in public relations and advertising to begin to collect material. It is also advisable to seek internships with professional organizations—or, at least, it's advisable to try to work part-time for those organizations.

And then, I went door-to-door in the neighborhood, checking to see if the DOH and DEP had indeed notified folks about condemned wells close by. They didn't, at least not fully.

Now I've got a story.

Then I did something I've learned is essential to delivering top-notch journalism, something that is so important. I called back all the people I spoke with about this story one more time and went over the chronology of events, spelling names again, checking dates, asking for their story one more time.

I'm not trying to trip anyone up, or at least not intentionally. It's just so easy to lose credibility; it happens one drip at a time, one false or misinterpreted sequence at a time. And it only takes one screwup to ruin a ton of research and effort. So get it right. Call back. Tell them, "I was listening intently the first time, but let me make sure I've got this right." Most people will appreciate it, they will understand, they will feel like they are being heard. And every time I've done this, with nearly every subject, you get one little fact, one little aspect they didn't tell you the first time.

By about 2:30 p.m. all my material was assembled. But before I started writing, I had to call my editors, something I do at least three times a day to let them know where I'm at with a story. They like that. Just do it, it'll keep you employed.

Then I called the cops and fire guys one more time to make sure I didn't miss anything while I was out all day. Thankfully, all was clear.

Then I wrote.

The story was in by 4:30. Edits came back about 5:30. During that hour, I grabbed a quick slice of pizza (cold, leftover from the circulation department during their lazy two-hour lunch break) and checked in with other reporters on our team about stuff they had going that day, if they needed any help, if they needed any last minute calls for quotes. We were one reporter down today; she worked Sunday shift out of her rotation so she got Friday off.

Talk to other reporters during the day, even if they get grouchy during deadlines. It breaks tension and helps others know they are not on their own. There's going to be a time you need it. If you've got a half hour to kill, help somebody out.

When the edits came back, my editor had about 12 questions, most of them really digging to provide readers with bigger understanding. How deep are these wells? Does that matter? Where do these folks go from here? Are they talking about lawsuits? How about the source of the contaminants? My story was slight on this aspect, because the DEP had not yet determined the source, but I spoke to the experts for about a combined hour over the course of three conversations over three days. So I spilled my notebook out to my editor and sure enough, there were enough attributable nuggets in there to at least narrow down likely sources.

By then it's 6:30. I'm almost done. Just have to fill out an overnight log, which lets the next day's editors and photographers know what each reporter will probably be working on.

The best part is, though, you never know what can break. The day went by fast. I walk away satisfied. ∎

Just as this textbook went to print, John Wing earned a promotion to night police reporter for The Tampa Tribune.

To repeat: The diploma just isn't enough to get you a job in modern mass media.

Key Points

▶ Professionals expect to see that you can produce professional work.

▶ Clips from campus publications or equivalents are a start, but one cannot underestimate the value of succeeding at an internship.

▶ In mass communication jobs, the applicant pool is larger than only specialized majors. The more skills you have, the more employable you may be. This is especially true for developing Internet-related skills.

▶ Joining student organizations related to mass communication can help show employers that you care about the field.

Web Links

Here are a few interesting Web sites where you can find useful information on jobs in the media writing field.

http://www.spj.org (Society of Professional Journalists site)
http://www.prsa.org (Public Relations Society of America site)
http://www.aaaa.org (American Association of Advertising Agencies site)
http://www.ajr.com (*American Journalism Review* site)
http://epclassifieds.com (Classified pages site of *Editor & Publisher*)
http://ww.jaws.org/jobs (Journalism and Women Symposium site)
http://www.dowjones.com/newsfund.college (Site for the prestigious Dow Jones Newspaper Fund internships)

Exercises

On the CD-ROM that accompanies this text, *CD-ROM for Modern Media Writing,* are electronic study resources for this chapter:

▶ Exercises for Appendix C.

▶ Quick access to the **World Wide Web.**

▶ A demo of **Web Tutor** for *Modern Media Writing.*

▶ The **Modern Media Writing Web Site** at the Wadsworth Communication Café, which offers activities for this chapter at **http://www.wadsworth.com/modernmedia_a.**

Glossary

Advance A preliminary story concerning a future event.

Advertising The crafting of messages that are delivered on paid space in or on a medium.

Advertising agency A company that specializes in producing advertisements for clients.

Appropriation A privacy tort that forbids the taking of a person's image without compensation or permission. Newsworthiness usually protects journalists here, but advertisers must be careful.

Associated Press (AP) A worldwide news-gathering service (see *Wire service*) run as a cooperative between all member news organizations.

Audition tape A compilation of a broadcast reporter's best material. An applicant sends this tape to news directors when job hunting.

Backgrounder (1) A meeting with the press in which a source gives information not for publication. (2) An informative, factual story that relates the history or background of a current news event in order to aid audience understanding.

Beat A reporter's regular assignment, such as the city hall beat or the police beat.

Break (1) The point at which a story moves from one column or page to another (see *Jump*). (2) The time when a story becomes available for publication. News is said to "break" when it happens.

Bright A type of feature story offering a lighter, more entertaining aspect of some newsworthy person or thing.

Byline The printed names of the reporter or reporters at the beginning of a story, usually preceded by the word *by,* as in "by Jane Doe."

Champagne glass A graphic model for showing a story's structure, often with a feature-style lead, followed by a chronology and an ending that refers in some way to the lead.

Chronology A type of news or feature story that uses time as its structure, from beginning to end. A detailed chronology is sometimes called a "tick-tock."

Circle kicker A term describing an ending that refers back in some way to the lead (see *Kicker*).

City editor The editor in charge of the collection, writing and editing of local news.

Clips Samples of a journalist's news stories, headlines, or other journalistic works. (Note: Editors will ask job applicants for these.)

Column (1) The area on a news page usually 10 to 14 picas (about 1 5/8 to 2 1/4 inches) wide. (2) An article appearing regularly, written by a particular writer, or columnist (see *Columnist*).

Column inch A unit of measurement one-inch deep and one-column wide, commonly used to describe a story's length (as in "a 15-inch story").

Columnist A writer using the same space daily or weekly to generally write about the same broad area of interest.

Conjunctive adverbs Words that often serve as effective transitions between one element of a story and another. Common conjunctive adverbs are *accordingly, also, anyway, besides, certainly, consequently, finally, further, furthermore, hence, however, incidentally, indeed, instead, likewise, meanwhile, moreover, namely, nevertheless, next, nonetheless, now, otherwise, similarly, still, then, thereafter, therefore, thus, undoubtedly.*

Copy (1) All written material in a newspaper. (2) To reproduce material using a photocopier.

Copy desk The desk where copy is edited, headlined and placed on the page it will appear on in the newspaper.

Copy editor A newspaper worker who edits reporters' stories for clarity, accuracy and style. Copy editors almost always write a story's headline.

Copyediting Correcting, improving and marking copy to be printed.

Copyright Legal protection of an author's exclusive right to his or her work for a specified period of time.

Corporate public relations Public relations within a corporation. Workers in this field are responsible for producing news releases and performing other public relations functions within the corporation.

Correspondent A reporter assigned to cover work away from the home office in another city, state or country. A "string" correspondent is not a full-time employee of the newspaper (see *Stringer*).

Cover To get all the available news about an event.

Cutline In newspapers, the words beneath a photograph that describe the photograph. In magazines, this is called a "caption."

Dateline The line at the beginning of a story that indicates both the place and the date of origin of the story.

Deadline The last moment to get copy in for an edition.

Descriptive lead A lead that uses detailed description to interest and inform the reader; most often used in feature stories.

Editorial (1) An article that expresses the opinion of the newspaper's editors and usually also reflects the opinion of the publisher or owner of the newspaper. (2) The department of the newspaper where news is gathered, written, edited and readied for publication.

Edition A particular print run of a newspaper, meant for a particular place or time of day, as "City Edition," "Lakeshore Edition," "Early Edition," or "Late Edition."

Editorial cartoon A cartoon, usually found near the editorial, that expresses an opinion about a news personality, issue or event.

Editorial department Specifically refers to the staff that produces written editorials and other opinion articles.

Editorialize To express an opinion in a news story or a headline. Editorializing in a news story is not considered good journalism.

Fair comment A libel defense that protects journalists who criticize performers and others who have thrust themselves into the light of public opinion.

Feature lead A lead that differs from a summary lead, often using descriptive or narrative techniques; also known as a "soft lead."

Feature story A work of nonfiction meant to entertain and inform the reader while paying special attention to the human interest aspects of storytelling.

First Amendment The first article of the Bill of Rights of the Constitution of the United States, guaranteeing Americans freedom of religion, speech, press, assembly and petition. The wording is "Congress shall make no law respecting an establishment of religion, or prohibiting the free exercise thereof; or abridging the freedom of speech, or of the press; or the right of the people peaceably to assemble, and to petition the Government for a redress of grievances."

First-day story A story published for the first time and dealing with something that has just happened (see *Follow-up story*).

Five *W's* and *H* Phrase used to describe the questions who, what, when, where, why and how.

Flag The printed title (that is, name and logo) of a newspaper at the top of the front page.

Flash The first brief bulletin from a press association with information about an important news event.

Folio The newspaper name, the date and the page number that appear at the top of each page.

Follow-up story A story giving later developments of an event already reported (see *First-day story*).

General assignment reporter A reporter who covers a variety of stories rather than a single beat (see *Beat*).

Ghostwriter Someone who writes stories for another's signature.

Graf A paragraph.

Handout A specially prepared news release for the media (see *Press release*).

Headline (1) Display type placed over a story summarizing the story for the reader. (2) Commonly thought of as the largest line of type across the top of a newspaper calling attention to the most important story of that edition.

Hourglass structure A structure that combines an inverted pyramid beginning with a narrative or chronological following.

Human interest Emotional appeal in the news based on material that affects the people in the news.

IABC International Association of Business Communicators.

Inch See column inch.

Interview A conversation between a reporter and a subject, meant to give the reporter information that he or she can use in writing a story.

Intrusion A privacy tort that keeps journalists from entering a home or other nonpublic forum without permission. Photographers usually get signed permission forms when shooting a picture within a home or office.

Invasion of privacy A civil tort that journalists must be aware of while doing their jobs. Newsworthiness is traditionally a defense against some privacy suits.

Inverted pyramid The traditional structure used in many news stories, placing the most important information at the top of the story, with subsequent paragraphs holding material of declining importance.

Jump (1) To continue a story from one page to another. (2) The continued material itself.

Kicker (1) A small headline, often in italics and usually underlined, above and slightly to the left of the main head. (2) An effective ending to a story.

Kill To eliminate all or part of a story.

Lead (pronounced "leed.") (1) The first few sentences or the first paragraph of a story. (2) A tip that may lead to a story.

Letter to the editor A letter in which a reader expresses his or her views in the newspaper; usually printed on the editorial page or the page opposite the editorial page

Libel Published words that harm or injure someone's reputation.

Library A newspaper's collection of clippings, books, files, etc. (see *Morgue*).

Linotype A trademarked name. Until the 1970s, most newspapers were produced on Linotype machines, which used hot lead type and required highly skilled operators.

Malice The reckless disregard of whether information is factual or not.

Managing editor Generally, the top assistant to a newspaper's editor in chief and the person directly responsible for managing the content of a daily newspaper.

Morgue In newspapers, the old term for a room where old stories were filed and kept for reference (see *Library*).

News hole The amount of space left for news after advertisements have been arranged on the page.

News service A news-gathering agency, such as the Associated Press and Reuters, that distributes news to subscribing newspapers (see *Wire service*).

Newsprint A grade of paper made from recycled paper and wood pulp; used primarily for printing newspapers.

Nonprofit public relations Public relations work done for charities and foundations and other not-for-profit entities.

Obit Abbreviation for *obituary*. A biography of a dead person. Sometimes "canned obits" are kept on file in the newspaper's library to be used at the time of a prominent person's death.

Off the record Information, often from an interview, not for publication, or at least not to be attributed to the source if used as background (see *On the record*).

Offset press A method of printing in which the inked image is transferred from a plate to a rubber roller, which in turn puts the ink onto the paper.

On the record Information, often from an interview, for publication, usually with full attribution (see *Off the record*).

Op-ed Abbreviation for *opinion-editorial*. A page featuring editorials and opinion columns. Also said to stand for material that is "opposite the editorial page."

Play The amount of emphasis given a piece of news. A story may be "played down" or "played up."

Portfolio A collection of advertisements, designs, public relations releases and other work that an advertising or public relations professional or student has worked on. Job applicants use portfolios to show prospective employers their best work.

Press agent A publicity or public relations person.

Press conference A meeting called to give information to the news media.

Press release A specially prepared statement for the news media (see *Handout*).

Privilege The protection granted to journalists who report on the official meetings of government, such as trials or meetings of government bodies. Such material is generally considered safe from libel.

Public relations The practice of developing understanding and goodwill between a person, firm or institution and the public.

Public relations agency A freestanding company that provides public relations services for individual and corporate clients.

Publisher The chief executive and often the owner of a newspaper or other publishing firm.

Puff Editorialized, complimentary statement in a news story. Writing puff is not considered good journalism.

Question lead   A lead that asks a question. It is best used very, very sparingly.

Quote   Interview material used in a story and placed within quotation marks.

Review   A writer's critical evaluation of a public occurrence or place, such as a movie, play, music performance, restaurant, or art show.

Revision   The process of improving a story through changes, corrections, additions or deletions.

Sacred cow   A person, subject or institution given special favor or treatment in a newspaper. Treating a subject like a sacred cow is not usually considered good journalism.

Schedule   (1) A news editor's record of assignments. (2) The copy editor's record of stories handled.

Scoop   An exclusive first-run story or photograph or a new element to an ongoing story.

Second-day story   A follow-up story giving new developments on one that has already appeared in the newspaper.

Shovel work   The act of taking a newspaper story and putting it onto the newspaper's Web site.

Sidebar   A secondary story that supports or amplifies a major story. Often, but not always, a sidebar is written with a feature approach.

Skyline   A banner head that runs above the flag.

Slander   Spoken defamation.

Slant   An angle of a story. A story is slanted when a certain aspect is played up for policy or other reasons.

Soft copy   Copy seen on a computer screen.

Sound bite   (1) The broadcast version of a quote. (2) That part of a broadcast story where the subject speaks directly to the listener or viewer.

Source   A supplier of information. A source can be a person, document, etc.

Spot news   News obtained on the scene of an event, usually unexpectedly.

Spread   The display given to an important story. A double spread is one across facing pages.

Stet   An editing notation mark meaning "let it stand," informing the printer to ignore a change marked on a proof; from the Latin *stare*, meaning "to stand."

Story   The general term applied to any newspaper article written by a reporter.

Straight news   A plain account of news facts written in standard style and structure, without coloring or embellishments.

Stringer   A correspondent for a newspaper or a news agency, usually part-time, who often covers a certain subject or geographic area. The person is usually paid according to the number or length of stories printed by the newspaper.

Style book A compilation of typographical and other rules formulated by a newspaper to make uniform its treatment of spelling, capitalization, abbreviations, punctuation, typography, etc. Most newspapers provide stylebooks for the use of their staff. *The Associated Press Stylebook* is the accepted standard for most newspapers, which then add their own local variations or additions.

Subhead A small, one-line headline inserted in the body of a story to break up the monotony of a solid column of small type.

Summary lead A lead that summarizes the most important point or points of a story, usually in fewer than 30 words; also known as a "basic lead" or "hard-news lead."

Syndicate An organization that buys and sells feature material of all kinds; for example, comic strips, gossip columns, and crossword puzzles.

Tabloid A newspaper of small page size, usually 11 inches wide and 16 to 18 inches deep.

Transitions Words, sentences or paragraphs that move the reader smoothly from one element of the story to the next (see *Conjunctive adverbs*).

Truth The best defense against libel suits. No matter how damaging the information, truth is an absolute defense in the United States.

Widow A single word or short line of type at the end of a paragraph, particularly at the top or bottom of a column or page.

Wire copy Editorial matter supplied by outside sources, especially that transmitted by telegraph or Teletype from news services.

Wire service A news collection and transmission service. News services include AFP (Agence France-Presse, based in France), AP (the Associated Press, based in the United States), Reuters (based in the United Kingdom), CP (Canadian Press news service, based in Canada).

Yellow journalism Sensational journalism. Yellow journalism is not considered good journalism.

Note: Significant portions of this glossary are from Wowcom.net, at:
http://www.wowcom.net/education/nie/glossary1.htm
a Web site of *The Holland* (Mich.) *Sentinel.* Reprinted by permission.

Index

A

AAAA. *See* American Association of
Advertising Agencies (AAAA)
Abbreviations, 334–335, 337
abcnews.com, 355
Abolitionism, 8
Absolute privilege for government
officials, 286
Access to information, 97–98, 291–292
Accountability, 307
Accuracy. *See also* Research
of health and medicine features, 140
of Internet information, 95–96,
213–214
of quotes, 118–119
research to avoid errors, 92
Active voice for leads, 74
Actual malice, 286
Actualities, 188
Adams, John, 6
Adams, Samuel, 6
A Day in the Life of..., 104–105,
125–127, 157–159, 178–180,
202–203, 221–223, 239–240,
241–242, 261–263, 279–281,
357–359
Addison, Joseph, 4
Adjectives
commas with, 337–338
definition of, 61
predicate adjectives, 65
types of, 61
Adverbs
conjunctive adverbs, 64, 337, 338
definition of, 61
types of, 62
Advertising copywriting

advantages and disadvantages for
different media, 252–255
advertorials, 261
audience for, 248–251
awareness and, 251
billboards, 255
brand names and, 256–257
brevity in, 257–258
catalog copy, 260–261
compared with public relations, 248
creativity and, 246
daily schedule for advertising
copywriter, 261–263
direct-mail campaigns, 255, 260–261
ethics code for, 307–309
fund-raising letters, 260–261
headlines and, 256
HUBBA guidelines for, 256–258
image advertising, 259
for Internet, 255
leads for print advertisements, 70
for magazines, 253–254
motivation and, 259–260
for newspapers, 252–253
promises in, 258
for radio, 254
research resources for, 94
research skills and, 92
samples of, 246–248
STARCH numbers in, 99, 101
substance over format in, 258–259
summary and key points on,
262–264
survey and, 99
team of copywriter and artist for,
246
for television, 252, 254–255